Migration, Health and Development

IIPS

International Institute for Population Sciences

Mumbai

Vision

To position IIPS as a premier teaching and research institution in population sciences responsive to emerging national and global needs based on values of inclusion, sensitivity and rights protection.

Mission

The Institute will strive to be a centre of excellence on population, health and development issues through high quality education, teaching and research. This will be achieved by (a) creating competent professionals, (b) generating and disseminating scientific knowledge and evidence, (c) collaboration and exchange of knowledge, and (d) advocacy and awareness.

Migration, Health and Development

Editors

S. Lahiri, B. Paswan and K.C. Das

International Institute for Population Sciences, Mumbai

RAWAT PUBLICATIONS

Jaipur • New Delhi • Bangalore • Hyderabad • Guwahati

ISBN 978-81-316-0398-7

Published by
Prem Rawat for **Rawat Publications**
Satyam Apts, Sector 3, Jawahar Nagar, Jaipur 302 004 (India)
Phone: 0141 265 1748 / 7006 Fax: 0141 265 1748
E-mail: info@rawatbooks.com
Website: www.rawatbooks.com

New Delhi Office
4858/24, Ansari Road, Daryaganj, New Delhi 110 002
Phone: 011 2326 3290

Also at *Bangalore, Hyderabad* and *Guwahati*

Printed at Chaman Enterprises, New Delhi

Dedicated in fond memory of

Late Prof. P.N. Mari Bhat,

Former Director (2005–2007),

International Institute for Population Sciences, Mumbai

Contents

Preface xi

Introduction xiii

Part I
Migration and Urbanisation

1 Household Remittances, Inequality and Poverty: Evidence from the State of Kerala, India 3
Adeline Pelletier

2 Female Labour Mobility and Urban Employment in India 40
Brinda Viswanathan and K. Shanthi

3 Some Facets of Migration to Districts of Maharashtra 66
Dipti Mukherji and V.S. Phadke

4 Population Trends of an Emerging City: The Case of Navi Mumbai 80
Deepak Kapoor and Rita Abbi

5 Migration and Development: Migration Patterns of the Hmong in Vietnam Through History 92
Nguyen Tran Lam

6 Impact of Urbanisation on Work-life Balance 132
Elizabeth Mathews

Part II
Population, Development and Environment

7 Changing Pattern of Population Growth and Socio-Economic Characteristics in the Fringe Villages of Guwahati City 141

Semim Wara Begum and Bimal K. Kar

8 Effects of Population Growth on Environmental Degradation in India 152

C.M. Lakshmana

9 Understanding Environmental Concern: Application of New Environmental Paradigm Scale in Rural West Bengal 170

Pradip Swarnakar and Arun Kumar Sharma

10 Projection of Cancer Incident Cases for India till 2016 202

N.S. Murthy, M. Dhar and K. Chaudhury

11 Trends in Cancer Incidence in Greater Mumbai: An Epidemiological Assessment 216

Balkrishna B. Yeole

Part III
Ageing

12 Rapid Fertility Decline and Age-Structural Transition in Iran: Causes and Consequences 229

Amir H. Mehryar, S. Ahmad-Nia and Shahla Kazemipour

13 Harnessing Human Resource of Older Persons for Promoting Social Interaction and Environment Protection 268

Ng Sor Tho

14 A Geographical Perspective on the Patterns of Ageing in the Tribal Areas of the North-Eastern Region of India 279

Debendra Kumar Nayak

Part IV
Demography of Ethnic Groups

15 Ethnic Differences in Fertility in Uplands of Kanchanaburi, Thailand 301

Jian Hu

16 Whom to 'Marry'? Spouse Selection in the Small Tribes of Nilambur Valley, South India 315

Seetha Kakkoth

17 Inequality in the Society in terms of Standard of Living Index 333

R.C. Yadava and Arvind K. Shukla

Part V
Population Policies and Programmes

18 Reproductive Health Services Remain Missing at the Grassroots Level: Evidence From a Time-Use Study of Service Providers in Rural Gujarat 351

N.P. Das and Urvi Shah

19 Health Modernity and Utilisation of Health Services: A Pilot Study in Madhya Pradesh 384

A.S. Dey and A. Shrivastava

20 The Road Map to Hospitalisation: Tackling Health Problem in Rural Meghalaya 409

Sandip Mitra, Chaiti S. Biswas, Dilip C. Nath, Manoranjan Pal and Biswanath Bhattacharya

Contributors 431

Preface

The International Conference on "Emerging Population Issues in the Asia-Pacific Region: Challenges for the 21st Century" was organised as a part of the golden jubilee celebrations of the International Institute for Population Sciences (IIPS) during December 10–13,2006, in Mumbai. This was attended by about 500 delegates (one-fourth of them from outside India) and provided an ideal platform for population experts, social scientists, policy makers and researchers to discuss and debate the recent developments in the Asian demographic scenario and their implications for coming decades. Keeping this in mind, the plenary, technical and poster sessions were organised by giving enough scope for exchange of different views and perspectives.

The conference received an overwhelming response from all over the world for our call for papers and abstracts. We received about 1,000 abstracts, of which 174 were selected for oral presentation and 114 for poster presentations. The 174 oral presentations were spread over 29 technical sessions, each focusing on a particular theme. Besides, there were five plenary sessions on important themes, which generated a healthy debate on many contemporary population and health issues, such as population and development, gender concerns in health and population, fertility and family planning, managing migration and urbanisation, and public health challenges.

The present volume contains 20 selected research papers divided into five major themes, namely, (a) Migration and Urbanisation, (b) Population, Development and Environment, (c) Ageing, (d) Demography of Ethnic Groups, and (e) Population Policies and Programmes. The papers on migration and urbanisation highlight the current patterns, trends and some emerging issues both on the internal as well as international migration in the Asia-Pacific region. Population and development in the context of environment is an emerging issue in the contemporary research. Health, including reproductive health, and ageing are also important issues, which have been much debated and attracted the attention of the researchers and policy makers. Therefore, an attempt has also been made to understand the linkages among population, health and development. We hope that the readers will find this volume useful for further research teaching policy formulation and programme implementation.

The conference organising committee is grateful to all those who have made the conference a great success. In organising the conference various organisations and individuals have provided financial, technical and logistic support in various capacities at different stages. We would like to thank all of them.

First and foremost, we would like to thank the Ministry of Health and Family Welfare, Government of India, for its generous financial assistance and overall technical guidance. We also thank Prof. F. Ram, Director of IIPS for his constant support and cooperation in bringing out this volume. Our special thanks are due to late Prof. P.N. Mari Bhat, who was also instrumental in organising this conference. This book is dedicated to him.

We gratefully acknowledge the technical support and partial funding provided by international organisations such as UNFPA, Packard Foundation, WHO, Wellcome Trust, UNAIDS and Population Foundation of India.

Last but not the least, we thank Ms Archana Basu and Ms Namita Sahoo for their secretarial assistance.

—Editors

Introduction

The present book is a compilation of twenty research papers written by distinguished scholars both from India and abroad in the concerned areas. These papers were presented in the international conference on "Emerging Population Issues in the Asia-Pacific Region: Challenges for the Twenty-first Century" held during December 10–13, 2006 in Mumbai, India. The papers are divided into five parts. The first part deals with issues of migration and urbanisation. The second part is devoted to various aspects of population, development and environment. The issues related to ageing are covered in part three. The fourth part contains papers highlighting the demography of ethnic groups. The last part addresses the issues related to population policies and programmes.

Part I: Migration and Urbanisation

There are total six papers in the first part of the book. The first paper, **"Household Remittances, Inequality and Poverty: Evidence from the State of Kerala, India"** by Adeline Pelletier, discusses the impact of international as well as internal remittances on household's poverty and inequality in Kerala. With high remittances sustained over a long period, industrial development has remained low and Kerala's impressive development achievements and reduction in poverty of the past decades has not been matched by adequate employment generation. In this context, the impacts of remittances on poverty and inequality are crucial to the sustainability of the development achievements. The data from the Kerala Migration Survey has been used in this study. The findings show that internal and international remittances do not have the same effect on poverty alleviation as they are not undertaken by the same type of migrants. Internal migration through the channel of remittances has very little poverty reducing effects and deepens inter-household inequalities on the whole and even within the migrant household as well. The impact of international migration is more positive in terms of poverty alleviation.

It is found that even though international remittances proved to be poor-friendly than internal remittances, they did not produce wealth redistribution favourable to the poorest families in the state.

In the second paper **"Female Labour Mobility and Urban Employment in India"** by Brinda Viswanathan and K. Shanthi, the authors argue that there is enough evidence across countries to show that the globalisation, has increased the demand for female labour force. Accepting the same logic, a similar trend may be expected in India too. Based on the employment-unemployment data for the economically active age group collected by the NSSO (1999–2000), this study highlights the regional variations and temporal changes in female migrants in the urban labour market. The results indicate that even though the dominant category for reasons of migration among currently working women is marriage, there is an increase in the share of associated migrants in the labour force and more significantly related to the work-oriented women migrants in the past decade. There is also a higher share of illiterates among the total working female migrants. However, significant proportion of the female migrants is comprised of diploma holders and graduates, when compared with non-migrant working women. The migrant women are predominantly self-employed or casual labourers. Besides, there are clear regional differences across the country with four southern states dominating the other states in terms of total female migrants in the labour market.

The next paper **"Some Facets of Migration to Districts of Maharashtra"** by Dipti Mukherji and V.S. Phadke discusses the patterns and trends of migration in Maharashtra using census data of 2001. Migration leads to growth of destination areas and depopulation of origin areas. The study analyses certain interesting spatial patterns associated with such migration in Maharashtra districts. Districts under the shadow of metropolitan cities show a high rate of migration compared to other districts. The sources of migrants also vary spatially. Local migrants predominate in economically less developed areas. With increase in distance of the origin places, the share of districts under the shadow of metropolitan cities significantly increases. The level of skill and education enables migrants to overcome the friction of distance. Weaver's crop combination technique has been adopted in order to fix the combination of states sending migrants. Six districts have a predominance of only one state in their in-migrant population. It is observed that these districts get slowly eliminated as the number of states in the combination increases. Rural migrants come from either the neighbouring or less developed states but urban migrants come from distant or more developed states. Duration of stay of migrant population shows a negative relation to distance but positive correlation with development. It is only recently that one finds a higher proportion of migrants in districts of Maharashtra coming from distant states.

The paper **"Population Trends of an Emerging City: The Case of Navi Mumbai"** by Deepak Kapoor and Rita Abbi. delineates the salient features of an emerging modern city, which was originally planned as a satellite city to decongest the already overcrowded Mumbai. The authors argue that Navi Mumbai offers all the advantages of a business and commercial town of the future. The city is all set to emerge as a new vibrant city of the 21st century with quality infrastructure and strong economic base. The rapid urbanisation, coupled with economic growth, has turned the area into an economic engine driving the economy of the entire coastal belt of Maharashtra. The planned developmental activities by City and Industrial Development Corporation (CIDCO) of Maharashtra on a continuous basis have resulted in the metamorphosis of the whole region into a brand new and modern city.

In the next paper on **"Migration and Development: Migration Patterns of the Hmong in Vietnam Through History"** by Nguyen Tran Lam, it is stated that migration is often opted by the poor to respond to adverse circumstances in order to seek a better life, even if they have to give up traditional values and relatives behind. In turn, migration may influence rural livelihood and shape people's reactions to change. The paper also describes the complex relationships between migration and livelihood in the context of socio-political changes taking place in the Northern Mountain Region (NMR) of Vietnam during the past 150 years. Analysing the different patterns of migration among the Hmong community during the major historical periods of Vietnam, the author makes on attempt to show how the migration among the Hmong is shaped by wars, policies and livelihoods. The author concludes by saying that the relationship between migration and development is very complex and historically contextualised. Therefore, further research is required to find out how migration patterns are structured and changed in the context of globalisation and to see the impact of migration on development in different settings.

The last paper in this section is on **"Impact of Urbanisation on Work-Life Balance"** by Elizabeth Mathews. The author defines work-life balance as the harmonious and holistic integration of work and non-work so that people can achieve their optimum level of potential across the domain in which they live. The paper makes an attempt to study the impact of urbanisation on work-life balance exploiting both primary and secondary sources of data. The author concludes that urbanisation has both positive and negative effects on the lives of the people. On the one hand, it offers a lot of opportunities and promises to improve ones life but on the other hand it is tilting the work-life balance in a wrong way affecting adversely the life of the people. Hence, there is a need in maintaining the work-life balance of the modern urban population.

Part II: Population, Development and Environment

The second part contains five papers. The first paper **"Changing Pattern of Population Growth and Socio-Economic Characteristics in the Fringe Villages of Guwahati City"** by Semim Wara Begum and Bimal K. Kar, begins with explaining that considerable change in the population growth and socio-economic characteristics in the fringe villages of Guwahati city due to the influence of the city is noticeable. Using both the primary and secondary data, the study explores the dimensions and context of this change in 80 fringe villages located up to 15 km from municipal boundary of the city. The population growth is generally high in the fringe villages. The socio-economic development has been taking place more in the non-tribal villages as compared to tribal fringe villages.

In the next paper **"Effects of Population Growth on Environmental Degradation in India"** by C.M. Lakshmana, data from census of India, reports and environment statistics published by the Ministry of Statistics are utilised to investigate the impact of population growth on environmental degradation in India. The author computed the environment degradation index (EDI) to understand the level of degradation. The high population growth and high deforestation in Uttar Pradesh, Bihar, Madhya Pradesh, Orissa, Maharashtra and Rajasthan seem to be the major causes of environmental degradation in these states. The Indian states witnessing higher industrial growth are facing more environmental degradation. The decadal growth of industries of India increased from 7 per cent in 1971–81 to 19 per cent during the decade 1991–2001. Some of the states like Tamil Nadu, Haryana, Kerala, Himachal Pradesh, Arunachal Pradesh, Rajasthan, Andhra Pradesh, Orissa, Maharashtra and Karnataka have higher industrial growth with rapid increase in the number of motor vehicles and rate of this growth is found to be higher than the growth of human population.

The increasing number of vehicles is the main source of pollution in most of our cities.

The paper **"Understanding Environmental Concern: Application of New Environmental Paradigm Scale in Rural West Bengal"** by Pradip Swarnakar and Arun Kumar Sharma explores the environmental concern of rural people facing the problem of quantity and quality with an upward shift in age at marriage in the younger cohorts.

The study is based on primary data collected from two blocks of two West Bengal districts covering 320 households. The important part of the study is the examination of the reliability of 'New Environment Paradigm' (NEP) scale administered for comparison. The study suggests that the 15-item NEP scale is well-suited to explore environmental consciousness in the rural setting of West Bengal. It is evident that arsenic affected people are environmentally more concerned (mean 3.34) than people facing scarcity of water (mean 2.90). The difference is statistically significant. Overall, fourteen out of fifteen cases of arsenic villages show greater pro-environmental beliefs than in the water-deficit villages.

The next paper **"Projection of Cancer Incident Cases for India till 2016"** by N.S. Murthy, M. Dhar and K. Chaudhury is based on data collected from the population-based cancer registries from various parts of the country working under National Cancer Registry Programme of the ICMR. The authors tried to present an estimate of the magnitude of incident cases of the cancer at the country as well as state level for quinquennial years from 2001 to 2016. The age-specific rates of cancer increase substantially after the age of 40 years. The pooled crude incidence rate and age standardised incidence rate were found to be 66.7 and 76.1 and 100.9 and 108.8 for males and females, respectively. The estimates suggest a 1.5–fold increase in the number of incident cases from 2001 to 2016 both at the all-India level as well as state level. Lung, esophagus, stomach, oral and pharyngeal cancers are much higher in men while in women, cancer in cervix and breast are predominant. The estimated number of tobacco-related cancer cases in males would rise from 0.171 million to 0.262 million merely as a result of change in size and age structure of populations. The study also suggests that the existing treatment facilities are woefully inadequate to combat this deadly disease.

The last paper in this part **"Trends in Cancer Incidence in Greater Mumbai: An Epidemiological Assessment"** by Balkrishna B. Yeole, investigates trends in age-adjusted incidence rate of cancer for the period 1982 to 2001 for prominent sites in Greater Mumbai patients after fitting the logarithmic model. Increasing trends in the incidence are seen among males for cancers involving liver, gall bladder, prostate, urinary bladder, kidney, brain, lymphomas and leukemia and among female for cancers involving the gall bladder, breast, uterus, ovary, urinary bladder, kidney, brain, lymphomas, and leukemia. Amongst the females, cancer of the breast, cervix and ovary contribute about 50 per cent of the total incidence. A statistically significant increasing trend was observed for ovarian cancers while decreasing trends was observed for cancer of the cervix.

Part III: Ageing

This part comprises three papers. The first paper, **"Rapid Fertility Decline and Age-Structural Transition in Iran: Causes and Consequences"** by Amir H. Mehryar, S. Ahmad-Nia and Shahla Kazemipour, after reviewing the process of demographic changes and fertility decline in Iran during the second half of the 20th century, assesses its possible demographic phenomenon and consequences during the first half of the 21st century. It then reviews the process of the age-structural transition that has resulted from these changes and also discusses the short-term and long-term implications for the Iranian society and economy. Census and some survey data for the period 1956–2003, along with projections for the period 2000–2050, of Iran have been utilised in this study.

The next paper, **"Harnessing Human Resource of Older Persons for Promoting Social Interaction and Environment Protection"** by Ng Sor Tho deals with issues relating to elderly persons in the context of promoting social interactions and environment protection in Malaysia. During the span of approximately 30 years since 1975–1980, the life expectancies for females and males increased by 10 years and 8 years respectively. Furthermore, in addition to substantial increase in the proportion of elderly persons aged 60 years and above and their substantial increase in educational attainment in Malaysia, the author opines that in future elderly persons will be better trained. Thus, as the author feels, there would be strong demand for maintenance of standard of living, and hence necessary opportunities and choices should be created for the elderly persons so as to enjoy independence, self-fulfilment, dignity etc. The author finally recommends that the expertise and the resource of the elderly persons should be fully tapped so as to integrate them in development programmes and as fully participating members of the society as per the experience of Petaling Jaya Community Centre (PJCC).

The last paper in this part, **"A Geographical Perspective on the Patterns of Ageing in the Tribal Areas of the North-Eastern Region of India"** by Debendra Kumar Nayak assesses the nature of the demographic and social changes among the tribal population in the north-east region of India, which experiences an unusual demographic situation of continuously high fertility along with an increase in life expectancy. Such a phenomenon of increased life expectancy in spite of high fertility level caused considerable increase in the proportion of elderly persons out of the total population. An attempt has also been made to understand the problems of ever-increasing number of the aged in context of tribal values towards the aged segment of the population. After a good deal of analyses and discussions, the author finds that the level and pattern of population ageing in the context of continued high fertility in the north-east region varies widely within various sub-regions and among different ethnic groups. Thus, it becomes a highly complex phenomenon in explaining the demographic situation in the north-east region, particularly in the tribal belt.

Part IV: Demography of Ethnic Groups

This part also consists of three papers. The main focus of the first paper, **"Ethnic Differences in Fertility in Uplands of Kanchanaburi, Thailand"** by Jian Hu is to study the differences in the number of children ever born (CEB) in relation to some socio-economic characteristics and language integration of the minority ethnic groups along with Thai population. This study makes use of the round 3 individual data set of the 2002 Demographic Surveillance System (DSS) in the Kanchanaburi province, Thailand. The main findings of this study are as follows: (i) Mon ethnic women had the highest cumulative fertility whereas the Thai women had the lowest one; (ii) The Mon, Karen, Burmese and other ethnic minority categories of respondents had lower educational attainment and higher child mortality than those of Thai; and (iii) The ethnic minorities, viz., Mon, Karen and Burmese women had higher mean CEB than that of Thai. The group of women other than Thai had lower educational attainment and higher proportion of child death than that of Thai. Thus, the author recommends that the human development indicators including educational level should be strengthened among the ethnic minorities so as to reduce infant and child mortality.

The next paper **"Whom to 'Marry'? Spouse Selection in the Small Tribes of Nilambur Valley, South India"** by Seetha Kakkoth deals with marriage-related issues in the two tribes—Aranadan and Kattupaniyan of Nilambur Valley. Both the communities have low sex ratio and the number of the unmarried males is much higher than that of females. Due to such imbalances in the sex ratio, younger men are compelled to marry older women and vice versa. Both these tribes follow exogamy and endogamy. Though cross-cousin marriages are preferable but owing to the lack of cross-cousins within the marriageable age, they even marry paternal or maternal parallel cousins, uncles, nieces, deceased wife's sisters, deceased husband's brothers, etc. There is thus no effective social control mechanism to regulate the various types of marital relations such as brother-in-law, sister-in-law, etc. The author also feels that commercialisation of forest, settler influx and deforestation have affected the ecosystem and economic base of these tribes. It helps them to get in contact with other communities and thus provide them ample opportunities in developing exogamous alliances among these tribes. It was found that the spouse selection in the forest-depended tribes is affected by the factors like geography, demography, society and economy. The author further commented that it is highly improbable for the communities with low population size, low sex ratio, relative isolation, disrupted economic base and week social control mechanism to follow prescribed marital rules. Hence, as a result, for survival strategy they resort alliance with their consanguine or with the communities with whom they have commonality or frequent interactions.

In the last paper of this part, **"Inequality in the Society in Terms of Standard of Living Index"** by R.C. Yadava and Arvind K. Shukla, an attempt has been made to study the relative inequality through the use of a standard living index (SLI), constructed by them assigning different weights to some household facilities and ownership status. The authors make use of Lorenz curves along with Gini-coefficients for better understanding the inequalities in various social groups as identified by them. The study makes use of the relevant data from the National Family Health Survey, 1998–99 (NFHS–2), carried out by the International Institute for Population Sciences, Mumbai. The study indicates that there exists a wide variation in inequality based on SLI, measured by the Gini-coefficients amongst various major Indian states. After ranking the Gini-coefficients in ascending order, the authors found that Punjab shows minimum inequality whereas the status in Orissa is most unequal even compared to Uttar Pradesh, Madhya Pradesh and Karnataka which occupy the middle position with respect to inequality. The second lowest and second highest ranks are occupied by Maharashtra and Bihar respectively. On the basis of average SLI alone, the authors observed that "as average development (SLI) increases, disparity decreases almost as a rule". The authors finally conclude that even after the lapse of more than half a century since independence, striking inter- and intra-state differentials in inequality and development levels as well are still observed among various Indian states. The authors also recommend that the Government of India should take appropriate steps in formulation of suitable policies so as to reduce the inequalities among the states and the Indian societies at large for a brighter future of the country as a whole.

Part V: Population Policies and Programmes

The last part has three papers too. The first paper **"Reproductive Health Services Remain Missing at the Grassroots Level: Evidence from a Time-Use Study of Service Providers in Rural Gujarat"** by N.P. Das and Urvi Shah is based on data collected from 24 primary health centres from five regions in the rural Gujarat. The basic objective is to assess the daily work pattern of various health and medical staff of PHCs, and time spent on various components of RCH programme. The staff of PHCs in Gujarat is well aware about RCH programmes. It is found that medical officers spent 45.5 hours per week in carrying out their various duties in the field as well as at the clinic, 21 hours on conducting OPD and remaining time on other programmes. The health supervisors devoted about 40–43 hours weekly in carrying out their responsibilities while other health workers spent about 43 hours in service provision. Fifty-five per cent of the respondents were not satisfied with the amount of time they could devote to various activities under the RCH programme. The RCH staff felt that RCH programme is good because it addresses new activities and initiatives. They also expressed that they need refresher training in RCH programme. It was reported that RCH programme suffered due to inadequacies in logistics, supplies and sub-centre facilities.

The next paper **"Health Modernity and Utilisation of Health Services: A Pilot Study in Madhya Pradesh"** by A.S. Dey and A. Shrivastava. is aimed to assess health modernity, attitudinal and behavioural scale and relationship between level of health, modernisation and utilisation of the health services in Sagar district of Madhya Pradesh based on data collected from 500 eligible women age 15–44 years through pilot survey. Forty per cent of women have 'very poor' health modernity having modernity score less than 25 per cent of total score. Seven per cent of women have 'good' score having 75 per cent or more of the total score. The factors affecting the modernity are mainly illiteracy and poverty. Women also believe in certain myths or have misconceptions and ignorance. It is found that couples having low level of obstetric modernity also utilised obstetric service in a limited way. Only 46 per cent low scoring couples had three or more ANC check-ups. About three-fourths of low scoring women had not taken IFA tablets.

The last paper **"The Road Map to Hospitalisation: Tackling Health Problem in Rural Meghalaya"** has been jointly authored by Sandip Mitra, Chaiti S. Biswas, Dilip C. Nath, Manoranjan Pal and Biswanath Bhattacharya. This study is based on household survey of all hospitalisation cases during 2002–03 from six villages of four CHCs in West Khasi Hill district of Meghalaya. All those households with at least one case of hospitalisation in preceding one year were considered for the study. The main objective was to know the socio-demographical profile of households and its relation with the hospitalisation. Total 135 cases of hospitalisation were identified from all six villages in four CHCs. The socio-economic profile of diseased families is illustrated without any real motive of generalisation. A more comprehensive study is essential to understand the health profile of individuals. It has been seen that older generation and educated families are more prone to observing hygienic conditions.

PART I

Migration and Urbanisation

1

Household Remittances, Inequality and Poverty

Evidence from the State of Kerala, India

Adeline Pelletier

The purpose of this paper is to analyse the impact of international as well as internal remittances[1] on households' poverty and inequality in Kerala. During the last quarter of the twentieth century, the cash remittances received by Kerala households, mainly from emigrants to the Gulf region, and popularly known as 'Gulf Money', have emerged as the most dynamic factor that contributed to sustain the economic development of the state, in the context of agricultural failure, industrial growth stagnation and increasing unemployment. The amount of remittances received by Kerala households has been rising during the last decade and the state economy has become more and more dependent on these capital flows. In 2003, the remittances represented 22 per cent of the net state domestic product.

With high remittances sustained over a long period, industrial investment has remained low, and Kerala's impressive development achievements and reduction in poverty of the past decades has not been matched by adequate employment generation. Unemployment and poverty are increasingly concentrated among casual labour, and poverty has also spread across caste groups. The persistence of the economic crisis has raised concerns about the sustainability of the achievements already made in health, education and other human development spheres and the further efforts to improve the quality of life of the people. In this context, the impacts remittances might have on poverty and inequality are crucial to the sustainability of the development achievements. Do remittances in Kerala help to sustain the achievements made in social and economic spheres or do they exacerbate inequalities without being poor-friendly?

This paper seeks to contribute to a better understanding of the impacts of remittances on the Kerala economy by focusing on the direct first-order effects of households' remittances. Their second order effects on employment and wages have been extensively studied by Zachariah et al. (2002, 2003, 2006).[2] The available literature on remittances and their macroeconomic or microeconomic impacts on inequities and poverty is mostly based on income variables to determine the effect of remittances on Gini coefficient, or to assess the impact of remittances on households' expenditures. It has been found that remittances directly affect poverty by increasing and broadening the opportunities to increase the income of the recipient. Evidence from households' survey shows that remittances increase savings and asset accumulation (liquid and non-liquid assets), help to smooth income and consumption (Kannan and Hari, 2002) and act as an insurance mechanism by responding positively to adverse shocks[3] (Lucas and Stark, 1985; Yang and Choi, 2005). Moreover, remittances lead to an increase of household expenditures in areas considered to be important for development, particularly education, health and entrepreneurship (World Bank, 2006). Unlike previous studies, the following analysis will be based on poverty indicators such as housing quality, facilities and possession of consumer durables and on socio-demographic variables determining the household's structure and which are likely to influence the reception of remittances and their uses. Moreover, most of the patterns of migration studied in the literature are either permanent international migration—generally to the United States—or temporal internal migration from rural to urban areas. Kerala constitutes an interesting case study for it is concerned both by international and internal migration—from Kerala to other Indian states; and international migration, mainly to Gulf countries. Different remitting behaviour might be expected from the emigrants who have to return eventually to their home country and those who intend to settle in the host countries. These different remitting behaviours might in turn affect the extent to which the households can rely on remittances to follow poverty-alleviation strategies.

From the standpoint of poverty and equity concerns the main questions regarding remittances addressed in the empirical analysis (part II) are the following:

1. Who goes to work abroad? If migrants are drawn from wealthier groups, this may have important negative effects on income

distribution in the studied area. The first section of part II outlines the influencing factors of migration, that is, the individual characteristics of the migrants.

2. What is the impact of remittances on the standard of living? The second section assesses the effects of remittances on the standard of living of selected recipient households.
3. Who is sending remittances and what is the composition of the households receiving remittances? If the poorer migrants have the higher propensity to remit, then remittances will be poor-friendly. The third section examines these issues.
4. How do migrants use their monies? Do remittance-receiving households spend more on health and education, which are strategic investments to lift people out of poverty? The fourth section sheds some light on households' pattern of expenditure.

The first part presents the data set, approach and methodology used in this paper, the second part is dedicated to the presentation of the empirical results and the third part summarises the results and concludes.

I

Study Area, Data Set and Methodology

Data Set

The following empirical analysis is based on two migration surveys done in the state of Kerala in 1998 and 2003—Kerala Migration Study (KMS 1998) and South Asia Migration Study (SMS 2003). KMS 1998 and SMS 2003 collected migration-related information only on Kerala migrants, that is, those emigrants and out-migrants who have their families living in Kerala and are included in the registers of local bodies in Kerala. Information about the migrants was collected from the families in Kerala. The methodology of estimation and analysis followed in both studies are quite similar, though their objectives were slightly different. The main aim of KMS had been the assessment of the migration situation in 1998 and its consequences while SMS not only assessed the situation in 2003, but also the dynamics during 1998–2003. Although the coverage is limited in SMS compared with that of the KMS, both studies are quite comparable with respect to the data collected and the method of analysis. Around 125 localities (or panchayat/municipal wards) out of 200 in KMS were included in SMS.

About 4,795 out of the total of 10,000 households in the SMS sample were the same as those included in KMS, and in these 4,795 households, about 23,000 individuals were the same in both surveys.

As a consequence, this gives an opportunity to study the dynamics of migration and remittances' impacts during 1998–2003, especially the changes in housing quality and possession of amenities that occurred for the households included in both studies.

Moreover, contrary to most of the papers focusing on households' remittances which use data sets from households' budget surveys, these two surveys are specifically designed to examine migration and remittances issues.

Methodology

The surveys examine the migration status of the individuals.

Following are the four types of migrants:

REM (return migrants), that is, members of the household who, in the past, had emigrated out of India but had returned to Kerala and were now the members of the household.

EMI (emigrants), that is, persons who had moved out of Kerala after 1980 and were living outside India at the time of the survey.

ROM (return out-migrants), that is, members of a household who had moved out of Kerala after 1980 and were living outside India at the time of the survey.

OMI (out-migrants), that is, persons who had moved out of Kerala after 1980 and were living outside Kerala but within India.

Migrant households (EMI HHs and OMI HHs) are households with at least one migrant member.

Information on remittances and migrants has been treated separately. The data provide information on the migrants, and the characteristics of their migration (year of the first emigration, country or state of residence, occupation ...). Information on remittances comes to four specific questions: about the amount of money received during the last year, the estimated value of goods received last year and pocket transfers—that is, cash brought with migrants on their visits to purchase or renovate land or house or for any other purpose. The surveys encompass the various forms of remittances. However, they do not determine who has sent the money. When there is more than one migrant in the family, it is not possible to determine how much each migrant has remitted, and for the recipient families with both emigrants and out-migrants it is not possible to know whether the remittances were internal or international. Thus, in the following analysis the sample will be divided into two sub-groups: families with only emigrants and families with only out-migrants.[4] In order to assess the individual characteristics influencing the propensity to remit, a sample including migrant families with only one migrant will be used.

Framework of Analysis

The framework used to assess the impacts of migration on poverty and inequality draws on models elaborated in different studies on remittances.

Following Stark, Taylor and Yitzhaki (1986, 1988) and Rodriguez (1988), we hypothesise that the dynamics of migration and remittances may be represented by an inverted U-shaped curve: in the presence of liquidity constraints and initially high migration costs, only high-income groups have access to higher income opportunities abroad and, consequently, remittances tend to increase inter-household inequality. Over time, access to migrant labour markets becomes diffused across sending-area households through the growth and elaboration of migrant networks, thus making migration affordable to low-income households so that ultimately economic inequality at origin decreases.

The diffusion of opportunities across households determines to a great extent the impact remittances will have on inequality. Emigration to the Gulf is not a recent phenomenon in Kerala, and it increased sharply after the oil price hike in 1973 and the rapid growth of job opportunities. It is neither a declining phenomenon, as evidenced by Zachariah and Rajan (2006). Indeed, it happens that contrary to previous expectations, external as well as internal migration has continued to increase steadily during the five-year period 1999–2004. In 1998, there were 13.6 lakh[5] emigrants and 18.4 lakh in 2003. During this five-year period, the number of emigrants from Kerala has increased by 35 per cent. They represented roughly 21 per cent of the households in 1998 and 27 per cent in 2003. Thus, we assume that Kerala's Gulf emigration has reached a mature stage. International, as well as internal migration from Kerala is neither a recent phenomenon nor a declining one. As the Gulf migration is long established, the migrant networks have already been established. This implies that the barriers due to information costs have largely been removed, and the opportunities to migrate in the Gulf region are much diffused. Thus, in the case of Kerala it is not correct to assume, as it can be at the initial stage of a migration process, that the non-migrants are dissuaded to move because of the very restricted access to relevant information, or because they are not innovative enough. Given that, have international and internal remittances helped to decrease economic inequality? To answer this question it is necessary to assess to what extent the poorest segments of the population have access to migration.

Another important point is the geographic scale of analysis. As evidenced by Jones (1998), two factors help to explain the divergence of views on migration inequality. One already mentioned is the place's stage of migration. Another is the geographic level of analysis: interregional, inter-urban, rural-urban or interfamilial. Most of the studies on remittances, inequality and poverty are based on surveys conducted at the local level—in communities or villages or inter-urban scale. In Kerala, rural-urban differences are generally small for many of the social indicators, and this is also true with respect to the unemployment rate (see Ramachandran, 1996, Zachariah et al., 2003). Thus discriminating the households by living area to assess the impact of remittances on poverty is not very relevant for this study. The data available from Kerala migration surveys enables us to extend the scope of analysis to a state level. The following analysis focuses on inequities between emigrant, out-migrant and non-migrant households in an area encompassing a state.

A more crucial issue concerning the methodology employed deals with the tools and concepts used to scrutinise poverty and inequality. The evaluation of the impacts of remittances is highly sensitive to the methodological choices, specifically how poverty and inequality are defined and how they are measured. Although poverty has been traditionally measured in monetary terms it is by now widely acknowledged that poverty is a multidimensional concept, involving not only economic deprivation but other forms of social and political deprivation as well. In the following discussion, poverty will not be approached in quantitative terms using monetary indicators of poverty such as headcount index or poverty gaps, or of inequality such as Gini coefficients, since the migrant surveys do not provide income or budget expenditure data. Instead, the focus will be on relative and qualitative poverty and on inter-household inequities. While absolute poverty refers to subsistence below minimum, relative poverty compares the lowest segments of a population with upper segments, usually measured in income quintiles or deciles. Indicators such as educational levels, housing quality or possession of specific consumer durables will be used to assess the inter-household inequities and the relative poverty of particular sub-groups of population. In the literature on remittances, inequality always refers to income inequality which is the extent of disparity between high and low incomes. It is assessed by indicators of income inequality such as Gini coefficients. To our knowledge, there is no study on the impact of remittances on inequality which broadens the concept of inequality to disparities in health or in standards of living. The conflicting results obtained from household income data as well as the shortcomings of income inequality indicators[6] make a strong case for a new approach measuring inequality in qualitative terms. This analysis will focus on inter-household socio-economic inequalities. The term 'socio-economic inequality' is used in the paper to signify inequality in a broader sense, i.e., inequality with respect to standards of living, and access to health services and education.

II

Empirical Analysis

Migration as a Highly Selective Process: Who Goes to Work Abroad?

The process of migration selects particular sub-groups of the population. In turn these sub-groups send remittances income back to their families. The selection is both demographic and socio-economic (Stark, Taylor, and Yitzhaki, 1986, 1988; Jones, 1998). The human capital model of migration predicts that migrants are better-off and are better-educated. This section outlines the individual characteristics of emigrants and out-migrants and compares individual characteristics of migrants and non-migrants. It analyses the structure of migration in order to test the selection hypothesis of the human capital migration theory. Are migrants from Kerala drawn from above-average income households or is migration a survival strategy for the poorer families?

Educational Status of the Migrant at the Time of Migration

If migrants have a higher educational level than the non-migrant population, the selection hypothesis holds true.

Table 1 ***Educational Level of Individuals Over 18 Years Old according to their Migration Status***

(in percentage)

Educational Level[a] *(%)*	*Emigrant*		*Out-migrant*		*Non-migrant*	
	1998	*2003*	*1998*	*2003*	*1998*	*2003*
Illiterate	0.7	0.5	0.8	0.2	9.2	7.2
Below primary	11.7	1.9	6.5	1.4	24.2	11.5
Primary	73.9	46.5	76.3	29.0	54.8	49.7
Secondary	10.7	31.0	15.7	43.0	6.7	22.4
Degree holders	3.2	20.1	0.8	26.3	5.1	9.1
Total	100.0	100.0	100.0	100.0	100.0	100.0

Source: Own calculations based on KMS 1998 and SMS 2003.

a Indicates the educational level of migrants at the time of migration.

In 2003, 2.4 per cent of the emigrants and 1.6 per cent of the out-migrants were illiterate or could only read or write simple sentence whereas as much as 18.7 per cent of the non-migrants were illiterate or did not attend primary school. The educational achievement of migrants and non-migrants yield significant differentials, consistent with the selection hypothesis. The *t*-tests done with SMS 2003 data revealed that the difference in educational achievements between emigrants and non-migrants is significant at 5 per cent (t = 27.32). The difference between out-migrants and non-migrants is also significant at 5 per cent (t = 11.92). Since the age distribution of the migrants is different from that of the non-migrants, with lesser elders among migrants, this may influence the distribution and may account for the lower educational level of the non-migrants—the educational level of the young generation being higher than that of the older generations. Given that the majority of the migrants are between 20 and 30 years old, the distribution of the educational status was estimated again for individuals between 20 and 30 years old of the three groups, using SMS 2003. After correcting for age, the differential is reduced: 53.9 per cent of the emigrants and 74.8 of the out-migrants between 20 and 30 years old hold a secondary certificate or are degree holders, while the figure is 47.8 per cent for non-migrants. T-tests done with SMS 2003 data revealed that the differentials between emigrant and non-migrant and between out-migrant and non-migrant were not significant at 10 per cent. The results obtained are not wholly consistent with the selection hypothesis that predicts that migrants are better educated than non-migrants.

Among the different groups, the out-migrants had achieved the highest educational levels. In 2003, 69.3 per cent of the out-migrants had at least a secondary certificate as against 51.1 per cent for the emigrants. The proportion of degree holders has increased by 16.9 percentage points among the emigrants and by 25.5 percentage points among the out-migrants, while it has only increased by 4.0 percentage points among the non-migrant population. These differentials may stem from two factors: first, the proportion of students who leave their state to study outside, be it abroad—the United States—or in another state of India, has increased between 1998 and 2003. Second, a shift in job opportunities in Gulf countries, evidenced by the increase in the number of emigrants with high status occupations in the host country, may explain this particular educational trend. In the early phase of Gulf emigration from Kerala, the emigrants were mostly non-agricultural labourers working in construction or semi-skilled workers. In 2003, the proportion of emigrants working as labourers in non-agricultural sectors lessened by nearly 10 percentage points, all host countries included. The demand for low-skilled emigrants has shrunk, while the demand for educated emigrants in the semi-government sector has increased.

Education is a major migration-facilitating factor. However, it must be kept in mind that the educational level of the migrants varies accordingly to the job opportunities abroad or in the neighbouring states within the country. For instance, contrary to rural Mexico (Taylor et al., 2005) and Kerala, where emigrants are less educated than out-migrants, external migration from rural Pakistan studied by Adams (1996) contained a larger positive reward to education than internal migration. The Pakistanis who pursued external migration were more educated than the internal migrants, because they could find jobs as clerks and small business operators in the Arab Gulf, positions for which some educational skills were appropriate. These findings highlight the fact that although migration tends to be positively related to education, which accords with human capital theory, the relation varies according to the job opportunities outside, and the correlation between education and migration is not necessarily positive.

Occupational Status at the Time of Migration

Another important factor to consider when scrutinising a migration process is the occupational status of the migrant at his or her place of origin. The scarcity of jobs is often one of the major factors influencing the decision to migrate.

Table 2 Occupation of the Population above 18 Years by Migration Status

(in percentage)

Occupational Status[a]	*Emigrant*		*Out-migrant*		*Non-migrant*	
	1998	*2003*	*1998*	*2003*	*1998*	*2003*
Employed in state/central govt.	2.2	1.4	3.2	2.9	3.7	3.5
Employed in semi-govt. aided school/college, cooperative/local administrative bodies.	0.6	2.7	0.5	1.5	1.1	1.5
Employed in private sector	15.4	9.1	7.3	2.0	4.5	2.5
Self-employment	13.9	7.2	4.7	2.1	12.8	9.0
Unpaid family worker	0.8	0.9	2.3	0.5	1.2	0.8
Agricultural labour	1.8	1.8	0.7	1.1	7.6	6.7
Labourers in non-agricultural sector	34.1	33.0	15.9	10.0	16.7	20.7
Job seekers	26.5	33.8	45.5	47.7	5.0	9.1
Job not required	0.2	0.4	0.3	0.9	7.7	6.1
Student	1.5	5.3	14.1	20.4	9.8	9.9
Household duties	3.2	4.2	5.6	10.7	29.2	28.0
Old-age/Handicapped pension	0.1	0.1	—	0.2	0.6	2.3
Total	100.0	100.0	100.0	100.0	100.0	100.0

Source: Own calculations based on KMS 1998 and SMS 2003.

a Indicates the occupation of migrants at the time of migration.

The pre-migration occupational distribution in Graph 1 indicates that nearly half of the out-migrants and more than 30 per cent of the emigrants were unemployed before moving from Kerala. The occupational statuses of out-migrants do not differ much from those of emigrants: majority of the migrants were labourers in the non-agricultural sector or job seekers at the time of migration. The higher percentage of people employed in household duties in the non-migrant population may be explained by the higher number of females and the elderly than among the migrant population, household duties being predominantly a women's occupation in Kerala. Migration is more and more driven by unemployment as evidenced by the increase of job seekers in the migrant population between 1998 and 2003. However, the number of unemployed also increased in the non-migrant population. Unemployment is a major concern for the overall population. Zachariah and Rajan (2006) estimated that the unemployment rate was 12 per cent for 1999 and 18.6 per cent for 2004.[7] The migration rate figures are not wholly consistent with migration theory. While that theory hypothesises the migration of the more skilled, the data indicate little evidence of occupational selectivity. For instance, a large part of the emigrants were labourers in the non-agricultural sector which is a low-skill occupation. Since a large majority is composed of job seekers, it is necessary to scrutinise the educational status of these unemployed migrants to determine whether migrants from Kerala selects the higher skilled unemployed or the lower-skilled ones.

Graph 1 ***Migration Rate in Kerala by Occupational Status in 2003***

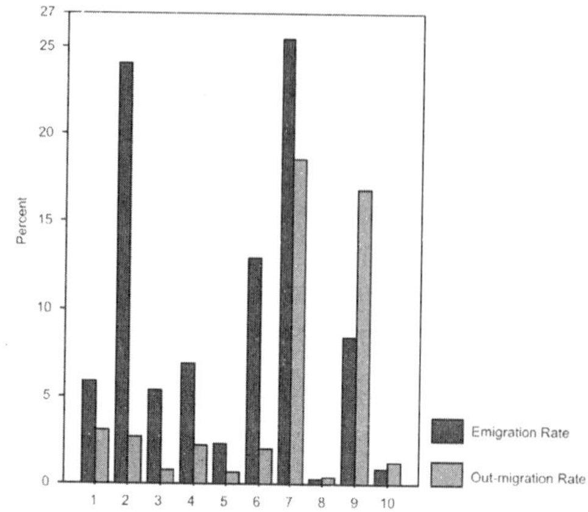

Source: Own calculations based on SMS 2003.

Note: Indicates the occupation of migrants before migration.
1: Employed in state/central govt./local administrative bodies, 2: Employed in private sector, 3: Self-employment, 4: Unpaid family work, 5: Agricultural labour, 6: Labourers in non-agricultural sector, 7: Job seekers, 8: Job not required, 9: Student, 10: Household duties.

Educational Status of the Migrants Unemployed before Migration

As reported above, the largest part of the emigrants in 2003 were unemployed ("job seekers") at the time of migration. Migration is often a way to escape poverty and unemployment. The premise of the New Economics of Labour (Stark, 1991) posits that the migration of the family member is often a survival strategy of households in poor developing countries. By migrating, finding a job outside the country and remitting a part of their salary, the unemployed can improve their family's living conditions. The hypothesis that migration is a cause of poverty holds particularly true if the majority of unemployed migrants are among the less skilled workers, with low economic status. The table below reports the educational status of the unemployed before migration to determine whether upward mobility through employment abroad was enjoyed by the less educated, and presumably poorer emigrants, or if it was the higher educated unemployed who could migrate.

Table 3 ***Educational Status of the Unemployed Population in 2003***

Educational Status (%)	*Emigrant*[a]	*Out-migrant*[b]	*Non-migrant*
Below primary	0.4	1.2	0.8
Primary	33.8	28.7	27.5
Secondary	38.8	47.4	51.3
Degree holders	27.0	22.7	20.4
Total	100.0	100.0	100.0

Source: Own calculations based on SMS 2003.

a and b: Individuals unemployed before migration.

Consistent with the findings concerning the educational status of the overall migrants, the figures in Table 3 show that migrants unemployed at the time of migration have achieved higher educational levels than unemployed non-migrants. However, t-tests done with SMS 2003 data revealed that the difference in educational levels between emigrant and non-migrant is not significant at 10 per cent ($t = 0.32$). The difference between out-migrant and non-migrant is also not significant at 10 per cent ($t = -0.25$). Then, with respect to educational level, unemployed migrants and unemployed non-migrants do not differ significantly and out-migrants tend to be slightly less educated than non-migrants and emigrants. These results neither indicate the degree of educational selectivity that is predicted by the human capital model of migration, nor do they indicate that migration was a survival strategy mainly opted by low skilled unemployed Keralites.

Migrants are drawn selectively from specific communities—particularly the Muslim community—as well as specific educational levels and occupations. The average level of education of emigrants is substantially higher than the average level in the state and unemployment is strongly influencing the decision to migrate. However, the pre-migration occupational distribution, and the educational level of the unemployed are not wholly consistent with the human capital migration theory given that those in high status jobs were negatively selected. This fact implies that in Kerala, working migration, especially emigration, is not a strategy or investment undertaken by those who are in the above-average income group, except for the very few emigrating to faraway places such as the United States. Then, the effects of migration through remittances are likely to be poor-friendly. Section II turns to the effects of remittances on recipients' standards of living.

Looking at the Impacts of Remittances on Inequality and Poverty through Households' Standards of Living

KMS 1998 and SMS 2003 provide rich details of the households' standards of living, scarcely available in the data sets commonly used in the literature on remittances. This data will be used to determine the households' position in the income distribution of the state.

Table 2 in Appendix shows that migrant households are better-off than non-migrant households in terms of housing quality, housing facilities and possession of consumer durables. However, these simple comparisons do not exactly reflect the effects of remittances on living standards as it might be that a higher proportion of migrant households compared to non-migrant households already had the items reported or already lived in houses of good quality before the departure of the migrant. To what extent do remittances contribute to improve the living conditions of the recipient households?

For the analytical purpose in view, a sample of households which did not receive remittances in 1998 but which did in 2003 is selected and denominated "Households *R*" (N = 358). The five-year period between the two surveys is long enough for the households to reap the benefits of migration and for the present study to assess the effects of remittances on the households' living standard. Since at the overall level the living conditions had bettered during this period, the figures for the *R* group are compared to those obtained for all the households interviewed both in 1998 and 2003 (N = 4,796). The aim is to evaluate the magnitude of the improvements in living conditions between two periods, one without remittances and one with.

Electrification

Table 4 ***Distribution of Electricity among Households***

Electrification (%)	*Households R*	*All Households*
Electrified in 1998 and 2003	74.0	71.7
Non-electrified in1998 and 2003	4.2	12.0
Non-electrified in 1998 but electrified in 2003	21.4	14.2
Electrified in 1998 and non-electrified in 2003	0.0	2.1
Total	100.0	100.0

Source: Own calculations based on KMS 1998 and SMS 2003.

The results are clear-cut: the households belonging to the group *R* are more likely to be electrified in 2003 and to have electricity installed in their house between 1998 and 2003 than the average household.

Housing Conditions

Housing improvement is measured using a scale ranging from –3 to + 3, using the five categories in the survey: Kutcha, poor, good, very good, luxurious. +3 indicates that the housing quality has improved by three points (e.g., from Kutcha to very good), –3 indicates that the housing quality has deteriorated by three points (e.g. from luxurious to poor). And 0 indicates that the housing condition of the household has remained unchanged between 1998 and 2003.

Table 5 ***Housing Improvement Between 1998 and 2003***

Housing Improvement (%)	*Households R*	*All Households*
+3	1.2	0.5
+2	5.5	5.6
+1	24.5	22.6
0	60.9	57.5
-1	7.9	12.6
-2	0.0	1.1
-3	0.0	0.1
Total	100.0	100.0

Source: Own calculations based on KMS 1998 and SMS 2003.

The figures show that households belonging to the group *R* have improved their housing quality to a greater extent than the overall households. Fewer households in the group *R* have experienced a deterioration of their housing conditions.

Possession of Consumer Durables

KMS 1998 and SMS 2003 record the possession by households of 8 consumer durables: motor car, taxi, motorcycle, telephone, mobile phone, television, VCR/VCP and fridge (see Table 2 in Appendix).

A composite index using all the 8 items is calculated by giving appropriate weights to each of the 8 items. The sum of the weights is 100 so that the index varies from 0 to 100. If the household has all the 8 items, the index will be 100. If the household does not have any of the items, the index will be 0 (see in appendix for the computation of the index).

Table 6 ***Changes in Possession of Goods Between 1998 and 2003***

Index of Possession of Goods (IPG)	*Households R*	*All Households*
Index IPG 1998 (Mean)	14.0	12.2
Index IPG 2003 (Mean)	26.9	20.0
Index increase (%)	+ 92.1	+ 63.9
Index IPG 1998 is null (%)	52.5	57.6
Index IPG 2003 is null (%)	18.2	32.6
Index score has improved (% of HHs)	67.0	50.5
No change (% of HHs)	16.5	29.7
Index score has deteriorated (% of HHs)	16.5	19.8
Total (% of HHs)	100.0	100.0
Index IPG 2003 for HHs with index deterioration (mean)	30.3	23.5

Source: Own calculations based on KMS 1998 and SMS 2003.

A large majority of households, both group considered, possessed more consumer durables in 2003 than in 1998, but the increase is sharper for the group *R* than for the overall households. Around 67 per cent of the families belonging to the group *R* have more consumer durables in 2003 than in 1998; when all households are considered, only half of the families have a higher IPG score in 2003 than in 1998. Households for which score decreased between the five-year period are still better off in 2003 than the average household of their respective group. Thus, their impoverishment was relative and they did not end up poorer than the average households.

The intertemporal comparisons of housing quality and possession of consumer durables indicate that the effects of remittances on standards of living are significant and positive. Of course, the improvements can not be exclusively attributed to these earnings from abroad, other variables likely to affect positively the households' living conditions might have changed during the five-year period. However, the fact that the households who started to receive remittances between 1998 and 2003 have improved their living conditions to a greater extent than the overall households highlights the positive role played by remittances in the observed changes.

Who Sends and Who Receives Remittances? Analysis of the Remitting Pattern

The preceding sections have highlighted the fact that migration is highly selective, the very poor not being able to migrate, and that remittances have large positive effects on recipient households' standards of living. This section aims at linking the migration process to the remitting process. Among those who migrate, not everyone is sending remittances. If migrants from households with low economic status have a higher propensity to remit than higher skilled migrants, with presumably higher incomes, then remittances will have positive effects on both poverty and inequality. The aim of the following analysis is (i) to examine the remitting behaviour of different categories of migrants (ii) to determine what the socio-demographic characteristics of the recipient households are and to what extent they differ from the non-recipient households.

Proportion of Migrants Remitting by Selected Socio-Economic Variables

As mentioned in part I, KMS and SMS surveys do not indicate the provenance of the remittances. In order to assess the individual characteristics influencing the propensity to remit, I have divided the data into two samples. One sample is composed of emigrant households with only one emigrant and without any out-migrant. Another sample composed of out-migrant households with only one out-migrant and without any emigrant. The selected samples remain large: in SMS 2003, only 17 per cent of the emigrant households had more than one emigrant. For out-migrant households, the sample size is, however, more reduced (N=625) given that 46 per cent of the households had more than one out-migrant.

Emigrant's Remitting Behaviour

With respect to emigrants, the figures highlight the fact that those with less education display a higher propensity to remit. The proportion of remitters decreases with the years of education. Consistent with the human capital theory which posits that education explains much of the differences in salaries between individuals, the results in Table 7 indicate that a high-educated migrant remits a larger amount than his or her less educated counterparts. The amount of cash or goods remitted is positively correlated with the educational level of the emigrant. With respect to the occupation of emigrants abroad, those with low status jobs are more prone to remit than those in private sector or self-employed. As expected, the sums remitted vary accordingly to the occupational status: emigrants with higher skilled jobs send a larger amount than manual workers. It may well be argued that high-skill emigration of Forward Caste to developed countries has increased long-term inequality since these immigrants have incomes much higher than other emigrants, thus

Table 7 *Proportion of Migrants Remitting and Amount Remitted According to Selected Socio-economic Variables*

Socio-economic Characteristics	*Number of Migrants*[c]		*Per cent of Migrants Remitting*		*Total Remittances in Cash and Kind per Household Member*[d] *(mean)*	
	Emi-grant	*Out-migrant*	*Emi-grant*	*Out-migrant*	*Emi-grant*	*Out-migrant*
Educational Level[a]						
Below primary	177	16	88.9	6.2	8,358	13,000
Primary	1,173	187	83.5	19.2	12,425	8,023
Secondary	777	302	80.1	18.5	15,870	29,127
Degree holder	488	115	63.7	18.3	17,165	18,522
Occupational Status[b]						
Employed in state/central govt. or local administrative bodies	272	134	81.6	15.7	24,227	11,683
Private secto.	926	179	79.7	21.8	14,439	12,676
Labourers in non-agricultural sector	930	109	84.4	19.3	10,884	39,993
Self-employment	142	28	77.0	21.4	11,659	5,198
Caste or Community						
SC/ST	29	39	86.4	2.6	6,826	12,500
Ezhavas	352	101	83.5	17.8	11,099	15,178
Nair	273	135	78.0	16.2	15,895	35,031
Brahmins	49	9	58.8	—	15,678	—
Christians	637	217	73.5	21.6	24,688	15,834
Muslims	1,179	70	86.3	34.3	11,136	9,790

Source: Own calculations based on SMS 2003.

SC/ST: Scheduled Castes, Scheduled Tribes.

a Indicate the educational level of the migrants before migration.

b Indicate the occupation of the migrants at the place of destination.

c Total number of migrants (remitters and non-remitters).

d Calculations of the mean total of remittances including only recipient households.

a higher capacity to remit. However, if one considers that the increase in inequality entailed by the migration process is mainly due to the fact that households receiving remittances are among the best-off, it is not possible to conclude that emigration severely affects the income distribution. Indeed, the proportion of remitting emigrants from the Forward

Hindu castes—Brahmins and Nairs—is lower than that of the Backward and Scheduled Castes. Almost 41.2 per cent of the Brahmin emigrants do not remit cash or goods, while the proportion drops to 16.5 per cent among the Ezhavas emigrants, 13.6 per cent among Scheduled Caste or Scheduled Tribe emigrants and 13.7 among Muslims. The Brahmin or Nair families are already relatively rich and there is no need or no pressure for the migrants to send money home. The remitting is negatively related to the wealth of the family. The Backward Castes (Ezahvas or Muslims) are rather mobile and for these communities migration is often associated with upward mobility prospects. The high propensity to remit of Ezhava emigrants suggests that they consider migration as a strategy to enhance the economic status of their family, if not to escape poverty.[8] A large proportion of Muslims, whose community have the highest illiteracy rate, are equally committed to remit a part of their earnings, suggesting a redistribution of the wealth in the state favourable to the poor. The large discrepancy in the means of remittances in cash per household members between the Christians and the Muslims is not explained by the family size, which is in fact lower for the Christians with a mean of respectively 4 persons in Christian households and 6 persons in Muslim households,[9] but by their educational level. Almost 78.6 per cent of the Christian emigrants who send remittances have a secondary certificate or are degree holders, whereas they are only 24.5 per cent among the Muslims. Having a higher educational level, Christian emigrants are employed in more skilled sectors. Then, they are able to remit a higher amount of cash than other emigrants.

These results indicate that the remitting behaviour of emigrants depends upon their socio-economic characteristics. Poorer emigrants are more prone to remit. Remittances made by these migrants are crucial resources for the origin households to overcome capital constraints or to create the conditions necessary to lift them out of poverty. However, they remit a lower amount of cash than the better-off emigrants. Although remittance flows are particularly directed towards households of lower economic status, the large differentials in the amount remitted might exacerbate inequalities between recipient households. I calculated the total amount sent by the emigrants whose educational level was equivalent to primary or below, and the amount sent by those who achieved secondary certificate or are degree holders. I found that among emigrants with low educational level—primary or below—563 sent remittances to their households, with an average amount of Rs 48,030 per household, whereas among emigrants with high educational level, secondary or degree, 437 sent remittances, with an average amount of Rs 56,396. Then, as the households of educated—and the assumed wealthier—emigrants received more in total than those of less educated emigrants, the wealth redistribution through international remittances has not been equalitarian and international remittances have increased inter-(emigrant) family inequalities.

Out-migrants' Remitting Behaviour

The figures for internal migration are very surprising. Contrary to what was observed for emigration, it is found that out-migrants with very low educational level, employed in low skilled jobs or from Backward or Scheduled Castes are less likely to remit than the better-off out-migrants. I calculated the amount of remittances sent by two groups of out-migrants: the high educated and the low educated in 2003. I found that among out-migrants with low educational level, primary or below, 31 sent remittances to their households, with an average amount of Rs 39,000 per household, whereas among out-migrants with high educational level—secondary certificate or degree—76 sent remittances, with an average amount of Rs 64,388. These results indicate that out-migration has had no large positive effect on poverty and that on the contrary, it has exacerbated income inequalities since the poorest out-migrant households were very few to receive remittances. Two explanations for these striking findings can be put forward. First, as mentioned earlier, out-migration is often a survival strategy chosen by individuals with very low financial or educational resources who can not afford emigration. The revenues of this category of out-migrants may be so meagre that they are not able to remit a part of their earnings to their family. A second explanation is that nearly three quarters of out-migrants were single, whereas they were only 56 per cent among emigrants. Without a spouse or children left behind, they were less inclined to remit.

Regression Analysis of Emigrants' Propensity to Remit

A regression analysis is done to determine which individual and household variables studied above are significant determinants of the propensity to remit. Given that emigration has a higher potential of poverty reduction than out-migration, the analysis is done for the emigrant group. Moreover, the sample of out-migrant households with only one migrant receiving remittances is too small (N=113) to substantiate any argument at the state level. The propensity of emigrants remitting to their households is examined through a logistic regression model. A single indicator of remitters, those sending either cash or goods is used. A sample of 1,228 individuals between 18 and 65 years old was available for the analysis, of which 974 were remitters and 254 non-remitters. The remittance status is the binary dependent variable indicating whether or not the emigrant had sent remittances in the year preceding the survey. Independent individual and household variables included in the analysis were chosen because they proved to be important factors explaining the sending or reception of remittances in the prior analysis. A set of independent variables representing individual characteristics is composed of dummy variables such as the age of the emigrant, the educational level (1 if secondary or degree, 0 otherwise), the occupation at the place of destination (1 if labourer in non-agricultural sector, 0 otherwise), the caste of origin (1 if Backward Caste, Scheduled Caste or Scheduled Tribe, 0 otherwise), and the family status (1 if children of the head, 0 otherwise; and 1 if husband or wife, 0 otherwise). Two variables are related to the pattern of emigration: the time spent abroad in years, and the country of residence (1 if developed country, 0 otherwise). The sex could not be a predictor given that in this sample there was no woman. Among the characteristics of the household of origin, variables indicating the structure of the household are the number of males above 15 and the number of children. A dummy variable indicating the economic status of the household is also selected: "poor housing quality" (1 if poor or Kutcha house, 0 otherwise). It is expected that migrants originating from poorer households will be more likely to remit. Three variables are expected to affect negatively the propensity to remit: the high educational level, the residence in a developed country and the number of males above 15 years old in the households.

Table 8 shows the results of the regression analysis. A variety of factors are significant in predicting the decision to remit. The fact that emigrants from Backward or Scheduled Castes are 1.6 times more likely to remit than those from other castes or communities, and that labourers are 1.6 times more likely to remit than migrants with higher status occupations indicates that remittances are reaching the poor. Conversely, living in a developed country—mainly the United States or United Kingdom—and holding a degree are negatively associated with the probability of remitting. The poor housing quality, which was expected to influence positively the decision to remit, turns out to have a negative and significant influence on the propensity to remit. It might stem from the fact that remittances having a strong potential of poverty alleviation, households receiving remittances could have improved their housing quality in a short span of time. The positive influence of time on the probability to remit might also account for this result; as it is possible that emigrants from households with poor housing quality had moved recently and were not able to send remittances yet.

Husband or wife as the head of the household has a much higher propensity to remit than children as the head. The demographic characteristics of households of origin, which are the number of children and the number of males above 15, appear to be poor predictors of remittance behaviour of emigrants. The equation was run with the dependency ratio instead of these two demographic variables, and even though the sign was positive, it was not significant.

Table 8 ***Variables Influencing the Decision to Remit among Emigrants***

Variables	*B*	*S.E.*	*Exp (B)*
Characteristics of Emigrant			
Time abroad (years)	0.078***	0.015	1.081
Age	-0.003	0.013	0.957
Degree holder[a]	-0.596**	0.207	0.551
Labourer in non-agricultural sector[b]	0.468**	0.163	1.597
Backward Caste or SC/ST	0.458*	0.211	1.581
Relationship with the head			
Children of the head	0.226	0.199	1.253
Husband or wife	0.785**	0.269	2.202
Reside in a developed country (US, UK)	-0.863*	0.385	0.422
Characteristics of Household of Origin			
Number of children	0.069	0.057	1.072
Number of males above 15	-0.054	0.067	0.947
Poor housing quality	-0.678**	0.262	0.507
Constant	0.383	0.511	1.467
Degrees of freedom = 11 N = 1,228	Likelihood ratio $\chi2$ (11) =116.04 p. $\chi2$ < 0.001		
-2 Log likelihood = 1,135.88			

Source: Own calculations based on SMS 2003.

Note: p. values: *p<.05, **p<.01, ***p<.001.

a Educational status before migration.

b Occupation abroad.

The fact that the propensity of emigrants to remit is negatively associated with their human and financial capital indicates that remittance flows are mostly explained by households' economic necessities.

Thus, in the state, a large population with a low economic status is able to reap the benefits of migration. However, the stark differences in the amount of cash or goods remitted between low-skilled and high-skilled migrants and the fact that even if high-educated migrants are less prone to remit than migrants with a low educational level, they are no less than 60 per cent to remit, indicate that remittances exacerbate the inter-household inequities, both at the overall level *and* within the migrant group. The findings for the out-migrant group point to a negative effect of remittances on inequality, and even on poverty reduction, given that there are fewer out-migrants from poorer background who remit than other categories.

Poverty-reducing Effects of Remittances: Short-term or Long-term? Looking at the Expenditure Patterns

A medium/long-term horizon is required to evaluate the extent to which remittances provide a path out of poverty. Poverty reduction includes building the capacity to accumulate assets that reduce vulnerability to financial shocks and gaining access to services such as education and care. Remittances in themselves do not ensure that the recipients will be permanently out of poverty, but they have marginal benefits in the medium and long term, enhancing the recipients' ability to participate in social and economic institutions that may have the power to alleviate poverty in the long term (Maimbo and Ratha, 2005).

Investments in health and education have been acknowledged to have positive impact on poverty alleviation. Education has also been reported to lessen inequalities. Do recipient households invest more in health and education than other households? This is a crucial question since higher investment in health and education may imply better opportunities for the children of the recipients, with prospects of social mobility through education. When invested in health or education, the remittances go beyond conversion into prestige for the immediate benefit of the current household, towards investment in long-term improvements of the family. But they also deepen the inequality of opportunities when children of recipient households attend better schools than those of non-recipient households.

SMS and KMS provide data on annual education and health expenses. Recipient households are expected to spend more on education than non-recipients, since they get external earnings and the data on the use of remittances indicate that a significant proportion of the remittances is used for educational purposes—see Table 3 in

Appendix. The same is expected for health expenditures. Table 9 reports the educational expenses per child and the health expenses per household member per year in rupees, according to the migrant status and the remittance status of the households. Given that migration is a selective and endogenous mechanism, households that participate in migration and receive remittances differ fundamentally from those that do not. Because of this, it is important to control for the determinants of migration when estimating the impacts of remittances on household expenditures. A control group is defined by the non-recipient households of each group, the emigrant group and the out-migrant group.

Table 9 ***Health and Educational Expenses by Migration Status***

		Emigrant Households		*Out-migrant Households*				
Type of Expenses[a]	*Non-migrant HHs*	*Recipient HHs*	*Non-recipient HHs*	*Recipient HHs*	*Non-recipient HHs*	*All HHs*	*t-test 1*	*t-test 2*
Educational expenses per child	3,943	3,881	6,912	7,491	7,867	4,078	-0.78	1.70
Health expenses per capita	1,107	2,185	2,186	1,173	1,814	1,314	2.80**	0.10

Source: Own calculations based on SMS 2003.

Note: Standard deviations are in parentheses. t-test 1: emigrant recipient HHs vs non-migrant HHs. t-test 2: out-migrant recipient HHs vs. non-migrant HHs.** significant at the 0.01 level.

a Mean in Rs per year.

Educational Expenditures

The figures indicate that the differences between migrant and non-migrant are not significant as far as educational expenses are concerned. Contrary to what was expected, emigrant recipient households even spend slightly less on education per child than non-migrant households. The lack of clear-cut differentials could be partly due to the selective nature of migration. If emigrants are selected from below-average income households, with less money to spend on education, they can still be below the average household in terms of educational expenditures. When controlling for the endogeneity of migration I find that emigrant households receiving remittances still have lower educational expenditures than non-recipient emigrant households. This does not indicate an unwillingness to invest in education on behalf of recipient households but rather the fact that remittances are received by households with fewer resources. Even though a significant proportion of these earnings are channelled towards education, recipient families are not able to close the gap with non-recipients. These results can also be explained by the fact that recipient families have more children. I calculated the total of educational expenditures per households and I found that households with international remittances spend on average Rs 6,742, non-migrant households spend Rs 6,322 and the figure is Rs 6,581 for the overall households. Remittances to emigrant households compensate partially the imbalances in educational needs but are not sufficient to give the children of recipient households the same schooling opportunities as those of non-recipient households. The families receiving internal remittances are spending most on education and the opted strategy for upward mobility through education may result in more inequalities between internal remittance receiving households and the others. As for emigrant households, out-migrant households which receive remittances spend less on education per child than those which do not receive external earnings. Although it was found earlier that recipient households were substantially better-off than non-recipient ones in terms of living standards, it does not seem that the reception of remittances will increase long-term inequality between recipient and non-recipient households if those are to be measured by households' educational expenditures.

Health Expenditures

The results indicate that the expenses of emigrant recipient households are twice as large as those of the non-migrant households, the difference in health expenses per capita is significant at 1 per cent. The difference between out-migrant recipient households and non-migrant households is not statistically significant. These figures might indicate the opportunity given by the additional remittance earnings to attend private health services, better and more expensive than those provided by the government hospital. Higher health expenditures by emigrant households may also be explained by the higher proportion of elders and children among these households (see Table 4 in appendix) because elders and children require more health care. Thus, the long-term impact of health investment on inter-household inequality is not clear. It is not possible to conclude that remittances to emigrant households will exacerbate inequality of access to health care services between migrant and non-migrant households.

The analysis of health and education expenditures did not reveal that remittances contribute to increasing long-term inequalities in access to education and healthcare services between recipient and non-recipient households. Actually, non-recipients spend slightly more on education per children than emigrant households receiving remittances. This result indicates that for the recipient households, remittances are crucial to secure access to education for their children. With respect to health expenses the difference between households receiving international remittances and the others exists—recipients have higher health expenditures—but with more elders and children recipients are also likely to require more healthcare services.

III

Summary and Concluding Remarks

Migration is a selective process and its impacts on poverty and inequity through the channel of remittances depend upon the destination of migration. Internal and international remittances do not have the same effect on poverty alleviation as they are not undertaken by the same category of migrants. Internal migration selects two different types of migrants. One is the group of very poor migrants pushed away by unemployment for whom migration is a survival strategy and who are deterred to emigrate because of the high entry costs entailed by any emigration project. Another group is composed of high educated Keralites, students or high skilled persons for whom internal migration is associated with upward occupational mobility. Evidence has also shown that those who were most committed to remit cash or goods to their family came from privileged backgrounds, whereas the practice of remitting was very uncommon among poor out-migrants. Hence, internal migration, through the channel of remittances, has very little poverty-reducing effects and deepens inter-household inequalities at the overall level and within the migrant group.

The scenario for international migration is more positive in terms of poverty alleviation and smoothing of inequalities. Although international migrants have spent more years in school than their non-migrants counterparts, they are less educated than the average out-migrants. The large majority is employed as non-agricultural labourers or semi-skilled workers in Gulf countries. Emigration to the Gulf selects negatively the highest educated, for whom the United States or the United Kingdom are the favourite destinations. Contrary to internal migrants, emigrants with low socio-economic status are particularly inclined to send a part of their earnings to their families. As a consequence, a large section of households receiving remittances belongs to below-average income groups. Emigrants' remitting behaviour is partly explained by the nature of emigration and the place of destination. Indeed, immigration in Gulf countries is bound to be temporal due to specific migration laws in the region preventing naturalisation. Moreover, a strict separation between migrant workers and the local population is observed. Emigrants having no prospect to settle, they endure hardships and work assiduously in order to maximise their savings and enjoy the accumulated wealth with their family when they return home. Contrary to permanent migration, the ties between a Gulf emigrant and his or her family do not loosen over time and emigrants' propensity to remit remains intact. Somehow, even though international remittances proved to be more poor-friendly than internal remittances, they did not produce a wealth redistribution favourable to the families at the bottom end of the socio-economic spectrum. Actually, a large bulk of remittances was received by wealthier families whose high educated migrants had the means to remit a substantial part of his or her earnings.

Emigration and internal migration from Kerala have reached a mature stage, and contrary to previous case study in Pakistan, Mexico and Egypt, where emigration exacerbated income inequalities while out-migration was income-equalising, I found that both emigration and out-migration increase inequality, and out-migration to a greater extent than emigration. On the whole, migration has not lessened the inequalities through the channel of remittances but has confirmed them both at the overall level and within each migrant group. However, it does not seem that remittances will sharpen long-term inter-household inequities in the state if those are to be measured in terms of access to education—and health services. For diverse cultural and sociological reasons, Kerala families are particularly committed to the education of their offsprings and the discrepancy between non-migrant and migrant households with respect to educational expenditure is not significant. Contrary to previous expectations, I found that the capacity to provide their children with high quality education—to pay for private schools—is slightly weaker for emigrant recipient households than for non-migrant households, and the difference in educational expenditures is even larger between emigrant recipient households and other migrant households. Remittances help recipient households to meet their higher educational and healthcare needs. Recipient and non-recipient households differ in their human capital endowments. Recipient households have on average a higher dependency ratio, more children and elders than non-recipient households. Although these demographic variables did not prove to be reliable predictors of the reception of remittances, they set the boundaries to which remittances can increase the living quality of the recipient households. For the large majority of recipient households the monies are absorbed by daily consumption, by educational expenses or debt repayments. Very few households are able to finance business projects or to invest in agriculture with remittances. As a consequence, the demographic factors influencing migration—household size, number of males above 15 years old, number of children and elders—also limit the deepening of imbalances between recipient and non-recipient households. Remittances do not exacerbate inequality of opportunities—especially schooling opportunities—between recipient and non-recipient household.

With these limitations in mind, it remains that recipient households have been able to modernise their living standards faster than their non-recipient counterparts. Households that receive remittances rapidly attain standards of living greater than those that do not have family members working abroad. One of the most pernicious effect of remittances emerges with the strengthening of self-perceived (relative) poverty. The host countries, by offering a wide range of new products have reshaped the preference of the migrants and migrant households have imposed their consumption pattern as a new norm, inclining non-migrants to emulate their pattern of consumption. All these factors have increased the demand for—often imported—consumer goods of the overall population. To follow the same lifestyle most of the households, anxious not to 'lag behind', have no choice but to invest in migration, given the lack of economic dynamism in Kerala. Then, migration has became progressively independent of the economic conditions that originally caused it. It is a self-perpetuating process because migration itself has created the social structure needed to sustain it. By increasing and strengthening the migrant network, every new migrant reduces the costs of subsequent migration for a set of friends and relatives. By displaying enhanced status, remittance-receiving families foster the desire of non-migrant families to acquire a new range of consumer goods. In most of the cases, the only way to fulfil these new aspirations is to undertake migration.

Finally, given the different remitting behaviour of emigrants and out-migrants the promotion of internal migration by policy makers will not have the same effects on poverty and inequality than the promotion of emigration. Steady flows of high educated internal migrants from Kerala are likely to reinforce the existing inequities at the place of origin by generating new sources of incomes for already well-off households. On the contrary, by widening the access to international migration to the poorest segments of the population, the redistribution of income through remittances is likely to be more even.

Method of Computation of the Index of Possession of Goods

The index is computed for the eight items: motor car, taxi, motorcycle, telephone, mobile phone, television, VCR/VCP, fridge by giving them appropriate weights.

The weight given to each item is determined by the percentage of households possessing such item according to their migration status. For example, 9.3 per cent of the emigrant households possess a motor car, then the weight given to the possession of a motor car is 0.907 (1–0.093) for the emigrant households. Nearly 4.2 per cent of the non-migrant households possess a car, then if a non-migrant household possesses a car, it receives the score of 0.958 (1–0.042). Consequently, when fewer households possess a specific item, the value attached to this item is higher. For each household, the index is computed by summing up the weights of the items in its possession, so if it does not possess any item it gets a 0. This sum is then divided by the total sum of the weights, that is, the score obtained if all the goods are possessed. The result is multiplied by 100 so that the index ranges from 0 to 100. Finally, the mean of the index is computed for each category of households.

Notes

1. For a taxonomy, see Wahba (1991).
2. The second order effects are related to the multiplier effects of remittances on the recipient area. If migrants' families buy local products, this can have a positive impact on multipliers, creating more economic opportunities locally which also benefit the non-recipients—through the creation of jobs, a consumption boom, etc. In Kerala, the multiplier effects of remittances have not decreased the unemployment rate in the state, as it could be expected. The money sent back by emigrants actually accelerated the construction industry

and the service sector but the scarcity of low skilled labour led to an increase in wage rates. At present, Kerala has the highest wage rate among the states in India. The wage gaps between Kerala and the neighbouring states have led to a steady flow of workers from other states moving into Kerala to take up work which used to be done by Kerala workers, especially in the construction sector. This phenomenon is known as "replacement migration". See Zachariah and Irudaya Rajan (2006).

3. Yang and Choi (2005) found that in the Philippines, in households with overseas migrants, exogenous changes in income lead to changes in remittances of the opposite sign, consistent with an insurance motivation for remittances. In such households, roughly 60 per cent of exogenous decrease in income is replaced by remittance inflows from overseas.
4. Households with both emigrants and out-migrants, which account for 1.6 per cent of the total households of the sample, will not be considered. Some non-migrant households also receive remittances, but their number is negligible, thus they have not been considered (in SMS 2003, 2.7 per cent of non-migrant households received remittances).
5. One lakh = one hundred thousand.
6. As far as measurement of income inequality is concerned, a vast literature is available on various methods and their merits and shortcomings. (See, for example: Amartya Sen 1973. *On Economic Inequality*, Oxford: Clarendon Press). A detailed discussion on these topics is therefore not included in the paper.
7. Zachariah and Irudaya Rajan (2006) also found that emigration reduced unemployment directly and indirectly through employment creation following the use of remittances sent home by emigrants and the money and expertise brought back by return emigrants. They estimated that the unemployment rate would have been 21.4 per cent instead of the observed 19.2 per cent, if it was not for emigration.
8. In recent decades, Ezahvas have sought to improve their position by accumulating economic, symbolic and cultural capital especially through migration (to the Gulf region), employment, marriage and education, and have tried to assert their right to mobility, often in the face of opposition from the higher status Christians and Nairs. Although some have experienced absolute mobility, Osella and Osella (2000) argue that it has not led to relative mobility within a society which remains stratified and prone to new forms of social exclusion.
9. Own calculations based on SMS 2003.
10. Very Good: 2 bed rooms with attached bathrooms, concrete roof, mosaic floor; Good: 1 bed room, brick and cement walls, concrete or tile roof; Poor: brick walls, cement floor, tin or asbestos roof and *kutcha*: mud walls, mud floor and thatched roof.

References

Adams, R. 1989. Worker Remittances and Inequality in Rural Egypt. *Economic Development and Cultural Change*, Vol. 38, No. 1, 45–71.

——. 1991. The Effects of International Remittances on Poverty, Inequality and Development in Rural Egypt. IFPRI Research Report No. 86.

——. 1996. "Remittances, Inequality and Asset Accumulation: The Case of Rural Pakistan" in D. O'Connor and L. Farsakh (eds.), *Development Strategy, Employment and Migration, Country Experiences*. Paris: OCDE, 259.

——. 2004. Remittances and Poverty in Guatemala. World Bank Policy Research Working Paper 3,418, September, Washington DC: World Bank.

——. 2005a. International Remittances and the Household: Analysis and Review of Global Evidence. Paper presented at the Plenary Session of the African Economic Research Consortium, May 29, Nairobi.

——. 2005b. Remittances, Household Expenditure and Investment in Guatemala. World Bank Policy Research Working Paper 3,532, March, Washington DC: The World Bank.

Adams, R. and J. Page. 2003. International Migration, Remittances and Poverty in Developing Countries. World Bank Policy Research Working Paper 3,179, December, Washington DC: The World Bank.

Government of Kerala. 1999. Economic Review 1999. State Planning Board, Thiruvananthapuram.

——. 2003. Economic Review 2003. State Planning Board, Thiruvananthapuram.

Harris, J. and M. Todaro. 1970. Migration, Unemployment and Development: A Two Sector Analysis. *American Economic Review*, Vol. 60, No. 1, March, 126–42.

Isaac, T. 1992. Economic Consequences of the Gulf Crisis: A Study of India with Special Reference to Kerala, ARTEP. New Delhi: ILO, 51.

Jones, R.C. 1998. Remittances and Inequality: A Question of Migration Stage and Geographic Scale. *Economic Geography*, Vol. 74, No. 1, January, 8–25.

Kannan, K. and K. Hari. 2002. Kerala's Gulf Connection: Emigration, Remittances and their Macroeconomic Impact, 1972–2000. CDS Working Paper 328, Thiruvananthapuram: Centre for Development Studies.

Lipton, M. 1980. Migration from Rural Areas of Poor Countries: The Impact on Rural Productivity and Income Distribution. *World Development*, Vol. 8, No. 1, 1–24.

Lowell, L. and R. De la Garza (eds.). 2002. *Sending Money Home: Hispanic Remittances and Community Development*. Oxford: Rowman and Littlefield, 256.

Lucas, R. and O. Stark. 1985. Motivations to Remit: Evidence from Botswana. *Journal of Political Economy*, Vol. 93, No. 5, 901–17.

Maimbo Munzele, S. and Dilip Ratha (eds.). 2005. *Remittances, Development Impacts and Future Prospects*. Washington DC: The World Bank, 378.

Maimbo Munzele, S., R. Adams, R. Aggarwal and N. Passas. 2005. *Migrant Labour Remittances in South Asia*. Washington DC: The World Bank, 77.

Nair, P.R.G. 1986. *Asian Migration to the Arab World: Migration from Kerala (India)*. Thiruvananthapuram: Centre for Development Studies.

Osella, F. and C. Osella. 2000. *Social Mobility in Kerala: Modernity and Identity in Conflict*. Anthropology, Culture and Society Series, edited by Richard Wilson and Thomas Hylland Eriksen, London: Pluto Press, 320.

Ralph, C., C. Fullenkamp and S. Jahjah. 2003. Are Immigrant Remittance Flows a Source of Capital for Development? IMF Working Paper *03/189*, September, Washington D.C.

Ramachandran, V.K. 1996. "On Kerala's Development Achievements" in J. Drèze and A. Sen (eds.), *Indian Development: Selected Regional Perspectives*. New Delhi: Oxford University Press, 205–356.

Rodriguez, Edgar R. 1998. International Migration and Income Distribution in the Philippines. *Economic Development and Cultural Change*, Vol. 46, No. 2, January, 329–50.

Stark, O. 1991. *The Migration of Labour*. Cambridge, MA: Basil Blackwell.

Stark, O. and D. Bloom. 1985. The New Economics of Labour Migration. *American Economic Review*, Vol. 25, 173–8.

Stark, O. and E.J. Taylor. 1989. Relative Deprivation and International Migration. *Demography*, Vol. 26, No. 1, February.

———. 1991. Migration Incentives, Migration Types: The Role of Relative Deprivation. *The Economic Journal*, Vol. 101, No. 408, 1163–78.

Stark, O. and R. Lucas 1988. Migration, Remittances and the Family. *Economic Development and Cultural Change*, Vol. 36, No. 3, 465–81.

Stark, O., E.J. Taylor and S. Yitzhaki. 1982. Migration, Growth, Distribution and Welfare. *Economics Letters*, Vol. 25, 191–6.

———. 1986. Remittances and Inequality. *The Economic Journal*, Vol. 96, 722–40.

Stark, O., E.J. Taylor and S. Yitzhaki. 1988. Labour Migration as a Response to Relative Deprivation. *Journal of Population Economics*, Vol. 1, 57–70.

Taylor, J.E., J. Mora, R. Adams and A. Lopez-Feldman. 2005. Remittances, Inequality and Poverty: Evidence from Rural Mexico. Selected Paper prepared for presentation at the American Agricultural Economics Association Annual Meeting, Providence, Rhode Island, July 24–27.

Taylor, J.E. and J. Mora. 2006. Does Migration Reshape Expenditures in Rural Households? World Bank Policy Research Working Paper *3,842*, February, Washington DC: The World Bank.

Wahba, S. 1991. What Determines Workers Remittances? *Finance and Development*, December, Vol. 28, No. 4.

World Bank. 2006. *Economic Implications of Remittances and Migration*. Washington DC: The World Bank, 157.

Yang, D. and H.J. Choi. 2005. Are Remittances Insurance? Evidence from Rainfall Shocks in the Philippines. Ford School of Public Policy Working Paper No. 05-04, July.

Zachariah, K.C., K.P. Kannan and S. Irudaya Rajan (eds.). 2002. *Kerala's Gulf Connection.* CDS Studies on International Labour Migration from Kerala State in India, Thiruvananthapuram: Centre for Development Studies, 230.

Zachariah, K.C., E.T. Mathew and S. Irudaya Rajan. 2003. *Dynamics of Migration in Kerala: Dimensions, Differentials and Consequences*. New Delhi: Orient Longman, 476.

Zachariah, K.C. and S. Irudaya Rajan. 2006. *Gulf Revisited*. Thiruvananthapuram: Centre for Development Studies, 231.

Appendix

Table 1 ***Summary of Selected Individual Characteristics of the Migrants***

Characteristics of the Migrants	*Emigrant*	*Out-migrant*
Sample	N=2,694	N=1,533
Households with migrants (%)	17.6	8.7
Number of emigrants/out-migrants in respective migrant HHs (Mean)	1.52	1.84
Age (mean)	26.47 (12.25)	22.32 (7.63)
Sex (%)		
Male	83.1	65.1
Female	16.9	34.9
Marital status (%)		
Unmarried	55.7	74.5
Married	44.2	25.3
Widow/Widower	0.1	0.2
Relationship with the head (%)		
Head of the HHs	1.0	0.5
Husband/wife	13.7	3.6
Unmarried children	12.8	29.1
Married children	43.7	28.6
Son-in-law/Daughter-in-law	14.9	15.7
Grand child	8.2	16.2
Father/Mother/Mother-in-law	0.3	0.5
Others	5.4	5.8
Living in rural area at the time of migration (%)	58.5	62.0
Country of residence (%)	—	—
Gulf countries	88.9	—
Others	11.1	—
United States	5.3	—
England	1.2	—

Table 2 ***Descriptive Statistics of the Households by Migration Status***

Characteristics of Households (%)	*Emigrant HHs*		*Out-migrant HHs*		*Return-emigrant HHs*		*Return Out-migrant HHs*		*Non-Migrant HHs*		*All HHs*	
Year	*1998*	*2003*	*1998*	*2003*	*1998*	*2003*	*1998*	*2003*	*1998*	*2003*	*1998*	*2003*
Housing quality[10]												
Luxurious	2.5	7.0	0.8	4.8	2.4	6.1	1.3	2.7	1.0	1.9	1.3	3.1
Very good	22.4	33.9	13.1	23.2	22.0	31.0	14.5	26.9	9.6	12.9	13.2	19.1
Good	64.4	53.3	65.9	62.4	60.1	53.3	60.5	60.2	54.3	58.1	57.2	57.7
Poor	7.1	4.7	13.3	8.0	10.7	8.0	13.9	7.8	21.9	20.3	17.7	15.2
Kutcha	3.7	1.1	6.9	1.6	4.8	1.6	9.7	2.3	13.3	6.9	10.5	4.9
High housing quality	89.3	94.2	79.8	90.4	84.5	90.4	76.3	89.8	64.9	72.9	71.7	79.9
Housing Facilities												
House electrified	89.9	96.4	83.4	92.2	87.4	93.5	81.3	91.3	66.4	80.1	73.6	85.3
Fuel used for cooking												
Wood	67.8	63.9	72.5	66.8	66.6	68.1	69.2	63.4	83.7	79.7	78.2	76.0
Electricity	0.2	0.3	0.0	0.1	0.2	0.3	0.4	0.5	0.1	0.0	0.1	0.2
Kerosene	1.9	3.4	1.6	5.4	3.0	3.9	3.3	4.0	2.7	4.6	2.6	4.3
L.P. Gas	30.2	54.6	25.8	53.2	30.2	46.1	27.1	54.6	13.6	26.5	19.1	35.6

Cont'd...

Cont'd…

Consumer Durables												
Motor car	3.7	9.3	2.8	8.6	5.2	10.2	3.6	10.9	1.8	4.2	2.5	6.0
Taxi/truck	2.4	3.2	0.9	1.6	4.3	4.3	1.5	2.6	1.7	2.6	2.0	2.8
Motorcycle/scooter	10.4	18.0	9.8	20.4	15.2	22.4	14.5	25.3	7.6	13.1	9.1	15.8
Telephone	27.5	72.7	16.8	61.2	26.1	61.5	18.2	59.7	10.7	31.5	15.0	43.6
Mobile phone	n.a.	10.1	n.a.	7.8	n.a.	12.2	n.a.	9.8	n.a.	5.0	n.a.	6.8
Television	50.9	76.6	45.1	71.2	50.7	71.2	43.7	73.1	32.1	52.1	37.8	59.9
VCR/VCP	24.1	33.2	9.6	24.1	23.4	27.5	10.8	24.6	5.2	11.0	9.9	17.1
Fridge	35.2	54.1	23.4	41.4	35.6	46.3	26.1	45.7	12.6	20.4	19.3	30.2

Source: Own calculations based on KMS 1998 and SMS 2003.

Note: Respondents can report multiple uses of fuel, so the total will not add up to 100. "High housing quality": good, very good or luxurious.

Table 3 ***End Use of Remittances According to the Educational Status of the Head of the Household in 1998 and 2003***

End-use of Remittances (%)	*Below Primary*		*Primary*		*Secondary*		*Degree*	
Year	*1998*	*2003*	*1998*	*2003*	*1998*	*2003*	*1998*	*2003*
Sample size	499	439	949	760	244	190	69	76
For day-to-day life	95.0	93.4	88.1	88.1	81.9	89.8	75.3	77.5
Education	35.2	44.2	37.7	41.1	34.0	46.7	43.4	38.1
To repay debts incurred	29.4	20.3	29.6	15.5	17.1	12.5	8.6	10.5
To purchase land	1.4	2.1	2.6	1.7	3.2	5.2	4.2	2.6
Maintain agricultural land	2.8	1.5	4.5	2.3	1.6	2.6	7.2	3.9
Housing purpose	6.0	9.8	11.7	8.6	11.4	13.4	15.8	14.3
Business	0.6	0.7	1.9	0.9	1.6	0.5	4.3	3.9
Dowry payment of relatives	3.0	4.1	4.8	5.8	3.6	3.0	5.8	3.9
Deposited into bank	5.0	7.0	4.6	9.3	14.3	12.1	20.1	26.3
Others	0.8	14.9	2.3	8.8	3.0	13.0	—	10.5
Characteristics of the Household								
Age of the head (mean)	61	64	53	55	49	52	45	53
Household size	6.34	6.20	5.24	4.92	4.13	4.06	3.84	3.84
	(3.15)	(2.98)	(4.59)	(2.60)	(1.78)	(2.16)	(1.69)	(2.34)
Number of children below 15 (mean)	2.13	1.91	1.68	1.39	1.21	1.12	1.26	1.05
	(1.87)	(1.63)	(1.50)	(1.47)	(1.14)	(1.25)	(1.15)	(1.41)
Number of elderly (60 or above) (mean)	0.83	0.94	0.61	0.62	0.53	0.74	0.46	0.75
	(0.70)	(0.71)	(0.75)	(0.72)	(0.76)	(0.81)	(0.74)	(0.88)
High housing quality (%)	15.0	10.1	23.8	19.6	41.0	42.4	56.5	64.8

Source: Own calculations based on KMS 1998 and SMS 2003.

Note: Standard deviations are in parentheses. Respondents can report multiple uses, so the total will not add up to 100.

Table 4 *Demographic Characteristics of the Households According to Remittance Status*

Variable (Mean)	*Receive no Remi-ttances*	*Receive Inter-national Remittances*	*Receive Internal Remittances*	*All Households*	*T-test (Remittances vs. No Remittances)*
Household size	4.71 (2.11)	5.18 (2.77)	4.76 (2.71)	4.78 (2.23)	5.75**
Age of household head (years)	54.80 (13.17)	57.04 (14.71)	60.08 (12.70)	56.46 (13.43)	5.56**
Number of females over age 15	1.89 (0.92)	2.27 (1.16)	2.08 (1.24)	1.95 (1.02)	11.42**
Number of males over age 15	1.83 (1.06)	1.36 (1.13)	1.42 (1.03)	1.76 (1.08)	-13.83**
Number of elders (60 years or above)	0.62 (0.75)	0.75 (0.75)	0.89 (0.71)	0.64 (0.76)	6.15**
Number of children	0.99 (1.15)	1.54 1.52)	1.24 (1.35)	1.06 (1.23)	12.06**
Dependency ratio	0.53 (0.59)	0.90 (0.94)	0.73 (0.87)	0.58 (0.66)	14.16**
N	8,297	1,428	157	10,012	—

Source: Own calculations based on SMS 2003.

Note: Household size include migrant members. Standard deviations are in parentheses.
* significant at the 0.05 level. ** significant at the 0.01 level.

2

Female Labour Mobility and Urban Employment in India

Brinda Viswanathan and K. Shanthi

The theories on migration have been analysed by scholars belonging to different disciplines of social sciences, thereby giving different perspectives. During the process of economic development a typical feature observed is the sectoral shift from agriculture towards industry. This has been characterised by a change in the labour allocated to these two sectors; the high wage industrial sector attracts the surplus labour from low productivity agriculture (Lewis, 1955). Commonly referred to as the Lewis model dealt with the issue of labour migration implicitly but it was the well-known analytical model of Harris and Todaro (1970) that explained labour mobility arising out of differential wages between rural and urban areas during the process of economic development. These attempts by economists to explain migration concerned primarily rural to urban migration which were also added on by those of demographers whose concern was the issue of migration as the movement of people in general leading to the process of urbanisation (Stark, 1984; Williamson 1988). The mainstream literature on internal migration in both economics and demography has predominantly focussed on labour migration of men (Lucas, 1997).[1] However, several studies particularly in sociology analyse the gender dimensions of migration in more detail (Wright, 1995). The focus of this study is on the pattern of female migration in India.

In most parts of the world, either (a) women stay back in the rural areas to look after the agricultural work and other family members are left behind while the men migrate alone to urban areas, or (b) that women migrate in association with the male breadwinner, or (c) women migrate after marriage to the husband's village or town but commonly observed in South Asia (Thadani and Todaro, 1984).[2] Thus, in the case of women, the cultural and social norms which restrict their participation in the labour market due to their confinement primarily to the household chores also restrict their mobility for employment reasons. Further, these same norms undermine the efforts of those women who after migrating (in their associated or married status) take up employment but unlike men do not cite that as the prime reason for movement. Since these two aspects did not confound to the standard framework of male migration, the general models of migration seem to ignore the gendered aspects in female migration (Sundari, 2005a).

Since early 1980s, globalisation was slowly setting in bringing about structural changes in several developing economies from agriculture towards services sector resulting in demand for labour in lower end services like domestic maids to higher end as in financial and banking sectors. The former types of jobs typically performed by women resulted in great demand for women with low skill levels or no education while limited supply of skilled men in latter types of jobs increased the demand for women having higher levels of education and skill. Further, textile and pharmaceuticals industries were also in demand for cheap labour to reduce costs and improve competitiveness. This had given rise to the movement of large number of (single) women for employment—from rural to urban areas, from smaller towns and cities to large business and industrial centres and from developing countries to the developed nations. Thereby the share of women among internal migrants rose and quite prominently among international migrants and came to be referred as *autonomous female migration* as opposed to *associated female migration* (Fawcett et al., 1984; United Nations, 2004). Since the motive for this movement of women was similar in nature to those of men, it started drawing attention of the analysts and policy makers and led to a surge of literature dealing with different facets of female migration. Nevertheless, very few studies exist on internal migration by women, from developing countries particularly covering large geographic regions. This study based on a large-scale survey data for India attempts to analyse the regional differences in pattern of female migration.

This paper is organised as follows. The next section gives a brief overview of the issues addressed on female migration with a focus on employment migration in India. Section III presents the objectives of the study while section IV discusses the features of the database used for this study. Section V discusses the pattern of female migrants engaged in the labour market from several aspects and section VI concludes the paper.

II

Female Migration: A Brief Overview

Female migration as noted in Shanti (2006) can be classified into three groups. (a) *Associated migration* or family migration when the woman moves with the male members of the household. (b) *Autonomous migration* when a woman moves unaccompanied mainly for work and a sub-component of this is the *relay migration*[3], (c) *Marriage migration* where a woman after getting married leaves the natal village/town to join the husband's family in another village/town due to the customary practice of exogamy observed in some countries.

The onset of globalisation and in particular, trade liberalisation impacted countries at different time points and in different ways in terms of the gender-specific labour demand for mainly unskilled and semi-skilled labour (Fernandez-Kelly, 1983; Khoo, 1984). This led to a sudden surge in the movement of women across and within national boundaries mainly for employment. This increased labour mobility of women brought into discussion on the one hand whether there was really any autonomy in the decision to take up job away from home and on the other, what impact it had on women's empowerment, that is, improvement in their social and economic status (Connell et al., 1976; Kabeer, 2000; Hugo, 2000; Chantavanich, 2001).

General Pattern of Migration in India

In India, the overall migration rate has declined in the 1990s compared to the earlier two decades and was based on the nation-wide data collected by National Sample Survey Organisation (Sivaramakrishnan et al., 2005; De Haan and Dubey, 2006). Given that this decade had shown rapid economic growth in India and the associated structural transformation from agriculture to industry and services, some authors find this unexpected. However, as is now well-known that during this period though the value added from the industrial and services sector showed a very high growth rate but this did not increase employment at the same rate. The additional job creation was mainly in the skilled sector and hence adversely affected the rural-urban migration (Sivaramakrishnan et al., 2005).

Since rural to urban migration constitutes a large proportion of the total migration in India a reduction in this rate affects the overall rate but Srivastava and Bhattacharya (2003) based on the same data source find that between 1993–94 and 1999–2000 there has been an increase in urban migration particularly the urban-urban migration. Unlike the earlier studies which have a very limited focus on female migrants, there is some more attention to this aspect here. An important result is that female migration for employment reasons has declined between the two periods while that for males it has increased. Though no explanation per se has been attributed to this, this declining trend could be because the overall female labour force participation in the urban labour market had declined in the age group of 15 to 60 years during this period.[4]

Female Migration and Workforce Participation in India: Concerns and Issues

Among the early studies on female migration in India, Premi (1980) had raised the concern that even though women constituted over two times more migrants than men, attributing it to marriage and associated migrants may not be correct. Widowhood and abandonment makes women move out in search of livelihoods. An important finding of this study was that about 58 per cent of the female workers in the country were migrants based on 1971 census and that the labour force participation rates among women migrants were higher than average rate of female labour force participation. Thus, even though women may not migrate solely for economic reasons but may actively participate in the labour market after migration.

Karlekar (1995) gives a broader overview of the gender dimensions in migration where the issue of survival migration by women was highlighted and clearly led to a preponderance of women migrants from the lower economic strata. Regional variations in female migration, causes of female migration and their overall economic and social status at the migration destination were discussed in this study with illustrations from several case studies in the 1980s. In an annotated bibliography on women and migration compiled by Lingam (1998), the migrant woman's active participation in labour market as survival strategies (e.g., noticed among slum dwellers in Mumbai) as well as seasonal rural migration by rural women had been highlighted. One study cited here clearly demarcates a 'life-cycle pattern' in female migration revolving around the marital phase—the 'pre-marital' phase and the 'dissolved marriage' phase both positively impacted their labour market participation rates. Further, increased economic participation of women was also observed in those regions where male migrants left behind their families. Several studies in this compilation further brought out that, women actively participated in the labour market after migration and may not just be 'passively' attaching themselves to male migrants and that their economic contributions were very important for the family's survival.

This last issue had been further emphasised in a recent study by Neetha (2004) based on the study of migrant female domestic workers in Delhi. Not only did the women contribute significantly to the household's economic well-being but they also assisted in the job search and settling down process due to their social networking abilities. As discussed earlier, export-oriented firms particularly in the textile manufacturing sector have been female labour intensive. The sudden increase in such jobs in some small pockets in India led to increased female migration as noted in other parts of the world. Sundari (2005b) while analysing the female migrant women in the Tiruppur garment factories in Tamil Nadu found that though migration substantially improved their standard of living above the subsistence level, for a large proportion of them, the impact had not been very effective particularly for the more vulnerable female-headed households.

Some of these findings mentioned above based on data from a single region were further highlighted in Shanti (2006) using the large survey data by NSSO across all parts of India. There was a predominance of single women (includes widowed, separated and never married women) among those who stated work as the reason for migration. Similarly, female-headed households dominated among the livelihood-oriented migration. Being unattached to a male head gave them the 'option' to move though in most situations it may be the need to survive. At the same time to escape social restrictions given their subordinate status in the society may also have compelled them to escape their existing surrounding. There was an increase in participation in the post-migration stage compared to low participation in the pre-migration stage by these same women. No doubt, labour force participation rate (LFPR) among women is always higher after migration and this is clearly captured by this data as well. This gives credence to the fact that there is a demand for female labour in the urban centres (perhaps exploitative in nature) and that the supply of labour by these women may also be imperative for the household's survival.[5]

As this study is based on a large survey data across states in India, regional variations in female migration as well as their workforce participation are brought out clearly. There is a predominance of southern and western states over the northern and north-western states of India. However, in all the states of India, labour force participation in the post-migration stage increases. This is mainly due to the fact that a large proportion of women in their pre-migration status attended to only domestic duties while post-migration they participated in the labour market as well. The present study is a further extension of the earlier study cited above, to understand the pattern of labour force participation among migrant women.

Thus, even though the general literature on migration has considered migration mainly as a livelihood strategy pursued mostly by men, the studies above clearly highlight the different patterns in the labour market activities of female migrants. This study based on large scale survey attempts to add further to the understanding of the role of women in migrant households and the forces that shape female labour mobility.

III

Objectives of the Study

Given this background, this study analyses different features of migrant women in India who participated in the urban labour market during the survey period of July 1999 to June 2000 in the age group of 15 to 60 years. As was discussed in the previous section, there is some gap in the literature on female labour migration. Firstly, the studies based on large scale data for all India discuss mainly the general features of migrant labourers with less attention on female migration and even lesser on female labour migration. Secondly, regional studies based on primary survey data on issues concerning employed women migrants do not lend a comparative perspective with other regions in the country or with non-migrant employed women in their own region.

As other country and recent in-country experiences suggest there are likely to be changes in the female labour migration in India during (a) the process of economic and human development and (b) changes in the economic environment arising from the economic reform process initiated since early 1990s as well as globalisation. Several studies highlight how these two have affected different sectors (for instance, the industry and service sectors) of the economy in general and the labour market in particular. Indeed, very few studies highlight changes, if any, in the labour market features for migrant women over the past two decades.

This paper thus, tries to concentrate on some of these concerns raised above as permitted by the data based on urban areas. In particular the following questions are addressed in this study:

1. How does the labour force participation rate of migrant women differ from that of non-migrant women and male migrants?

2. What is the pattern of employed women migrants when the classification is based on the reason for migration? How does this compare with male migrants?
3. Has there been any change in this pattern as in (b) over time? Even though this study is based only on a single year survey data, the information on duration of stay of the migrants at the time of enumeration is used to capture the changes based on the migrants who (i) arrived within the last 10 years (at the time of survey) and (ii) arrived before that.
4. What is the quality of the migrant labour force? This is analysed based on the education attainment and the employment status with a regional perspective and as mentioned above a comparison between the two time periods is also carried out.

The database used for this analysis collects information on several socio-demographic and economic variables at the individual level for in-migrants and some features of the data are discussed below.

IV

Database

The individual and household level (unit record) data on employment and unemployment surveyed by the NSSO also collect some important details on migrants. The data on migration details is collected periodically once in five years and the present study uses the data for the year 1999–2000 (55th round).

The analysis takes the NSSO definition of *labour force* which is the population that supplies or seeks to supply labour for production activities. Consequently, labour force includes those who are actively engaged in the labour market as well as the unemployed. The labour force participation rate is the ratio of population in the labour force to the total population. The NSSO uses three different reference periods for determining the activity status of an individual. In this analysis, we use the activity status during the previous 365 days referred to as the *usual activity status* and includes both the *principal status* in which the person spent the major time as well as the *subsidiary status* in which the person spent minor time. It has been observed that many women are commonly in the subsidiary status of employment which has of course been on the decline over the years.

The NSSO collects information on in-migrants in their quinquennial round (large sample rounds) employment-unemployment surveys. The definition of a migrant according to NSSO is as follows:

> A member of the sample household was treated as a migrant if he/she had stayed continuously for at least six months or more in a place (village/town) other than the village/town where he/she was enumerated. The village/town where the person had stayed continuously for at least six months or more prior to moving to the place of enumeration (village/town) was referred to as the 'last usual place of residence' of that migrated person. Shifting of residence within village/town was not considered as an event of migration. (GoI, 2001: 14).

Along with other socio-economic and demographic details, information on three important aspects pertaining to migrants is collected. These are: *period since leaving the last usual place of residence* in completed years till the date of survey, *location of last usual place of residence* classified based on rural or urban from within the country or abroad. The in-country migrants are further classified based on whether they belong to a different state, same state but different district or same district in a given state. Finally, *the reason for leaving the last usual place of residence* is also asked, categorised into 13 aspects and includes migration for employment, marriage, or as associated migrants and other reasons (GoI, 2001: 14).

This information on migrants is part of the regular employment-unemployment survey of the NSSO information on occupation status, industry classification and employment status. The employment status includes the (a) *self-employed:* the persons who have the autonomy and independence for carrying out their economic activity and the remuneration received by them comprises of their share of labour and profit of the enterprise; (b) *regular salaried/wage employee*: the person works in other's farm or non-farm enterprise (both household and non-household) and in turn receives salary or wages on a regular basis; and the (c) *casual wage labour*: the person is casually engaged in other's farm or non-farm enterprise (both household and non-household) and receives wages according to the terms of the daily or periodic work contract.

To reiterate once again, the current study is based on:

1. The unit record data of the NSSO employment-unemployment survey for the year 1999–2000;

2. Migrant women who are in the labour force in the age group of 15–60 years;
3. Migration into urban areas;
4. The usual activity status including principal and subsidiary status;
5. 16 major states in India giving a regional perspective;

V

Employment Pattern of Female Migrants: Results and Discussion

The total in-migrant population in the age group of 15 to 60 years is very unequally distributed across states as shown in Table 1. This may be expected as the states (and more importantly the urban centres within) have varied levels of economic development. Moreover, due to industrial agglomeration (which are predominantly in the southern parts of the country) and hence the demand for related services, only some cities within these states have large employment opportunities resulting in a concentration of migrants in select states. States like Bihar and Uttar Pradesh have more out-migrants than in-migrants (GoI 2003). If we focus only on the age group of 15–60 years and those who are in the labour force there are about 85 lakh migrant women while migrant men in the same category are about 211 lakh as shown in Table 1. Of these Maharashtra has the highest number of about 12 lakh women and 49 lakh men in 1999–2000. Andhra Pradesh, Tamil Nadu and Uttar Pradesh are other three states with next highest number (about 10 lakh each) of women in-migrants in the labour force. Among men, apart from these three states where the migrants range between 20–25 lakh, Gujarat, Karnataka and West Bengal also have between 10–15 lakh migrants in the labour force. Women in these states constitute a very small proportion.

The following sub-sections present results on labour force participation rate among migrants and inter-regional variations, the reason for migration and labour force participation rate of migrant women, quality of the migrant female labour force and the origin and destination of the women migrants.

Labour Force Participation Rate among Migrants

Overall the female participation rate among urban women in India is lower than men when compared to several other countries with similar level of development. As shown in Table 1, women in general have a far lower participation rate of about 27 per cent while men have about 81 per cent. Cultural reasons not withstanding, the four southern states of

Kerala (36.3%), Tamil Nadu (32.6%), Andhra Pradesh (27.1%) and Karnataka (26.6%) have a far higher participation rate than the all India average while at the lower end are Bihar (12.7%), Uttar Pradesh (15.5%) and Haryana and Chandigarh (16.7%). This general pattern of workforce participation across states is more or less replicated for the migrant population as well but few states have higher and few lower rates than the general population. However, such a discernible difference between the southern states and other states as is observed among women is not so for men.

Further, contrast between women and men arises when one considers the proportion of migrants in the labour force. At the all India level 54.7 per cent of migrants constitute the female labour force while for males it is 33 per cent. Most states have similar proportion of migrants as that of all India average but in states like Punjab, Rajasthan and Uttar Pradesh about 70 per cent of the female labour force is constituted by migrants. Thus, states with lower female LFPR in general have a substantially higher proportion of migrant women in the labour force. A comparison of LFPR of these women before and after migration further substantiates that women migrants indeed have an important role to play by participating in the labour market. In all the states post-migration LFPR increases substantially compared to their pre-migration status (Srivastava and Bhattacharya, 2003). These changes are the largest in the three states mentioned above and that this increase in post-migration LFPR is naturally offset by a significant decline in proportion of women reporting 'carry out domestic duties alone' (Shanti, 2006).

As for their distribution across states, the two southern states of Tamil Nadu and Andhra Pradesh together account for about 25 per cent of the urban migrant women while Maharashtra has the highest share with nearly 15 per cent. Since Maharashtra also has a very high share of male migrants and this perhaps explains the large proportion of women migrants in the labour force who may have taken up a job either after migrating along with their family members or after being married to the male migrant.

Reasons for Migration and LFPR

This brings us to the next issue that if women migrants have a large share in the female labour force, what is the prime reason they cite for migration? As discussed in Section II above, marriage migration constitutes a very high proportion for women, followed by associated migration while migration for employment constitutes a very small share.

Table 1 ***Characteristics of Urban Labour Force Participation Rates for Women and Men Migrants Aged 15–60 Years Across States (%)***

	Migrant Labour Force (Lakh)		Labour Force Participation Rate[1]				Share of Migrants in the Respective Labour Force		Distribution of Migrant Labour Force Across States[4]	
	Women	Men	Women		Men		Women	Men	Women	Men
			Tot[2]	Migr[3]	Tot[2]	Migr[3]				
Andhra Pradesh	10.1	20.6	27.1	29.6	80.9	81.9	56.0	36.7	12.9	9.7
Assam	0.3	0.8	18.5	20.1	81.9	80.5	20.1	11.1	0.4	0.4
Bihar	2.0	4.5	12.7	12.2	77.8	72.8	46.5	15.6	2.7	2.1
Gujarat	5.4	12.7	19.8	19.6	82.3	83.5	60.5	32.4	6.4	6.0
Haryana and Chandigarh	2.1	7.9	16.7	16.2	79.2	82.1	73.4	49.3	1.9	3.8
Himachal Pradesh	0.3	0.8	21.4	21.5	77.0	79.4	79.9	60.2	0.3	0.4
Karnataka	5.8	12.0	26.6	26.8	82.3	85.9	50.6	33.0	7.6	5.7
Kerala	4.9	5.9	36.3	36.6	83.1	81.9	54.7	31.7	5.6	2.8
Madhya Pradesh	6.5	9.7	21.3	22.0	80.7	81.2	61.3	22.2	8.4	4.6
Maharashtra	12.2	48.8	21.8	20.3	82.7	88.5	54.1	49.2	15.4	23.1
Orissa	1.8	5.7	22.8	18.7	79.3	81.2	45.7	38.7	2.0	2.7
Punjab	2.9	7.1	18.5	19.8	84.3	92.2	76.2	35.6	2.4	3.3

Cont'd...

Cont'd...

Rajasthan	4.6	8.9	22.5	24.2	78.9	81.7	74.5	34.8	4.2	4.2
Tamil Nadu	10.2	19.5	32.6	30.7	84.3	86.7	46.9	33.4	13.1	9.4
Uttar Pradesh	9.8	26.2	15.5	15.6	82.0	85.6	71.4	31.0	9.4	12.2
West Bengal	5.0	16.2	18.1	17.4	85.9	89.2	56.8	34.3	6.2	7.8
All India	84.8	211.6	27.1	29.6	80.9	81.9	56.0	36.7	100	100

Note: 1. Labour Force Participation Rate (LFPR): Ratio of the proportion of people in the labour force to the population in the age group of 15–60 years.
2. Tot is LFPR in the total population, migrant and non-migrant.
3. Migr is LFPR in the migrant population alone.
4. The distribution here pertains to the migrants in the labour force for women and men separately.

Source: Tabulation by the authors using unit record data of the NSSO on employment and unemployment for 1999–2000 (55th round).

This is also observed in the data as shown in Table 2 below while the order is exactly reversed for men. The issue of interest revolves around two aspects, that is, what are the changes observed in the past decade in this pattern and what is the variation across states in this change? Based on the information on period since leaving last usual place of residence, the total period of stay is classified into those who migrated recently, that is, have the duration of stay below 10 years and those who have stayed for 10 years or more since migration. As discussed in Section IV the single period cross-section data is being used to capture the changes that could have possibly taken place since the onset of liberalisation policies in India along with the globalisation process around the world.

The reasons for migration in the NSSO data are broadly classified into (i) marriage, (ii) associated, (iii) work, (iv) studies and (v) others. Due to the subordinate status attached to a woman's participation in the labour market they may cite marriage or association as the reason for migration but are likely to work in the new destination. Similarly, many women though may cite work as the reason for migration but could possibly drop out of labour market after getting married. It is in fact observed in the data wherein only 68 per cent of those who cite work as the reason for migration continued working while about 20 per cent each among the married and associated migrants also work. From a regional dimension, the same picture arises but since the southern states in India have a higher LFPR among women this results in a higher proportion for these states in all these groups of migrants.

As was briefly highlighted in Section II above, due to the practise of exogamy, women migrate after marriage and hence marriage is the main reason for migration. In the 1999–2000 NSSO data (Table 2), marriage migration (64.2%) is the dominant reason followed by associated migrants (26.6%), and migration for work constitutes a minuscule (3.2%) proportion even lower than those who cite 'other' reasons (5.0%). Unlike this, men (61%) cite work as the prime reason for migration followed by associated migration (19%). Marriage migration is a very small proportion (1.7%). This all India pattern is replicated across all the states except for Andhra Pradesh where lower proportion (about 48%) of women migrants cite marriage as the reason and a higher than average (41%) are associated according to this survey. More importantly, *among the migrant women who participate in the labour market* a very similar distribution of the reason for migration is noted except that work migration increases to about 10 per cent while the share of marriage migration declines to about 60 per cent. This pattern is by and large the same for all the states in India.

Thus, on the one hand this reflects that women who migrate due to marriage also seem to have the aspiration to work and perhaps use this to seek better opportunities for themselves given the social fabric that women may not be allowed to move alone but also need to be accompanied by male escorts. On the other hand, when men migrate they also take into account the fact that women can also participate in labour market to enhance the standard of living in the newly settled area which perhaps helps the household to smoothen the stream of income due to this change. One micro study on internal female migration in Nicaragua observes that young females migrate not for just economic gains and marital purposes; they consider a wide range of factors, such as work aspirations, consumption patterns in urban areas, enhancement of their skills and knowledge and career development (Behrman and Wolfe, 1984).

Interestingly, the pattern of female migration with marriage as the dominant reason seems to have changed to some extent in the recent times in general and more importantly among those who participate in the labour market. If the group of migrants are classified into those who moved ten or more years prior to the survey time and those who moved in within the last ten years, the change is rather dramatic. Among the earlier settlers, the proportion of total married migrants constituted more than 70 per cent while among the recent ones they are about 48 per cent. The associated migrants were earlier 21 per cent and have increased their share to 32.6 per cent in the past decade. The most notable change comes in the work-related migrants increasing their share from about 6 per cent to about 19 per cent.

Table 2 ***Distribution of the Women Migrants in the Labour Force by Reasons for Migration Classified According to Duration of Stay (%)***

States	*Duration of Stay for*					
	10 Years or More			*Less than 10 Years*		
	Employ	*Marriage*	*Associate*	*Employ*	*Marriage*	*Associate*
Andhra Pradesh	11.2	63.4	25.4	19.1 (54.7)	36.2 (27.5)	44.7 (56.5)
Assam	16.8	80.0	3.3	49.9 (75.6)	25.5 (13.3)	24.6 (89.3)
Bihar	6.0	87.2	6.8	28.0 (33.4)	53.5 (10.6)	18.4 (27.8)
Gujarat	3.3	79.2	17.6	19.0 (62.6)	47.8 (14.5)	33.2 (35.4)

Cont'd...

Cont'd...

Haryana and Chandigarh	5.3	58.8	35.9	8.7 (38.2)	65.0 (40.7)	26.3 (29.5)
Himachal Pradesh	22.5	64.2	13.3	29.7 (36.5)	52.4 (26.8)	17.8 (36.5)
Karnataka	6.1	73.8	20.2	22.6 (74.9)	48.2 (29.5)	29.2 (51.5)
Kerala	3.6	81.9	14.5	15.2 (76.8)	57.8 (33.3)	27.0 (56.9)
Madhya Pradesh	5.4	86.7	7.9	11.9 (46.7)	75.1 (24.5)	13.0 (39.0)
Maharashtra	7.5	66.7	25.8	25.4 (60.8)	41.9 (21.6)	32.8 (34.6)
Orissa	5.7	83.8	10.5	26.3 (69.5)	55.6 (21.1)	18.1 (44.3)
Punjab	4.1	74.4	21.5	15.5 (62.8)	46.5 (20.0)	38.0 (35.1)
Rajasthan	5.9	75.1	19.0	10.9 (46.9)	61.4 (29.5)	27.7 (42.7)
Tamil Nadu	7.7	68.1	24.2	17.8 (61.2)	42.9 (29.0)	39.3 (49.7)
Uttar Pradesh	3.1	72.0	24.8	11.9 (57.3)	53.8 (19.4)	34.4 (31.0)
West Bengal	6.8	75.6	17.6	24.6 (68.3)	44.2 (23.9)	31.1 (52.1)
All India	6.3	73.0	20.7	18.8 (60.8)	48.6 (24.5)	32.6 (43.8)

Note: The values in parentheses are the share of less than ten-year duration migrants within each reason category.

Source: Same as Table 1.

Table 2 also shows that broadly similar pattern is observed across states but some variations among them are noteworthy. Kinship marriage is more common among the southern states and this may to some extent explain the lower proportions of marriage migration in the states of Andhra Pradesh, Maharashtra and Tamil Nadu. Among the states with high LFPR, like Andhra Pradesh, Maharashtra, and Tamil Nadu, the decline in the share of marriage migration is large and so is also noted among one of the lower LFPR states like Bihar. Associated migrants on the other hand have also increased their share which varies between one-third to one-half of the total migrants in the labour force, across the states.

There is a significant jump in the share of employment-related migrants in Bihar as well as smaller states like Assam and Himachal Pradesh. Among the larger states Karnataka, Maharashtra, Orissa and West Bengal show substantial changes in the share of employment related migrants. In Assam, Karnataka and Kerala, the recent migrants have a very high share among the total employed migrants (shown within parentheses in Table 2). In Karnataka, the change is perhaps the result of Bangalore which became a hub for software, biotechnology and textile exports industries further spawning demand for other related services and thereby attracting lot of migrants from far and near. It is further noted that when the last ten-year period is further split into two five-year periods, the change has been very significant in the last five years. The changes in Assam and Kerala seem less explainable.

Given these recent changes, the next section examines the quality of the female migrant workforce by focussing on the educational attainment and current employment status.

Quality of Workforce and Migration Status

The quality of the workforce is usually discussed based on their wages earned and their economic standard of living based on poverty status. Since wages earned are not reported by the self-employed (who constitute a substantial proportion) in this survey, this study is unable to use wages as one of the basis to judge the economic status. Further, the information on economic standard of living as well as wages is available only for the current period of survey and not at the time of migration. The migrants who moved earlier may have substantially improved their position over time (and reverse may also be possible) while the recent entrants may be differentially positioned. This would bias the analysis based on current income.[6] Consequently, the quality aspect is addressed on the basis of level of education and employment status. This analysis is carried out by comparing (a) the migrants with non-migrants and male migrants and (b) the migrants who arrived in the last ten years and those who moved earlier than that.

Educational Attainment

It is a well-known fact that higher levels of education have higher returns (wages) and this aspect is being used to assess the quality of the labour force. In the Indian context, due to bias against female children and women, one finds that the average level of education is lower than the males and this is one of the reasons for labour market segmentation between these two groups. The interest here is to see if the gap between

Figure 1(a) *Level of Education Among Migrants and Non-Migrants: Women*

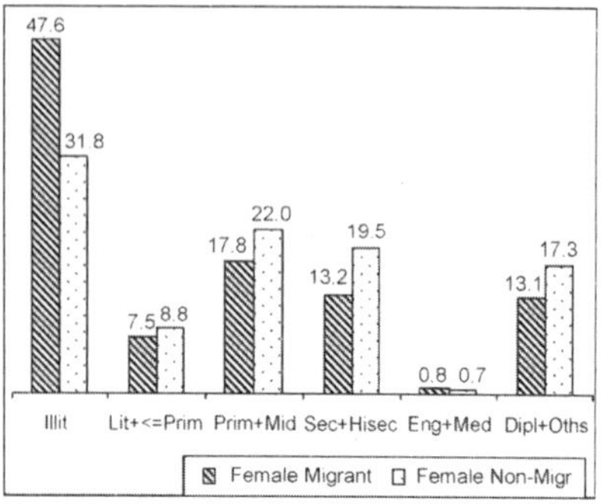

Figure 1(b) *Level of Education Among Migrants and Non-Migrants: Men*

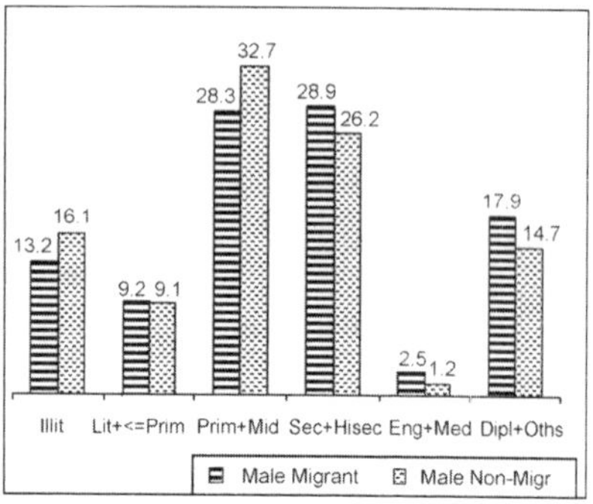

males and females is lower among the migrants compared to the non-migrants and to further assess the level of education among these migrants.

The proportion of females across education levels among total migrant and non-migrant labour force presents a mixed picture as shown in Figure 1(a) for all India. Among the different educational groups migrant women have higher proportions in all the segments. The gap is of course substantial among the illiterates perhaps reflecting the fact that migrant women may be forced to participate in the labour market if the migration has taken place due to push factors for whom the general economic condition would have been lower prior to migration or that urban centres have higher cost of living which may need augmentation of household income by women. This situation does not seem to persist across all education groups and that they have higher educational attainment as well wherein women with secondary level of education are about 16 per cent among migrants while it is 10 per cent among non-migrants. The same is true for others which include diploma holders, non-engineering graduates and non-medical graduates wherein the gap between migrant and non-migrant women is significant enough to merit attention.

In comparison to male migrants, the female migrants seem to be worse-off in their overall education status as shown in Figure 1(b) below. Unlike male migrants, female migrants have a larger proportion of illiterates and lower proportion among all the higher levels of educational attainment. The only exception to that is among engineers and medical degree holders who anyway constitute a minuscule proportion among both migrants and non-migrants. All the states show a similar pattern barring Kerala, wherein the pattern is reverse, with fewer migrants among the illiterates but more in all other categories (results not reported here).

Figures 1(a) and (b) though paint a dismal picture of the quality of migrant women labour force, the proportion of migrants in each education group across states brings out variations in this pattern. The migrants who constitute a little more than half (55%) of the total female labour force, there are two different clusters of states among these as shown in Table 3. The first are those states where the migrants constitute more than 70 per cent of the workforce and are predominantly the northern and north-western states of Haryana and Chandigarh, Himachal Pradesh, Punjab, Rajasthan and Uttar Pradesh. The second are among the southern and eastern states with similar rate as that of all India average with values between 45–55 per cent. Gujarat and Madhya Pradesh have about 60 per cent migrants and somewhere in between these two.

We further contrast the education level across migrants who have moved in the last 10 years (Table 3). As observed earlier, due to age and time factor, these migrants constitute a lower proportion (35%) in the entire labour force. Despite this, the newer migrants in the labour force seem to be better educated with fewer illiterates and more are among the higher levels of education compared to their senior counterparts signifying an improvement in the quality of the labour force. Though some of the improvement in the education level can be attributed to overall improvement in the country over the years and this is perhaps best reflected by lower proportion of these migrants among the illiterates and the lower education segment. However, not all of it could be attributed to this aspect alone. Not only are there fewer illiterates among these new migrant women, but also their representation increases to nearly 50 per cent at the all India level beyond the secondary levels of education. In the southern states of Andhra Pradesh, Karnataka, Kerala and Tamil Nadu where their total proportion is larger than the all India average, they seem to be having substantially higher proportions in the higher education segments.

Current Employment Status

The employment status in the urban labour market is classified by the NSSO into self-employed, regular salaried, casual labour and the unemployed as discussed in Section IV above. The first three of these

Table 3 *Level of Education among Female Migrants*

	Proportion of Migrants							*Proportion of Below 10 Years of Stay among the Migrants*						
States	*Illiter*	*Liter and Bel Prim*	*Prim and Mid*	*Sec and Hisec*	*Engg and Medc*	*Others*	*All*	*Illiter*	*Liter and Bel Prim*	*Prim and Mid*	*Sec and Hisec*	*Engg and Medc*	*Others*	*All*
Andhra Pradesh	61.8	58.5	51.2	36.9	63.3	45.9	56.0	36.7	38.2	66.5	55.3	65.0	51.2	42.9
Assam	15.3	31.9	21.0	12.1	0.0	30.1	19.8	14.4	54.9	66.6	69.0	0.0	43.0	47.4
Bihar	50.4	48.8	22.5	29.9	95.6	47.3	46.5	10.0	28.5	20.8	17.7	29.7	28.5	14.3
Gujarat	76.3	61.5	48.4	48.8	50.5	50.6	60.5	18.2	28.8	19.9	49.5	17.5	22.5	23.9
Haryana and Chandigarh	86.3	74.8	68.7	58.0	97.7	72.3	73.4	30.4	37.9	54.3	40.9	1.7	35.4	36.8
Himachal Pradesh	90.4	88.1	74.8	76.6	99.6	75.1	79.9	18.2	17.7	34.7	34.8	83.5	38.7	32.0
Karnataka	52.3	44.7	49.1	50.1	44.7	52.4	50.6	29.1	45.5	41.3	63.2	74.2	44.0	42.2
Kerala	45.0	51.9	56.0	51.4	70.1	64.6	54.6	7.1	20.4	32.2	54.4	54.6	71.0	43.0
Madhya Pradesh	67.5	63.8	50.6	53.2	100.0	38.6	61.3	25.8	23.3	33.1	46.3	42.2	39.6	28.7
Maharashtra	69.9	48.4	53.4	41.7	56.5	42.3	54.1	20.6	29.9	36.4	43.0	53.5	51.4	33.1
Orissa	46.3	41.1	55.5	39.8	0.0	42.5	45.7	23.0	40.2	28.6	54.2	0.0	52.0	30.9
Punjab	91.9	96.0	72.9	63.1	100.0	59.7	76.2	25.6	1.2	37.4	27.7	79.9	36.5	28.8
Rajasthan	85.5	57.6	45.5	59.0	100.0	74.2	74.5	28.6	52.6	46.8	42.8	47.5	54.4	35.2
Tamil Nadu	52.1	45.1	41.1	43.7	28.0	53.2	46.9	23.4	45.5	44.1	52.7	84.5	63.3	41.1
Uttar Pradesh	78.0	44.7	63.6	54.9	96.1	70.9	71.4	18.6	43.4	54.5	37.5	11.2	36.3	27.0
West Bengal	63.8	54.1	60.1	42.0	100.0	51.0	56.8	40.3	44.9	32.3	32.5	100.0	39.8	38.3
All India	64.4	50.6	49.5	45.0	58.3	47.8	54.7	25.9	35.9	40.0	48.2	50.1	46.7	35.0

Source: Same as Table 1.

Figure 2(a) ***Distribution of Women in Each Employment Group by Migrant Status***

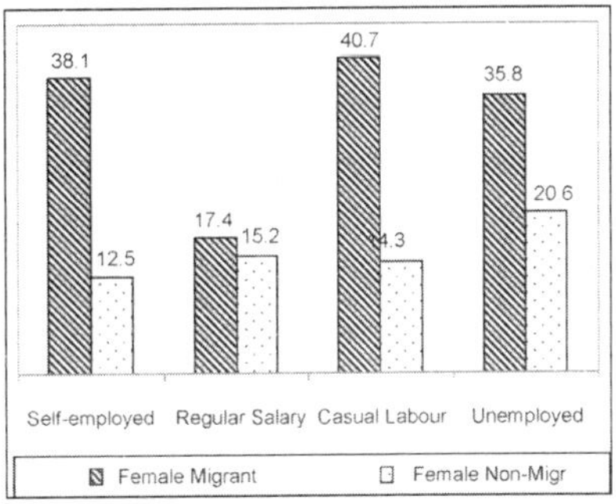

Figure 2(b) ***Distribution of Women Across Employment Groups by Migrant Status***

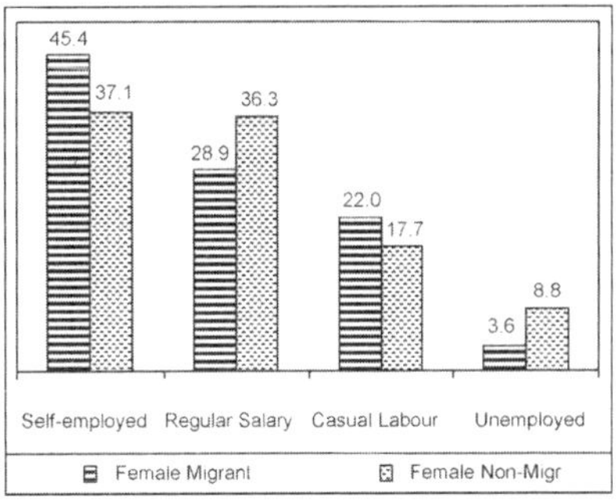

groups constitute the workforce and are among the actively employed. It is also well known that when the households are classified on the basis of their members' employment status, the regular salaried are among the top followed by the self-employed, and then the casual labour. The unemployed in India as observed from this data source constitute a very small segment and may be spread among all economic classes.

Based on this classification of employment status, both migrant and non-migrant women form a very small proportion among the regular salaried and the gap between these two groups is rather small, as shown in Figure 2(a). This in a way may reflect the discrimination between men and women in the labour market wherein the better paid jobs (regular salaried) are male dominated. The overall higher participation rates by the migrant women in a way seem to further accentuate their subordinate position as they form a large proportion among the casual labour and the self-employed compared to their non-migrant counterparts.

Figure 2(b) compares the distribution of migrant and non-migrant women separately across the employment sub-groups. The migrant women have a larger share among the casual labour and self-employed and smaller share among the regular salaried when compared to the non-migrant women. Looking at it in another way, the migrant women constitute nearly 60 per cent each of the total self-employed women and total women casual labourers while for men it is 25 per cent each respectively (results not reported here). This further seems to indicate that migrant women are not as better placed compared to the non-migrant women. The unemployed among the non-migrants seem to be much higher perhaps reflecting an aspiration effect while the migrants may be forced to accept jobs to have a better status in the migrated area.

Table 4 below shows that there are indeed state level variations. Uttar Pradesh tops among the self-employed followed by Maharashtra, Andhra Pradesh and Tamil Nadu. Maharashtra and Tamil Nadu dominate among the regular salaried with 15 per cent each from these states followed by Uttar Pradesh and Andhra Pradesh having about 10 per cent each. The next highest among these are Karnataka and West Bengal at about 7 per cent each. All other states have far lower values. This distribution of the regular salaried perhaps reflects the effect of large metropolitan cities in most of these states like Mumbai, Chennai, Hyderabad, Bangalore and Kolkata. Uttar Pradesh though may not have a metro city may be capturing either the large population effect or the presence of a large urban agglomeration in Uttar Pradesh adjacent to Delhi. This last aspect is also observed among male migrants but a major difference lies in the fact that Tamil Nadu and Andhra Pradesh are not as prominent and Maharashtra has a significant lead among all other states in each of the employment groups for male migrants. West Bengal, Gujarat and Bihar also have significant presence of male migrants thereby reducing the share of the southern states.

Table 4 ***Distribution of Migrant Women for the Employment Across States***

	Distribution Across States For			*Proportion of Migrants Below 10 Years of Stay For*		
	Self-employed	*Regular Salary*	*Casual Labour*	*Self-employed*	*Regular Salary*	*Casual Labour*
Andhra Pradesh	10.2	10.0	18.6	35.6 (38.7)	42.5 (24.2)	48.8 (34.2)
Assam	0.1	0.6	0.4	40.1 (19.5)[3]	46.4 (51.8)	49.2 (24.1)
Bihar	2.2	2.4	2.1	12.9 (43.6)	16.5 (30.7)	16.2 (19.6)
Gujarat	5.6	5.1	10.7	22.8 (39.8)	31.4 (23.0)	20.4 (36.9)
Haryana and Chandigarh	2.6	3.2	1.4	46.5 (47.8)	23.4 (37.1)	29.4 (12.6)
Himachal Pradesh	0.3	0.4	0.1	24.3 (48.4)	35.1 (39.6)	23.2 (5.4)

Cont'd...

Cont'd...

Karnataka	5.9	7.3	8.4	28.8 (39.0)	55.7 (30.9)	46.6 (27.0)
Kerala	5.1	5.7	3.4	27.4 (40.5)	48.4 (28.4)	28.7 (12.9)
Madhya Pradesh	8.5	4.2	11.7	27.9 (50.3)	30.3 (15.7)	28.1 (33.6)
Maharashtra	13.7	14.4	16.1	28.5 (43.3)	44.4 (28.9)	23.4 (24.7)
Orissa	1.9	2.3	2.6	34.2 (41.0)	30.1 (31.1)	26.5 (26.8)
Punjab	3.5	5.2	1.2	24.8 (47.1)	34.4 (44.3)	19.6 (7.6)
Rajasthan	7.6	3.9	3.9	31.9 (63.7)	44.3 (20.6)	36.7 (15.7)
Tamil Nadu	10.2	15.4	10.6	36.5 (38.6)	45.3 (37.1)	30.4 (19.5)
Uttar Pradesh	16.1	10.6	4.0	26.1 (63.5)	22.0 (26.6)	30.6 (7.6)
West Bengal	5.6	7.6	4.2	29.4 (42.5)	47.0 (36.9)	38.1 (15.6)
All India	100	100	100	29.9 (45.4)	44.0 (28.9)	33.0 (22.0)

Note: (1) The values in parentheses represent the distribution of migrant women for all durations of stay across the three employment groups for each state. These values do not add up to hundred as the unemployed group is not reported here.

Source: Same as Table 1.

The migrant casual labourers seem to have a different distribution. Andhra Pradesh picks up a significant share of about 19 per cent followed by Maharashtra with 16 per cent, Gujarat and Madhya Pradesh join Tamil Nadu with about 10 per cent each followed by Karnataka at about 8 per cent while in Uttar Pradesh the share of female migrant casual labourers is very small. This picture is also somewhat different from that of males where Maharashtra (19.4%) has the largest share followed by Andhra Pradesh (13.5%), Tamil Nadu (11.3%) while Gujarat (10.5%) and Madhya Pradesh (4%) are lower in the order.

With the onset of globalisation, there has been an increase in the demand for female labour and this has led to significant increase in internal migrants as noted in the case of China, Indonesia and other East-Asian countries (Zhang, 1999). How has the situation been for an in-migrant woman in India in the last 10 years given that this country has liberalised its economy towards a more outward looking policy than before and hence would also be influenced by the globalisation process? Though it is not apparent from this analysis if the women benefited from the ongoing changes but there has surely been a change among the recent migrants towards better jobs.

The recent migrants have a large share of about 40 per cent among the regular salaried at the all India level but there are substantial state level variations. This may be due to the fact that recent women migrants are better qualified and hence able to access better jobs in the urban centres. All the southern states as well as Maharashtra and West Bengal have a larger than the all India average value while states like Bihar, Uttar Pradesh have far lower representation of the recent in-migrants. Even states like Gujarat and Punjab have lower mobility in this category. Among the self-employed and the casual labourers they are about 30 per cent which is similar to their proportion in the overall migrant female labour force. This brings into picture a very clear aspect that in the southern states of Andhra Pradesh, Kerala, Karnataka and Tamil Nadu, there has been a higher labour mobility in the last 10 years. In all these states, the recent migrants constitute more than 40 per cent of the female migrant labour force and perhaps have been able to do so due to higher levels of education and the demand for certain type of skills in the labour market.

VI

Summary and Conclusion

With the feminisation of international migration the issue of female labour mobility has gained importance. However, the issue of internal migration of women with employment as the objective of migration is not well-researched. This study is an attempt to fill this gap from an empirical perspective using the Indian data. There is enough evidence across countries to show that during the process of globalisation female labour is much in demand and with the onset of economic liberalisation in India a similar trend may be expected.

This is one of the few recent studies that have analysed female migration based on a large scale survey data while highlighting the regional dimensions as well. Moreover, the study for the first time brings in a dynamic component to this analysis by using the information on duration of stay, to compare changes across two periods, in the pattern of female migrants engaged in the labour market. In a country where marriage is still the dominant reason for migration several women take up employment post-marriage and so it is true of those women who accompany male migrants. These women are predominantly illiterate and are either self-employed or casual labourers. From a policy perspective not only improvements need to be made in their skill level but also in their living conditions.

The important issue is that even though the overall migration rates have declined in the past years, more women are migrating to cities from rural areas for employment in the age-group of 15–60 years. There is also a significantly high proportion of women migrants among the professionals like engineers and doctors primarily indicating aspiration effect of the well-educated. The data set has permitted limited analysis of the pre- and post-migration economic status and more regional studies are required to understand the impact of liberalisation and globalisation on female labour force participation as well as its impact on their social and economic status.

Notes

1. See Karlekar (1995) for a more detailed discussion of the theories of migration.
2. In countries like India where marriage migration is very pronounced in several parts of the country, women migrants outnumber men migrants substantially.
3. A common practice has been that a young girl from a rural area is sent to work as domestic help to a household in an urban centre mainly to augment the family income who, after getting married is replaced by a younger female sibling (or a female cousin).
4. Though the LFPR for rural women, urban men and rural men has also declined in the 1990s, the decline for urban women has been more (Viswanathan, 2003).
5. Better educated women may also use this mode of getting married to men in urban centres where job opportunities may be better and hence easy for them to pursue their 'ambitions'.
6. NSSO data provides information on monthly per capita expenditure (mpce) of the households and not incomes of the individual or the households. This mpce data is usually used to classify them either as poor or otherwise based on a poverty line or grouping them into mpce deciles or quintiles.

References

Behrman, J.R. and B.L. Wolfe. 1984. Micro Determinants of Female Migration in a Developing Country: Labour Market, Demographic, Marriage Market and Economic Marriage Market Incentives. *Research in Population Economics,* 5: 131–66.

Chantavanich, S. 2001. Female Labour Migration in South East Asia: Change and Continuity. Research Monograph, ARCM Institute of Asian Studies, Chulanlongkorn University.

Connell, J., B. Das Gupta, Laish Ley and M. Lipton. 1976. *Migration from Rural Areas: The Evidence from Village Studies*. New Delhi: Oxford University Press.

De Haan, A. and A. Dubey. 2006. "Are Migrants Worse or Better Off? Asking the Right Questions" in A. Dubey, M. Satish Kumar, N. Srivastava and E.D. Thomas (eds.), *Globalisation and North-East India: Some Developmental Issues*.

Fawcett, J.T., S. Khoo and P.C. Smith. 1984. *Women in the Cities of Asia: Migration and Urban Adaptation.* Boulder, Colorado: Westview Press.

Fernandez-Kelly and Maria Patricia. 1983. "Mexican Border, Industrialisation, Female Labour Force Participation and Migration" in June Nash, Maria Patricia and Fernandez-Kelly (eds.), *Women, Men and International Division of Labour.* State University of New York Press, New York: Albany, 205–23.

GoI. 2001. Migration in India· 1999–2000. Report Number 470, National Sample Survey Organisation, Ministry of Planning and Programme Implementation, New Delhi: Government of India.

Harris, J.R. and M.P. Todaro. 1970. Migration, Unemployment and Development: A Two Sector Analysis. *American Economic Review,* 60: 126–42.

Hugo, G. 2000. "Migration and Women's Empowerment" in H.B. Presser and Gita Sen (eds.), *Women's Empowerment and Demographic Processes: Moving Beyond Cairo.* New York: Oxford University Press.

Kabeer, N. 2000. *The Power to Choose, Bangladeshi Women and Labour Market Decisions in London and Dhaka*. London: Verso Press.

Karlekar, M. 1995. "Gender Dimensions in Labour Migration: An Overview" in Schenk Sandbergen (ed.), *Women and Seasonal Migration.* New Delhi: IDPAD and Sage Publications.

Khoo, Siew-Ean. 1984. "Urbanward Migration and Employment of Women in South East and East Asian Cities: Patterns and Policy Issues" in Gavin W. Jones (ed.), *Women in the Urban and Industrial Workforce*. Southeast and East Asia Development Studies Centre, Monograph No. 33, Canberra: Australian National University, 277–92.

Lewis, W.A. 1955. Economic Development with Unlimited Supplies of Labour. *Manchester School* 28: 139–91.

Lingam, L. 1998. Women and Migration: An Annotated Bibliography. *Indian Journal of Social Work* 59: 864–82.

Lucas, R.E.B. 1997. "Internal Migration in Developing Countries" in M.R. Rosenzweig and O. Stark (eds.), *Handbook of Population and Family Economics*. North-Holland: Elsevier Science Publishers, 721–98.

Neetha, N. 2004. Making of Female Breadwinners: Migration and Social Networking of Women Domestics in Delhi. *Economic and Political Weekly*, April 24: 1681–8.

Premi, M.K. 1980. Aspects of Female Migration in India. *Economic and Political Weekly of India,* April 12: 714–20.

Shanti, K. 2006. Female Labour Migration in India: Insights from NSSO Data. Working Paper No. 4/2006, Chennai: Madras School of Economics.

Sivaramakrishnan, K.C., A. Kundu and B.N. Singh. 2005. *Handbook of Urbanisation in India*. New Delhi: Oxford University Press.

Stark, O. 1984. Rural-to-Urban Migration in LDCs: A Relative Deprivation Approach. *Economic Development and Cultural Change* 32: 475–86.

Sundari, S. 2005a. Female Migration in Tamil Nadu: An Inter-District Analysis. *Demography India* 34: 103–26.

Sundari, S. 2005b. Migration as Livelihood Strategy: A Gender Perspective. *Economic and Political Weekly*, May 28: 2295–303.

Srivastava, R. and S. Bhattacharya. 2003. Globalisation, Reforms and Internal Labour Mobility: Analysis of Recent Indian Trends. *Labour and Development* 9: 31–55.

Thandani, V. and M.P. Todaro. 1984. "Female Migration: A Conceptual Framework" in J.T. Fawcett, S. Khoo and P.C. Smith (eds.), *Women in the Cities of Asia: Migration and Urban Adaptation.*

United Nations. 2004. Report of the Consultative Meeting on Migration and Mobility and How this Affects Women, New York.

Viswanathan, B. 2003. Demography and Employment in Tamil Nadu State Development Report, Union Planning Commission, New Delhi: Government of India.

Williamson, J.G. 1988. "Migration and Urbanisation" in H. Chenery and T.N. Srinivasan (eds.), *Handbook of Development Economics.* Vol. I, North-Holland: Elsevier Science Publishers, 425–65.

Wright, C. 1995. Gender Awareness in Migration Theory: Synthesising Actor and Structure in Southern Africa. *Development and Change* 26: 771–91.

Zhang, H.X. 1999. Female Migration and Urban Labour Markets in Tianjin. *Development and Change* 30: 21–41.

3

Some Facets of Migration to Districts of Maharashtra

Dipti Mukherji and V.S. Phadke

The Problem

Migration is an important component in the growth of population of an area, the other being natural growth. The process leads to growth of destination areas, on the one hand, and depopulation of sending areas, on the other; thus, it not only affects the migrant population but also the population of absorbing areas. Of late, it is, therefore, becoming an important socio-economic issue, especially in the areas of destination which are receiving migrants in numbers disproportionate to the opportunities and amenities (Roy, 1980); this also leads to deterioration in quality of life of mega cities (Srinivasan, 1990). In the past, only the landless used to migrate, but today, even those possessing land follow suit (Smita, 2007); this entails social tension. It is substantially changing the social structure and traditional face of the mega cities.

Traditionally, regional planners looked at migration as a mechanism to minimise regional and thereby socio-economic disparities, and thus considered it to be an integral part of the regional development process (Holland, 1976; Brown and Burrows, 1977). Migration was a natural process in which surplus labour was gradually withdrawn from the rural farm sector to provide manpower needed for urban industrial growth. This was socially beneficial because human resources were being shifted from locations, where their social marginal product was often assumed to be negative, to places where this marginal product was not only positive but also rapidly growing as a result of capital accumulation and technological progress. It helped to reduce the pressure of population on the resources of the less developed, rural areas and provided labour for the activities of the destination, urban areas. Migrants sought employment and earned income which was partly repatriated to source areas thereby providing some monetary benefit; this led to the famous 'money order economy'. Such migration, however, had always been selective and hence created problems for the sending areas by depriving them of the necessary skilled manpower leading to their further stagnation. Moreover, although it did not create problem for the destination areas immediately, it did so with passage of time, as the latter could not address the inflow smoothly which has increased day by day.

Around two-fifths of the total urban growth in the Third World is accounted for by the rural-to-urban migration. This leads to misallocation of labour between rural and urban sectors and raises urban unemployment, underemployment and poverty; it also increases the social cost of providing amenities to migrant population. This increases the growth rate of urban job seekers, rather disproportionately, and tends to swell the urban labour supply. Urban job creation is generally more difficult to accomplish because of the need for substantial complementary resource inputs for most of the jobs in the industrial sector. The pressure of rising urban wages, in combination with the non-availability of appropriate, more labour-intensive production technologies, results in a growing share of modern sector output which is accounted for by increases in labour productivity. This induces "jobless growth" which tends to convert a short-run problem of resource imbalances into a long-run situation of chronic and rising urban surplus labour.

The level of urbanisation in the world increased from 30 per cent in 1950 to 47 per cent in 2000 and is projected to attain 60 per cent by 2030. Rapid urbanisation is witnessed in developing countries, where the urban population ratios doubled. This, with a high population growth, has exerted enormous pressure on cities. Access to labour, capital and markets, basic infrastructure, skills, technical know-how, networks and market linkages make cities efficient in modern production (Burgess and Venables, 2004). As a result, the poor from under-developed regions migrate to them in search of better livelihoods. It is not surprising then that the number of cities in the world with a population of more than 1 million went up from 115 in 1960 to 416 in 2000; for cities over 4 million the increase was from 18 to 53 and for those over 12 million it was from 1 to 11 (Henderson and Wang, 2003). Dominance of mega cities is particularly common in poor countries.

In the developed countries, rural to urban migration and the resulting urbanisation are associated with a vertical shift in the labour force from the agricultural sector to the urbanised-industrial sector, whereas in the developing countries, it is from rural agricultural sector to urban informal sector. This is a typical manifestation of underdevelopment, poverty, and spatial disorganisation of economy of underdeveloped sectors of the society, which arose partially as a result of past colonisation and its adverse consequences on space economy (Dasgupta et al., 2004). These displacements are not due to structural changes within the labour force as seen in the West, but as a dislocation of uprooted workers and peasants from the marginalised countryside to urban centres. This displacement in India is a typical characteristic of urban growth that has outpaced industrialisation. It is a system of underdevelopment, and tends to compound the same further (Mukherji, 2002).

Though the rate of migration is not necessarily very high in the countries like India, the situation of excess-supply-limited-demand cannot be ruled out in the urban areas as the natural growth of urban population represents an unprecedented phenomenon. In large cities, for example, a large initial base tends to keep the annual rate of population growth modest; the migration rate does not appear to be exceptionally high, but it implies phenomenal increase in absolute terms. With a significant fall in the mortality rate, this has maintained the natural growth of urban population at a high level thus raising the long run supply of labour substantially.

Uneven level of development in developing countries is reflected in uneven rate of migration to different areas (Breman and Das, 2000). However, apart from the factor of development, there are historical and cultural factors that also tend to influence the spatial pattern of migration (Srivastava and Sasikumar, 2003). This produces an interesting pattern in states which have been reorganised on a linguistic basis by incorporating areas from different administrative segments in the past. The thrust of the present paper is, therefore, on analysing some such facets of migration to districts of one such state, viz. Maharashtra.

Data Base and Methodology

The Census of India, 2001, has published some useful data on migration at a district level for Maharashtra and the present paper aims at bringing out certain spatial patterns related to migration. The data relate to persons born at the place of present residence, elsewhere in the district of enumeration, in other districts of the state, outside the state, and outside India. Since the analysis is at the district level, the percentage of persons born outside the country is too low to be considered. The data are analysed at three levels. While working on data at the inter-state level an attempt has been made to identify the diversified nature of the sources of migration using Weaver's technique which has been originally used to identify crop combination regions. This has helped to fix the number of states from which different districts have drawn their migrant population as also the extent of influence exerted by each of these states. The data have been analysed cartographically as well as quantitatively, and interpreted to draw valid inferences.

Pattern of Migrants and Their Sources

There is a considerable spatial variation in the extent of immigration (Figure 1). While Thane and Satara districts record over 50 per cent of their population comprising migrants, the lowest figure of below 35 per

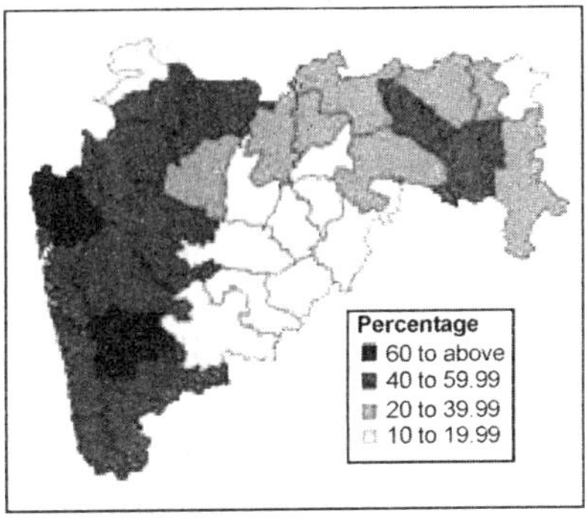

Figure 1 ***Distribution of Migrants in Districts of Maharashtra***

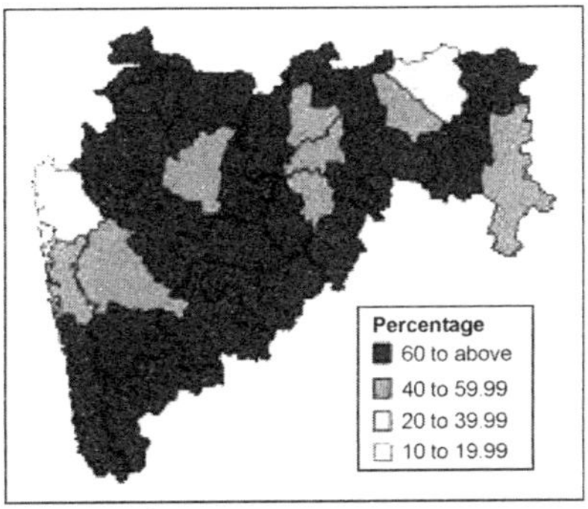

Figure 1a ***Distribution of Intra-District Migrants in Maharashtra***

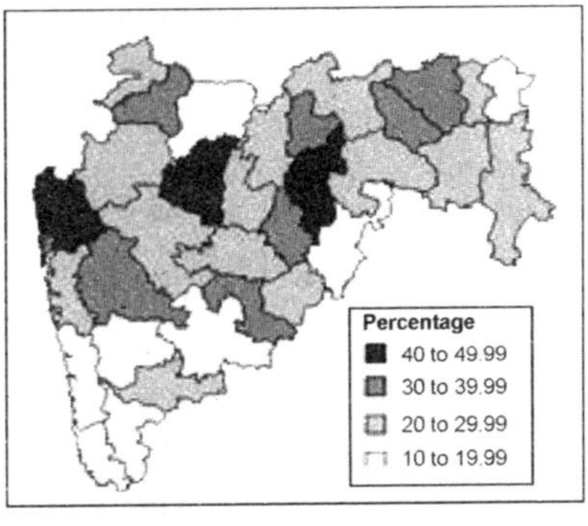

Figure 1b ***Distribution of Inter-District Migrants in Maharashtra***

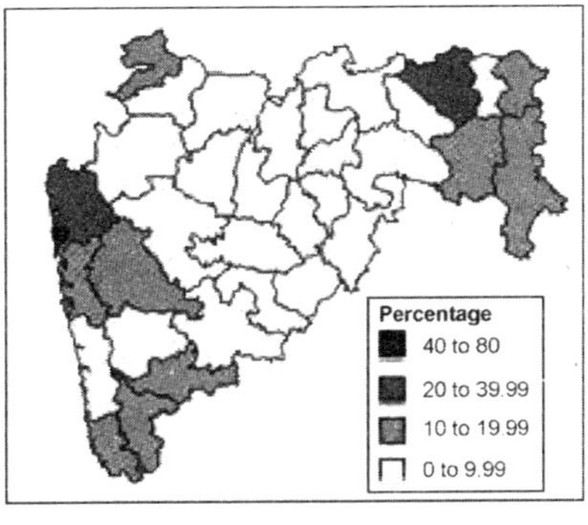

Figure 1c ***Distribution of Inter-State Migrants in Maharashtra***

cent is recorded by all the districts of Marathwada except Aurangabad, Gondiya district of Vidarbha as also Nandurbar and Solapur districts of western Maharashtra plateau; surprisingly, this is not the case with districts of South Konkan. The districts under the shadow of large cities like Mumbai, Pune and Nagpur show a higher rate (40–50%) compared to other districts, where it is 35–40 per cent. Surprisingly, the city district of Mumbai fails to show a high proportion of immigrants; this is also the case with Nagpur district. In the case of Mumbai this is primarily the result of the absence of intra-district migration, the district being the smallest unit; in Nagpur, as well as in Mumbai, saturation is also responsible for such small proportion. This can be seen from the higher proportion of immigrants in Thane district. Even Satara shows a higher proportion than Pune, but the margin is very small.

Source areas of migrant population also show a significant spatial variation (Figure 1a). For almost the entire state, over two-fifth of the migrant population is from within the district. In predominantly agricultural areas of western Maharashtra, Marathwada and Vidarbha this proportion goes up to over three-fifths. The migrant population in this case belongs primarily to agricultural labour category. This proportion progressively comes down as agriculture becomes less important relatively. This is indicated by low percentage for Nagpur and lowest for Thane. Mumbai city and suburban districts do not record any intra-district migration as no internal divisions have been recognised for the purpose of recording data.

The pattern is almost reversed when inter-district migration is considered (Figure 1b). All the districts predominating in non-agricultural activities get projected with high proportion. Even here, Mumbai suburban district fails to come up to the expected position, but this is only relative as out of state sources contribute substantially to total migrants (Figure 1c). The contribution of out of state sources was expected to intensify the pattern shown by inter-district sources. However, the picture is complicated as the factors other than non-agricultural employment play an important role in shaping this pattern. Access by transport lines, historical ties and location, whether at the core or periphery, all play an important role. Thus, a higher proportion in the districts like Nandurbar, Gadchiroli or Sindhudurg could only be explained in terms of border location and historical ties. Low proportion in the heart of the state as also that in Satara district, could be explained in terms of their locations which do not have contiguity with bordering states. Despite this, it is true that as the distance of the source areas of migrants increases, the share of districts containing cities like Mumbai, Nagpur, Pune, Kolhapur or districts under their shadow significantly increases. One thus finds a positive relationship between the distance and the level of opportunity, on the one hand, and skill or education possessed by the migrants, on the other; these factors alone enable them to overcome the friction of distance.

Pattern of Out-of-State Migrants

Among different sources of migration, out-of-state source is more important qualitatively and hence this has been analysed in greater detail. Here, the problem arose because almost all the districts of the state received some migrants from every other state. It was, therefore, necessary to separate out more important states sending the migrants from those which were less important. The analysis could have been performed in different ways, but there was a need to separate out the influence of historical ties and border location from the development variable, including access. This was sought to be achieved by identifying the number of states contributing to out-of-state migrants to each district, by employing Weaver's combination technique. Their location vis-à-vis the district concerned along with the historical ties, if any, was then analysed. The analysis reveals certain interesting results.

Six out of thirty-five districts have predominance of only one source state in sending migrant population (Figure 2). As only has been expected, districts lying on the border of the state show this feature. Moreover, the neighbouring state is sending these migrants substantiating the near neighbourhood effect in the process. Five of these lie along the border of Karnataka and this is primarily because the adjoining part of Karnataka formed a part of Bombay Province before state reorganisation in 1956. The same effect is shown by Amaravati which had connections with Madhya Pradesh of which it was a part till 1956; in fact, Amaravati is the traditional destination for the people from Sagar-Damoh plateau. The difference in the nature of boundary is also evident; hilly border in the north is less influential than valleys of the Bhima and the Krishna in the south.

The districts at the junction of two neighbouring states, show influence of both of them as exemplified by two-state combinations. This is clearly seen, if one observes the districts at four different corners of the state. Nandurbar and Dhule receive migrants from two states, viz. Gujarat and Madhya Pradesh. It is interesting to note, however, that while Gujarat is more important than Madhya Pradesh to Nandurbar, it

Figure 2 ***Distribution of Migrants from other States in Districts of Maharashtra***

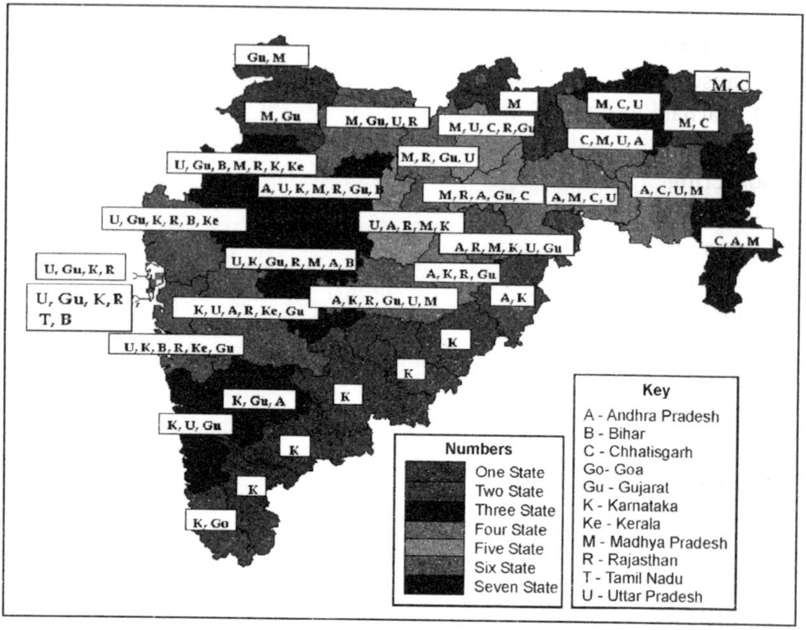

is the other way round for Dhule and here access plays a more important role. Bhandara and Gondiya draw migrants from Madhya Pradesh in the north and Chhattisgarh in the east in that order. Nature of population has played an important role in determining the relative strength. Historical contacts have influenced the order of importance of Andhra Pradesh and Karnataka in contributing to migrants in bordering district of Nanded. This should have been borne out by Sindhudurg too, but Karnataka is sending more migrants to it than Goa which is closer to it in all the respects. Probably, the size and princely ties with Belgaum have played a more important role.

The districts slightly inward from the border, e.g., Ratnagiri or Satara, draw migrants from three different states which is quite explicable; this becomes quite difficult to appreciate in the case of the district of Gadchiroli. It is observed that the districts get slowly eliminated this way as the number of states in the combination increases, first from the southern part and then from the eastern part. Thus, districts of the western Maharashtra are characterised by more diversified sources of migration, reflecting on greater opportunities present there.

In twenty-eight out of thirty-five districts, the first ranking state in terms of number of migrants is the neighbouring state; Madhya Pradesh, Karnataka and Andhra Pradesh dominate in this respect primarily because of the length of the border they share with Maharashtra (Figure 2). Karnataka is, however, more consistent in terms of higher proportion than the other states. The share of Gujarat and Chhattisgarh, the other bordering states, as the first ranking states in terms of the number of districts receiving such migrants is less than expected. In the case of the former, it is because of the developed nature of districts like Thane or Mumbai which attract more migrants from the labour-rich state of Uttar Pradesh. Here again, Ahmadnagar and Jalna are rather the surprises; both of them have probably religious affiliations coming to their help.

Six districts do not have significant contribution from the second ranking state as the first ranking state itself sends overwhelming number of migrants, over 60 per cent; all these, except Amaravati, are bordering Karnataka. In others, it is invariably the neighbouring state which could not rank first for some reason (Figure 2). Only in some districts like Pune, Aurangabad, Akola or Ratnagiri that Uttar Pradesh has scored over the neighbouring states. In neither of these districts the proportion exceeds 60 per cent.

Six more districts do not have any third ranking state as the first and second ranking states send overwhelming number of migrants to make the proportion of the third too small to count (Figure 2). These are the corner districts seen earlier. In the rest, it is either the bordering state or those which are opportunity-poor, such as, Uttar Pradesh, Bihar or Rajasthan that become important; migrants from the first two states predominate in industrially developed districts, such as, Nashik or Nagpur while those from Rajasthan become important in rather inaccessible districts, viz., Bid, Parbhani and Jalna. In neither of the districts the proportion of migrants exceeds 20 per cent.

Madhya Pradesh and Gujarat continue to dominate as senders among the fourth ranking state (Figure 2). The other senders are Uttar Pradesh and Rajasthan. Although the spatial contiguity exists in the pattern, explanation is rather difficult. Moreover, district is too large a unit and inter-district variations are not ruled out. It is noteworthy, however, that these areas are a part of geographical core which do not have an overwhelming influence of any one of the bordering states. Moreover, none of these districts receives over 15 per cent of the migrants.

None of the districts having a land border with other states, barring Thane and Nashik, appear to be receiving migrants from the fifth ranking state (Figure 2). Surprisingly, Mumbai suburban district fails to stand in this group. Moreover, the continuity shown so far has been broken by the districts of Buldana and Parabhani which are less developed. The districts, with contribution from the fifth state, are diversified in activities and, naturally, sources of migrants are also distant and diversified; Rajasthan, Uttar Pradesh, Bihar and Kerala are the major senders. None of the states contribute more than 10 per cent migrants.

Figure 3 ***Flow of Migrants from other States to***

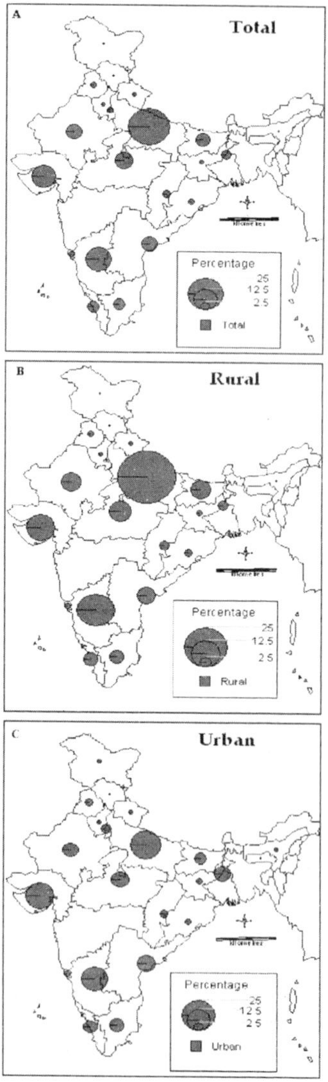

The districts with significant proportion of migrants from the sixth ranking states are almost all concentrated in the north-western part of the state around Mumbai and Pune (Figure 2). The senders are all the neighbouring states, except Kerala. None of the districts receives more than 10 per cent of the migrants from this source.

There are only three districts having migrants from the seventh ranking state; none of these are highly industrialised (Figure 2). The source regions are distant, viz., Bihar and Kerala. None of the districts receives more than 10 per cent of the migrants from this source. Religious ties appear to have brought these migrants to these districts.

Share of States in Out of State Migrants

The state of Uttar Pradesh has the highest share among migrants to the state; this is obviously due to its rank in absolute population as also the lack of enough employment opportunities (Figure 3A). Neighbouring states of Gujarat and Karnataka follow, partly due to proximity and also, in part, due to historical ties. Distance plays an important role in the share of other states; this is clear from near absence of migrants from the north-east and north which are rather inaccessible spatially as well as socially. But this is not strictly so as can be seen from the small size from the nearby states like Chhattisgarh and Orissa vis-à-vis the states of Kerala and Tamil Nadu. Role of information appears to play an important role in this respect.

The patterns of rural and urban migrants are nearly replica of the above pattern (Figure 3B and C). While rural migrants are drawn primarily from less developed states, such as, Uttar Pradesh and Bihar, urban migrants also come from the developed states like Gujarat, Karnataka, West Bengal, Kerala and Tamil Nadu. An analysis of relative proportion of migrants from the states coming from rural and urban areas suggests that migrants of the former type come primarily drawn from either the neighbouring or less developed states but those of the latter category come from the distant or more developed states.

Duration of Migrants from States

Duration of stay of migrant population suggests that it is negatively related to distance but shows a positive correlation with development (Figure 4A-D). Older residents have come from the neighbouring states and those from the south. Punjab is the only northern state sending over 55 per cent of the migrants which are 10 or more years old. The next stream of migrants has come from the central and north-eastern states of the peninsular India; Assam and Tripura are the only states outside the peninsula. All these are population surplus opportunity-poor areas. It is only recently that one finds a higher proportion of migrants from the distant states like those of the north-east and the north; the proportion of migrants is, however, small.

The pattern for migrants from the rural areas matches that for the total migrants, with slight extensions during the older period and corresponding contraction during more recent period (Figure 5A-D). However, urban migrants show a slight variation (Figure 6A-D). The state of Andhra Pradesh, for example, is only a recent participant in sending migrants from the urban areas. Although historical ties have sent people to Marathwada region of Maharashtra, they were mainly agricultural labourers. Since the ruling elite during the princely statehood did not pay sufficient attention in developing skills or providing education, number of migrants from urban areas was very limited. It is only after state reorganisation that such efforts were made and this is reflected in the recent migration from the urban areas of that state.

Figure 4 ***Duration of Stay of Migrants in Maharashtra (Total)***

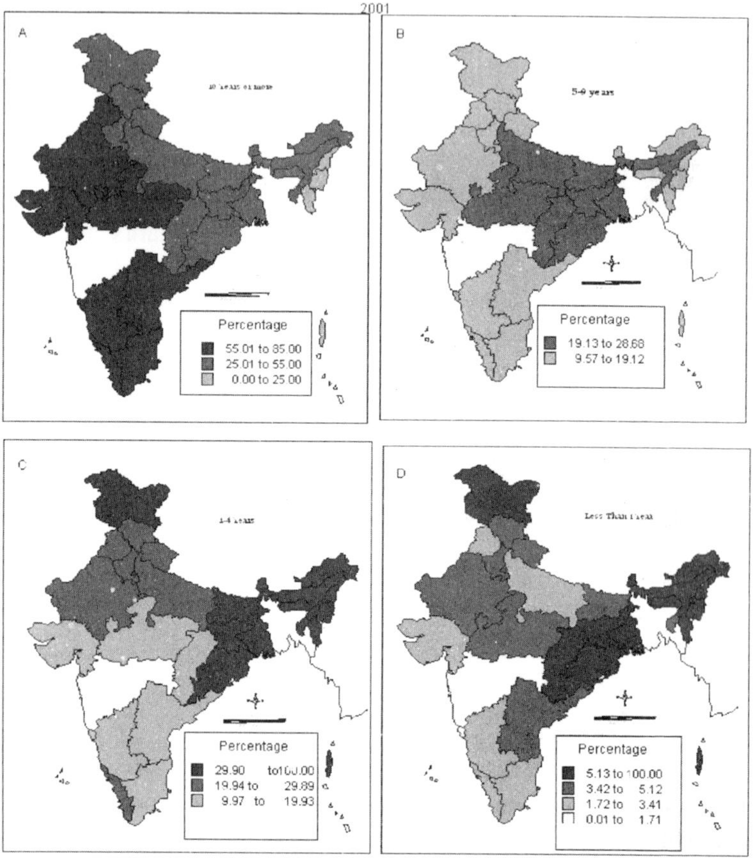

Concluding Remarks

The foregoing discussion on migrants to Maharashtra reveals some interesting patterns. Only a little over two-fifths of the population has changed the place of residence and for nearly half of this, the shift is within the district; this is primarily the migration of agricultural labour and reflects on unequal distribution of resources among the villages, as reported from elsewhere (Singh and Sharma, 1984). A little over a tenth of the population has crossed the district border; this is partly a result of push factors such as drought or unfavourable terrain and, in part, due to pull of cities like Mumbai (Mukherjee and Sita, 1982). Development of transport and communication, as also attainment of higher level of education, has facilitated the process (Phadke and Mukherji, 2004).

Figure 5 ***Duration of Stay of Migrants in Maharashtra (Rural)***

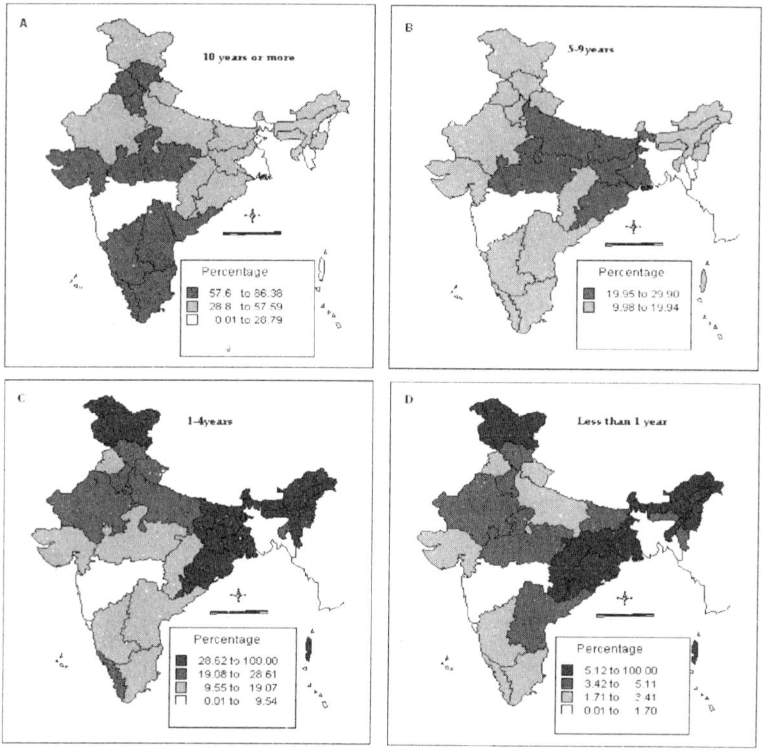

Slightly less than a tenth of the migrants have come from outside the state. Thus, there is a phenomenon of distance decay in the proportion of migrants. These results tally with those obtained earlier for the entire country (Mukherjee and Banerjee, 1992). This general pattern is not strictly adhered to by all the districts, however, and there are variations from one district to the other depending on the level of development and scope for absorbing migrants.

The out-of-state migrants are primarily from the neighbouring states, but labour surplus and opportunity-poor states of the BIMARU belt like Bihar, Uttar Pradesh and Rajasthan are forerunners among the distant senders. While the duration of residence is generally negatively related to distance, there is a slight variation among the urban migrants. Traditionally, progressive states like Kerala and Tamil Nadu have sent urban migrants compared to those, like Andhra Pradesh, which have developed their human resources rather recently. The fact that nearly a

Figure 6 *Duration of Stay of Migrants in Maharashtra (Urban)*

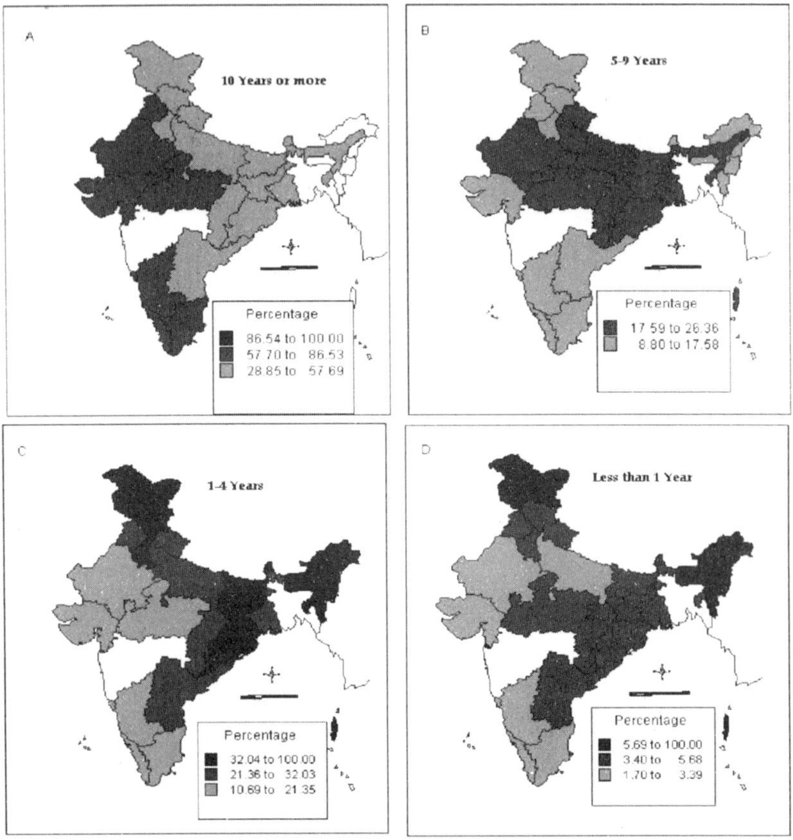

tenth of the population of Maharashtra has come from outside the state is clearly a reflection on opportunities here vis-à-vis lack of opportunities elsewhere. The problem becomes complicated when the sending states continue to have high birth rate and, therefore, population surplus; it leads to changes in the face of the cities where they settle. That mounts the tension and all the subsequent problems of social rivalry.

Migration for improving livelihood opportunities has been a characteristic of rural India, but its incidence has increased considerably during the past few decades. This is on account of persistent drought and environmental degradation in some areas. Simultaneously, agricultural infrastructure has been created in other areas resulting in flows from the areas of distress to those of opportunities. It is, therefore, necessary to look into the problem in inter-regional perspective and undertake measures to create more opportunities in the sending states so that the absorbing states would get some relief, as the latter cannot permanently act as a refuge to surplus population of the sending states as they also face limits to their growth.

References

Breman, J. and A.N. Das. 2000. *Down and Out: Labouring under Global Capitalism*. Delhi: Oxford University Press.

Brown, A.J. and E.M. Burrows. 1977. *Regional Economic Problems*. London: George Allen and Unwin.

Burgess, R. and A.J. Venables. 2004. Toward a Microeconomics of Growth. Policy Research Working Paper Series 3257, The World Bank. http://ideas.repec.org/e/pve7.html

Dasgupta, P., R. Kumar and A. Mitra. 2004. Urbanisation, Poverty and Slums in India. www.igidr.ac.in/.../Purnamita%20Dasgupta-urbanisation_Poverty_and_Slums_in_India__final_draft21_sept.doc

Henderson, V.J. and H.G. Wang. 2003. Aspects of the Rural-Urban Transformation of Countries. Working Paper, Brown University. http://www.arts.cornell.edu/poverty/kanbur/KanRap.pdf

Holland, S. 1976. *The Regional Problem*. London: The Macmillan Press.

Mukherji, D. and K. Sita. 1982. Spatial Patterns of Out-migration in Maharashtra: 1961–71. *Population Geography* 4(1–2): 76–80.

Mukherjee, S.R. and S.K. Banerjee. 1992. Some Aspects of Internal Annual Migration in India. *Asian Pacific Migration Journal* 1(1): 168–92.

Mukherji, S. 2002. Urbanisation and Migration in India: A Different Scene. M.A.: Edward Elgar Pub. http://www.wscsd.org/ejournal /article.php3?id_article=109

Phadke, V.S. and D. Mukherji. 2004. Urbanisation and Development Scenario in Maharashtra, 1961–91. Project Report Submitted to ICSSR, New Delhi.

Roy, B.K. 1980. Internal Migration in India: An Evaluation of 1971 Census Data. *Transactions, I.I.G.* 2(1): 33–57.

Singh, S.N. and H.I. Sharma. 1984. A Study of Pattern of Out-migration: A Regression Analysis. *Man in India* 64(2): 143–53.

Smita. 2007. *Locked Homes, Empty Schools: The Impact of Distress Seasonal Migration on the Rural Poor.* New Delhi: Zubaan.

Srinivasan, K. 1990. Exodus to Cities and Quality of Life. *Yojana* 34: 14–5.

Srivastava, R. and S.K. Sasikumar. 2003. An Overview of Migration in India: Its Impact and Key Issues. http://www.livelihoods.org/hot_topics/docs/Dhaka_CP_2.pdf

4

Population Trends of an Emerging City

The Case of Navi Mumbai

Deepak Kapoor and Rita Abbi

Need for the New City

While as per census of India in 1951 and 1961, the number of cities with a population of one million increased from 5 to 6. (Gupta, 1986). This number went up to 35 in the year 2001. Nearly 37 per cent of the population of the country stays in million plus cities. The increasing population of Mumbai has put tremendous strain on the housing and urban services which failed to keep abreast with the increase in demand. Thus, it is seen that the housing demand is much higher than the total supply from private sector, government and housing board. This has left huge gap between demand and supply.

Large urban centres in India and many parts of the world are literally exploding with the population growth during the last three and half decades. About 30 years later, more than 9 million people had crowded the Mumbai city exploding urbanisation, throwing housing, transport, water supply and other amenities into disarray. Bursting at the seams of the city spilled over into surrounding areas, straggling north and east towards Kalyan and across the harbour to the main land. Clearly Mumbai needed redesigning and reshaping, plan for future would have to draw in other areas. The new growth centre would have to be identified and developed so that jobs and population could be distributed over a wider spread, easing pressure on the heart of the city. Navi Mumbai was obviously important for the Mumbai of the future. The background and the rationale behind the decision to set up Navi Mumbai was to achieve a common objective (CIDCO, 1992)

Objective

To reduce the growth of population in Greater Mumbai by creating an attractive urban centre on the main line across the harbour which will:

- Absorb the immigrants who would otherwise come to Mumbai.
- Attract some of the Mumbai's present population so that overall population of Greater Mumbai can be contained within the manageable limits.
- To provide physical and social services to raise the living standard and reduce the disparities in the amenities available to the different sections of the population.
- To provide an environment, which would permit the citizen of Navi Mumbai to live cooler and richer lives as far as possible, free from the physical and social tensions, which would be commonly associated with urban means.

Nodal Development in Navi Mumbai

Navi Mumbai is a series of 14 self-contained townships called 'nodes', each developed at a different point of time having independent physical and social infrastructure system, and linked by mass transport rail system and trunk roads. This was strategy adopted to bring development progressively. The characteristics of the developed nodes are housing areas, higher property values, and better amenities. The land use pattern of Navi Mumbai is as follows:

Figure 1 ***Percentage Distribution of Land Use Pattern in Navi Mumbai***

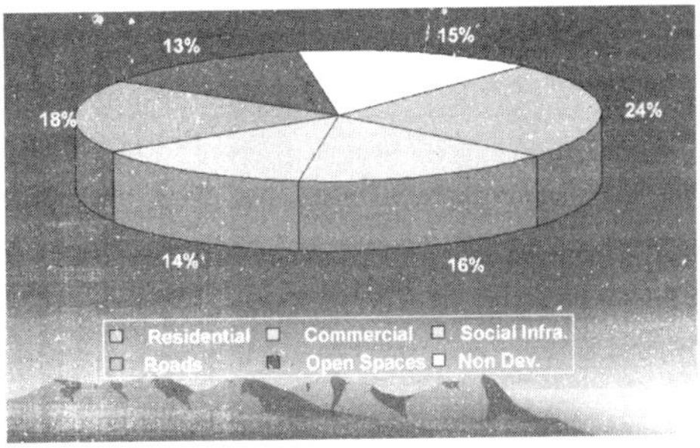

Table 1 ***Land Use Pattern in Navi Mumbai***

(in per cent)

Residential	24
Commercial/Service industries	16
Social facilities/institutions and health facilities	07
Public utilities	07
Open space	13
Roads	18
Non developable area	15
Total	100

City and Industrial Development Corporation of Maharashtra Limited (CIDCO) was entrusted with a seed capital of Rs 3.95 crore, with 344 square kilometres of marshy land to plan and create an environment-friendly and self-sustainable city with full-fledged infrastructure to meet its residential, commercial needs for the future generation. CIDCO'S land pricing and land sale policy has shown a strong pattern of continuity. The rules, which guide the price and sale of land, are rooted in the concept of the use of land as resource. The following table gives the hike in base price of land (reserve price of Vashi node) the table shows the changes in reserve price, in current price and in constant 1980–81 price over a period of 19 years. There was similar price rise in 1990's. (Shaw, 2004: Chapter 5, p. 141).

Table 2 ***Reserve Land Price of Vashi Node***

Date	*Land Price Rs/sq m (Reserve Price)*	*% Growth*	*Index of Reserve Price (RP)*	*RP in Constant 80–81 Prices*	*Index of RP*
8.6.1977	85	—	100	85	100
6.11.1981	120	10.2	141	110	129
24.2.1984	150	8.3	176	121	142
24.2.1986	400	83	470	323	380
05.1.1989	600	12.5	706	331	389
22.3.1991	1,000	33	1,235	467	549
23.3.1992	1,250	25	1,471	517	608
15.1.1993	1,500	20	1,765	570	671
21.5.1993	2,000	33	2,353	694	816
26.5.1995	2,800	20	3,294	823	968
26.5.1996	3,220	15	3,788	887	1,043
25.7.1997	3,220	0	3,788	887	1,043
28.2.2000	3,220	0	3,788	887	1,043

Population Growth of Navi Mumbai

Housing need in any town is a function of the present and the projected population. In the development plan of Navi Mumbai, which was adopted in 1975, it was projected that city would acquire a population of 2 million by the year 1990, which was later extended to 2000. As of 1991, the population reached a level of 5.35 lakh only. Considering the trend of population growth and the possible changes in the variables, which affect population growth, it was necessary to review the projected population. The following table reveals that in every decade, there is almost 100 per cent increase in the population of Navi Mumbai. (District Census Handbook, Thane – 1981 and 1991, Town Survey Report, Panvel – 1981, District Census Handbook, Raigard – 1981 and 1991, website censusindia.net – 2001).

Table 3 ***Population Growth Rate of Navi Mumbai***

Navi Mumbai	*1981*	*1991*	*2001*	*1981–91*	*1991–2001*
Nodes	21,657	2,09,676	5,49,511	86.82	16.21
Villages[1]	1,76,638	2,65,625	4,26,500	5.04	6.06
Municipal Councils	52,241	59,908	1,27,285	1.47	11.25
Total	2,50,536	5,35,209	11,03,296	11.36	10.26

[1] In Census 2001, villages under Navi Mumbai Municipal Corporation were declared as urban population.

Decelerated growth rate of Mumbai city means higher rate of growth of population in suburbs. This phenomenon was more pronounced in 1991–2001 decade due to scarcity of land in the main city and very high prices of land. This factor was given a fair weightage while projecting the Navi Mumbai population. Thus, there are two factors which will determine the future population of Navi Mumbai; natural growth, migration due to overflow from Mumbai and direct migration to Navi Mumbai from the hinterland.

1. Natural growth: Considering the mixed population—both economically and socially—the national average growth rate can be applied to determine the contribution by this factor.
2. Overflow from Mumbai, increased growth of Mumbai attracts large migration from all parts of the country.

Emerging Population Trend

The following table shows the growth of population in Mumbai during the last 3 decades (District Census Handbook Thane, 1971 and 1981 and 1991, Town Survey Report Panvel, 1981, District Census Handbook Raigard, 1981 and 1991, website censusindia.net-2001)

Table 4 ***Population of Greater Mumbai and Its Constituent Units***

(in lakhs)

Census group	*1971*	*1981*	*1991*	*2001*
Greater Mumbai	59.71	82.43	99.26	119.14
Thane	1.71	4.74	8.04	12.62
Kalyan Dombivli	1.51	5.78	8.20	11.93
Navi Mumbai	1.56	2.50	5.35	11.03

Table 5 ***Growth Rate of Greater Mumbai and Its Constituent Units***

Census group	*1971–81*	*1981–91*	*1991–2001*
Greater Mumbai	3.81	2.04	2.00
Thane	8.13	15.68	5.85
Kalyan–Dombivli[2]	28.28	4.19	4.55
Navi Mumbai	6.03	11.36	10.26
	4.55	2.87	2.81

[2] Increase in Kalyan is due to change of census group.

From Table 5, the impact of Navi Mumbai city shows the reduction in the growth rate of population in Greater Mumbai. The growth rate of Greater Mumbai in 1971 to 1981 was 3.81, which was reduced to 2.04, and during the decade 1991 and 2001 it was 2.0. The migration pattern of the population of Navi Mumbai is shown in the Table 6. (Socio-Economic Survey in planned nodes in New Bombay, 1987–88, Socio-Economic Survey of households in various nodes and villages in New Bombay,1995, Socio-Economic Survey in planned nodes in Navi Mumbai, 2000, Socio-Economic Survey in planned nodes in Navi Mumbai, 2005)

Figure 2 ***Growth Rate of Population in Greater Mumbai***

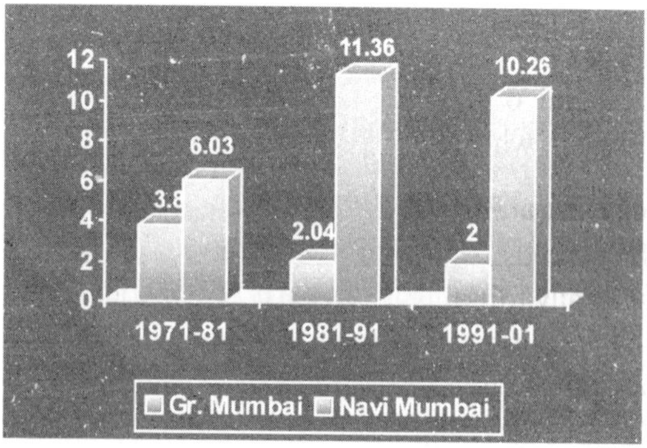

Migration Pattern of Population of Navi Mumbai

The migration trend during the last 35 years can be observed from the chart. From 2000–2005, the total migration is 60 per cent out of that 48 per cent of the population migrated from Mumbai.

Figure 3 ***Migration Pattern of Population in Navi Mumbai***

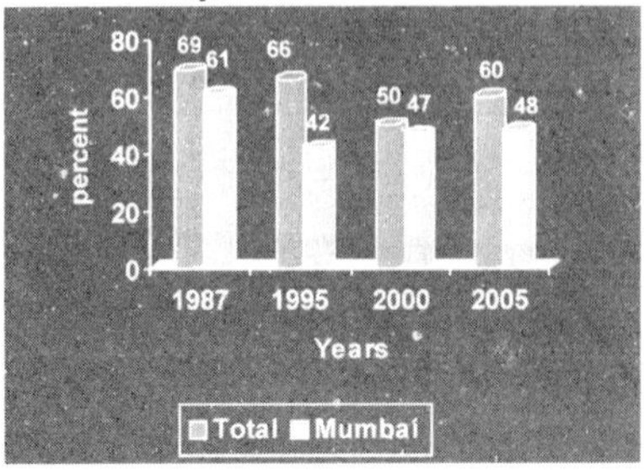

Table 6 ***Place of Last Residence of Households Shifted to Navi Mumbai***

Last Place of Residence	*1987 Survey*	*1995 Survey*	*2000 Survey*	*2005 Survey*
Island (%)	21	12.48	11.0	30.0
Western Suburbs (%)	6	4.73	13.2	4.4
Eastern Suburbs (%)	21	19.42	18.2	5.7
Thane-Kalyan (%)	6	3.97	4.2	6.1
Other MMR[3] (%)	7	1.06	.4	2.0
Total (%)	61	41.6	47.0	48.2

[3] Mumbai Metropolitan Region.

The above table presents that 30 per cent of households shifted from Island city-Mumbai, 5 per cent from western suburbs of Mumbai around 6 per cent each from eastern suburbs and Thane, 2 per cent from other metro region. The survey report–2005 also shows 9 per cent from villages of Navi Mumbai, 7 per cent from other district of Maharashtra state and 6 per cent from other parts of the country shifted in Navi Mumbai, while 30 per cent stay in nodes of Navi Mumbai.

Behavioural Pattern of Population

Households in India are divided into various income categories especially for the purpose of housing for every stratum. The large industrial working force, domestic workers and hawkers constituted the low income group in Navi Mumbai which can be revealed from the Table 7 (Adusumilli, 2003). (Socio Economic Survey of household in planned nodes–2000, Socio Economic Survey of household in planned nodes–2005, Socio-Economic Survey of households in various nodes and villages–1995, Socio-Economic Survey of households in various nodes–1987–88).

Table 7 ***Income Distribution of Households in Navi Mumbai***

Income Group	*As per Survey 1987*		*As per Survey 1995*		*As per Survey 2000*		*As per Survey 2005*	
	Monthly Income of Households (in Rs)	*% Population*	*Monthly Income of Households (in Rs)*	*% Population*	*Monthly Income of Households (in Rs)*	*% Population*	*Monthly Income of Households (in Rs)*	*% Population*
LIG	Upto 1,500	52	Upto 2,650	48	Upto 5,000	36	Upto 10,000	27
MIG	1,501 to 3,500	25	2,651 to 4,450	27	5,001 to 10,000	32	10,001 to13,000	59
HIG	>3,500	23	>4,450	25	>10,000	32	>13,000	14

LIG: Low Income Group, MIG: Middle Income Group and HIG: High Income Group.

Households Characteristics

The average household size for Greater Mumbai was 4.74 as per census 2001. The average household size for Navi Mumbai is reduced from 4.05 to 3.8 as presented in the Table 8. It can be observed that over the period there is reduction in family size and increase in built up area of the dwelling units. The average accommodation trend in the formal sector has increased from 35 sq mt to 45 sq mt.

Table 8 ***Family Size of Population Living in Navi Mumbai***

Description	*Survey 1987*	*Survey 1995*	*Survey 2000*	*Survey 2005*
Average family size	3.86	4.01	4.05	3.8
Average built-up area of dwelling unit	35 sq mt	33 sq mt	42 sq mt	45 sq mt

The average age of the population is 28 years as against the national average nearly 24 years.

Educational Status

The literacy rate of Maharashtra is 86.4 per cent based on the 2001 census. In case of Navi Mumbai 2 per cent of the population is illiterate which declined from the survey 2000 to 2005 by 2 per cent. The trend of graduates, postgraduates, professionals in engineering, medicine, law and computer skills have increased reasonably. The following table shows the numbers of graduates are doubled in 2005 as compared to the survey result of 1987. This factor may be attributed to the educational

Table 9 ***Educational Level of the Residents in Navi Mumbai***

Description	*Survey 1987*	*Survey 1995*	*Survey 2000*	*Survey 2005*
Literacy rate (%)	93	94	96	98
Graduates and above (%)	15	17	27	28
% of households happy with education amenities	Not recorded	Not recorded	75	86

facilities existing in the new city. Nearly 86 per cent of the population is satisfied with the educational amenities available in the city.

Job Profile

Employment is an important indicator to know the status of economic profile of any settlement. The socio-economic study reveals that 32 per cent of the population is working. It was observed that 45 per cent of the working population is working in private offices and around 30 per cent in government and public sector/banks and remaining represents commercial/ industrial units. More than 60 per cent of the working and residing in Navi Mumbai.

Figure 4 ***Average Age of Population in Navi Mumbai***

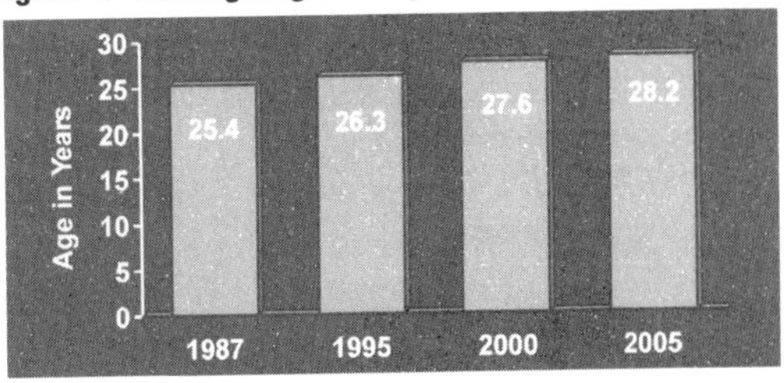

Table 10 ***Job Profile of Residents in Navi Mumbai***

Description	*1987*	*1995*	*2000*	*2005*
Type of employer				
Private sector offices (%)	14	6	37.4	45.3
Government (%) offices/Public sector banks	30	21	22.6	29.0
Commercial units (%)	17	26	14.0	9.6
Industrial units (%)	25	25	8.5	9.4
Others (%)	10	15	13.1	6.7
Working population (%)	32.8	33.15	31.5	32
Population working and residing in Navi Mumbai (%)	48	60	63	60

Economic Status

The average income of the household in Navi Mumbai is higher than the average income of household in Mumbai. Even if the inflation component is taken care of there is distinct increase in the income of residents in Navi Mumbai. It could be attributed to the factors like IT parks, private sector and increase in the incomes due to fifth pay commission of salaried class families employed in public sector and possibly the higher gains through business due to improved market strategy. Table 11 presents that the ownership of dwelling units was more than three-fourth households due to loan facilities and easy accommodation in Navi Mumbai at economical price.

Table 11 ***Economic Status of Households in Navi Mumbai***

Description	*Survey 1987*	*Survey 1995*	*Survey 2000*	*Survey 2005*
Average family income (Rs/month)	2,112	3,740	9,549	12,591
% of ownership houses	68	89	72	74
Ownership of vehicles	18	28	46	49

From the Table 11 we can conclude that the ownership of vehicle was 28 per cent in 1995, which is almost doubled in 2005.

Infrastructure

Creation of infrastructure—both physical and social—is crucial to the success of evolution of a planned city. In fact, given the proximity of work to residents of the main city Mumbai, one of the consideration that could attract them to a newly planned city (Navi Mumbai). CIDCO made efforts to fulfil the conditions by spending massive funds on creating infrastructure in a low-lying coastal land which was improved upon for developing the city. The level of satisfaction of its residents with both social and physical infrastructure became an important aspect to be highlighted through the survey. Here physical infrastructure means good roads, water supply, storm water drain, electric supply, garbage disposal, transport facility, overall cleanliness in the area. Social facilities mean the availability of religious facilities, hospital/private clinics, recreational facilities and public amenities. More than 80 per cent of the population satisfied with the physical and social infrastructure (Socio-Economic Survey of households in planned nodes in Navi Mumbai 2005).

Table 12 ***Residents' Satisfaction on Infrastructure in Navi Mumbai***

Households	*Survey 1987*	*Survey 1995*	*Survey 2000*	*Survey 2005*
Happy with physical infrastructure	Not recorded	40%	67%	80%
Happy with the social facilities	Not recorded	Not recorded	75%	82%

Transportation

Transport is the lifeline in a multi-million city like Mumbai and is a crucial factor in determining one's place of residence or even place of work. Given the stress and time spent in travelling for work, city residents not only seek effective transport for their travel but also quicker and cost effective one. Travel factor is so important that in its early years of formation—for over a decade—Navi Mumbai was not considered to be a suitable place to stay due to its poor linkage with the city. Till then, the railway line between Mankhurd and Navi Mumbai was not commissioned. Moreover, its linkage with the western suburbs was very poor and time-consuming. It is only when the railway link was established with the main city and BEST (an effective road transport system) started operating its buses between the main city and Navi Mumbai then staying at Navi Mumbai became a viable proposition—particularly for those families who were in search of purchasing a house at an affordable price.

Table 13 ***Time Spent on Travelling to Work Place by Residents in Navi Mumbai***

Description	*Survey 1987*	*Survey 1995*	*Survey 2000*	*Survey 2005*
% of non-work trips to Mumbai	61%	10%	13%	1%
Average travel time[4] (all trips)	—	—	42 minutes	28 minutes

[4] One-way trip (for work, education, social).

The above table reveals the per cent of non-work trips to Mumbai reduced from 61 per cent to 1 per cent over the decades, which shows the self-dependency of the city. The average travel time also reduced from 42 minutes to 28 minutes, which indicates drastic improvement in transportation system and also creation of jobs at close proximity.

Success of a 'Super City'

The major achievement of Navi Mumbai Project is its financial viability. It can be observed from the socio-economic studies that Navi Mumbai is self-sufficient in each and every aspect. The population is enjoying much high standard of living. It is well-balanced and landscaped city designed and planned for life and commerce for twenty-first century. The city has world class infrastructure and also preserved environment, 45 per cent land reserved for green zone, as given in Table 1, such as open space, hill slopes, gardens, holding ponds etc. It has excellent educational and social facilities as per the development plan. One of the major achievements is shifting of wholesale market of agricultural produce. The railway stations-cum-commercial complexes are the city's architectural wonder. The railway network of Navi Mumbai is the life line of the city. Another major accomplishment is IT sectors, the info tech international parks, millennium business park and so on. The socio-economic status of this city has improved due to highly paid IT sectors and also due to substantial private employment and investments.

The population and employment growth is much higher than any other new city/town, but not at the projected rate. The population of 2 million and corresponding employment was supposed to be attained in 1990 and later on in 2000 is not yet achieved. The Central Business District of Navi Mumbai, CBD Belapur was planned to shift majority of the government offices. But instead of government offices more private/public sector offices were shifted which can be clearly seen from the Table 10. CIDCO had planned to shift the wholesale steel market to Navi Mumbai, which could not be achieved because of the change in economic climate of India and the region particularly. The initial plan was to develop the Navi Mumbai as a city where a common man can find an affordable shelter. But it clearly reveals from the survey reports that this is the city of middle and upper middle class. Improved economic status, loan facilities, and the automobile growth lead to deficiency in parking place.

To sum up, it can be seen that the city has applied two-dimensional approach instead of three-dimensional. This means the city has concentrated more on physical infrastructure but not towards the affordable legal housing for all, resulting into a sizeable population living in slums and other unauthorised settlement. The rapid and mass urbanisation, as witnessed in the last decade, coupled with economic growth has turned the area into an economic engine driving the whole economy of this coastal belt. Last 35 years saw slackness in the development of Central Business District (CBD), erosion of manufacturing base, slump in the market based development and changing economic scenario. This had direct impact on the growth of the city but even these growth retarding developments have not been able to hinder or halt the transformation of the city into a viable entity, as this is a living testimony to planned development. The planned development by CIDCO on a continuous basis has resulted in the metamorphosis of the whole region into a brand new and modern city.

References

Adusumilli, U. 2003. Housing Development Types and Low Income Group Housing: Public Housing by CIDCO in Navi Mumbai.

CIDCO. 1992. Two Decades of Planning and Development. District Census Handbook.1971, Thana, Part A and B, Mumbai: Maharashtra Census Office.

District Census Handbook. 1981. Series 12, Maharashtra, Part XIII A and B, Thane District, Directorate of Census Operations, Maharashtra.

District Census Handbook. 1981. Series 12. Maharashtra, Part XIII A and B, Raigarh.

District Census Handbook. 1991. Raigarh, Maharashtra.

District Census Handbook. 1991. Thane, Maharashtra.

District Directorate of Census Operations, Maharashtra.

Economics Section, CIDCO. 1987–88. Socio Economic Survey of Households in Various Nodes in New Bombay.

Economics Section, CIDCO. 1995. Socio Economic Survey of Households in Various Nodes and Villages in New Bombay

Economics Section, CIDCO. 2000. Socio Economic Survey of Households in Planned Nodes in Navi Mumbai.

Economics Section, CIDCO. 2005. Socio Economic Survey of Households in Planned Nodes in Navi Mumbai.

Final Population Totals. 1991. Series–1, Paper–1 of 1992, Vol. 11, New Delhi. http://www.censusindia.net, 2001.

Gupta, L.C. 1986. Housing for Low Income Groups: New Bombay Experience. Vice Chairman and Managing Director, CIDCO.

Shaw, A. 2004. *The Making of Navi Mumbai*, New Delhi: Orient Longman Private Limited.

Town Survey Report Panvel. 1981. Directorate of Census Operations, Maharashtra, Part XB, Series 12, Maharashtra.

5

Migration and Development

Migration Patterns of the Hmong in Vietnam Through History

Nguyen Tran Lam

The Northern Mountain Region of Vietnam (NMR) is home to more than 30 different ethnic groups and is characterised by very high levels of ecological and social diversity, as well as a rapid but unevenly distributed process of change (Rambo, 1997; Jamieson et al., 1998). The special feature of the NMR is that it has a very long history of migration, and my ongoing work is a historical study of this, trying to describe the way migration affects the development of this area, and the livelihood of the ethnic minorities living there. Using historical approach in migration may help to take us away from the sedentary bias of development studies, and understand migration as a central aspect of rural development (Mcdowell and De Haan, 1997; De Haan, 2002). In Vietnam, historians point to four major periods in recent history with distinct patterns of population mobility. These are: the French colonial period 1859–1954, the Indo-Chinese War from 1954–1975, the post-war reconstruction period 1975–1986, and the post-Renovation period 1986 to date. Although some authors have studied migration issues in these historical periods (Dang et al., 1997; Hardy, 2003; Desbarats, 1987; Dery, 2000), little is known about migration dynamics among ethnic minorities in the NMR and how its migration forms have changed overtime.

In this paper, I analyse the relationships between migration and livelihood in the context of social changes in the NMR, focusing on one of its ethnic groups—the Hmong people. The study draws on literature reviews and ethnography conducted in the NMR between 2002–2004 and interrupted trips to the NMR and Central Highlands during 2005–2006. Ethnographic interviews were held with 92 indigenous villagers of whom 68 were Hmong living in 8 communes across seven districts of six provinces (Ha Giang, Yen Bai, Son La, Dien Bien, Nghe An, and Dac Lac), and with village, commune, district, provincial, and national level authorities in various ministries, departments, and mass organisations. Researchers and staff of international development projects were also interviewed. Especially interviews were held with 8 geologists who provided interesting data about the historical migrations among ethnic minorities. The paper is structured as follows: after the introduction, I analyse some academic debates that deal with the development—livelihood—migration relationships. Next, I describe different patterns of migration among the Hmong in the four historical periods of Vietnam, dating back from the colonial period up to date. Then five case studies of the districts occupied by the Hmong are presented. The last section concludes the paper. Throughout the paper, attention is paid to the varied trends and patterns of migration at the individual and household levels and the underlying factors contributing to these variations and changes. Geographically, my analysis focuses on the NMR, while some contexts in the Central Highlands are also compared. Chronologically, emphasis is put more on post-Renovation period.

Migration and Livelihood

Migration plays a significant role in the livelihood of poor people yet little attention is paid to the nature of this relationship in the context of social change. Under globalisation, livelihood has become increasingly multidimensional (Carney, 1999; Ellis, 2000; Scoones, 1998), with an increased rearrangement of strategies using various capitals, and in different locations (De Haan and Zoomers, 2003; Kaag et al., 2003). Because of individualisation, more and more households break up. Poor people nowadays are not only involved in multi-activities, but are increasingly moving over multiple areas. The ability of people to cope with social change is often determined by geographical factors (sites and situations). Often, people in resource-rich places (well-connected to global space) are in a position to benefit, yet the majority of the poor are located in resource-poor places, that are in marginal and isolated areas. The only way to benefit from global opportunities is to break up and diversify their economic activities (Ellis, 2000), to enable them to perform multi-activities and to live in different places. For the majority of the poor, having a personal relationship with people at various locations has become a key element for their ability to cope with change, and establish a secure livelihood either within the country or abroad, even if this means giving up their traditional cultural practices (Winkels and Adger, 2002; Hardy, 2003; De Haan and Zoomers, 2003). Such migration dynamics may affect local development and people's livelihoods and shape people's reactions towards change (Ballard, 1983; Skeldon, 1997; De Haan, 2000).

The Context of Migration in the Northern Mountain Region

Worldwide there are more than six million Hmongs living in different countries.[1] In Vietnam, about 7,80,000 Hmong are living in 13 provinces (2004). Table below shows the Hmong population of ten provinces in the National Census 1999. The Hmong in Vietnam live in the so-called 'Region III', the poorest areas according to the government classification.[2]

Hmong Populations in their Most Concentrated Provinces (1999)

Province	*Hmong Population*	*Province*	*Hmong Population*
Ha Giang	1,83,994	Tuyen Quang	14,658
Lai Chau	1,70,460	Hoa Binh	3,962
Lao Cai	1,23,778	Cao Bang	41,737
Son La	1,14,578	Nghe An	26,045
Yen Bai	60,736	Daklak	10,891

Source: National Census 1999.

Throughout history, the Hmong in Vietnam have been known by different names: *Man, Miao, Meo, Mong* and *Hmong*. The Hmong language belongs to the Hmong-Zdao linguistic group, a branch of the Sino-Tibetan family. There are six branches of the Hmong family, including: the Hmong Dau (the White Hmong), the Hmong Si (the Red Hmong), the Hmong Du (the Black Hmong), the Hmong Sua (the Mixed Hmong), the Hmong Linh (Flower Hmong), and the Na Meo (the Water Hmong). These Hmong sub-groups can be differentiated by their dress, language, customs, and home architecture. Although this distinction is not made in official statistics but it does play an important role in social affairs.

Hmong social structure has been described by most researchers as one characterised by patrilineal descent groups (clans), virilocal or patrilocal residence, and a preference for matrilateral cross-cousin marriage. The number of Hmong family names hardly exceeds 20 throughout the whole country, with the most common ones being Giang, Vang, Vu, Thao and Nua (Lam Tam, 1972). Religious rituals, such as weddings, funerals, and new house ceremonies, are considered as a shared responsibility of all clan members. For example, "*Tu Su*", "*Sau Su*", and "*Thi Su*" are three important rituals that signify the cohesion among the Hmong. During these ceremonies, members of the same clan gather round the communal house, give their contributions, and share event tasks. The village old folks and family clan's chiefs are very important and they not only influence the enforcement of customary laws and cultural life of the village but they also play a decisive role in the management of land and natural resources, of development of production and even migration.

Hmong are pantheists-believing in a variety of natural and supernatural spiritual forces (Tapp, 1989: 59). For them, death is simply the passage from this world to another world, the migration of the soul of the deceased from his body to another body. In the Hmong's cosmology, three different worlds exist: the higher world where heaven is and the souls of people dying a natural death—death from old-age or illness; the middle world, that of men; and the lower world where are confined the souls of people dying from accidents—those struck by lightning or killed by drowning, a snake bite, a tiger's attack, or a blow dealt by another man. The soul, in the course of its migration, finds itself at the crossroads of the different worlds, and so it is the *txi nenh's* (Hmong shaman) duty to act as a guide.

According to Hmong legend, human settlement is arranged by God in which the highland is for Hmong, the lowland for the Viet, and the midland for the Tay. The history of their migration is written in the funeral song called Khua Ke, which shows the dead the way leading from the Land of Light (*yang*) to the ancestors' Land of Shadows (*yin*) (Giang Seo Ga, 2005: 27).[3]

Hmong settlement patterns are characterised by geographical, spiritual and habitual features. Hmong villages cling to the mountain slopes where the configuration of the ground must necessarily determine the orientation of the house: leaning against the mountain and facing the valley. The choice of a new place for the village was dependent on the proximity of the bush, the indispensable agricultural requirement for the practice of slash-and-burn cultivation, the existence of streams, and a mountain flank which should not slope too steeply, the absence of tombs or of certain trees considered to be haunted. Those conditions fulfiled, the clan chieftain and the cult master go to the chosen place to consult the spirits of the forest, the mountain and the earth by means of bamboo strings or of rice, and also by oneiromancy. The rite could be repeated upto three times; if, on the last time, the spirits proved to be still unfavourable, the Hmong looked for another place. When he has chosen a place, he asserts his right as first occupier by planting a few forks into the ground or by rapidly clearing the spot of brushwood.

As the Hmong mostly carry on shifting cultivation on burnt-out clearings, their villages are not fixed but are moved to another region once the soil has been exhausted. In the old days, villages were frequently moved to other sites due to natural calamities and epizootic diseases, in which the Hmong man saw the baneful action of the spirits. Another pull factor for a new settlement is poppy. Historically, the Hmong is considered the ethnic group that has grown poppy crops on the acreage larger than other groups in Vietnam. (Dang, 1978: 296). William Geddes (1976) found that Hmong decide where to live and with whom to associate based on the availability of land for cultivation of the opium poppy, and secondarily, for rice.

Information about the earliest arrival of Hmong in Indo-China is inaccurate but 1750 is a credible date (Culas and Michaud, 2004: 72). The Hmong entered North Vietnam very late, when the fertile valleys and the middle altitudes had been occupied by other ethnic groups. They were then obliged to settle on heights ranging from 800 m to 2,000 m. According to Vietnamese ethnologists (Lam, 1972; Dien, 2002; Son, 2005), the Hmong came to Vietnam in three waves. The first wave dates back 14 or 15 generations ago, numbering about 80 families coming from Kweichow (Southern China) before entering Dong Van and Meo Vac (Ha Giang). The second wave dates back nine or ten generations ago. It took two different roads: about 100 families entered Ha Giang and settled at Dong Van, Meo Vac and Hoang Su Phi; other 80 families entered Lao Cai and settled at Si Ma Cai and Bac Ha district, before going farther into the north-west. All these 180 families also came from Kweichow. The last wave included more than 10,000 Hmong of the Chinese provinces of Kweichow, Yunnan and Kwangsi, having taken part in the Taiping Movement against the Ching Dynasty, fled to Vietnam after the bloody repression of 1868. They settled in the provinces of Ha Giang, Lao Cai, Lai Chau, Son La, and Nghia Lo, before going farther south (Hoa Binh, Thanh Hoa and Nghe An). Since then the Hmong in China had continued to migrate into Vietnam (until 1954) but in a rather sporadic way (Mai, 1968; Lam Tam 1972).

The Chinese origin of this group is still reflected by the arrangement of the altars seen today in each Hmong house in Dong Van and Meo Vac. The ancestors' altar, always sticked in the central place against the back wall, is simply a rectangle-shaped paper made of the bark of *cay zo*, most often coloured red. It bears some Chinese ideograms and is adorned with three feathers of a cock. The second sign of the Chinese origin is the flag on the front door of each Hmong house, which is considered the Hmong flag. Old people in Meo Vac explain that upon arrival in Vietnam, the big flag is torn into pieces, which is then distributed to each Hmong so that they can recognise each other wherever in the world. The last sign is reflected by the Chinese Han names of villages occupied by the Hmong, such as Si Ma Cai (new horse street); Lao Chai (old village); Sin Chai (new village), Ta Phin (large plateau). I also observed that Hmong people pronounce Chinese words more easily than they do Viet words.

Migration During the French Colonial (1859–1954)[4]

The last wave of the Hmong immigration corresponded with the period of the war launched by France against feudal Vietnam. French armies occupied three provinces of Southern Vietnam (Cochinchina) in 1859–1862, the remainder of the Mekong estuary in 1867 and central northern Vietnam in 1883–1885; Pacification gradually made headway: in the delta from 1890–1892 and in the mountains from 1895–1900 (Chesneaux, 1955: 66).

Under colonial domination, Hmong society went through a very unequal development owing to the scattering of the settlements and to the difference in their livelihood conditions. While the Hmong of Ha Giang already led a sedentary life, the Hmong in Nghia Lo combined shifting cultivation and terraced rice field, the Hmong in Nghe An and Thanh Hoa still practiced shifting cultivation on burn-out clearings (Lam, 1972). For all Hmong, however, poppy was a mainstay and the opium trading was widespread, although this was a limited radius of action around their own areas of settlement (UNODC, 2003: 47).

The Hmong of the Northeast had to bow their heads to the rule of the *Tho Ty* or *Tay*, *Nung* and *Lolo* despots, while their ethnic brothers of the Northwest were dependent on the *phia tao* or *Thai* local despots (Lam, 1972). Living under the yokes of the French administrators and local chiefs,[5] the Hmong did not submit themselves to the oppressors. During the 40 years preceding the August 1945 Revolution, the French colonialists had to face at least seven Hmong revolts which broke out in 1904, 1911, 1917, 1925, 1930, 1936 and 1943, the most important being those of 1911 and 1917.[6] (Lam, 1972)

During 1940s, the Hmong and other ethnic groups in Northern Tonkin had to bear the impact of The Second Sino-Japanese War (1937–1945), the largest Asian war in the twentieth century. In the autumn of 1940, the French colonial government had to confront different revolts. At the Chinese border, various gangs, notably Vietnamese partisans of Prince Cuong De (1882–1951), attacked French outposts, killing isolated soldiers and local notables. With Japanese support these gangs freely plundered the population and villages. On both sides of the frontier, people were struck with panic, and left their villages to live in the forests (Ba, 1968: 7). The French colonists had then capitulated to the Japanese, but mustered their forces to fight the insurgents: in 1941, around 4,000 troops launched sweeps through the region for 8 months on end; many militants were arrested or killed and many villages burnt down or razed (Mai Quang, 1968: 10). French columns were making their way to China fighting against the Japanese as well as illness (Jackson, 1969: 317).

Because of the war impact, the famine of 1945 (Nan dói Ât Dâu) and epidemic in Northern Vietnam broke out, leading to the death of at least one million people.[7] The highland labourers suffering from the famine and diseases were overburdened by a massive immigration of lowland farmers who were driven by famine thus rushing to the NMR for a hope to survive. People had to live on wild vegetables or use bamboo ashes as a substitute. Among some tribes, a bit of rocksalt was carefully kept in the house for the family to lick after each meal. Epidemics of malaria, cholera, small pox, tuberculosis, leprosy, and syphilis were rampant. Broncho-pneumonia and intestinal diseases caused catastrophic infant mortality.

Patterns of Hmong Migration

The launching of the war of reconquest by the French colonialists then compelled Vietnam to engage in nine years (1946–1954) of armed liberation struggle. When French forces successfully established themselves in the Red River Delta in 1946–1947, the Vietminh as a tactical manoeuver allied itself with the sympathetic NMR. Some of the Vietminh's crack infantry divisions were recruited almost exclusively from the NMR; thus a policy of limited self-government began to evolve as early as 1946; and reached its final stages after Geneva armistice in 1954 (Jackson, 1969: 317–319). Millions of peasants thus participated in guerilla warfare, joined the army, or worked as volunteers for the supply of the front. Ardent patriots, the Hmong took an active part in the August 1945 Revolution, then in the 1946–1954 war. The Hmong played an outstanding role in the liberation of the north-west where their solid guerilla bases, scattered on the steepest heights, served as bases for the People's Army. Many of their names have become famous in the history of the first resistance such as Pu Nhung, Ta Sin Thang (Lai Chau), Long He, Nam Khat (Son La), Tram Tau, Than Uyen (Nghia Lo).[8]

Other Hmong had to move to nearby provinces bordering with Laos, such as Dien Bien, Son La, Nghe An, as a response to the war and the high taxes imposed by the French on opium. The tax level was said to be heavier than those in Indonesia, India, Malaysia, and Japan (Popkin, 1976).

Another pattern of migration emerged since 1940s yet little mentioned was the first flow of NMR people moving south to the Central Highlands (Tay Nguyen), including Han, Thai, Tay, Nung, Dao, Hmong, the total of these northern migrants then took up only 5 per cent of Tay Nguyen population (IOE, 2005). The reasons behind this flow were possibly due to the war, famine, and epidemics at the China border.

Migration during the Second Indo-Chinese War (1954–1975)

In 1954, following the departure of the French, Vietnam was partitioned into two parts: the North and the South.

Population movements in this period were thus greatly influenced by the different political ideologies of the two regimes. For the ethnic minorities and the Hmong in the NMR, six factors affect their livelihood and mobility, including:

- the land reform (1953–1956)
- the establishment of autonomous zones (1955–1956)[9]
- the agricultural collectivisation (started, 1956)
- the in-migration policy (started, 1958)
- the sedentary policy (started, 1964); and
- the arrival of the US troop (1968)

Patterns of Hmong Migration

Migrating Abroad

During the French colonial rule, numerous Hmong sided with Vietminh but a smaller portion of Hmong collaborated with the French. After the 1954 armistice, a number of these pro-French Hmong from the east of the Red River valley fled to Laos, following the wave of pro-French Tai to the same destination. These Hmong (and Tai) fleeing to Laos, later, in 1975 were among the first to flee from Laos to seek refuge in Thailand (Culas and Michaud, 2004: 78). The migration of the Hmong living in Dien Bien and Son La to Laos went on until 1990s yet in a sporadic way.

The Triple Policy and the Mobility of the Hmong

Right after the Land Reform,[10] the agricultural collectivisation in the north started in late 1956,[11] with first labour exchange brigades established, then small cooperatives consolidated into larger ones.[12] By the end of 1961, 70 per cent of highland farmers had joined the cooperatives (Quang Canh, 1968). In Hmong concentrated areas such as Ha Giang, Yen Bai, Lao Cai, the village cooperatives were set up during 1960s when the highlanders had taken over from the local chiefs the management of public affairs. The state then gave highlanders access to paddy land but nationalised sloping land and limited villages' use of the forest land. The shifting cultivators such as Hmong and Dao were thus restricted with their favourite technique that requires periodic migration.

In parallel with the collectivisation process, the government began to launch the in-migration policy[13] via the three-year plan (1958–1960), then the first five-year plan (1961–1965) by moving lowlanders, mainly Kinh, from densely populated areas of the Red River Delta to the sparsely inhabited upland provinces in the North, through the establishment of New Economic Zones (NEZs).[14] To attract lowland migrants, many state forestry enterprises were formed in the highlands and concentrated on crops such as rubber, coffee or oranges. One million migrants were sent to the NMR between 1961–1966, according to De Koninck (2000: 15).[15] Since then more than 3,00,000 Hmong in the NMR[16] began to receive (and interact with) lowlanders who came to 'clear the wilderness' (*khai hoang*). In the two districts of Bat Sat (Lao Cai) and Mai Chau (Son La), for example, thousands of Kinh people, both cadres and peasants, from Nam Dinh arrived during 1962–1964. The in-migration policy, under the name of the NEZ programme, could have a more profound effect on Vietnam than any other events in the twentieth century (Pike, 1978: 71)

Six years after the launching of the in-migration policy, in 1964 the government went ahead with sedentary policy, aiming to resettle "nomadic tribes" practicing shifting cultivation under state control, and to introduce permanent agriculture (UNHCR, 2002). This policy was based on the euphemism that shifting cultivation (*du canh du cu*) is a primitive and backward agricultural technology which is harmful to the environment. Thus, the Hmong community, blamed as environment destroyers, had experienced a new period of *ha son* (moving down to the lowland). The programme is intensified by the Resolution 71/TW detailing the fixed cultivation and settlement programme (dinh canh dinh cu) in 1968. Until 1972, about 70 per cent of the shifting cultivators were sedentarised at lower altitudes, with majority being the Hmong who were said to be very adaptable once resettled (Kahin, 1972: 583).

The Impact of the Triple Policy

While the mixing and interactions of the Hmong with other ethnic minority groups living in the valleys such as the Tay, Nung, Thai and Muong became more intensified as the result of *hason* policy and NEZ policies, a greater impact of the triple policy (collectivisation, in-migration and sedentarisation) is the land conflict, which can be explained by several reasons. First, as cooperatives were formed there was a natural tension between poorer peasants who wanted the crops to be divided among the members in proportion to the amount of work each family did, and wealthier ones who wanted those families which had contributed more land and draft animals to the cooperative to get a larger share of the crops (Moise, 1976: 88). Second, the policies were at odds with Hmong customary laws over land use rights. Among the Hmong, persons who are not members of the kinship groups have no rights to infringe on its land, and those who do not respect customary law can be excluded from the group and its land (Corlin, 2004: 306) while land belongs to those who cleared it or those who inherited it from ancestors. As the in-migration and sedentary policy came into force, such traditional land rights were not recognised; forestland was returned to the state and farmland was unequally redistributed to new settlers, including Hmong, Tay, Kinh, and others.

As the result, in the areas occupied both by Hmong and Tay such as Cao Bang or Langson, a series of land conflicts arose: as Tay farmers repossessed the land that their forefathers had contributed to the cooperatives, Hmong groups (and the Zdao) were left out without paddy fields[17] Additionally, such conflicts also broke out between the Hmong and the Kinh authorities (Forest Protection Unit, Agriculture and Cadastral, Forest Enterprise, Commune People's Committee) who were involved in the decision-making process for land allocation, and in the Hmong view, had 'eaten their land', violating their ancestors' and spirits' rule. The land conflict was fired by relational tensions from the past, when the Hmong distrusted the lowland Vietnamese, viewing them as foreigners (Jackson, 1969: 315). These conflicts and the resultant distrust were the key factors for the massive movement to the Central Highlands at a later stage.

The Arrival of US Troop and the Southward Movement

After the Gulf of Tonkin incident, on 14 June 1965 the US planes started their bombing attacks against the NMR (Hop, 1967),[18] leading to a massive campaign among ethnic groups to join the army. Thousands of highlanders and Hmong men became soldiers and went to the Central Highlands battlefield in response to the party mottoes 'all for the bloody south' and 'each village is a fortress, each person is a soldier'.[19] In Hoa Binh, for example, nearly 12,000 men joined the army and more than 15,000 youths were ready to go south. Indeed, mountainous areas and their ethnic minorities played a strategic role in the different wars in Vietnam.

Migration During Post-War Decade (1975–1986)

Migration patterns among highlanders and the Hmong in this period are influenced by three key factors: (a) the conflicts with Cambodia in the south-west (1975–1979); (b) the conflicts with China in the north (1979); and (c) the resettlement policies.[20] Four migration patterns among the Hmong are analysed below.

Fleeing Abroad

Right after the historical victory on 30 April 1975, a large number of people, many from the NMR, risked boarding a boat to China, Hong Kong, Australia, the US, and other countries,[21] a process that continued until mid-1980s. While data about Hmong emigrants is scarce, this is true for most highland migrants, such as the Nung living on the north-east border of the NMR, who, upon arrival at the Nei Ku Chau detention camp in Hong Kong, were considered refugees with confusing or 'negative identity', as illustrated by a famous quote "when in China we were Vietnamese, when in Vietnam we were Chinese" (Hutton, 1998).

Migration Due to War

In February 1979 the NMR became chaotic as the Vietnam-China war[22] broke out when 6,00,000 Chinese troops were launched against the border provinces of Vietnam (Vien, 2004), occupying and plundering most of Hmong—presided provinces, such as Lang Son, Cao Bang, Ha Giang, and Lao Cai.

Right after the war, a large number of Hoa and other ethnic minorities left Vietnam. While number of Hmong who fled was unknown, according to Hardy (2003: 117–18),[23] around 2,50,000 Vietnamese crossed the border into China; 68,748 arrived in Hong Kong alone. Meanwhile in the NMR, inter-provincial migration occurred on a large scale. Hmong people moved within their districts or migrated to neighbouring provinces at Laos-Viet border, chiefly Son La and Lai Chau; others went far off the order such as Thai Nguyen, Bac Giang, Hoa Binh, forming purely Hmong villages as we see today.[24]

Migration within the NMR

The main objective of the post-war resettlement programme was to redress the imbalance of population density both between the north and the south, and between the two delta regions and the mountainous areas.[25] Between 1976–1980 at least 30 related migration legislations were issued to resettle the border provinces. Borderlines between provinces were rearranged, leading to numerous Hmong villages being merged with other villages to form the new ones.

The in-migration policy[26] was continued. The ambitious plan of the government at the beginning of the 1980s was to move 10 million people by the end of the century and to reclaim five million hectares of uncultivated land for farming in the NEZs, mostly in the frontier uplands.[27] The organised resettlement programme initiated during war-time is continued with the Red River Delta residents being encouraged to settle in the NMR where NEZs are now functioning as a buffer zone to alleviate the country's economic crises after reunification (Desbarats, 1987; Jones and Fraser, 1982). While this campaign had partly achieved its aim, the arrivals of massive lowlanders brought about a severe population pressure for the NMR,[28] thus pushing some ethnic groups, such as Dao and Hmong, further to higher slope.

The sedentary policy or mountain-valley resettlement went on to achieve the target of settling down three million people by the year 2000 (Pholsena, 2003: 21). Having bad experience from the past stories, many Hmong refused to join this programme by means of moving away, either higher in the mountains or deeper in the forests, to continue their favourite swiddening beyond the authorities' control.

Another migration pattern among the Hmong during this period was due to the construction of the Hoa Binh hydropower plant on the Black River, which started in November 1979 (and completed 1994; with the capacity of 1,920 MW and annual energy production of 8.4 billion kWh, equivalent to 40 per cent of the national energy production). While it is vital to the industrialisation, the project led to a relocation of 56,294 people, mainly ethnic groups (Hmong, Muong, Zdao, Thai) of 10 districts of Hoa Binh and Son La provinces. Around 11,000 hectares of arable land were flooded, and hundreds of thousands of square metres of homestead areas, offices, schools, and heath care centres and many working places were inundated. Thirty years after the relocation,[29] today many of those settlers, including the Hmong, are still suffering negative effects of their resettlement. In Son La Province, for example, 1,000 families affected by the Hoa Binh reservoir are now under programme 1,382, a programme designed to help resettled families.

Moving Southward

After 1975, some new economic zones and state farms were established in the Central Highlands to attract a large number of migrants from the crowded provinces in the northern and the central coastal regions of the country. The main objective of encouraging migration to the Central Highlands by the government is to utilise national resources to achieve economic growth and social security.

The first planned migration led to the settlement of 40,000 inhabitants in different coffee plantations in the Central Highlands (Anh, 2006: 60). However, the free or 'spontaneous' migration was much larger in scope. The period 1981–1989 witnessed the first flow of tens of thousands of Han, Thai, Tay, Nung, Dao, and Hmong from Lang Son, Cao Bang, Lao Cai, Lai Chau, Ha giang moving to the Central Highlands,[30] or as far as Binh Phuoc, Dong Nai and Ho Chi Minh City.[31] Often, the ethnic groups migrated in family groups or clans. My study in Lao Cai and Dak Lak (Lam, 2006b) shows five reasons for this pattern of migration among the NMR migrants:

- avoid the Vietnam-China conflict (which in fact went on several years after 1979);
- become landless by population pressure and the resultant land conflicts during 1970s
- be attracted by the abundant forests and fertile land in the Central Highlands;
- follow the call of their relatives who went southward during 1965–1968 as soldiers or cadres;
- unify with their relatives who were forced to migrate to the Central Highlands since 1954.

Migration Since Doi Moi (1986 to date)

Patterns of population mobility have shifted dramatically since the start of the economic renovation known as *Doi Moi*, marked by decollectivisation and land reforms. The ongoing resettlement programme has become intensified and overshadowed by the growing spontaneous population flows, both rural-rural and rural-urban (Dang et al., 1997; Scott, 2000; Hardy, 2003). Several new policies were issued (such as Decision 116/HDBT dated 9/4/1990), the most important being the change from NEZ migration policy to project-based migration policy, under the banner of socio-economic development. As such policies and social dynamics go along, new forms of mobility emerge to respond to the changing situations. Among the Hmong, eight patterns of migration could be identified.

Migration Due to Sedentarisation

Since 1986 until now, settlement and sedentary farming of the Hmong have undergone ups and downs. For example, in the former province of Hoang Lien Son (now comprising Yen Bai, Nghia Lo and Lao Cai), by 1988, of the total 118,799 Hmong only 42,343 people had been settled down to sedentary farming. In Lai Chau Province, 85 per cent among 4,000 Hmong households migrated to Si Pa Phin are still doing shifting cultivation. In Bac Can more than 10,000 Hmong were sedentarised in 1999 but many returned to their native village after several months. In Thanh Hoa, the majority of more than 1,000 Hmong in Muong Lat continue shifting cultivation.

In the NMR and the Central Highlands, there has been a rearrangement of border districts with the involvement of the Ministry of Defense. Combined with sedentary programme, the so-called 'new settlement villages' (*ban dinh cu moi*) or 'border population clusters' (*quan cu bien gioi*) are set up with the average of 20–40 households for each hamlet. In Cao Bang, for example, 4,832 households (26,470 inhabitants) had to resettle back to Chinese border region within 7 years 1989–1996 (Anh, 2006: 86)

While such new border villages are put in strict control, many ethnic groups in question refused to stay there. Thousands of Hmong from resettlement areas, such as Na Hy (Dien Bien), Don Den (Bac Can), Ban Ve (Nghe An), Dak Rlap (Đac Nong), Ro Men (Lam Dong) decided to return to their origin villages after a while. Most of the interviewees complained about the small amount of state compensations,[32] corruptions of the local authorities, and the hard conditions in the new settlement areas.

Migration to the Central Highlands

Since 1990, hundreds of thousands of NMR ethnic minorities, of which 25 per cent are Hmong, continued to move to the Central Highlands in larger waves, a process just like the Exodus of the Israelites in the Old Testament or as described by Dery (2000) "agricultural colonisation".[33] It was estimated that the Hmong took up 25 per cent of these northern movers. The influx peaked between 1991–1995[34] and goes on until now. Dak Lak is the most attractive area for these northern highlanders. In Cu Jut district, for example as of July 1997, out of 87,500 total populations 30,000 were immigrants (Lam, 2006b). The Hmong population in Dak Lak has increased very rapidly: in 1979 there were no Hmong in the province; in 1989: only 8 persons; in 1999, the number went up to 10,891 (GSO, 1979, 1989, 1999). During 1995–2005, more than 18,000 Hmong from Lai Chau, Lao Cai, Ha Giang, Cao Bang, Tuyen Quang, Bac Can migrated to this province.

Before 1990, the Hmong often went to the Central Highlands in groups, sometimes the husband went first, and then returned home to bring their dependents, sometimes the whole family, or even the whole village. However, due to policy pressure, since 2001 this pattern has changed: people tend to migrate in the forms of households or individuals (Anh, 2006; Lam, 2006b). Some studies highlighted the negative impacts associated with both movers and stayers, namely: social disorder, land conflicts, deforestation, disintegration of ethnic relations, and the incidence of infectious diseases (Hardy, 2003; Xuan, 1998; Lam, 2006a).

An important point to note is that this migration pattern echoes with the massive conversion to Protestantism among the Hmong nationwide, the process started in 1989 and continues until now.[35] The Hmong may convert religion before or after travelling to the Central Highlands. This conversion among the Hmong echoes with the similar trend among other ethnic groups in the Central Highlands (Stieng, Mnong, Koho, Ede, Jarai) and other countries in South East and East Asia (UNHCR, 2002: 16). The followers demolished their ancestors' shrines, gave up funeral and wedding ceremonies, and threw dead people into canyons instead of burying them.

Fleeing to Laos and Cambodia

During mid-1990s, about 10,000 Hmong people migrated from NMR to the Northern Lao (Lam, 2006b). Most of these Hmong are from Dien Bien, Son La, Thanh Hoa, and Nghe An, the provinces adjacent to the Laos border. Before making such decision to go abroad, these highlanders had undergone different migrations within the NMR. The reasons for their migration are simply due to lack of arable land for production and scarcity of clean water. In Huoi Moi 2 (Que Phong, Nghe An), a small commune of 32 Hmong households, twenty-six families migrated to Laos within four months due to scarcity of paddy fields and water in their native village.

A similar situation is found among the Hmong living in the south-west provinces bordering with Cambodia. During 2001–2004, different waves of Hmong from Pleiku and Buon Ma Thuot crossed the border to Cambodia. This is certainly relating to the population pressure, the chronic poverty, and the political chaos in this region since 2001[36] when thousands of ethnic groups in the Central Highlands, including the Hmong migrants from the north, converted to Protestantism before their move (Lam, 2006b)

Migration Due to Disaster

In Vietnam, the NMR and the Central Highlands are the most disaster-prone regions. Severe storms with strong winds are often engaged with heavy rains, causing river water level to rise and flood. Rainy season is often accompanied by landslides, causing traffic interruptions and human tragedies. Over the last decade, such disasters tend to become increasingly complicated. Hail, whirlwind, landslide, flash flood, mud and rock flood come suddenly with unforeseen severity and scale, devastating thousands of villages mostly inhabited by ethnic minorities, causing serious losses in term of human lives, properties and ecological environment.

The historical disastrous events that affected the Hmong during the last decade include: flash floods in Lai Chau and Son La (1994, 1996, 2000, 2002); Lao Cai, Ha Giang, and Cao Bang (2000, 2001, 2002, 2004, 2005, 2007). The flood in Yen Minh (a district of Ha Giang with 34,000 Hmong) during two days 18–19 July 2004, the biggest one since the last 100 years, had swept away the whole Du Tien commune (510 households with 2,951 persons); 45 persons were missing or died; in some Hmong families, 14 members died leaving one person alive. The devastating Typhoon Damrey 2005, which reduced 0.5 per cent GDP of Vietnam, had led to the evacuation of hundred of thousands of households in Yen Bai and Lao Cai. In Cao Bang, flood and storms during 2001–2005 caused hundreds of deaths and thousands of houses collapsed. Currently, around 1,000 households in Bao Lam and Bao Lac (mostly inhabited by Hmong) still live in high risk areas of flood and landslide. In Ky Son, whirlwind and flood flash during April-September 2005 had washed away 1,000 houses and 15 irrigation works, leading to

Case Study in Lao Cai

Sa Pa district has 37,200 inhabitants of which 52 per cent Hmong. During the last decade, this tourist district has suffered numerous floods and landslides. The Cua Cai resettlement zone (Ta Giang Phinh) was set up in 2005, to accommodate 150 Hmong households who had moved here as the result of landslides. Like other Hmong families, Mr Sung A Seng received a subsidy of 5 million dong (300 US$) from Poverty Reduction Programme 135. Eight months after the arrival in Cua Cai, his family did not get any land for cultivation. Everyday he had to walk to his field, situated 25 km away.

Bat Xat district has a population of 56,000 with 27.8 per cent Hmong (1999). The flood flash and the resultant rock slide in Phin Ngan commune on 13 September 2004 had buried 23 people. District authority said 1,100 people (Hmong and Zdao) live in risky areas and need to be relocated to safe zone. However, many Hmong families do not want to relocate their ancestors' altar so they decided to stay there.

a relocation of 600 households, most of them are Hmong and Khomu. In the Central Highlands, the flood in November 1996 inundated almost the entire region. The recent flood in August 2007 has inundated 16,000 ha in Dak Lak, mostly affecting the districts of Buon Don, Chu M'ga, Ea Sup. In Ea Sup alone, a district with highest number of Hmong migrants, the flood had washed away 6,600 ha of land and destroyed 40 per cent irrigation works just within 3 days.[37]

As a result of such frequent disasters, hundreds of thousands of ethnic highlanders in the NMR and the Central Highlands had to move to new settlement areas arranged by the government. The problem for the Hmong is that, such new locations do not match with their traditional livelihoods and cultural habits. In many cases, Hmong farmers refuse to move, thus accepting to live with disasters and death risks. My research in Ha Giang and Lao Cai shows that in addition to economic losses, the bureaucratic procedures, the limited (and delayed) compensation, and corruption lead them to fall back into chronic poverty.

Drug and Sex Mobile

Over the last ten years, crossing of border has increased together with drug, sex, and human trafficking. Transborder migration of the highlanders is common, as they often do not recognise the border demarcation. However, entering into unfamiliar world, ethnic minorities could be vulnerable to HIV through sexual transmission, or through injecting drug use. Ethnic women are also induced into marriage markets, especially in remote areas where men can not find wives. At the Vietnam-China border, the border crossings among ethnic minorities take different forms with different purposes: (a) to marry Chinese men; (b) to work in domestic services; (c) to work as sex workers; and (d) to involve in drug trafficking.

Although the number of Hmong women working as sex workers is unknown, studies show proxy indicators of their vulnerability to this service. A large majority of Vietnamese sex workers in Hekou (China) are illiterate and originated from Lao Cai, Hagiang, Lai Chau, and Yen Bai, the provinces populated by many Hmong. These sex workers are visited by Chinese businessmen, including those from Hong Kong, Singapore, Malaysia, Thailand, for whom, 'virgins can bring auspicious luck' and the price for such exotic and virgin girls is around 300–500 US$ per night (Zhixiong, 2003).

Those ethnic women who live in tourist areas may be vulnerable to sex work as they may involve in tourist related jobs such as tourist guides. This is the case of Hmong girls in Sapa and Bac Ha, who work as embroidery traders-cum-tourist guides, and because of cash need and innocence, sometimes stay overnight with tourists or wood cutters in the caves, accepting the risk of becoming prostitutes and therefore the risk of HIV and sexually transmitted diseases (Quang, 1996; Lam, 2006a). In other cases, some Hmong boys and girls may work as street traders and combine opium selling service (UNODC, 2003: 86)

Opium use among the Hmong is not new but the concern is related to its impact: becoming drug traffickers and vulnerable to HIV. The current number of drug users reported (2,00,000) also means that everyday hundred of kilograms of drugs are used. This level of consumption is certainly related to the increasing of drug trafficking from Laos and China into Vietnam via border routes where thousands of Hmong are presiding. Drug trading routes are changing directions. Heroin and amphetamines are beginning to replace opium. Number of Hmong arrested due to drug sentences is increasing and so is the number of Hmong trainees in rehabilitation centres.[38]

High number of Hmong drug users-cum-traffickers is recorded in all border provinces. In Nangum commune (Dien Bien), 80 per cent of 87 households (the majority being Hmong) are related to drug; in some families, the husband went to prison, the wife continued to smuggle drug. In another family, the husband was sentenced death due to drug trafficking, leaving a sick wife and six children. There were tens of

Mai Chau Case Study[39]

Hang Kia and Pa Co are two communes of Mai Chau district, Hoa Binh province. These two communes are inhabited by 99.7 per cent Hmong (Flowery Hmong in Hang Kia; Black Hmong in Pa Co). Hmong population in Hang Kia over years: 466 (1960); 1228 (1979); 1513 (1989); 2226 (1999). Hmong population in Paco: 585 (1960); 968 (1979); 1388 (1989); 1864 (1999).

Historically, these two communes were inhabited by the Tai (Hang Kia means 'Bat Grotto' and Pa Co means 'Goat Forest' in Tai language). Before 1954, these two villages belonged to Son La before merging into Hoa Binh. This is why Hmong people in Hoa Binh and Son La today still maintain good relationships. The Hmong of these communes moved here from Son La, about 5–6 generations ago; Sung and Mua are the most popular among the total seven family names. Drug business, including opium planting, is key for income among Hmong households also plant cash crops such as corns, dong rieng, and fruit trees.

The two communes are considered as 'hot spot' of drug trafficking rings from Laos to Vietnam. During the French time, the Hmong planted opium for smoking; paying taxes (20 gram/person/year), and selling for cash. After 1954, the government encouraged opium growing so they sold opium to government in exchange for daily necessities. Before the 1992 opium ban, on the average, each household planted 500 ha of poppy and harvested two tons of opium. Since 1996, people have changed from trafficking opium to heroin from Laos. Accordingly, youths also changed from smoking opium to injecting heroin.

According to village authority, among the current 435 Hmong households of Pa Co, more than 100 are drug users of whom 16 people were arrested due to trafficking, 1 person was with life imprisonment. In Hang Kia, four Hmong got death sentence, some tens Hmong got life imprisonment.

families where three generations get addicted. In Yen Bai, as of October 2006 there were 2,651 drug users reported, mostly Hmong. Van Chan, Tram Tau and Mu Cang Chai are the three districts having high rate of Hmong drug users. In Lai Chau, a study conducted by UNODC (2003) showed different trafficking routes and high level of Hmong drug users in the two communes of Na U and Muong Nha.

The Hunt for Fortune

During the last five years, a new business has emerged in the NMR: hunting for gold or other ore mines. Illegal gold mining activities have been reported by all provinces occupied by the Hmong. And that's what is happening on the slopes of Lua Cay, the tallest peak in Dien Bien Dong (Dien Bien province), where ethnic villagers in their thousands are making the one-hour trek from Phi Nhu Commune every day in the hope of unearthing the metal of kings. The gold reserves in the area have yet to be calculated but they are contained in several beds near the ground and therefore easy to get at. The local authorities have forbidden the illegal mining and told the chiefs of 18 villages to keep their people in line, but no avail.

In Minh Luong (Van Ban) Lao Cai, 11 digging areas are full of Tay and Hmong who were among the first to join the gold rush. At least 80 per cent of local labourers and 95 per cent of households are involved in illegal mining. The work also lures children, who quit schools to join these digging groups. Very few Hmong get lucky, and many have fallen prey to poverty or drug addiction. A Hmong man from the village, who usually digs several holes a day without luck, says, "It is hard work. If I get lucky, I get some gold dust." In nearby areas of the village, gangs of mud-covered people with digging tools work tirelessly sifting soil for gold. Some men can make 10–50 US$ per day, but such money is often frittered away in luxurious motorbikes, gambling and drugs. The problem is much larger, as many mines lay scattered in hundreds of hectares stretching across tens of kilometres.

In Lai Chau, since May 2006, hundreds of Hmong have begun flocking to Pac Ta Commune of Than Uyen district in search of the king metal, hoping to make a fortune. The prospectors have not only dug up the area but widened the search to neighbouring Bai Giua, Rung Vau and Cay Da Doi, spanning 100 ha. The gold ore is stored in local houses nearby where merchandisers later come to collect it at around 4,000–5,000 dong (0.3 US$) per kilogram of ore (100 kg of ore yields 0.08 to 0.1 tael of pure gold). Most Hmong prospectors are farmers from neighbouring areas who dig for gold in their spare time, pinning their hopes on striking it rich while trying to tend their swidden fields afar.

In response to this problem, local authorities in these provinces have launched campaigns to close down illegal mining. In Lao Cai and Lai Chau, the working teams were established, with the help of military, police and forestry security forces, to limit the influx of the gold hunters. However, such interventions have failed, as the miners return.

Gold, however, has not helped Hmong households to improve their lives. To compound the problem, the gold mines and their surrounding areas have often become a popular destination for drug addicts. Many who have moved to these sites are people with criminal records, who may lure Hmong men into using and selling heroin. Gold mining has led to an increasing number of drug traffickers as well as robberies.

Migration due to Dam Construction

Since 2005, thousands of ethnic minorities in the NMR have moved to new settlement areas due to the construction of the Son La hydropower plant. This 2,400 MW dam, which is planned to be built 200 kilometres upstream of the existing Hoa Binh dam on the Da River, would be Vietnam's largest dam and would require the largest resettlement of people in Vietnam's history.[40] Ethnic minorities take up 96 per cent among those to be moved. By 2010, 91,000 people (or 18,968 households) in the three provinces of Son La, Lai Chau and Dien Bien are expected to be resettled. Most of them are Hmong and Tai, who will be moving between 50 to 100 kilometres away from their current homes and without access to the Da River—a source of livelihood for most of them.

Although the government provided some compensation[41] for their move, land-use rights and the small amount of arable land are the two most contentious aspects of the Son La resettlement project. Inter-related with these issues are ensuring sustainable livelihood for the affected people, and the impacts that resettlement will have on the cultural continuity and community values of the ethnic minority groups. For the Hmong, one of the biggest difficulties is the relocation of graves as they do not want the dead bodies to be reentered once buried. Another problem is that not being accustomed to saving and investing, some have used the compensation money to buy motorbikes, furniture or wasted it on drinking or drugs.

In the Central Highlands, with the rapid rate of constructing new hydropower plants, more and more Hmong and other ethnic groups will be affected.[42] In the case of Yali dam, for example, although only few Hmong were affected, it was said to bring death, disease and environmental devastation to as far as Cambodia even before the plant being put in full capacity.[43] (Lang, 2002)

Going to Work Oversea

Since 2004, a new trend has emerged among ethnic groups and the Hmong: the highlanders go abroad to work as cheap labourers. This is part of the government plan to send 1,00,000–2,00,000 workers abroad by 2010 (CSEARHAP, 2007) to deal with the increasing number of landless peasants due to urbanisation.[44] Milaco, a Hanoi based company has set up two branches in Cao Bang and Ho Chi Minh city to specifically recruit highland labourers to be sent abroad. Between 2005–2006, a number of Hmong (mostly men) from Yen Bai and Ha Giang were sent to Malaysia, a country is now hosting more than 100,000 Vietnamese guest labourers. Yen Bai Department of Labour reported that many of them have stayed beyond the contract and moved to another factory to earn additional money. A similar situation is found in other NMR provinces. A cadre in Xin Man (Hagiang) explained for their plan:

Among 53,000 inhabitants of the district, those at working age are 24,300 ... this is an important labour force for the district. However, farmers look to two crops per year and other cash crops—but it takes them only three months for all weeding, planting, harvesting—for other 9 months they don't know what to do ... this is why many of them are jobless and wanderers. At the beginning of 2006, we (Xin Man authority) worked with two companies in Hanoi to send them to Malaysia.

Moving South to Work in Industrial Parks

One reason for the recent migration of ethnic minorities to the south to seek employment is related to the rapid development of Industrial Parks (IPs) in Vietnam. Since the first IP was set up in 1991, by the end of 2006, 140 IPs and export processing zones were set up, mostly in the south; 85 per cent of projects licensed in these industrial zones are 100 per cent foreign-owned companies (Doanh, 2002). Over the last three years, in parallel with the flow of rural labourers going overseas to work, there is another flow of ethnic minorities from the NMR rushing to the south to work as cheap labourers in various IPs.

The Hmong, mostly men, tend to prefer this new type of employment. Youths give up their school work looking for a job in IPs. Thousands of Hmong men from the NMR are now working in IPs in the south. The advantage of this type of job is that the input investment is cheaper than overseas labouring; and one can sign a long-term contract with the employers, thus increasing the amount of remittances to send home. Many Hmong families in Yen Bai now receive regular money sent by their sons, although the receivers may not know what to do with such money. Authority people say that if this tendency is increasing, their economic target may not be achieved as they lose manpower.

Case Studies

Dong Van[45]

A north-east district of Ha Giang province. Consists of 1 township and 18 communes. Area: 446.6km^2. Population: 52,855 of which 46,848 Hmong (1999); population density 121 persons/km^2. Other ethnic groups: Tay, Dao, Kinh, Nung, Giay, Hoa, Co Lao, Lolo, Pubeo, Muong. Common Hmong families: Vuong, Giang, Sung, Mua, Ly, Lau, The, Vu, Va, Ha, Chu, Sinh, Cu, Cha, Lu.

Living with scarce water and a harsh climate, the Hmong practice unique rock pocket agriculture on the steep limestone peaks with an elevation exceeding 1,100 metres above sea level.

Dong Van elders say the Hmong came here from Kweichow (China) around ten generations ago.

1880s–1920s: different revolts against the French and local despots (such as the Lolo and Tay *tho ty*) took place due to colonial monopoly policy in the trading and taxing of opium and interethnic conflicts. In 1905 the first purchases of indigenous opium in Tonkin were made through the intermediary of a colonist who acquired about three tonnes of raw opium.

1950s–1960s: people lived under the yoke of landlords (a system called *ty sung)* as cheap servants (*ngau phang*) or seasonal workers. Hmong lived scattered over a large territory with isolated hamlets of 10–20 families.

1965–1968: US forces attacked the south then bombed the NMR. Many Hmong men joined the army; others went to Central Highland battlefield.

Since 1970s: the sedentary policy came in force. Villages were reorganised, thus merging the Hmong with other ethnic groups. Moving down to the lower elevations was troublesome since people have to climb up again everyday to care for their fields. The sedentarisation continued during 1980s–1990s and today several villages have moved back to border areas, for security reasons, to form the so-called 'border clusters'. The government program 134 compensates 7 million dong (430 US$) for their move.

Since 1989: a massive conversion to Protestantism took place among the Hmong (and the Zdao). During May 1996, hundreds of households left for Dak Lak. Since 2000, the conversion became more widespread. The Hmong and Dzao even sing Thanh ca (Hymn) in the

Cont'd...

Cont'd...

market. Households are requested by the authority to sign 'three don'ts pledges': don't listen, don't trust, and don't follow Vang Chu (God)

Since 2000: trafficking in women and children is alarming. Since 2006, a new pattern of trafficking in men has emerged. Typical scenario: Chinese traffickers (mostly from Yunnan and Quangxi) cross Chinese border into Dong Van; then collaborate with one or two local Hmong brokers who will trick single women into a forced marriage or sexual exploitation after offering a good marriage with a decent Chinese man or a good job. Women are sold with a price of 15,000 CNY (2003 US$), half of this amount is for brokers. Pho Cao, Pho La, Xin Cai are three communes where trafficking cases are prevalent. The fact that some Hmong women succeeded in marrying with Chinese men facilitates this human trafficking tendency.

Since March 2007: thousands of Hmong (and other ethnic groups) rush to Van Chai, Sung Trai and Ho Quang Phin (Dong Van) to hunt for the open-air chromium ore. They go in families, leaving behind hundreds of empty villages and thousands of ha of desolate fields. In Van Chai all 556 households (3,400 inhabitants) having someone to migrate. People can earn upto 1,00,000 dong (7 US$) per kg ore per day.

Tua Chua

A north-east district of Dien Bien province lies on the side of Black River. Previously belonging to Lai Chau but since 2003 belonged to Dien Bien. Area: 680 km^2; consists of one township and 11 communes. Population: 40.900 (2003); Population density: 55 persons/km2. Major ethnic groups: Tai, Hmong, Xa, Zdao, Kinh.

The Hmong in Tua Chua make up 76 per cent. Hmong subdivisions: Red, White, and Green. Lineage names: Thao, Hue, Sung, Vue, Vang, Lau, Lu, Hua. Previously, Hmong worked on terraced rice-fields but now combine it with cash crops (tea, cotton) and cattle raising

Prior and during colonial period: people lived under the yoke of local chiefs (*thong ly, song quan, and xeo xi*).

1945–1946: lowlanders from Thai Binh and Nam Dinh migrated here as the result of the Great Famine (1945).

1946–1954: Many Hmong participated in the guerrilla warfare

After 1954: new administrative system was set up

1960s: Paddy land and in some cases swidden land was collectivised.

Cont'd...

Cont'd...

1964: sedentarisation implemented and new villages set up. A sizable out-migration to another village across the Nam Muc River

1976: cooperatives disbanded. Villages re-established although no large out-migration occurred. Trung Thu and Sinh Phinh, the two communes with 100 per cent Hmong in 1994, but later mixed up with the Kinh.

Patterns of Migration After 1986

1. Drug use and trafficking: During Colonial period: opium was primary means of paying taxes and providing cash income. Cultivation of opium was severely restricted during 1960s, promoted during 1980s, and finally banned in 1993. However, today people still plant poppy in clandestine and inaccessible plots to avoid authority punishment. Since 1996, heroin became abundant and later amphetamines appeared. Hmong men imported the drugs from Hua Phan (Laos) and Hekou (China). Some Hmong men joined a gang of drug smugglers who trafficked from Laos. In one commune, 70 per cent Hmong families have an addict relative.
2. Dam migration. During 2006 and 2007, hundred of Hmong families were relocated to Huoi Luc resettled zone due to Son La dam building. However, land and loan were not allocated timely, leading to another move. Some households got compensation from the state but did not know what to do with the money; so they bought television and motorbike instead. Some managed to build a new house but faced water scarcity for both living and irrigation.
3. Gold migration. In mid-2007, Hmong from Tua Chua rushed to Dien Bien Dong district seeking the gold mine, joining thousands of people from all over the district. The hunt for gold coinsides with the drug trafficking and malaria break out.

Mu Cang Chai

A western district of Yen Bai province. Area: 1,200 km^2. Population: 38,200 (2004) of which 91 per cent are Hmong; population density: 32 persons/km2. Seven ethnic groups live in one township and 13 communes. For centuries, the Hmong work on terraced rice fields to plant rice and maize. Shifting cultivation is very common; and opium was the mainstay. Until now household income is based mainly on state subsidy.

Cont'd...

Cont'd...

Before 1957: the district belonged to Nghia Lo province; 1975–1991: belonged to Hoang Lien Son province; since 1992 belonged to Yen Bai province. The Hmong here migrated from China around 100 years ago. Lu families were the first settlers. Next came the lineages of Trang, Thao, Ly, Vang, Denh.

- 1940s: many Hmong participated in the guerilla warfare.
- 1959–1960: cooperatives and plantations were set up.
- 1960s–1970s: Thai Binh farmers came here when land was fertile. Some Hmong households moved to lower elevation due to sedentary policy.
- 1979: Hmong and other ethnic minorities in the district migrated to Thai Nguyen, Hoa Binh, Thanh Hoa due to China war.
- 1980s: Hmong households from Son La moved in due to Hoa Binh dam construction.
- 1987–1988: a large portion of Hmong moved within district or out-migrated to Van Ban district (Lao Cai) due to land shortage.
- 1993–1995: arable land and forest land were allocated for long-term use. This restricted the mobility of the Hmong shifting cultivators.
- 1998: 150 Hmong households moved to Van Chan (Yen Bai) and Van Ban (Lao Cai), forming the poorest hamlets at destination.
- Since 2000: number of drug users-cum-traffickers increases rapidly. In Nam Co commune, 40 per cent villagers use drugs. Daily trips to Son La made by Hmong men, both farmers and cadres, for drug purchase (opium and heroin). Due to drug cravings, since 1990s, a large number of Hmong youths go to forest to hunt for pomu (Fokienia)[46] to sell it for money.
- 2002: 50 Hmong households migrated to Central Highlands but some came back after 3 years.
- Since 2005: young Hmong (mostly men) out migrate to cities and the south to work as unskilled labourers in the industrial parks.

Yen Chau

Became a district of Son La since 1908. Borders with Laos in the west. Area 843.7km^2. Population 57,100 (1999); population density 68 persons/km^2. Major ethnic groups: Thai, Hmong, Xinh Mun, Lao, Kinh, and Muong. Contains 1 township and 14 communes. Three Hmong communities (920 inhabitants) are located at the base of limestone bluffs at elevations of 850–1,000m.

Cont'd...

Cont'd...

- 1955–1956: Hmong villages were re-organised as autonomous zones set up.
- 1969: a cooperative was established. The Hmong shift from swidden cultivation, involving continuous clearing of new forest fields to more sedentary systems of agriculture.
- 1960s–1970s: Hmong households moved within district due to the impact of sedentary policy and large-scale lowland immigrants.
- 1980s: a portion of Hmong and other ethnic groups moved to nearby provinces and Laos due to war impact.
- 1986–1993: substantial reduction of planted poppy area (from 178 ha in 1986 to 5ha in 1993) seriously affected Hmong livelihood (elders say 1 ha of poppy area brings in 5kg of opium, equivalent to 300 US$).
- 1994: land was allocated to lowland Tai but much delayed for highland Hmong. Then upper watershed forest plots were distributed to Hmong households for protection; but some of these plots were already divided previously between Tai and Kinh villages. The resultant land shortage and land conflicts forced some Hmong families to move to nearby areas and to Laos; others went farther into the uplands to exploit forest for additional dry land fields.
- Since mid-1990s: due to land shortage and poverty several Hmong households in Yen Chau converted to Protestantism and moved to Thanh Hoa, Nghe An, and Central Highlands, although before 1980, no religious activities were operational in the district.
- 2005: Hmong from Tan Lap and Phieng Tin resettlement sites moved to Yen Chau after getting cash compensation (400 US$). Each household is compensated 350 m^2 plot of land but far from sufficient for large Hmong families. Not accustomed to saving and investing, some have bought motorbikes, furniture or wasted money on alcohol or drugs.

Ky Son

A mountainous district of Nghe An province. Border with Laos via the Nam Can border gate (192 km borderline). Contains 20 communes and one town. Area: 2,094 km^2. Population: 57,800 (1999) of which 90 per cent belong to 6 ethnic groups (Thai, Kho Mu, Hmong, K' ho and Hoa). Population density: 28 persons/km^2. Highlanders live on farming,

Cont'd...

Cont'd...

forestry, and cattle raising. Traditionally, the Hmong practice shifting cultivation on burnt out clearings. Today, those who live near the road run shops at local markets or involve in trading cattle to Laos.

During colonial period: the district was the biggest producer of poppy crops in Vietnam; opium was used for income, smoking and medical treatment. After the opium ban 1992, each Hmong household still harvested dozens of kgs of opium per crop. Since mid-1990s, Ky Son has become notorious for cross-border drug trafficking from Laos, a business engaged by many Hmong.

Nam Can commune (with 3,300 inhabitants; 75% Hmong, 18% Khomu and 6% Thai), bordering with Noong Het district (Laos), is a bustling area for drug trading. Border crossers include traders, truck drivers, seasonal labourers, tourists, drug traffickers, etc. The Ky Son Hmong may go to Laos to visit their relatives or get married there.

Border drug goes with border sex. Sex workers, including ethnic minorities, come from both countries. A Lao brothel is formally operated near the border gate to recruit ethnic girls and serve clients. Interviewees say sex policy in Laos is looser than that in Vietnam. The Hmong, mostly men, tend to work as opium porters and the Tai tend to work as sex workers. Such border interactions, drug and sex, facilitate the spread of cross-border transmission of HIV and sexually transmitted diseases.

Ea Sup (or Ea Suop)

A north-west district of Dak Lak province. Set up in 1977 after separating from Krong Buk district. Borders with Cambodia in the west. Situated 85 km from Buon Ma Thuot, the capital of Daklak. Area: 1,765 km^2, with 80 per cent forest. Contains 1 township and 9 communes. Population: 31,000 (1999); 47,000 (2006) with the density being 26 persons/km^2. Major ethnic groups: Ede, Kinh, Gia Rai, Hmong, Tay, Nung, Tai. The fertile basaltic soil and water resources are suitable for coffee, pepper, cashew and other cash crops. These favourable conditions attract migrants from other regions. Ea Sup is the district with highest Hmong population among 16,000 Hmong currently living in Dak Lak.

- 1950s–1960s: Different waves of Kinh migrants from the north moved in.

Cont'd...

Cont'd...

- 1976: The first plantation was set up.
- 1980s: Few Hmong immigrants in the district
- 1991–1995: The Hmong from Northern provinces (Hà Giang, Tuyên Quang, Cao Bàng, Lào Cai, Thanh Hoa) migrated here in different waves. They live in clusters, work on coffee plantations and exploit deep forests.
- Since 1994: Some Hmong households and other ethnic minorities moved in as the impact of Ya Ly hydropower plant.
- 1995: Restructuring of district borders led to a flow of Hmong people from Buon Ma Thuot moving in Ea Sup
- 2001–2003: Some 12 Hmong households in the district migrated to Cambodia as the impact of the 2001 event.
- 2003–2004: Hmong moved within district due to the construction of Ea Sup water reservoir.
- November 2004: Some 20 Hmong households in La Lop commune were relocated due to flood risks. Each household receives 1 ha of land for production and 30 million dong (1,800 US$) as compensation.
- 2005: Hundreds of Hmong migrated from Krong Pac district due to water and land shortage.
- 2005–2006: Some Hmong migrants return to Lao Cai due to malaria endemics.
- January-April 2007: The (continued) arrival of 45 Hmong households (193 persons), among 75 Hmong households migrated to Dak Lak in the same period. These households settled down in Cu KBang commune.

Concluding Remarks

In this paper I have analysed various patterns of migration among the Hmong and how their causes are historically determined. After various generations of migration we have seen how the social contexts (wars, policies, livelihoods) determine the dynamics of Hmong migration. Since the time of fleeing China, the Hmong have suffered from numerous wars, conflicts, and unjust policies. The migration patterns during the French colonial be they inter-provincial or southward, are heavily dependent on the war policies imposed by both the French and the Vietnamese administrators. When the French left and the Americans came, the Hmong began to bear the repercussions of the war-driven triple policies (collectivisation, sedentary, in-migration) with land loss, land conflicts, and distrust being the final result. The war with China in 1979 and the continuing resettlement policies during 1980s brought additional burden to their livelihood, thus pushing them from the north and triggering a southward movement. Next, the fresh air of the renovation did not warm the Hmong soul. The rush for development, characterised by privatisation, industrialisation, or modernisation had left them behind, neglecting their customary rules and agricultural habits. The ambition to achieve GDP high rate (which is meaningless for the poor) is paid by the increasing number of landless minorities and so is the increasing number of Hmong men migrating south or abroad to work as cheap labourers and live in dilapidated houses. The construction of dams and industrial parks, in combination with red tape, corruption and natural disasters have made thousands of Hmong (and other ethnic minorities) to become short of land or landless and thus falling back into the trap of chronic poverty.

Having nothing to lose and in order to save themselves, migration has become a suitable solution adopted by the Hmong to enhance their livelihood. This tactic is so smart and adaptive, and has been so throughout history. Although migration is not a choice for many, both economic and spiritual miseries could be worse if migration opportunities did not exist. The massive Protestant conversion among the Hmong can be interpreted as a spiritual reaction to social discrimination in the globalising society.

Migration decisions among the Hmong make sense when they are seen as part of a continuing effort, consistent with traditional values, to solve, by well-tried means, recurrent problems. Indeed, migration does not undermine social cohesion but, on the contrary, reinforces and even widens the Hmong network. The visit of a Wisconsin Hmong to his relative in Dong Van on the occasion of Gau Tao (Hmong New Year festival) is a vivid example; so is the marriage of a Hmong Lao with his Hmong partner from Nghe An. In this sense, migration is a social process.

I have also shown that out-migration usually does not radically transform poverty for both movers and stayers and that moving to a new area may mean facing new sufferings and inequality (land conflicts, political chaos, water shortage, disasters). Remittances, in the case of working overseas or in industrial parks, may be not effective in the context of low investment capacity of the receivers. Involving in drug trafficking or gold digging also mean to face adverse consequences, such as arrests, disease, or addiction. As the last resort, many ethnic groups have continued their journeys by going deeper into forests, crossing border to a new land, or combining both ways.

After nearly 50 years of enforcing sedentarisation, the policy has not achieved its target as desired, and the shifting cultivation and opium planting are still going on, even more intensified. To deal with this problem, the National Conference on Sedentarisation for the Hmong (held in Hanoi during September 2004) has approved a big plan to settle down 3,00,000 Hmong doing shifting cultivation by 2010. My suggestion is that such plan may be a waste of money and that similar repercussions will be repeated like the past. This is because, for many years, migrations among the poor were hardly seen as a positive tactic for household survival but often perceived to be a negative factor for development, like environmental degradation and social insecurity.

The argument put forward here is that policies should be timely and sensibly supportive of migration among ethnic minorities rather than banning it, and taking into account the contexts that shape their migration and reactions. Patterns of migration (be they voluntary or involuntary, short-distance or long-distance, short-term, or long-term) should be seen as responsive and well-adaptive to the same things: poverty, insecurity, and inequality. The approach adopted here contributes to debates around the concept of sustainable (rural) livelihoods, which emphasises the need for a multi-disciplinary approach that looks at the interactions of migration and development. Analysing structural factors alone (e.g., poverty, conflicts, land shortage, unemployment) is not adequate to explain the dynamics of migration. Rather, we need a better understanding of the capabilities and tactics of the poor people, in their own perspective and reasoning, and that will help to improve development policies. Clearly, development may alter the patterns of migration but may not reduce migration. As such, further research should look at how migration patterns are structured and changed in the context of globalisation as well as the impacts of migration on development in different settings.

Notes

1. It is now estimated that the current total Miao population in China is 9 million; but only less than half of all the 'Miao' people in China are Hmong. Hmong populations in Thailand: 1,24,000 (1995), Laos: 3,16,000 (1995), Vietnam 5,58,000 (1989); outside Asia: 2,00,000 (Lee and Tapp, 2005)
2. Based on geographical and socio-economic condition, mountainous and remote areas are divided into three regions by the government: Region I: urban areas (centre); Region II: villages near urban and highways; Region

III: villages farther from the urban centre with difficult socio-economic conditions

3. This song, referred to as *Qhuabke*, is also used for the deceased Hmong in Wisconsin, who tried to find there way back to Laos via Ban Vinai refugee camp in Thailand and Mekong River (Vincent, 2005).
4. For further details about the French policy for Vietnamese minorities and the operations of French Catholic missions in Colonial Upper Tonkin, see Michaud (2000, 2004) and Salemink (1995).
5. By ranking top down, local chiefs include: *thong ly, song quan, xeo phai and xeo xi (Lam Tam: 12).*
6. The 1911 Hmong revolt took place in Dong Van under the lead of a poor local peasant Sung Mi Chang. This is the consequence of inter-ethnic conflicts and colonial monopoly policy in the commerce of salt and opium and restrictions in poppy cultivation (Lam Tam, 1972 and UNODC, 2003). The 1917 uprising, motivated by almost the same factors, took on much greater dimensions and was to last until 1922. Directed by Vu A Chay, it set ablaze the provinces of the North-west (Lai Chau, Son La and Nghia Lo), reached those of Yen Bai, Lao Cai and Ha Giang, and extended to the *Meo* settlements in Laos, also placed under French Protectorate. The insurgents achieved important victories in 1919, chiefly in the Dien Bien Phu valley. Towards the end of 1920, the Hmong succeeded in controlling an immense region of 40,000 km^2, including the whole of the North-west of Vietnam and a part of upper Laos.
7. From October 1944 to May 1945: about 4,00,000–20,00,000 people died due to hunger, war, disasters, and epidemics in the North.
8. For further information about the Hmong support for Vietnminh, see Michaud 2004: 76–79.
9. For purposes of more centralised administration and security, two autonomous zones were set up between 1955–56. The Thai Meo Autonomous Region, founded on May 7, 1955, the date of the first anniversary of the Dien Bien Phu victory, embraces the four provinces of Son La, Lai Chau, Lao Cai and Yen Bai. Covering an area of 19,000 sq miles (one-third of that of North Vietnam), the zone has 5,00,000 inhabitants belonging to 20 different ethnic groups, the greater portion belongs to the Thai and the Hmong (Jackson, 1969: 321). One year later (August 19, 1956), the Viet Bac Autonomous Region was set up, comprising the five North-eastern provinces: Lang Son, Cao Bang, Ha Giang, Tuyen Quang and Bac Thai. Its population, totalling 15,10,000 people belongs to 14 different ethnic groups, the largest being the Tay and the Nung; and about 1,00,000 Hmong. (Mai, 1968). With the creation of these zones, the Hmong organised themselves into 11 separate districts (Lam, 1972)
10. The land reform (December 1953-July 1956) is aimed at abolishing landlordism and distribute the land to peasant smallholders, thus paving the

way for a later transition to cooperative farming. Around 3,314 villages (or 1,05,00,000 inhabitants) underwent the reform (Moise, 1976: 70).

11. The collectivisation in the south started later, between 1976–78.
12. By the end of 1956, 13,52,000 peasant households out of a total of 23,00,000 were participating in labour exchange brigades (Shabad, 1958: 47); by the end of 1958, there were 2,44,000 labour exchange brigades and 4,800 co-ops.
13. From 1958–75: NMR is the primary destination of the resettlement policy because the war is still going on in the south.
14. NEZs large scale projects in which teams of labourers are sent to clear the jungle with bulldozers and build roads and houses; then peasants are brought in and given land. One reason for the establishment of NEZs is due to uneven population distribution of Vietnam's 30.5 million inhabitants in 1962 (16.5 million in the north and 14 million in the south), close to 29 million live on about 20% of the national territory, while the remaining, mostly ethnic minorities, roam over more than 1,00,000 square miles of plateau and mountain areas (Jackson, 1969: 314).
15. Different sources show the scope of this movement. Between 1960–64, around 6,00,000 persons from Red River Delta were resettled to the NMR (Ly and Quang, 2006). Between 1961–75, barely one million persons were moved, the total population of North Vietnam grew by 8 million people (Desbarats, 1987: 44).
16. According to the Census 1960, there were 3,13,998 Hmong living mainly in the North-west Autonomous Zone, Ha Giang and Lao Cai province (1960 census).
17. Another similar case is found among the Hmong in Hagiang (Lam, 2007).
18. Between 1965 and 1973, due to the US escalation against North Vietnam, thousands of people and hundreds of industrial centres and urban factories had to retreat to rural villages and forests; the operation is called *so tan* (evacuation and dispersal). According to US sources, 10 million rural people were forced to leave their homes to avoid the bombing, artillery shelling and chemical spraying (Vien, 2004: 321).
19. This well known southward movement is called by Vietnamese as 'phong trao di B'.
20. Between 1976–80, at least 30 migration related legislations were issued to resettle the border provinces
21. According to Amer (1991), as of September 1979, about 6,00,000 people had escaped by boat (excluding departures in April 1975). This refugee flow continued for several years, and by the 1980s, boarding a boat was no longer a response to specific fears or experiences of exclusion from Vietnam's new society but an expression of hope to find better livelihood (Hardy, 2003). The impact of the exodus was great, not only leaving a deep scar in the pain of the

nation but also contributing to the so-called "visions of paradise"—a tendency to respect foreign things among both movers and stayers.

22. The Vietnam China war took place right after the conflicts with Cambodia. Around 1,00,000 people moved to settle the border with China, and 'join the ethnic compatriots in fighting the war' (Hardy, 2003: 111).
23. By April 1980, around 3,31,725 were found in camps throughout Southeast Asia and a cumulative total of 8,39,228 in countries of first asylum by 1997 (Condominas and Pottier, 1982: 53).
24. For example, during 1979–89 Hmong migrated to Vo Nhai (Thai Nguyen) in different waves; often in groups or the whole lineage and settled down in the same place.
25. About 60 per cent of Vietnam's total population inhabits the two Deltas (Red River Delta and Mekong Delta) and the Southeast Region, representing about 24 per cent of the country's total area. In contrast, 20 per cent of the total population inhabits the NMR and the Central Highlands, which account for over 46 per cent of the nation's territory (GSO, 1991).
26. Decree 95/CP/1980 involving "The implementation of Resettlement Work and Labour Movement for NEZs".
27. According to Desbarats (1987: 50) and Jones and Fraser (1982: 126), between 6,00,000 to one million people were to be moved each year under this plan.
28. Different authors give different figures to describe the scope of this movement. According to Lam (2006a), during 1960–79, the inflow of migrants caused an annual increase of 3.4% of population in the NMR. Over 30 years to 1989, number of Kinh immigrants had increased from 6,40,000 to 2, 6 million, tripling the population density in the NMR (Rambo, 1997: 16–18). Between 1960–96, around 6 million people from Northern and Central Lowland were resettled in the NEZs (Anh, 2006: 23).
29. The resettlement planning started from 1975.
30. Until late 1970s, the total of northern migrants took up 50% of the Central Highlands population (IOE, 2005: 133).
31. During 1980–93, 21,801 households (102.204 people) migrated to southern provinces (Daklak, Lam Dong, Song be) (Anh, 2006: 105).
32. The movers get 7 million dong (US$ 437) from the Program 134 for housebuilding.
33. Different figures show the scope of this emigration. According to Rambo and Jamieson (2003), between 1976 and 1999, Tay Nguyen's population had doubled from 20,13,900 to 40,59,928. In Dak Lak, the population had increased from 3,60,000 to nearly 1.8 million during the same period (CCSC, 1999). De Koninck (2000) mentions two to five million northerners having moved to Tay Nguyen between 1976 and the late 1980s.

34. The massive migration during 1991–95 led to the issuance of the Instruction 393/CT-TTg (dated 10 June, 1996) to rearrange the resettlement and production in mountain regions; and the official telegram by the Prime Minister (1 April, 1997) sent to relevant provinces regarding the order to stop this flow to the Central Highlands
35. Protestantism is translated to Vietnamese as *Tin Lanh* or good news. Number of Hmong who converted to Protestantism has increased in all NMR provinces. For example, in Lai Chau 16,000 persons (as of 2005); in Son La 8,675 persons (as of 2002).
36. For more information about the events, see UNHCR (2002: 19).
37. Accessible at: http://www.dddn.com.vn/Desktop.aspx/Tin-DN/Tieu-diem/Tay_Nguyen-Noi_lu_vua_qua. Accesed on 7 August, 2007.
38. During 2006, I visited some drug rehabilitation centres in the NMR. In Yen Bai 06 centre for example, number of Hmong drug users has increased from 11 (1993) to 129 (2006); 100% are men and come from Son La, Lang Son, Lai Chau (HPI, 2007).
39. Population statistics are from Khong Dien (2001).
40. The dam construction formally started on 2 December, 2005 and will generate electricity in 2012. The project's cost is estimated at US$2.5 billion.
41. The compensations include: 30 kg of rice/month/person during 12 months; 3 million dong (200 US$)/household and 200 sq m of land; and some 100 US$ for medicines and books.
42. In 2006, as many as 22 hydropower plants with a combined capacity of 3,200 megawatts were under construction with a plan to relocate 200,000 people, mostly ethnic minorities. And 30 hydropower plants will be built in the central and central highlands regions in the 2006–15 period.
43. The 720 MW Ya Li dam (1992–2002) is located in Gia Lai and Kon Tum province, drains into the Se San River which runs through Cambodia to the Mekong. This is the second biggest in the country after the Son La project. Nearly 6,500 families in Kon Tum province were resettled under this project.
44. In Lao Cai, for example in 2006, 4,470 households had to yield their land to for the construction of industrial parks (DOLISA, 2007).
45. Based on LamTam (1972), UNODC (2003) and my fieldwork in Hagiang (Lam, 2007).
46. Pomu is a precious timber, often exported to China to make art works, cosmetics, and medicines.

References

Amer, R. 1991. *The Ethnic Chinese in Vietnam and Sino-Vietnamese Relations*. Kuala Lumpur Forum, 12.

Anh, D.N. (ed.). 2006. *Migration Policy in the Process of Socio-economic Development in Mountainous Provinces*. Hanoi: The Gioi Publishers, 250.

Ba, L.Q. 1968. Reminiscences of Underground Revolutionary Work. *Vietnamese Studies*, Hanoi, 15: 2–14.

Ballard, R. 1983. The Context and Consequences of Migration: Jullundur and Mirpur Compared. *New Community,* Utrecht, 11: 117–37.

Carney, D. 1999. *Livelihoods Approaches Compared.* London: Department for International Development, November 19.

CCSC. 1999. *The 1999 Census of Vietnam at a Glance*. Hanoi: The Gioi Publishers, 25.

Chesneaux, J. 1955. Stages in the Development of the Vietnam National Movement 1862–1940. *Past and Present*, Oxford University Press, 7: 63–75.

Condominas, G. and R. Pottier (eds.). 1982. *Les refugies originaires de l'Asie du Sud-Est.* Paris: La Documentation Francaise, 227.

Corlin, C. 2004. "Hmong and the Land Question in Vietnam: National Policy and Local Concepts of the Environment" in N. Tapp, J. Michaud, C. Culas and G.Y. Lee (eds.), *Hmong/Miao in Asia*. Chiang Mai, Silkworm Books, 295–320.

CSEARHAP (Canada South East Asia Regional HIV/AIDS Programme). 2007. Mobility and HIV Vulnerability in Vietnam: Implications for HIV/AIDS Prevention Programmes among Migrants and Mobile Populations. Hanoi, March, CSEARHAP Report, 44.

Culas, C. and J. Michaud. 2004. "A Contribution to the Study of Hmong (Miao) Migrations and History" in N. Tapp, J. Michaud, C. Culas and G.Y. Lee (eds.), *Hmong/Miao in Asia*, Chiang Mai, Silkworm Books, 61–96.

Dang, N.A., S. Goldstein and J. McNally. 1997. Internal Migration and Development in Vietnam. *Internal Migration Review,* New York, Summer, 31: 312–37.

Dang, B.V. (ed.). 1978. *Meo People*. Hanoi: Social Sciences Publishing House, 113.

De Haan, A. 2000. Migrants, Livelihoods and Rights: The Relevance of Migration in Development Policies. Social Development Working Paper No. 4, Brighton: Institute of Development Studies, 33.

——. 2002. Migration and Livelihoods in Historical Perspective: A Case Study of Bihar, India. *The Journal of Development Study*, London, 38: 115–42.

De Haan, L. and A. Zoomers. 2003. Development Geography at the Crossroads of Livelihood and Globalisation. *Tijdschrift voor Economische en Sociale Geographie* 94: 350–62.

De Koninck, R. 2000. The Theory and Practice of Frontier Development: Vietnam's Contribution. *Asia Pacific Viewpoint,* Victoria University of Wellington, 41: 7–21.

Dery, S. 2000. Agricultural Colonisation in Lam Dong Province, Vietnam. *Asia Pacific Viewpoint,* Victoria University of Wellington, 41: 35–49.

Desbarats, J. 1987. Population Redistribution in the Socialist Republic of Vietnam. *Population and Development Review,* Population Council, March, 13: 43–76.

Dien, Khong (ed.). 2001. *Population and Family Planning in Hoa Binh*. Hanoi: Social Science Publishing House, 232.

——. 2002. *Population and Ethno-demography in Vietnam*. Chiang Mai, Silkworm Books, 207.

Doanh, L.D. 2002. Foreign Direct Investment in VietNam: Results, Achievements, Challenges and Prospect. Hanoi (Vietnam), 16–17 August, paper presented at Hanoi International Monetary Fund Conference on Foreign Direct Investment, 14.

DOLISA Department of Labour, Invalids and Social Affairs. 2007. Socio-economic Development Report, Lao Cai (Vietnam), DOLISA Report, 34.

Ellis, F. (ed.). 2000. *Rural Livelihood Diversity in Developing Countries: Analysis, Policy, Methods.* Oxford: Oxford University Press, 267.

Geddes, W. (ed.). 1976. *Migrants of the Mountains: The Cultural Ecology of the Blue Miao (Hmong Njua) of Thailand,* Oxford: The Clarendon Press.

Giang Seo Ga. 2005. Characteristics of the Kruoz Ce. *Vietnamese Studies,* Hanoi, 2: 24–71.

General Statistics Organisation (GSO). 1979. *Vietnam Population Census.* Hanoi: Statistical Publishing House, 145.

——. 1989. *Vietnam Population Census.* Hanoi: Statistical Publishing House, 165.

——. 1991. *Statistical Analysis of Sample Results*. Hanoi: Statistical Publishing House, 98.

——. 1999. *Vietnam Population Census.* Hanoi: Statistical Publishing House, 234.

Hardy, A. 2003. "State Visions, Migrants' Decisions: Population Movements since the End of the Vietnam War" in H.V. Luong (ed.), *Postwar Vietnam*. Maryland: Rowman and Littlefield Publishers Inc., 107–37.

Hop, N.D. 1967. The Thai. *Vietnamese Studies* 15: 1–7.

HPI (Health Policy Initiative). Economics of Rehabilitation Programmes in Vietnam. Hanoi, HPI Report, 45.

Hutton, C. 1998. From Pre-modern to Modern: Ethnic Classification by Language and the Case of the Ngai/Nung of Vietnam. *Language and Communication* 18: 125–32.

IOE. 2005. Social Impact for Environment Issues during Industrialisation and Modernisation. January, Institute of Ethnology Report, 84.

Jackson, L. 1969. The Vietnamese Revolution and the Montagnards. *Asian Survey*, University of California, May, 9: 313–30.

Jamieson, N.L., L.T. Cuc and A.T. Rambo. 1998. The Development Crisis in Vietnam's Mountains. East-West Centre Special Report No. 6, Honolulu, East-West Centre.

Jones, G.W. and S.E. Fraser. 1982. Populations Trends and Policies in Vietnam. *Population and Development Review,* Population Council, 8: 783–810.

Kaag, M., R. Van Berkel, J. Brons, M. De Bruijn, H. Van Dijk, L. De Haan, G. Nooteboom and A. Zoomers. 2003. Poverty is Bad: Ways Forward in Livelihood Research. Utrecht (Netherlands), paper presented at the CERES Pathways Project Seminar, Inter-University Research School for Resource Studies for Development.

Kahin, G. 1972. Minorities in the Democratic Republic of Vietnam. *Asian Survey*, University of California Press, July, 12: 580–6.

Lam, Tam. 1972. A Survey of the Meo. *Vietnamese Studies*, Hanoi, 6: 1–29.

Lam, N.T. 2006a. "Social Change and Infectious Diseases in the Northern Mountains Vietnam" in A. Sleigh, C.H. Leng, P.K. Hong, et al. (eds.), *Population Dynamics and Infectious Diseases in Asia,* Singapore, World Scientific, 138–57.

——. The Dilemma of Development in Vietnam: Migration, Religion and Disease. Hawaii, 15–17 February, paper presented at Hawaii International Graduate Student Conference on "Continuity and Change in the Asia Pacific Community: People's, Places, Systems", 21.

——. Reproductive Health among Ethnic Minorities in Vietnam. Hanoi, Report to UNFPA, 47.

Lang, C. 2002. Dam in Vietnam Hits Cambodians. *World Rainforest Movement Bulletin*, Uruguay, July, No. 60

Lee, G. and N. Tapp. 2005. Current Hmong Issues: 10 Point Statement. Gary Yia Lee Homepage, http://members.ozemail.com.au/~yeulee/Topical/12point%20statement.html, 9.

Ly, P. and T. Quang. 2006. Migration in Yen Bai Province. Hanoi, Vietnam-Sweden Research Cooperation Programme 2004–2007, 17.

Mai, Quang. 1968. Viet Bac: From Cradle of the Revolution to Autonomous Zone. *Vietnamese Studies,* Hanoi, 15: 7–12.

McDowell, L.C. and A. De Haan. 1997. Migration and Sustainable Livelihoods: A Critical Review of the Literature. Working Paper No. 65, Institute of Development Studies, Brighton, University of Sussex, 29.

Michaud, J. 2000. The Montagnards and the State in Northern Vietnam from 1802 to 1975: A Historical Overview. *Ethnohistory*, Duke University Press, 47: 333–68.

Michaud, J. 2004. French Missionary Expansion in Colonial Upper Tonkin. *Journal of Southeast Asian Studies*, Cambridge, 35: 287–310.

Moise, E. 1976. Land Reform and Land Reform Errors in North Vietnam. *Pacific Affairs*, University of British Columbia, Spring, 49: 70–92.

Pholsena, V. 2003. Inclusion of Minorities in Public Life in Laos, Thailand and Vietnam, Singapore, 12–16 May. Paper presented at the Commission on Human Rights, Sub-Commission on Promotion and Protection of Human Rights, Working Group on Minorities, The Ninth Session, Asia Research Institute, National University of Singapore, 14.

Pike, D. 1978. Vietnam in 1977: More of the Same. *Asian Survey*, University of California, January, 18: 68–75.

Popkin, S. 1976. Corporatism and Colonialism: The Political Economy of Rural Change in Vietnam. *Comparative Politics*, City University of New York, April, 8 (3): 431–64.

Quang, Canh. 1968. Economic Transformation of Mountain Region. *Vietnamese Studies*, Hanoi, 15 (2), 9.

Quang, V.D. 1996. Report on the Result of the Survey on Risk Behaviours of HIV/AIDS Transmission among Mong and Dao Groups at Sa Pa, Lao Cai. Hanoi, May, UNAIDS Resource Centre, 12.

Rambo, A.T. 1997. "Development Trends in Vietnam's Northern Mountain Region" in D. Dorovan, T. Rambo, J. Fox, L.T. Cuc and T.D. Vien (eds.), *Development Trends in Vietnam's Northern Mountain Region*. Hanoi: National Political Publishing House, Vol. 1, 5–52.

Salemink, O. 1995. "Primitive Partisans: French Strategy and the Construction of Montagnard Ethnic Identity in Indochina" in H. Antlov and S. Stonneson (eds.), *Imperial Policy and Southeast Asian Nationalism, 1930–1957*. Richmond: Curzon Press, 261–93.

Scoones, I. 1998. Sustainable Rural Livelihoods: A Framework for Analysis. Brighton, Working Paper No. 72, Institute of Development Studies, 18.

Scott, S. 2000. Changing Rules of the Game: Local Responses to Decollectivisation in Thai Nguyen, Vietnam. *Asia Pacific Viewpoint*, Blackwell Publishing, 41: 69–84.

Shabad, T. 1958. Economic Development in North Vietnam. *Pacific Affairs*, University of British Columbia, March, 31: 36–53.

Skeldon, R. (ed.). 1997. *Migration and Development: A Global Perspective*. England: Longman, 253.

Son, C.T. (ed.). 2005. *The Hmong*. Hanoi: Youth Publishing House, 147.

Tapp, N. 1989. Hmong Religion. *Asian Folklore Studies*, Nanzan University, 48: 59–94.

UNHCR. 2002. Vietnam: Indigenous Minority Groups in the Central Highlands. UK, January, Centre for Documentation and Research /WRITENET Paper No. 05/2001, 32.

UNODC (United Nations Office on Drugs and Crime). 2003. *Ethnic Minorities, Drug Use and Harm in the Highlands of Northern Vietnam: A Contextual Analysis of the Situation in Six Communes from Son La, Lai Chau, and Lao Cai.* Hanoi: The Gioi Publishing House, 258.

Vien, N.K. (ed.). 2004. *Vietnam: A Long History.* Hanoi: The Gioi Publishers, 704.

Vincent, K.H. 2005. Hmong Cosmology: Proposed Model, Preliminary Insights. *Hmong Studies Journal* 6: 1–25.

Winkels, A. and N. Adger. 2002. Sustainable Livelihoods and Migration in Vietnam: The Importance of Social Capital as Access to Resources. Chiangmai (Thailand), 8–11 January, paper presented at Chiangmai Conference on "International Symposium Sustaining Food Security and Managing Natural Resources in Southeast Asia-Challenges for the Twenty-first Century, 16.

Xuan, H.T. 1998. *Social Impacts of Rural-Rural Migration on the Destination Province Dak Lak.* Hanoi, Population Council, 28.

Zhixiong, He. 2003. Migration and the Sex Industry in the Hekou-Lao Cai Border Region between Yunnan and Vietnam. Centre for Population and Policy Studies, Gadjah Mada University, 43.

6

Impact of Urbanisation on Work-life Balance

Elizabeth Mathews

Urbanisation, in general, is considered to be associated with the process of economic development and good quality of life because of the types of facilities and opportunities it offers to its inhabitants. Urbanisation is an economic and geographic necessity of today despite the massive environmental and ecological problems. The question to be answered is—has urbanisation contributed to work-life balance of an individual?

Considering urban India today, 27.8 per cent of India's people live in urban areas; in another 15 years almost 41 per cent of India's population will be urbanised. The population of the biggest cities in India will increase by 47 per cent in the next 10 years. The division of human habitats into 'urban' and 'rural' is based on certain attributes of the population of the habitat. Although the two are associated with the dichotomies of modern and traditional and industrial and agricultural attributes, apparently, one finds urban attributes in rural areas. Urbanisation then involves the transformation of rural attributes to urban ones.

Methodology

The study is based on primary and secondary data. The study is undertaken with a sample size of 100 executives working in various organisations selected on random basis, to whom structured questionnaires were circulated and responses obtained to study their views on urbanisation and work-life balance.

Aim and Rationale

With the rapid growth of urbanisation there is a need to study the impact of urbanisation on the work-life balance of an individual which is important to maintain the quality of work life and family life and an important employment factor. Work-life balance initiatives can help to bridge the gap between work and home responsibilities.

Background

Urbanisation

Urbanisation may be taken to mean the total change that is brought about in the population due to the concentration of people in areas that are designated as urban. The development in the social and economic set-up of the urban areas and the consequent impact on the cultural and behavioural aspects which could bring about a change in the very way of life not only in the cities but in the country as a whole, could be described as urbanisation. Bradshaw (1987) explained the causes of relative urbanisation. According to him, urban growth was a characteristic of societies undergoing a transition from an agrarian to an industrial service economy. Rural–urban production disparity and foreign investment in manufacturing were positively related to relative urbanisation. These findings suggested that rural inhabitants are drawn to the city when they perceive that it will offer them a superior quality of life.

But does this perception really offer them a better work-life balance?

Urbanisation: A Recent Phenomenon

The widespread urbanisation is truly a twentieth century phenomenon. As per Table 1, in 1800 only 2 per cent of the world's population was urbanised. By 1900, out of the world population of close to 1.5 to 1.7 billion, 15 per cent of the population, or about 250 million, lived and worked in urban areas. By 1950, this proportion of urban population to the total global population had risen to 30 per cent, whereas in 2000, 2.8 billion people lived in urban areas equalling approximately 49 per cent of the world's population (Mohan and Dasgupta, 2005). So, the pace of urbanisation witnessed in the twentieth century has been truly unprecedented.

Table 1 ***Percentage of World Urban Population (1800–2000)***

Year	*Percentage of Population*
1800	2
1900	15
1950	30
2000	49

Source: Economic and Political Weekly, XL, No. 3, January 15–21, 2005.

Work-Life Balance

Urbanisation has both positive and negative effects. It offers a lot of opportunities and promises to improve one's life but on the other hand, is it tilting the work-life balance the wrong way. Everyone faces the issue of time management at one point or another, but as more and more people are moving from rural to urban areas they have to deal with working at one or more jobs, travelling long distances, managing a household, attending school or other training, advent of nuclear families, raising one or more children, responding to increasing work and time pressures, of the shrinking workplace, and dealing with aging parents, the days often seem to last long into the night and vacation and leisure time seem to be consumed with issues other than relaxation and personal fulfilment.

Work-life balance means the harmonious and holistic integration of work and non-work, so that people can achieve their optimum potential across the domains in which they live. Researches have shown that employees are most productive when they are happy and motivated, and are getting the best out of life at work as well as at home. Many corporate bodies have recognised the importance of work/life balance and are trying to incorporate innovative methods to cope with it. Most employees across the globe see a balance between work-life as a more critical factor for job satisfaction.

The Indian Industry

In India, there are not many references to work-life balance policies and issues This is not to discount their existence in the country, but it does indicate its relative lack of importance as a strategic business issue in the country. A majority of Indian companies still do not offer managers opportunities to strike a healthy work-life balance. The IT Industry is probably the first mover in terms of introducing work-life balance policies. There have been pioneers in the country like NIIT, a premier IT training organisation, which several years ago introduced innovative allowances for employees who were dating, got engaged and so on. It made the news time and again because of what these policies did to recruit promising talent and ensure a motivated workforce.

IBM is one such company that offers many policies to help employees to overcome the challenges of balancing work and life. Some of the policies are:

Option for leave of absence: Employees can take longer breaks during their career at IBM.

Personal work/life: This policy helps employees to manage situations that range from attending school function of their children, shifting house, or to provide emergency care for elderly relatives.

Religious observation: IBM aims to help its employees to accommodate their personal beliefs while simultaneously meeting the business objectives.

Study plan: IBM provides opportunity for its employees to take certification programme for personal development.

In addition to annual vacations, IBM also provides flexibility to enhance employee personal work/life balance by having extra-personal leave, sick leave, maternity leave, paternity leave, compassionate leave, marriage leave, etc.

Work-life Balance Policies and Women

Work-life balance policies seem to be targeted at potential recruits rather than as a tool to further the entry and progress of women into the workplace as elsewhere in the world. The social constraints of women in the Indian workforce force them to leave work after marriage. They have a kid, go on leave, and do not come back. So much potential is wasted and management's confidence in a woman as an employee gets shaken. That can change only as more and more women come in and show a professional attitude that they have to work and manage the home too ...

Benefits of Work-life Balance Programmes

Attracts new talented employees,
Helps to retain existing staff,
Improves morale and confidence of employees,
Reduces sickness and absenteeism,
Enhances working relationships between colleagues,
Encourages employees to show more initiative and teamwork,
Increases levels of production and satisfaction, and decreases stress and conflicts.

How Balanced Are We?

The four important quadrants of life—work, family, friends and self, need to be balanced to strike a balance between work and life. In today's urbanised world, there is a negative tilt towards work and other aspects take a backseat. Organisations have realised the importance of work-life balance for their employees. Work, family, friends and self have to be balanced to increase the levels of production and decrease stress and conflict. A balanced individual is an asset to the society.

Urbanisation and Work-Life Balance

The findings of the study are tabulated as under in Table 2.

Table 2 *Impact of Urbanisation on Work-Life Balance*

Particulars	*Yes (%)*	*No (%)*
Feel pressure of work	84	16
Difficult to balance work and life	72	28
Spending more time on work related projects	88	12
Difficult to take time for family and friends	64	36
Feel overworked or overstretched	76	24
Feel lost or aimless at times	48	52
Use the allotted leaves	12	88
Do you have time for personal hobbies	36	64
Does your organisation take any initiative to improve work-life balance	28	72
Urbanisation has influenced work-life balance	96	04
It contributed to imbalance	88	12

Source: Compiled from the questionnaire.

Findings of the Study

About 84 per cent of the executives feel the pressure of work. Whereas 72 per cent feel that it is difficult to balance work and life. It is found that about 88 per cent feel that they are spending more time on work-related projects. Similarly, 64 per cent reported it is difficult to take time for family and friends. Whereas 76 per cent told that they are over-worked or overstretched. Again, it is found that 48 per cent feel lost or aimless at times. Only 12 per cent use their allotted leaves. Above one-third feel that they have time for personal hobbies and 28 per cent feel their organisation takes steps to improve their work-life balance. Majority (96%) feel that urbanisation has influenced work-life balance. Similarly, 88 per cent feel it has contributed to imbalance in work and life.

Figure 1 indicates that there is an adverse effect of urbanisation on work-life balance. The individuals are experiencing a tilt towards work and pressure and most of them find it difficult to balance work-life. On the part of organisations there is very little effort taken to tackle this serious problem.

The findings of the study clearly indicate that there is an imbalance in the work-life responsibilities. It is also found that urbanisation has an impact on work-life balance and it has contributed to the imbalance in work and life.

Figure 1 ***Impact of Urbanisation on Work-life Balance***

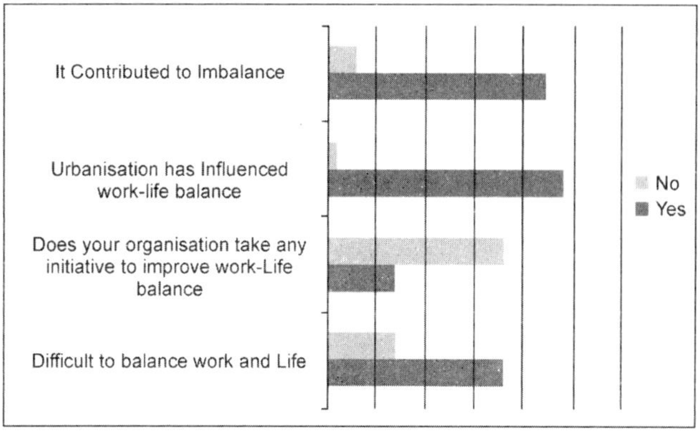

Urbanisation Tilting the Work-life Balance

The following are the causes for tilting the work-life balance:

Moving from rural to urban areas
Deal with working at one or more jobs
Travelling long distances
Long working hours
Growing numbers of women in formal work
Advent of nuclear families
Increasing work and time pressures
Shrinking workplace
The deterioration of boundaries between work and home
Dealing with aging parents
Days often seem to last long into the night.
Vacation and leisure time consumed with issues other than relaxation and personal fulfilment.
Lack of socio-cultural support system

Work-life balance initiatives that can help to bridge the gap between work and home responsibilities.

Flexible working hours
Onsite childcare
Seminars on stress
Fitness facilities, fitness membership assistance (financial)
Parental leave for adoptive parents
Flexible leave policies
Elder care initiatives
Family leave policies

Other leaves of absence policies such as educational leave, community service leaves.

Conclusion

An effort is made to relate urbanisation to work-life balance. Urbanisation has both positive and negative effects. It offers a lot of opportunities and promises to improve one's life but on the other hand, it is tilting the work-life balance the wrong way. Various initiatives listed above can help in maintaining the work-life balance. It will help the individual to balance the four vital quadrants of his life, i.e., work, family, friends and self which in the end will help him be a more balanced individual. In today's competitive environment, the challenge of integrating work and family life is part of everyday reality for majority of working families. The challenge cuts across all socio-economic levels and is felt directly by both women and men. A balance between work/life benefits both employers and employees. Employers reap the benefit in having a more motivated, productive and less stressed workforce and employees will be loyal and committed to the organisation.

References

Benedict, P. 2003. Are Indian Companies Striking a Work Life Balance. *Management Next*, Vol. 1, Issue 3.

Bradshaw, Y.W. 1987. Urbanisation and Under-Development: A Global Study of Modernisation, Urban Bias and Economic Dependency. *American Sociological Review* 52, No. 2, April.

Davidson, M.J. and C. Cooper. 1992. *Shattering the Glass Ceiling*. London: Paul Chapman Publishing.

Gupta, A. 1997. *Impact of Urbanisation on Rural Development*. New Delhi: Mohit Publications.

Mohan, R. and S. Dasgupta. 2005. The Twenty-first Century: Asia Becomes Urban, *Economic and Political Weekly* XL, No. 3, January 15–21, 213.

Thompson, W.S. 1935. "Urbanisation" in *Encyclopedia of Social Sciences*, Vol. XV, Macmillan.

PART II

Population, Development and Environment

7

Changing Pattern of Population Growth and Socio-Economic Characteristics in the Fringe Villages of Guwahati City

Semim Wara Begum and Bimal K. Kar

Although urbanisation in India is not a recent phenomenon, rapid urbanisation has taken place during the last few decades. With the rapid growth of industrialisation, improvement of transport and communication, increase of service activities along with better facilities, the cities draw people from surrounding areas seeking employment in different secondary and tertiary activities. This has led to an explosion of population in the city proper and as a consequence, it exerts tremendous pressure upon its fringe areas. The situation is no less true in the case of Guwahati, the largest city in the entire north-east India. As the administrative importance of Guwahati has increased significantly after shifting of the state capital from Shillong to Dispur in 1972, the commercial and industrial activities also increased to a great extent which attracted people from rural areas. This has resulted in a tremendous increase of population in Guwahati city. It is worth-mentioning that the city population has increased from 1.46 lakh to 8.1 lakh during 1971–2001. Due to this increasing population and multiplicity of functions, people living in the city centre have to face so many problems of diverse nature which compelled many of them to move to fringe areas. In fact, a remarkable change may be observed in the land-use pattern and other socio-economic aspects in the fringe areas of the city. With this background, an attempt is made in this paper to study the population growth and changing nature of socio-economic aspects in the fringe villages of Guwahati city.

Objectives

The main objectives of the study are:

- to study the population growth during the last three decades, i.e, during 1971–2001;
- to study the degree of Guwahati's influence on the fringe villages due to rapid growth of population;
- to analyse the changing pattern of socio-economic characteristics in the fringe villages of the city; and
- to suggest measures for socio-economic upliftment and a balanced development of the entire urban-fringe.

Database and Methodology

The base map of the study area has been prepared by consulting different maps collected from sources like Guwahati Municipal Corporation; Town and Country Planning, Assam; Census of India, etc. The study area is formed by an outer fringe which is a contiguous area, but outside the municipal boundary. The river Brahmaputra which forms the northern boundary of the city has been hampering physical expansion of the city towards north. That is why, no village on the north of the river Brahmaputra is included in the study area. In other three sides, altogether 80 villages have been considered for the present study being located up to a distance of about 15 km from the municipal boundary of the city. Again, as the southern fringe area is covered mostly by reserved forests and hills, most of the selected villages are lying towards eastern and western fringe of the city.

Both primary and secondary data have been used for the present study. The secondary data relating to the problem have been collected from various official published and unpublished reports and documents. Data for understanding the population growth and changing conditions of the demographic, social and economic characteristics of the fringe villages have been drawn from the District Census Handbooks of Kamrup district for 1971 through 2001. The data so obtained have been analysed by using simple statistical measures including correlation coefficient.

Geographical Context of Guwahati City Fringe

The study area, i.e., fringe villages of Guwahati city, covers southern part of Kamrup district in Assam. It is surrounded by river Brahmaputra in the north, Rani CD Block and Rani Reserved Forest in the west, Digaru river and a part of Dimoria CD Block in the east and Garbhanga Reserved Forest and the state of Meghalaya in the south (Figure 1). The study area comprises 80 villages covering an area of 172 km^2. So far as the relief is concerned, the area is not a smooth one. The western side is almost plain, while most of the area is covered by hills interspersed with low-lying areas in the eastern and southern part of the region.

Figure 1 *Fringe Areas of Guwahati City*

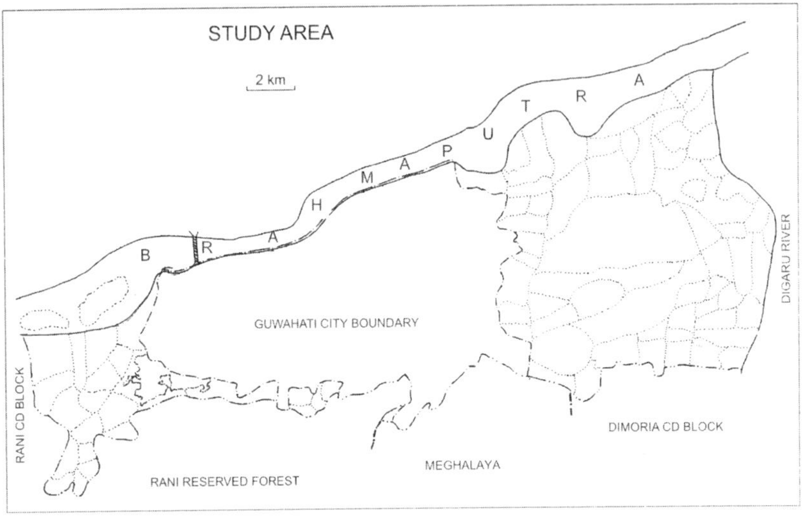

The study area has a total population of 1.14 lakh as per 2001 census. The state of Assam, which has significant diversity in ethnic, religious and linguistic composition, is witnessing a socio-spatially varied and complex demographic character (Kar, 2002). The situation is no less true in case of the fringe areas of Guwahati city. In the western side, non-tribal people belonging to both Hindu and Muslim religious groups are found in majority. On the other hand, the eastern and southern sides have a considerable proportion of scheduled caste and scheduled tribe population including hill tribes like Karbi, Garo, Khasi, etc., (Table 1). Most of the fringe villages are well-connected with Guwahati city by roads.

Table 1 *Percentage Distribution of Scheduled Caste and Scheduled Tribe Population in the Fringe Areas of Guwahati City, 1971 and 2001*

Region	*Percentage of SC in %*		*Percentage of ST in %*	
	1971	*2001*	*1971*	*2001*
Western Fringe	5.03	6.16	1.41	2.49
Southern Fringe	0.78	0.39	19.74	26.07
Eastern Fringe	4.35	8.08	11.07	11.02
Total Study Area	4.54	7.03	7.16	8.42
Guwahati City	4.54	4.96	1.17	3.76

Source: Primary Census Abstract, Kamrup District, Assam, Census of India, 1971 and 2001.

Population Growth

Due to rapid urbanisation, the cities are growing at a very fast rate today both in population and area. As a result of this, the cities are not only changed, but their influence on the fringe is also becoming more and more pronounced (Borah, 1985). The population of Guwahati city has increased from 1.23 lakh in 1971 to 8.09 lakh in 2001 at an average annual growth rate of 6.46 per cent. It shows how rapidly the population in the city has been increasing during the last 30 years. The areal expansion of the city boundary has also contributed significantly towards rapid increase of population in the city. But the explosion of population within the city has not been exerting pressure uniformly around the area. The degree and nature of influence of the city upon its fringe areas vary depending upon its accessibility from the city, terrain condition and socio-economic background of the different communities living there.

Although the overall annual growth rate of population in the study area is 2.13 per cent during 1971–2001, it has been found to vary significantly among its different parts. Inhabited largely by the tribal communities, the southern and eastern parts of the study area have witnessed population growth rate of as high as 3.64 per cent and 2.35 per cent respectively (Table 2). The southern fringe of Guwahati city has been remarkably changed in its demographic and socio-economic character during last ten years due to availability of levelled land located

Figure 2 ***Annual Population Growth Rate of Guwahati City 1971–2001***

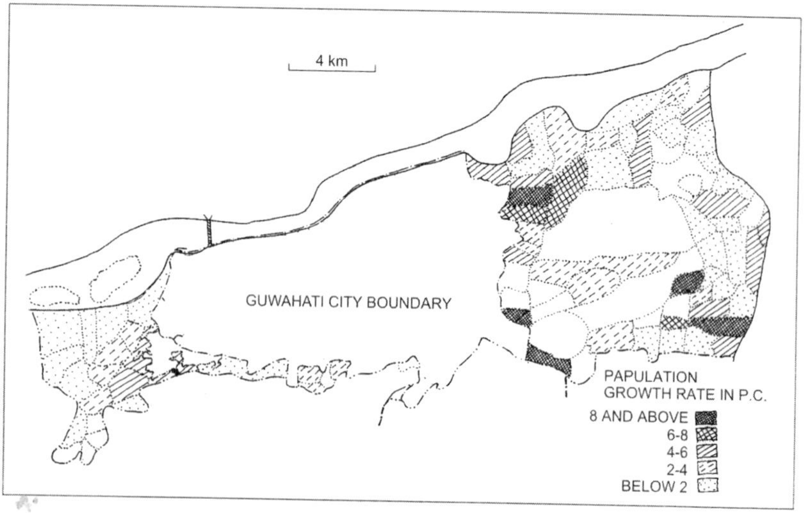

by the side of the NH–37. Besides, dominating tribal communities and their low level of literacy has also contributed to the high growth of population in the area (Figure 2). This is well indicated by the prevailing high annual growth rates of population among both scheduled castes (3.63%) and scheduled tribes (2.69%) in the study area (Table 2). Again, the higher population growth rates, particularly in southern and eastern fringes, have resulted in considerably higher proportion of 0–6 population in the study area (Table 3).

Table 2 ***Annual Growth Rate of Population in the Fringe Areas of Guwahati City, 1971–2001***

Region	*Annual Growth Rate*		
	Total Population	*SC Population*	*ST Population*
Western Fringe	1.72	2.41	3.66
Southern Fringe	3.64	1.27	4.6
Eastern Fringe	2.35	4.48	2.33
Total Study Area	2.13	3.63	2.69
Guwahati City	6.46	6.77	10.68

Source: Primary Census Abstract, Kamrup District, Assam, Census of India, 1971 and 2001.

Pattern of Socio-Economic Change

As stated earlier, the rapid growth of population exerts a great impact upon the socio-economic character of the fringe villages of Guwahati city. The population growth rate and the degree of socio-economic changes vary from one community to another depending on cultural practices and attitude (Barman, 1984). The decline of average household size in the study area from 6.33 in 1971 to 5.06 in 2001 (from 5.18 to 4.4 in Guwahati city), is indicative of urban influence in breaking down of the joint family system. Besides, lowering of fertility is another factor behind declining average household size in the study area. As expected the proportion of 0–6 populations is found to be slightly higher in the city fringe (13.38%) than that of the city area (11.02%). It is even more in the tribal dominated southern fringe (16.71%) (Table 3). The picture in this respect is, however, somewhat better in the western fringe inhabited largely by non-tribal people. This phenomenon of considerably higher proportion of 0–6 population can be well explained by literacy rate (r= –0.72).

Table 3 ***Average Household Size in the Fringe Areas of Guwahati City, 1971–2001***

Region	*Average Household Size*		*Percentage of 0–6 Population*
	1971	*2001*	*2001*
Western Fringe	6.25	5.15	10.85
Southern Fringe	6.02	5.08	16.71
Eastern Fringe	6.42	5.0	14.79
Total Study Area	6.33	5.06	13.38
Guwahati City	5.18	4.39	11.02

Source: Primary Census Abstract, Kamrup District, Assam, Census of India, 1971 and 2001.

Literacy, which is considered to be one of the basic ingredients of socio-economic development and transformation of any society (Kar and Sarma, 1997), has witnessed significant progress during 1971–2001. In 1971, the literacy rate in the fringe area was as low as 27.8 per cent as against 64.52 per cent in Guwahati city. It is quite satisfactory to note that the literacy rate of the entire fringe area has now reached 76.29 per cent (2001 census) as against the city average of 86.53 per cent (Table 4). There is, however, significant disparity in literacy in different parts of the fringe area. The western fringe occupies a better position with a literacy rate of 81.03 per cent in comparison to the southern fringe (73.18%) and eastern fringe (73.26%). Although female literacy in the fringe has witnessed a significant progress during 1971–2001 (20.6% to 68.73%), the male-female disparity is found to be quite high (male: 83.04%; female: 68.73%) as compared to the city (male: 90.44%; female: 81.01%) (Table 4) (Figure 3).

The picture is almost the same as regards the proportion of non-agricultural workers. It is found that the proportion of non-agricultural workers in the fringe area has significantly increased from 62.52 per cent to 81.58 per cent during 1971–2001 as against the city's unchanged average figure for 99 per cent. Although the tribal-dominated southern fringe witnessed a very high increase in the proportion of non-agricultural workers, at present it is as low as 53.88 per cent as compared to the eastern (80.50%) and western (86.92%) fringes (Table 4). It means still there is prevalence of agricultural practices largely among the scheduled tribe people in the area (Figure 4).

Figure 3 Literacy Rate of Population in the Fringe Areas of Guhawati City 1971–2001

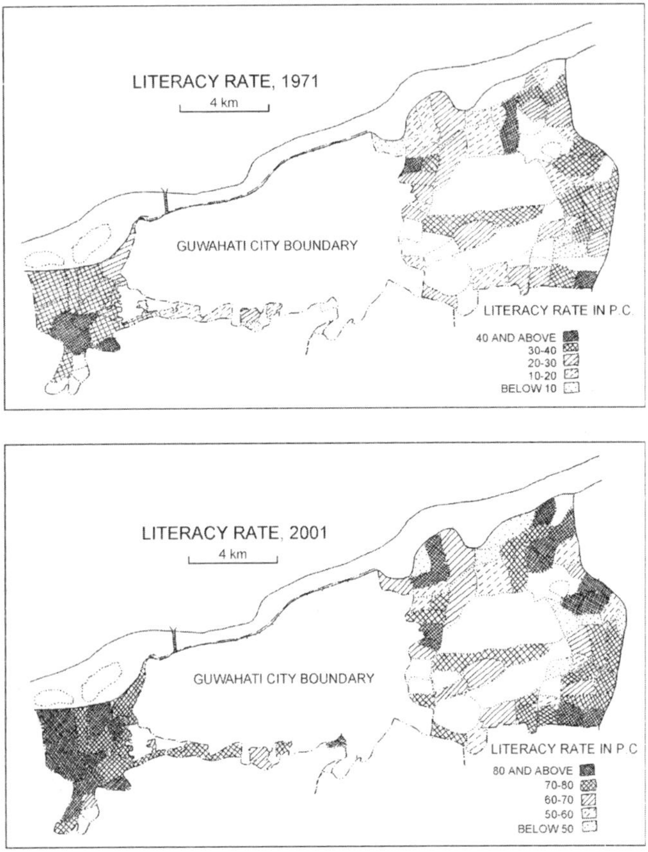

Table 4 Percentage of Literacy and Non-Agricultural Workers in the Fringe Areas of Guwahati City 1971–2001

Region	*Percentage of Literacy*						*Percentage of Non-Agricultural Workers*	
	1971			*2001*			*1971*	*2001*
	P	*M*	*F*	*P*	*M*	*F*	*Persons*	*Persons*
Western Fringe	35.14	44.16	23.8	81.01	86.53	75.0	67.90	86.92
Southern Fringe	20.89	31.32	10.49	73.18	80.63	65.34	10.65	53.88
Eastern Fringe	22.39	24.68	18.12	73.26	80.86	64.61	59.87	80.50
Total Study Area	27.82	32.5	20.60	76.29	83.04	68.73	62.52	81.58
Guwahati City	64.52	68.71	57.95	86.53	90.44	81.80	99.27	99.00

Source: Primary Census Abstract, Kamrup District, Assam, Census of India, 1971 and 2001.

Figure 4 ***Distribution of Non-Agricultural Workers in Fringe Areas of Guwahati City, 1971–2001***

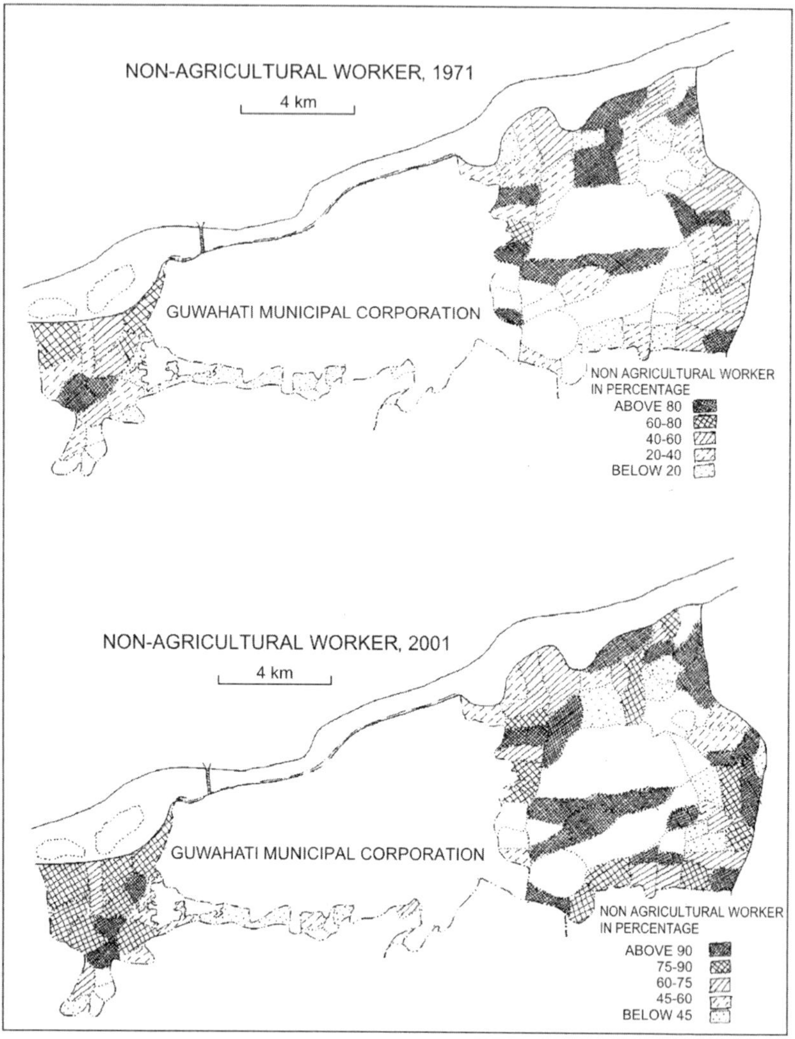

In order to get a more clear picture of educational attainment and other socio-economic aspects primary data have been collected from seven sample villages of the area considering different socio-cultural background. Accordingly, Kahikuchi, which is mostly inhabited by non-tribal people and situated in the western fringe of the city, witnesses considerably a high level of educational attainment with 62.23 per cent matriculates (Table 5). Mean female age at marriage is one of the important demographic indicators which play a significant role in determining fertility and natural growth of population in any area (Kar and Das, 2002). The prevalence of early female marriage among the socio-economically backward class people has kept the mean female age at marriage quite low in the area. Accordingly, Azara, Amerigog and Pamohi are witnessing low level mean female age at marriage in the area dominated by Muslim, Nepali and Karbi people respectively (Table 6). Again, the child-woman ratio is found to be higher where the mean female age at marriage is low since both of them are negatively correlated to each other (Table 6).

Table 5 ***Percentage of Matriculates and Above in the Fringe Areas of Selected Villages of Guwahati City***

Village Name	*Dominant Community*	*Percentage of Matriculates and Above*
Patgaon	Boro (ST)	25.5
Jugipara	Assamese Hindu (OBC)	43.4
Kahikuchi	Assamese Hindu (General Caste)	62.23
Azara	Indigenous Muslim	26.3
Pamohi	Karbi (ST)	22.4
Amerigog	Nepali	22.9
Tapesia	Karbi	39.8

Source: Primary Survey, 2006.

Table 6 ***Mean Female Age at Marriage (in Years) and Child-Woman Ratio in the Fringe Areas of Selected Villages of Guwahati City, 2006***

Village Name	*Dominant Community*	*Mean Female Age at Marriage in Different Age Groups of Currently Married Woman*		*Child-Woman Ratio*
		45 and Above	*Below 45*	
Patgaon	Boro (ST)	14.9	17.8	3.5
Jugipara	Assamese Hindu (OBC)	15.8	20.1	3.2
Kahikuchi	Assamese Hindu (General Caste)	17.4	21.2	3.1
Azara	Indigenous Muslim	14.2	17.7	4.8
Pamohi	Karbi (ST)	14.4	17.9	3.6
Amerigog	Nepali	14.3	15.9	4.2
Tapesia	Karbi	15.2	18.4	4.1

Source: Primary Survey, 2006.

So far as the improvement of infrastructural facilities is concerned, there has been moderate increase in educational facilities, health facilities and approached road conditions in the fringe areas during 1971–1991 (Table 7). In the case of road condition, the proportion of villages having *pucca* road approach has increased from 45 per cent to 57 per cent during 1971–1991. However, on the whole, it is observed that most of the fringe villages, more particularly in the east and south, still present a rural character.

Table 7 ***Infrastructural Facilities in the Fringe Areas of Guwahati City at Different Points of Time***

Region	*No. of Educational Institution Per Village*		*Percentage Pucca Roads Per Village*		*Hospital Facilities Per Lakh Population*		*Agricultural Landuse in Per Cent*	
	1971	*1991*	*1971*	*1991*	*1971*	*1991*	*1971*	*1991*
Study Area	0.9	1.3	45	57	13	20	48	37

Source: Primary Census Abstract, Kamrup District, Assam, Census of India, 1971and 2001.

Conclusion

The above discussion reveals that although the influence of Guwahati city upon its fringe areas is noticeably high, the picture is still far from satisfactory in some of the areas. It has been observed that the population growth is quite high in the southern fringe as well as eastern fringe villages, which are mainly dominated by tribal people. On the other hand, the socio-economic changes are found to be more in the locationally advantageous villages and among the non-tribal groups of people. Thus, it is found that the change and development is considerably higher in the western fringe. It is, therefore, highly essential for the authorities concerned to take up appropriate programmes of integrated balanced development of the fringe areas around Guwahati city.

References

Barman, R. 1984. Social Landscape of Bajali with special reference to social constraint. (Unpublished M. Phil. Dissertation), Gauhati University.

Bhagabati, A.K. 1996. Pattern of Urbanisation in the Peripheries of India: The Case of North-Eastern Boarder Region, *North-Eastern Geographer*, Vol. 27, Nos. 1 and 2.

Bhattacharyya, N.N. 1981. *Morphology of Towns of Assam with special Reference to the City of Guwahati*. Mani Manik Prakash, Guwahati.

Borah, J. 1985. *Spatial Structure of Urban Influence in the Neighbouring Areas of Guwahati City*. New Delhi: Inter India Publication.

Census of India. 1971, 1991 and 2001. District Census Handbook. Kamrup District.

Kar, B.K. and M. Das. 2002. Female Age at Marriage and Associated Correlates in Assam. *North-Eastern Geographer*, Vol. 32, Nos.1 and 2, 42–9.

Kar, B.K. 1999. Land Use Change in the Eastern Fringe of Dehradun City: A Study Using Remote Sensing and GIS. *North-Eastern Geographer*, Vol. 30, No. 182.

Kar, B.K. 2002. "Population of Assam" in A.K. Bhagabati et al., (eds.), *Geography Assam*. New Delhi: Rajesh Publications.

Kar, B.K. and H.N. Sharma. 1997. Socio-Economic Transformation in the Tribal Society of Assam. *North-Eastern Geographer*, Vol. 28, Nos.1 and 2, 32–41.

Ramachandran, R. 1989. *Urbanisation and Urban System in India*. Delhi: Oxford University Press.

Sharma, H.N. 1979. Urban Growth and Spatial Pattern of Urban Development in the Brahmaputra Valley, Assam. *North-Eastern Geographer*, Vol. XI, Nos. 1 and 2.

8

Effects of Population Growth on Environmental Degradation in India

C.M. Lakshmana

Degradation of environment today not only impacts human health but also has a negative influence on the global environment. Rapid growth of population has been the main cause of environmental degradation. Realisation came during 1960s and 1970s when people began to think that human existence would not be possible unless they adjusted their relationship with their environment. It has been fully realised that these environmental problems are not limited to local, regional and national level alone, but to the entire globe. Along with human resources, land, water and vegetation are the three important natural resources necessary for sustainable national growth. Rising population leads to overuse of natural resources, endangering the welfare of future generations. The global population increased from 3.85 billion in 1971 to 6.1 billion in 2000 and is currently (2006) growing by 77 million people a year. Most of the growth is concentrated in developing regions, with nearly two-thirds in Asia and Pacific. In India-population has grown steadily from 1901, except for a decrease in the decade 1911–1921. The total population of India was 23.8 crore in 1901 which increased to 36.1 crore in 1951 and 102.7 crore in 2001. India has got only 2.4 per cent of the total land area in the world but, it is the home for 16.7 per cent of the world's population.

An attempt has been made in the present investigation to understand the environmental degradation caused by the growth of population in India and its states. The analysis has been done for the last three decades: 1971–1981, 1981–1991 and 1991–2001. The three major aspects, deforestation, growth of industries and growth in the number of registered motor vehicles have been selected for the study. A detailed investigation has been done to understand the state-wise environmental degradation and its link with population growth. Overall understanding is arrived at by computing the environmental degradation index (EDI). In the concluding part, viable policy recommendations have also been drawn.

Objectives

1. To study the effects of population growth on environmental degradation in India by states,
2. To investigate the status of environmental degradation under aspects of deforestation, growth in the number of industries and growth in number of motor vehicles in India by states,
3. Preparation of Environmental Degradation Index (EDI) by states in India and link it up with population growth figures.

Methodology

The data for the study has been collected from the available census reports and Environment Statistics published by the Ministry of Statistics for the years 1971, 1981, 1991 and 2001. Collected data pertaining to the registered motor vehicles and industries have been converted into simple growth rates for the respective decades: 1971–1981, 1981–1991 and 1991–2001 and analysed to link it up with population growth. To understand thc overall status of environmental degradation the Index of Environmental Degradation (IED) has been prepared. Suitable illustrations have been drawn up and appropriate policy suggestions and conclusions have been stated in the study.

Hypothesis

1. Due to rapid growth of industries in states like Maharashtra, Gujarat, Tamil Nadu and Karnataka have sustained comparatively higher degree of environmental degradation.
2. With relatively lower growth of population and higher proportion of forest area in the total geographical area, the north-eastern states of India shown relatively less environmental degradation,
3. With higher population, economic backwardness and comparatively higher per cent of SCs/STs in total population, states of Madhya Pradesh, Orissa, Uttar Pradesh and Bihar seem to have higher deforestation and environmental degradation.

Human Impact on the Natural Environment

Increasing population has created several environmental problems, some of which are: overall reduction in agricultural land, lower productivity, deforestation, soil erosion, landslides and expansion of wasteland, problem of drinking water and malnutrition. Population pressure also leads to gradual change in climatic conditions like increasing frequency of floods and draughts. Increasing level of pollution has adverse effects on human health and quality of life.

In this view, if we examine the per capita land availability for agriculture in India from Table 1, it indicates that, over the census years it had shown a steady decline, while it was 0.30 hectares in 1971, it came down to 0.21 hectares in 1991 which was further reduced to 0.18 hectares by the year 2001. Of course, there are three reasons for such a decline, viz., (i) In general, increasing population leads to reduction of per capita land availability for agriculture (ii) Where land is inelastic in its availability and (iii) in recent years, especially after 1990s, rapid growth of industries and establishment of various institutions under liberalisation and globalisation, a large amount of agricultural land is used for various purposes (like residential, development projects like railways, industries, mining, river valley projects and defence, etc.). It is further evident that the average size of holdings had shown a steady decline over all the censuses; while it was 2.3 hectares in 1970–71 it came down to 1.84 hectares in 1980–81, which was further reduced to 1.55 hectares during 1990–91(All India Report on Agricultural Census (1991–92).

Of late, creating of Special Economic Zones (SEZs) in the name of promotion of exports through increased industrial development often on this shrinking agricultural land is a serious issue. This has directly influenced the reduction of gross agricultural land, and its further impact on reduction in net sown area, thus leading to extinction of flora and fauna. This process has been further damaging the whole bio-diversity which is also vital for our survival. Further in this regard it is important note that recently in Delhi our honourable President of India Dr A.P.J. Abdul Kalam has called a second green revolution, to meet future food grains needs necessitated by increasing population growth. By 2020, India would need to produce over 340 million tones of food grains. Our agricultural scientists and technologists have to work for doubling the productivity of the available land for agriculture as well as within the availability of water. The requirement of land for the increasing population as well as for greater afforestation and environment preservation activities would force a situation whereby the present 170 million hectares of arable land would not be fully available. It is estimated to shrink to 100 million hectares by 2020. Hence, in future it may create shortage of food production and also environmental problems.

Table 1 ***Per-capita Availability of Agriculture Land (in hectares) in India***

Year	*Population*	*Per-capita Land Availability for Agriculture*
1971	54.79,49,809	0.30
1981	68,51,84,692	0.25
1991	84,63,02,688	0.21
2001	1,02,70,15,247	0.18

Source: All India Report on Agricultural Census, 1990–91 and www.indiastat.com.

Population Growth, Deforestation and Environment

In India, deforestation is going on at a very fast rate. The overexploitation of forests started during World War II, when the British started clearing forests to meet their need for land, etc., (Saxena, 1999). In the post-independence period, the process of exploitation has been continuing to meet the needs of development projects like housing, railways, industries, mining, river valley projects and defense, etc. The impact of deforestation on the environment can be seen in the form of micro-climatic change, increase in temperature and decrease in humidity/rainfall flood and soil erosion.

Figure 1 (a) represents the overall growth rate of population by states in India for the decades 1971–1981, 1981–1991 and 1991–2001. Similarly, Figure 1 (b) shows percentage of forest area in total geographical area by states. The average growth rate of population of India in the decade 1971–1981 was 24.66 per cent, it decreased to 21.34 per cent by the decade 1991–2001. But there is a substantial rise in absolute growth of population in different states. In the last decade there has been a gradual decline in the growth rate of population in India, and its states except for a few states namely, Nagaland, Bihar and Uttar Pradesh.

This is mainly due to higher percentage of tribal and SC/ST population and also to some extent the backwardness. The per cent of forest area to total geographical area of the country has slightly increased to 23.38 per cent in 2001 from 22.41 per cent in 1981. It indicates a marginal increase in forest area. But, in many states this has been decreasing over the years. There was a drastic decline in forest area in Bihar (16.83% in 1981 to 6.45% in 2001), Uttar Pradesh (17.39% in 1981 to 6.98% in 2001), and Madhya Pradesh (34.63% in 1981 to 30.89% in 2001). Interestingly, these states have had relatively higher growth rate of population and higher proportion of SC/STs in the country (see Table 1). Hence, it is assumed that, higher growth rate and weaker sections of population lead to higher demand of land for agriculture, settlement of industries and infrastructure. Naturally, the demand is met by clearing the forest area. Also, as there is sizeable SC/ST population it denotes that there would be more dependence on forests for firewood, etc.

The prevailing forest use practice and the inherent contractor-government nexus often deprive the traditional rights of local tribes to go the fire wood, minor forest produce, etc., so much so that they indulge in overuse of accessible forests and often resort to unhealthy forest uses like cutting immature trees and stealing forest produce. These areas with higher percentage of forest area and lower absolute size of population suffer relatively lower environmental degradation. However, rising forest based industries demand for horticulture and floriculture crops, etc., have placed higher demand on forest lands with resultant degradation.

Figure 1a ***Decadal Growth of Population by States in India***

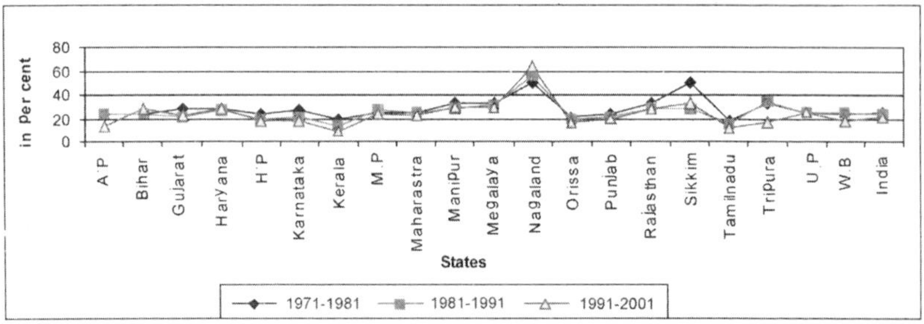

Figure 1b ***Percentage of Forest Area in Different States of India***

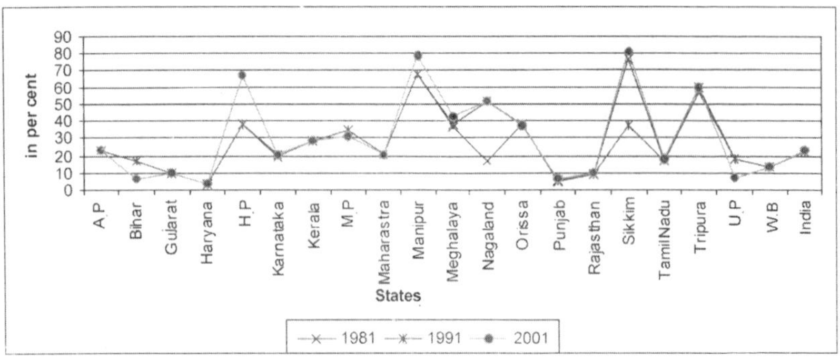

The north and north-eastern states of Sikkim, Nagaland, Manipur, Meghalaya, Mizoram, Arunachal Pradesh, Jammu&Kashmir have higher growth rate of population as compared to the southern states. But, these states also have higher per cent of forest area in their total geographical area. The state of Sikkim has 81.24 per cent, highest in the country, followed by Manipur – 78.01, Mizoram – 75.59, Himachal Pradesh – 66.52, the newly-constructed state of Uttaranchal – 64.81, Arunachal Pradesh – 61.55, Tripura – 60.01, Nagaland – 52.05, Chhattisgarh – 43.85 and Meghalaya – 43.34 per cent. It can be noted that from the following analysis these states have suffered relatively lower degree of environmental degradation. Figure 1(b) reveals that the percentage of forest area in the above said states is higher than the growth rate of human population. As they are hilly states and from these evidences, we could infer that, environmental sustainability and degradation are within limits in these states as compared to other states. But in the case of Madhya Pradesh., Arunachal Pradesh, Orissa, Maharashtra, Rajasthan, Bihar and Uttar Pradesh deforestation is more severe. The loss of forest is about 2 million hectares in Madhya Pradesh while in Maharashtra, Orissa, Andhra Pradesh, and Jammu & Kashmir, loss is over a million hectares. In Rajasthan and Himachal Pradesh it is over half a million hectares each (Saxena, 1999). Hence, in this regard urgent attention needs to be given to forest management. Action to halt deforestation and to conserve bio-diversity is absolutely necessary.

Population Growth, Industries and Environment

The rapid growth of industries post-1970s has resulted in environmental degradation. Various industrial processes release a large spectrum of pollutants into land, soil, water and air. Industries like cement, iron and steel, fertiliser, petrochemical, etc., are particularly harmful not only because of the difficulty in controlling the emission of pollutants by these industries, but also due to the rapid rise in their number with least concern for environment friendly in recent years.

The industrial units in India are largely located in the states of Gujarat, Maharashtra, Tamil Nadu, West Bengal, Karnataka, Uttar Pradesh and Bihar. The highest concentration of sulphur dioxide and oxides of nitrogen is therefore often found in cities located in these states. Improper management of industrial effluents and solid wastes from industrial estates of Delhi, Punjab, Rajasthan, Andhra Pradesh, Maharashtra, Tamil Nadu and Karnataka have been causing influenced to the environmental irreparable damage in these states.

Figure 2 represents the overall growth rate of industries in India by states for the decade 1981–1991 and 1991–2001. In the decade of 1981–1991 few states like Himachal Pradesh, Andhra Pradesh, Uttar Pradesh, Rajasthan and Gujarat recorded a higher growth in number of industries and comparatively low growth rate in registered industries in the country as a whole. But, in recent decades, due to liberalisation and globalisation, and of late creating of Special Economic Zones industrial growth rate has been higher in India. The average decadal rate of growth has increased from 7.08 per cent in the decade 1981–1991 to 19.04 per cent in 1991–2001. The state of Himachal Pradesh recorded the highest growth rate in industries in both the decades (see Table 2). Industrially, fast growing states like Rajasthan, Haryana, Tamil Nadu, Manipur, Karnataka and Maharashtra achieved 38.15 per cent, 37.93, 36.42, 25.84, 19.42 and 18.36 per cent growth respectively. Further, these have achieved a growth rate higher than that of human population. This has contributed a great extent in polluting land, air and water. The environmental degradation is more as a result of industrial pollution in the states of Himachal Pradesh, Rajasthan, Haryana, Tamil Nadu, Manipur, Karnataka and Maharashtra. Conversely, states of Assam, Bihar, Madhya Pradesh, and Tripura have negative growth rates of industries (Figure 2). While rest of the states, i.e., Meghalaya, Orissa, Punjab and West Bengal have comparatively low growth rate of industries and correspondingly as well as lower environmental degradation index. But some of these states have earlier industrial base (West Bengal, Tamil Nadu, Karnataka, Maharashtra and Gujarat) and some of them have sensitive forest and water ecosystem (Karnataka, Maharashtra, Bihar, Uttar Pradesh and Madhya Pradesh). There may be Western Ghats and

Figure 2 ***Decadal Growth Rate of Industries in States of India***

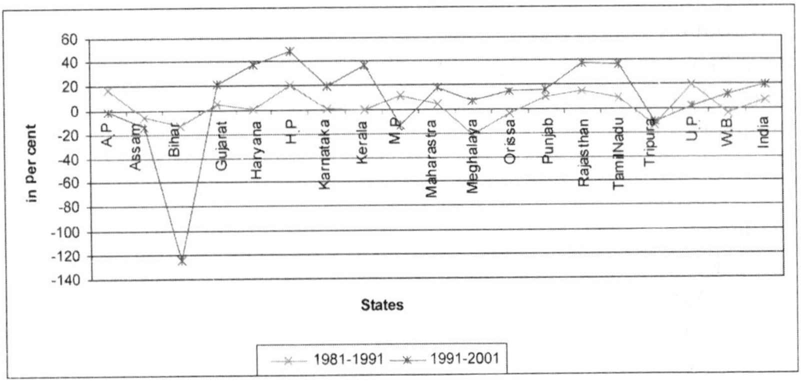

mid-Himalayan sections where mineral discharge and often industrial growth with least concern for environment has created ecological damages (Limestone quarrying in Uttarakhand, iron ore and coal mining in other states and establishment of aluminium and a host of cement industries, etc.).

States having either lower or negative growth of industries does not mean that they have low or negative index of environmental degradation. States which have had rapid growth industrially and consequent absolute rise in population (case of West Bengal, etc.), immigration to big industrial cities like Bangalore in Karnataka, Lucknow in Uttar Pradesh, Patna in Bihar, etc., too have recorded much higher levels of environmental damage. The recent policy of taking industries to backward areas is also adding to environmental degradation because in few cases this has necessitated the need to build coal-based thermal power stations. Increased infrastructure, though to some extent justified, has often resulted in such projects eating away useful agricultural lands. We have to wait and watch the impact of creation of Special Economic Zones on environment. However, there is a need to halt this mindless growth. Comparing Indian situation with that of industrial set-up in western nations and of late with China is not a healthy trend. There is a need to link growth with sustainability and to our needs rather than always competing with western standards.

Population Growth, Registered Vehicles and Environment

The environmental problems in India of late are getting aggravated by the kind of socio-economic development vis-à-vis the availability of natural resources as also the lifestyles of its population. In India, rapid growth of population, poverty, urbanisation, industrialisation and several related factors are responsible for the rapid degradation of the environment. A near lack of vision is apparent on part of our planners and they have instead of promoting means of mass public transport, allowed corporate automobile industry to market a dangerously high number of cars, two-wheelers, etc., in total disregard to environmental factors and carrying capacity of our road network.

Increasing vehicular traffic in India is the main source of air pollution in most of our cities. They emit carbon monoxide, sulphur dioxide, nitric oxide sulphur oxide and create dust particles in the air, etc. In India, the southern state of Tamil Nadu has recorded the higher growth rate (72.8%) of registered vehicles (Figure 3). This is followed in

Figure 3 ***Growth of Registered Vehicles in States of India***

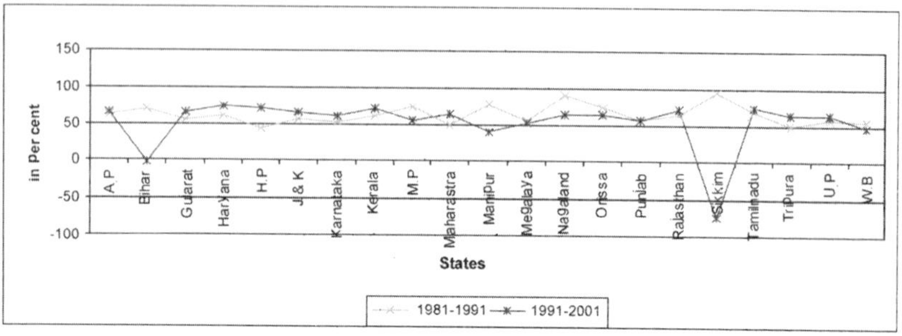

ranking order by states of Haryana, Rajasthan, Kerala, Himachal Pradesh, Arunachal Pradesh, Andhra Pradesh, Orissa, Gujarat, Goa, Nagaland, Maharashtra, Tripura, Uttar Pradesh and Karnataka (Refer Table 3). Further, these states have also registered higher growth rates in number of registered vehicles in the decade 1991–2001 over that of human population growth.

States of Sikkim and Bihar have shown negative growth in number of registered vehicles (–74.1 and –1.94% respectively). Comparatively, the state of Manipur registered lower rate of growth (39.27%). The rest of states have recorded growth ranging between 50 to 60 per cent.

From the above analysis, it is clear that, states of Sikkim and Bihar have less environmental degradation caused by vehicular pollution. The states of Tamil Nadu, Haryana, Kerala, Himachal Pradesh, Arunachal Pradesh, Rajasthan, Andhra Pradesh, Orissa, Gujarat, Nagaland, Maharashtra, Tripura, Uttar Pradesh and Karnataka have higher degree of vehicular pollution levels, due to increasing number of transport and non-transport vehicles.

Except West Bengal, other states have relatively lower levels of environmental degradation caused by vehicular pollution. But, industrialised states like West Bengal where generation of thermal power is the main polluter and affluent states like Punjab and Haryana have remarkable air pollution in urban areas. In general, it is the proliferation of motor vehicles (two- and three-wheelers) that has been causing significant levels of environmental degradation. There is a need for evolving of people and environmental-friendly transport policies (mass transit in cities) to prevent not only degrading environment but also conserve precious foreign exchange which otherwise would be spent on importing oil.

Environmental Degradation Index (EDI)

The Environmental Degradation Index (EDI) has been prepared to know the degradation in different states in India by selected indicators for the present decade (1991–2001). The appropriate weightages have been assigned to selected aspects of growth in number of industries, growth in number of registered motor vehicles and forest degraded area (per 1,000 sq km) and their link with population growth. If the growth rate is below 20 per cent, the scoring is 1; for growth rate between 21–40 per cent the scoring is 2; followed by 41–60 (3), 61–80 (4), and if the growth rate is negative the scoring assigned is 0.

As per the EDI the states of Madhya Pradesh, Himachal Pradesh, Haryana, Gujarat, Maharashtra, Orissa, Rajasthan and Jammu&Kashmir have relatively high degree of environmental degradation. The states of Andhra Pradesh, Manipur, Meghalaya, Punjab, Tripura, West Bengal, Karnataka, Kerala, Tamil Nadu and Uttar Pradesh show relatively medium level environmental degradation. The backward state of Bihar and the smaller state of Sikkim have relatively low environmental degradation (Appendix 1 b).

Similarly, an effort has been made to understand the EDI by individual aspects. According to this the southern states of Kerala and Tamil Nadu suffer from relatively low level environmental degradation due to deforestation. The states of Maharashtra, Nagaland, Orissa, Sikkim and Madhya Pradesh suffer from relatively high levels of environmental degradation due to deforestation. Rest of the states which have been listed in appendix 1 (c), suffer from relatively medium level environmental degradation due to deforestation.

Interestingly, in spite of hosting a very high in numbers of registered industries the southern state of Andhra Pradesh still shows relatively low environmental degradation. Environmental damage by growth of industries in the backward states of Bihar, M.P., and north-eastern state of Tripura is relatively moderate. States like Himachal Pradesh, Gujarat, Haryana, J&K, Manipur, and Rajasthan suffer from relatively very high environmental damage and rest of the states (Appendix 1 d) show relatively high levels of environmental degradation due to growth of registered industries.

If we examine the environmental degradation by the individual aspect of growth in number of registered motor vehicles, the states of Bihar and Manipur have relatively low levels of degradation (scores 2 and 3). States of Andhra Pradesh, Kerala, Madhya Pradesh, Manipur,

Meghalaya, Punjab, Tamil Nadu and West Bengal have show relatively moderate levels of environmental degradation (scores 4 and 5). The rest of the states, i.e., Nagaland, Gujarat, Haryana, Himachal Pradesh, J&K, Karnataka, Maharashtra, Orissa, Rajasthan, Tripura, and Uttar Pradesh, show relatively high levels of environmental degradation attributed to vehicular pollution (Appendix, e).

Summary and Conclusions

Currently, the global population is growing by 77 million a year, and India is the seventh largest country in the world, and home for 16.7 per cent of the world population. Due to drastic decline and its degradation in forest area witnessed in states of Bihar, Uttar Pradesh and Madhya Pradesh which have significantly higher growth of population. Hence, it is safe to infer that deforestation and degradation of forest areas in Bihar, Uttar Pradesh and Madhya Pradesh are the cause of environmental degradation in these states. Though, the north and north-eastern states of Sikkim, Manipur, Nagaland, Meghalaya, Mizoram, Arunachal Pradesh, Jammu&Kashmir have higher growth rate of population and are also endowed with a higher percentage of forest area to the total geographical area. Hence, the man-environment relationship is quite interesting and impressive in these states and to some extent degradation of environment is not so much deteriorated. One could note that, these states show less environmental degradation by deforestation. In the states of Madhya Pradesh, Arunachal Pradesh, Orissa, Maharashtra, Rajasthan, Bihar and Uttar Pradesh degraded forest area is more. Hence, more attention needs to be given to forest management and appropriate and useful steps to avoid further deforestation and conservation of bio-diversity are needed to be taken expeditiously.

The rapid rate of industrialisation since the 1970s has been causing massive environmental degradation. In the wake of globalisation and economic liberalisation , the growth rate of industries in the states of India was quite high in the decade 1991–2001, as compared to previous decades. The decadal growth of industries of India increased from 7.08 per cent in 1971–1981 to 19.04 per cent by the decade 1991–2001. The states of Himachal Pradesh, Rajasthan, Haryana, Tamil Nadu, Kerala, Jammu & Kashmir, Manipur, and Karnataka have a growth rate of industries which is higher than the national average of 19 per cent. Further, growth rate of industrialisation is higher than the rate of human population growth. Hence, environmental degradation is higher in these states compared to other states in India. Therefore, there is need to implement stringent industrial policies to control industrial pollution in order to ensure sustainable environment.

Increasing vehicular pollution in India is the main source of air pollution in most of the cities. The states of Tamil Nadu, Haryana, Kerala, Himachal Pradesh, Arunachal Pradesh, Rajasthan, Andhra Pradesh, Orissa, Maharashtra and Karnataka have higher industrial growth with rapid increase in number of motor vehicles and this rate of growth is found to be higher than the rate of human population growth. Hence, comparatively these states suffer from higher air pollution by the increased number of transport and non-transport vehicles. In this regard, what is most urgently needed is to implement strict vehicular emission norms by the respective state governments. The situation further warrants to follow CPCB's recommendations to prohibit twenty-year old vehicles from plying effect from December 1998, followed by phasing out of seventeen-year old vehicles from November 98 and fifteen-year old vehicles with effect from December 98. Above all, long range environment friendly mass transit system must be developed.

North-eastern state of Sikkim and the economically backward state of Bihar registered negative rates of growth in the number of registered motor vehicles. Therefore, there is comparatively less environmental pollution in these states caused by motor vehicles. Similarly, the states of Manipur, Meghalaya, Mizoram, West Bengal, Assam and Madhya Pradesh have low levels of environmental degradation caused by vehicular pollution as compared to other states.

Table 2 ***Population and Forest Area of the States 1971 and 2001***

State	*Decadal Growth Rate of Population*			*Percentage of Forest Area to the Total Geographic Area*			*Forest Degraded Area (per 1,000 sq km)*
	1971-1981	*1981-1991*	*1991-2001*	*1981*	*1991*	*2001*	*2000*
Andhra Pradesh	23.1	23.91	13.86	23.3	23.18	23.2	37.34
Arunachal Pradesh	*	35.86	26.21	61.54	61.54	61.55	N.A.
Assam	N.C.	52.44	18.85	36.47	39.14	34.45	7.95
Bihar	24.06	23.49	28.43	16.83	16.8	6.45	15.62

Cont'd...

Cont'd...

Chhattisgarh	@	@	18.06	@	@	43.85	N.A.
Goa	*	15.96	14.89	*	33.76	33.07	N.A.
Gujarat	27.67	20.8	22.48	9.96	9.85	9.69	6.83
Haryana	28.75	26.27	28.06	3.67	3.84	3.51	0.74
Himachal Pradesh	23.71	19.39	17.53	38.05	38.3	66.52	5.34
Jammu & Kashmir	29.69	N.A.	29.04	10.17	9.08	9.1	10.34
Jharkhand	@	@	23.19	@	@	29.61	N.A.
Karnataka	26.75	20.66	17.25	19.74	20.14	20.19	20.43
Kerala	19.24	14.06	9.42	28.95	28.86	28.87	2.26
Madhya Pradesh	25.27	26.75	24.34	34.63	35.04	30.89	71.95
Maharashtra	24.54	25.43	22.57	20.82	20.84	20.13	28.41
Manipur	32.46	28.56	30.02	67.87	67.87	78.01	14.24
Meghalaya	32.04	31.8	29.94	36.68	37.95	42.34	11.03
Mizoram	*	38.98	29.18	*	75.58	75.59	N.A.
Nagaland	50.05	56.86	64.41	17.25	52.02	52.05	8.78
Orissa	20.17	19.5	15.94	38.67	38.24	37.34	32.27
Punjab	23.89	20.26	19.76	4.45	5.6	6.07	0.79
Rajasthan	32.97	28.07	28.33	8.95	9.14	9.49	19.33
Sikkim	50.77	28.17	32.98	76.8	37.34	81.24	1.5
Tamil Nadu	17.5	14.94	11.19	16.75	17.2	17.59	10.09
Tripura	31.92	33.69	15.74	57.2	60.06	60.01	8.65
Uttar Pradesh	25.49	25.41	25.8	17.39	17.43	6.98	14.26
Uttaranchal	@	@	19.2	@	@	64.81	N.A.
West Bengal	23.17	24.55	17.84	13.33	13.38	13.38	3.59
India	24.66	23.5	21.34	22.41	22.41	23.38	

Source: (1) Compendium of Environment Statistics, India 2002.

(2) Statistical Abstract 1986, 1992 and 2003.

Note: @ New state.

* Union territory.

N.C.: Census was not conducted.

Table 3 Growth of Industries in States of India, 1971–2001

State	*Decadal Growth Rate of Poplation*			*Growth of Registered Industries (in %)*	
	1971–1981	*1981–1991*	*1991–2001*	*1981–1991*	*1991–2001*
Andhra Pradesh	23.1	23.91	13.86	17.18	-1.87
Arunachal Pradesh	*	35.86	26.21	*	N.A.
Assam	N.C.	52.44	18.85	-6.14	-14.56
Bihar	24.06	23.49	28.43	-13.19	-124.69
Chhattisgarh	@	@	18.06	@	@
Goa	*	15.96	14.89	*	*
Gujarat	27.67	20.8	22.48	5.49	21.2
Haryana	28.75	26.27	28.06	0.58	37.93
Himachal Pradesh	23.71	19.39	17.53	20.69	48.52
Jammu & Kashmir	29.69	N.A.	29.04	-40.53	25.84
Jharkhand	@	@	23.19	@	@
Karnataka	26.75	20.66	17.25	0.83	19.42
Kerala	19.24	14.06	9.42	-0.81	36.7
Madhya Pradesh	25.27	26.75	24.34	11.03	-12.88
Maharashtra	24.54	25.43	22.57	3.84	18.36
Manipur	32.46	28.56	30.02	0	25.42
Meghalaya	32.04	31.8	29.94	-21.43	6.67
Mizoram	*	38.98	29.18	*	N.A.
Nagaland	50.05	56.86	64.41	N.A.	N.A.
Orissa	20.17	19.5	15.94	-3.86	14.11
Punjab	23.89	20.26	19.76	10.29	15.97
Rajasthan	32.97	28.07	28.33	14.23	38.15
Sikkim	50.77	28.17	32.98	N.A.	N.A.
Tamil Nadu	17.5	14.94	11.19	9.02	36.42
Tripura	31.92	33.69	15.74	-14.29	-11.3
Uttar Pradesh	25.49	25.41	25.8	19.83	2.4
Uttaranchal	@	@	19.2	@	@
West Bengal	23.17	24.55	17.84	-3.99	11.03
India	24.66	23.5	21.34	7.08	19.04

Source: Statistical Abstract 1986, 1992 and 2003.

Note: @ Not existing.

* Union territory.

N.A.: Census was not conducted.

Table 4 *Growth of Motor Vehicles in States of India, 1971–2001*

State	*Decadal Growth Rate of Population*			*Growth of Registered Motor Vehicles (in %)*	
	1971–1981	*1981–1991*	*1991–2001*	*1981–1991*	*1991–2001*
Andhra Pradesh	23.1	23.91	13.86	62.46	66.31
Arunachal Pradesh	*	35.86	26.21	*	72.43
Assam	N.C.	52.44	18.85	60.05	52.41
Bihar	24.06	23.49	28.43	70.63	-1.94
Chhattisgarh	@	@	18.06	@	@
Goa	*	15.96	14.89	@	64.13
Gujarat	27.67	20.8	22.48	54.16	65.84
Haryana	28.75	26.27	28.06	60.54	72.65
Himachal Pradesh	23.71	19.39	17.53	43.69	72.53
Jammu & Kashmir	29.69	N.A.	29.04	57.47	65.65
Jharkhand	@	@	23.19	@	@
Karnataka	26.75	20.66	17.25	52.77	60.59
Kerala	19.24	14.06	9.42	60.8	72.02
Madhya Pradesh	25.27	26.75	24.34	72.9	53.97
Maharashtra	24.54	25.43	22.57	48.88	63.54
Manipur	32.46	28.56	30.02	77.4	39.27
Mehgalaya	32.04	31.8	29.94	55.09	52.86
Mizoram	*	38.98	29.18	*	53.34
Nagaland	50.05	56.86	64.41	90.94	63.55
Orissa	20.17	19.5	15.94	73.73	65.09
Punjab	23.89	20.26	19.76	56.95	57.16
Rajasthan	32.97	28.07	28.33	64	71.91
Sikkim	50.77	28.17	32.98	94.36	-74.1
Tamil Nadu	17.5	14.94	11.19	68.21	72.8
Tripura	31.92	33.69	15.74	50.01	63.36
Uttar Pradesh	25.49	25.41	25.8	58.24	63.3
Uttaranchal	@	@	19.2	@	@
West Bengal	23.17	24.55	17.84	44.47	46.91
India	24.66	23.5	21.34	54.03	67.49

Source: Statistical Abstract 1986, 1992 and 2003.

Note: @ Not existing.

* Union territory.

N.A.: Census was not conducted.

References

Centre for Science and Environment. 1982. The State of India's Environment, New Delhi.

Datta, Ray, H.K. Mazhari, P.M. Passah and M.C. Pandey. 2000. *Population Poverty and Environment in North East India.* New Delhi: Concept Publishing Company.

Government of India. 1991. *Statistical Abstract.* New Delhi: Central Statistical Organisation.

John, J. Fagan. 1974. *The Earth Environment.* London: Prentice Hall International Inc.

Registrar General of India. 2001. *Population Census Abstract 2001.* New Delhi.

Robertson, David and Aynsley Kellow. 2001. *Globalisation and the Environment.* UK: Edward Elgar Publishing Limited.

Sharma, Goutham. 1989. *Environment Man and Nature.* New Delhi: Reliance Publishing House.

——. 1992. All India Report on Agricultural Census, Department of Agriculture and Cooperation, Ministry of Agriculture, Krishi Bhavan, New Delhi, 110001.

——. 2001. *Statistical Abstract.* New Delhi: Central Statistical Organisation.

——. 2002a. *Compendium of Environment Statistics.* New Delhi: Central Statistical Organisation.

The World Bank. 2004. Sustaining Forests. The International Bank for Reconstruction and Development, Washington.

Timothy, M. Swanson. 1996. The Economics of Environmental Degradation. UK, UNEP.

UNEP. 2002b. *Global Environment Outlook 3.* London: Earthscan Publications Ltd.

United Nations. 1992. Nations of the Earth Report. UNCED, Geneva.

World Resources Institute. 2000–2001. People and Ecosystem. Washington www.indiastat.com.

Appendix 1a ***Environmental Degradation Index (EDI)***

S. No.	State	PG	IG	VG	FDA	PG+ IG	PG+VG	PG+FDA	Total
1.	Andhra Pradesh	1	0	4	2	1	5	3	7
2.	Arunachal Pradesh	–	–	4	–	–	–	–	–
3.	Assam	–	0	3	1	–	–	–	–
4.	Bihar	2	0	0	1	2	2	3	3
5.	Goa	–	–	4	–	–	–	–	–
6.	Gujarat	2	2	4	1	4	6	3	9
7.	Haryana	2	2	4	1	4	6	3	9
8.	Himachal Pradesh	2	3	4	1	5	6	3	10
9.	J&K	2	2	4	1	4	6	3	9
10.	Karnataka	2	1	4	1	3	6	3	8
11.	Kerala	1	2	4	1	3	5	2	8
12.	Madhya Pradesh	2	0	3	4	2	5	6	9
13.	Maharashtra	2	1	4	2	3	6	4	9
14.	Manipur	2	2	2	1	4	4	3	7
15.	Meghalaya	2	1	3	1	3	5	3	7
16.	Mizoram	–	–	3	–	–	–	–	–
17.	Nagaland	3	–	4	1	–	7	4	–
18.	Orissa	2	1	4	2	3	6	4	9
19.	Punjab	2	1	3	1	3	5	3	7
20.	Rajasthan	2	2	4	1	4	6	3	9
21.	Sikkim	3	–	0	1	–	–	4	4
22.	Tamil Nadu	1	2	4	1	3	5	2	8
23.	Tripura	2	0	4	1	2	6	3	7
24.	U.P.	2	1	4	1	3	6	3	8
25.	West Bengal	2	1	3	1	3	5	3	7

Source: Computed by the scoring from the individual aspects.

Note: P.G. refers to population growth, I.G., industrial growth, V.G., vehicle growth and FDA, forest degraded area in sq km. Population growth in percentage.

Appendix 1b ***Classification of Environmental Degradation by the Selected Aspects of P.G., I.G., V.G., and FDA by States of India***

Relatively Low (Total scoring 3 to 4)	*Bihar and Sikkim*
Relatively Medium (7–8)	Karnataka, Kerala, Tamil Nadu, U.P., Andhra Pradesh, Manipur, Meghalaya, Punjab, Tripura and West Bengal
Relatively High (9–10)	Himachal Pradesh, Gujarat, Haryana, J&K, Madhya Pradesh, Maharashtra, Orissa, Rajasthan

Appendix 1c ***Classification of Environmental Degradation by Forest Degraded Area in States of India***

Relatively Low (Total score 2)	*Kerala and Tamil Nadu*
Relatively Medium (3)	Andhra Pradesh, Bihar, Gujarat, Haryana, Himachal Pradesh, J&K, Karnataka, Manipur, Meghalaya, Punjab, Rajasthan, Tripura, U.P., West Bengal
Relatively High (4)	Maharashtra, Nagaland, Orissa, Sikkim
Relatively Very High (6)	Madhya Pradesh

Appendix 1d ***Classification of Environmental Degradation by Industrial Growth in States of India***

Classification	*States*
Relatively Low (Total Scoring 1or 2)	Andhra Pradesh, Bihar, M.P., Tripura
Relatively Moderate (Total Scoring 3)	Karnataka, Kerala, Maharashtra, Meghalaya, Orissa, Punjab, Tamil Nadu, U.P., West Bengal
Relatively High (Total Scoring 5)	Himachal Pradesh, Gujarat, Haryana, J&K, Manipur, Rajasthan

Appendix 1e ***Classification of Environmental Degradation by the Growth of Vehicles in States of India***

Relatively Low (Total score 3 and 4)	*Bihar, Manipur*
Relatively Moderate (Total score 5)	Andhra Pradesh, Kerala, Madhya Pradesh, Manipur, Meghalaya, Punjab, Tamil Nadu, West Bengal
Relatively High (Total score 6 and 7)	Nagaland, Gujarat, Haryana, Himachal Pradesh, J&K, Karnataka, Maharastra, Orissa, Rajasthan, Tripura, U.P.

Source: Computed From Table 1, 2 and 3.

9

Understanding Environmental Concern

Application of New Environmental Paradigm Scale in Rural West Bengal

Pradip Swarnakar and Arun Kumar Sharma

In India, life, prosperity and civilisation revolve around water. The picture of West Bengal state is not different from rest of the country. In the recent past, however, water, the most precious resource, has come under threat. There is evidence of widespread contamination and scarcity of water resources in many areas of this state. The present study deals with the relationship between *visibility of risk* and *environmental concerns* with respect to water consumption in West Bengal state of India. It may be noted that the rise of global environmentalism, environmental activism, and social movements due to ever-increasing environmental problems has led many social scientists to focus on environmental concern. However, the way in which the term environmental concern has been conceptualised and operationalised is still subject to debate. This study is based on application of New Environmental Scale (NEP) developed by Dunlap and others to measure general environmental beliefs.

A number of studies reveal that citizens in both industrialised and developing countries exhibit high degree of concern for the environment (Brechin and Kempton 1994; Dunlap, Gallup and Gallup 1993; Dunlap and Mertig 1995). Further, environmental concern has typically been associated with variables such as age, gender, income, education, urbanity, and political ideology (Guagnano and Markee 1995; Scott and Willis 1994; Stern, Dietz and Kalof 1993). Several researchers have shown that disadvantaged groups within a society have greater stake in environmental protection, given that they disproportionately experienced the costs of environmental degradation (Buttel and Flinn 1978; Neiman and Loveridge 1981; Martinez-Alier 1995). Dunlap et al. (1993) also show that the citizens of developing countries were no less concerned than citizens of industrialised countries. Brechin and Kempton (1994) back this by suggesting that concern for the environment should be seen as a global phenomenon, emerging from multiple sources, such as direct exposure to environmental degradation, the political and institutional framework in a given community, and the effects of mass media, rather than being determined only by the level of economic development. It has been suggested that special emphasis should be placed on 'concrete and specific' environmental issues rather than 'abstract and hypothetical' measures of general environmental concern (Wall 1995), and look at the geographical proximity of a particular environmental problem.

Dimensionality of Environmental Concern

Bamberg (2003: 21) states that environmental concern is used "to refer to the whole range of environmentally related perceptions, emotions, knowledge, attitude, values and behaviour." For several decades, environmental concern has been an extensively researched construct. Investigators have attempted to identify variables which influence the level of environmental concern. The variety and number of independent variables which relate to environmental concern is vast (Buttel and Johnson, 1977), and research results have sometimes been supportive of previous results and sometimes contradictory. Some studies appear to have treated environmental concern as a uni-dimensional construct, determined, of course, by either a single variable or a group of variables. For those who view environmental concern as a multi-dimensional construct, this way of thinking tends to promote the idea that people are either concerned about the environment or they are not, and largely ignores the (possibly different) motives that people may have for being concerned about the environment. Buttel and Johnson (1977: 50) claim that "environmentalists are not all cut from the same cloth", and add that the sometimes supportive and sometimes contradictory research results may originate from the multi-dimensional nature of environmental concern.

From various researches it has been found that in literature the term "dimension" is used rather loosely. Various researchers have approached the investigation and measurement of environmental issues from different viewpoints, and have employed concepts which may fall into the category of "multiple dimensions", such as ameliorative/redirective (Buttel and Johnson, 1977), environmental degradation/environmental action/overpopulation (Lounsbury and Tornatsky, 1977), substantive/theoretical (Van Liere and Dunlap, 1981), utilitarian/moral relevance (Seligman, 1989), instrumental/spiritual (Stokols, 1990), attitudinal/self-efficacy/desire for certain outcomes (Axelrod and Lehman, 1993), egoistic/social altruistic/biospheric (Stern, Dietz and Kalof, 1993), anthropocentric/ ecocentric (Gagnon, Thompson and Barton, 1994), and passive/active (Willers, 1996). From a study of 32 Wisconsin communities, Buttel and Johnson (1977) found that environmental concern issues are at least bi-dimensional, and proposed ameliorative and redirective dimensions. These two dimensions focus on two different approaches to solve environmental problems. The ameliorative dimension favours the seeking of solutions within the context in which problems presently occur, for example, financial incentives to encourage more efficient use of natural resources, or technological solutions to reduce pollution. The redirective dimension favours a more radical, aggressive approach to solving environmental problems by challenging the status quo and demanding, in effect, that proper environmental planning be seen as an integral part of industry and society, rather than something to be added on if the need arises.

Axelrod and Lehman (1993) state that past research identifies several factors or combinations of factors which relate to environmentally responsible behaviour, and suggest that these factors may be categorised into three domains: attitudinal, self-efficacy, and desire for certain outcomes. The attitudinal domain focuses on the ability of attitudes to predict behaviour, that is, people act in accordance with their beliefs relating to an attitude object. Self-efficacy refers to people's knowledge or perceived ability to act in accordance with their attitudes, and desire for outcomes refers to the confidence or expectation that actions will produce a desired result. Willers (1996) proposes that the two categories of concern, namely, passive and active, are indicative of the bi-dimensional nature of environmental concern. The association between the categories of passive and active concern, and an external versus internal locus of control, respectively, is evident.

Seligman (1989) distinguishes between two approaches to man's relationship with the natural environment. The first, utilitarian approach, assumes that the value of nature results from the degree to which it satisfies the needs and wants of human beings. The second approach assumes that non-human aspects of the natural environment have inherent value apart from their utilitarian value to human beings, and are, therefore, morally relevant.

Stokols (1990) suggests two philosophical approaches to man-environment interaction: the instrumentalist and the spiritualist. The former sees nature purely as a means which humans may use in order to achieve their goals, while the latter sees the natural environment as contributing to the spiritual enrichment of people, and, therefore, having value independent of its usefulness in facilitating the achievement of human materialistic goals.

Stern, Dietz and Kalof (1993) propose three values, each of which provides a different reason why people may be environmentally concerned. Egoistic values relate to the natural environment because of their importance to the self; social altruistic values focus on the natural environment because of their importance to other people; and biospheric values focus on the inherent values of all aspects of the natural environment itself. Egoistic and social altruistic values have a common characteristic that they both focus on outcomes for humans.

Gagnon Thompson and Barton (1994: 149) propose a bi-dimensional approach to understanding environmental concern, and suggest that there are (at least) two motives, or reasons, which motivate people to be concerned about the natural environment: ecocentric and anthropocentric. Individuals showing ecocentric motive value nature for its own sake, and, therefore, argue that it deserves protection. In contrast, individuals showing anthropocentric value feel that the environment should be protected because of its value in maintaining or enhancing the quality of life for humans but not for its own sake.

In the recent past, works by Schultz (2000, 2001) provide evidence in support of maintaining a distinction between the altruistic and egoistic value orientations proposed by Stern, Dietz and Kalof (1993). Recently, several researchers have conceptualised a global, more general measure of environmental concern, while still giving importance to the existence of local or specific factors (Lewis, 2003).

New Environmental Paradigm (NEP) Scale for Environmental Beliefs/Concern

Environmental concern and problems of measuring it emerged in the formative years of the sub-discipline of environmental sociology. Environmental sociology is the study of the reciprocal interactions between the physical environment, social organisation, and social behaviour. Within this approach, environment encompasses all physical and material bases of life on a scale ranging from the most micro level to the biosphere. Catton and Dunlap published their pioneering papers in *The American Sociologist* and *Annual Review of Sociology* in the late 1970s (Catton and Dunlap, 1978, 1980; Dunlap and Catton, 1979). Since then environmental sociology has made major strides and emerged as an important sub-discipline in the broad area of sociology.

A diversity of paradigms, themes and levels of analysis has characterised environmental sociology. However, despite this diversity, a minimal identity of the sub-discipline has been established through significant empirical research and a theoretical contribution "self-consciously fashioned as a critique to 'mainstream' sociology" (Buttel, 1987). One of the most crucial elements of the new approach to environmental thinking is: what are people's beliefs regarding environment. Environmental beliefs can be defined as ethical-normative cognitions concerning the relationship between humans and nature. Analogous to nature images, environmental beliefs are often classified according to their position on a dimension ranging from anthropocentric to ecocentric (Catton and Dunlap, 1980). Individuals holding anthropocentric environmental beliefs view nature as subordinate to humans, who are seen as rulers or managers of the natural world. Individuals holding ecocentric environmental beliefs regard nature as the most important reality, and view humans as only part of that reality. Environmental beliefs, or worldviews, of the relationship between humans and their natural surroundings have been mentioned as potential predictors of conservation behaviour (Scott and Willits, 1994). Gray (1985) posits environmental beliefs as underlying a system of attitudes and beliefs that determine behaviour towards the environment. According to these authors, environmental beliefs are referential frameworks, which are used when interacting with the environment.

In order to assess individual differences in environmental beliefs, Dunlap and Van Liere (1978) have developed the New Environmental Paradigm (NEP)[1] scale. In theory, pro-ecological beliefs like those constituting a "New Environmental Paradigm" are precedents to environmental actions. Conversely, anthropocentric beliefs like the "Human Exception Paradigm" would preclude the development of pro-ecological behaviours. According to Stern, Dietz and Guagnano (1995: 783), the NEP-HEP is "a paradigm or worldview—a set of generalised beliefs about human—environment relations". If, as they assert, these environmental beliefs are indirect predictors of specific pro-ecological behaviours, then their predictive ability should be assessed along with the mediating variables. In 1978, for the first time, Dunlap and Van Liere proposed a twelve-item scale to measure environmental beliefs. Each item was measured through a five-point Likert type scale using categories from 'strongly agree' to 'strongly disagree'.

Of late, NEP scale developed by Dunlap, Van Liere, Mertig, and Jones (2000) has been used frequently for the measurement of general attitudes/values/concerns/beliefs regarding man-nature relationship. It is a fifteen-item scale and presents an improvement over the twelve-item scale developed earlier. It may be noted that in such measurements, the terms like 'environmental belief', 'environmental attitude', 'environmental concern' and 'environmental worldview' are used interchangeably (Dunlap and Jones, 2002; Fransson and Gärling, 1999; Schultz and Zelezny, 1999, 2003). The present study too uses the term 'environmental beliefs' to depict the sum total of beliefs, affects, and behavioural intentions a person holds regarding environmentally related activities or issues. From this perspective, environmental concern is one aspect of the environmental attitude. The term 'environmental worldview' is used to refer to a person's beliefs about humanity's relationship with nature (Dunlap and Van Liere, 1978; Dunlap et al., 2000). Numerous applications of the scale—in integral or modified forms—have made it a well-tested instrument.

The 1978 scale of Dunlap and Van Liere, contained twelve items, which were subsequently separated into three dimensions of environmental beliefs: (a) a worldview of a 'natural balance' between humans and the rest of the nature; (b) a perspective emphasising the need to impose 'limits to growth' on human activities; and (c) a 'human exception' paradigm which sees humans as outside the rules of the natural world (Albretch, et al., 1982). Several authors argued that there is a need to revise NEP scale for both conceptual and operational reasons. In response to this, Dunlap et al. presented a revised NEP scale. The revised NEP scale is designed to improve upon the original one in several respects. Dunlap et al. claim that the revised scale has three desirable qualities: (a) it taps a wider range of facets of an ecological worldview; (b) it offers a balanced set of pro- and anti-NEP items; and (c) it claims to avoid outmoded terminology. A set of 15 items (including 6 from the original NEP scale, four of which are modified very slightly) is constructed to achieve these qualities. Three items are designed to tap each of the five hypothesised facets of an ecological worldview: the reality of limits to growth; anti-anthropocentricism; the fragility of nature's balance; rejection of exemptionalism; and the possibility of an eco-crisis. Although Dunlap et al., (2000) have somewhat broadened the definition of the measured subject, it is still too fragmentary for the measurement of ecological paradigm or ecological values. It seems that reluctance to define the subject more fully is based on their intention to construct a practical and uni-dimensional measure.

The measures developed and theories available in the West needed improvisation as the socio-economic and cultural context of India is not same as of the West. In the West most of the empirical studies use Dunlap scale (Dunlap et al., 1978, 2000) for measuring environmental concern. Some studies question its universality. In the context of less developed countries, essay on Nigerian environmentalism, Adeola (1996) questioned universal applicability of NEP scales. Freudenburg (1991) stresses on the requirement of conceptual and methodological refinement of available scale and indexes of environmental concern for a closer geographical focus. In this context, the present research attempts at validation of Dunlap's scale and theorisation of environmental beliefs and action in India.

This study uses the modified NEP scale (with a bit of explanation of some items). However, emphasis has been given to retain the original structure and meaning of the items. The language of the original scale was English, however, for the convenience of survey the entire scale was translated in local (Bengali) language. To maintain the clarity and consistency of the expressions the Bengali version of the schedule was retranslated back by three independent translators into English. This feedback helped to revise the wordings of the Bengali schedule. To make the scale free from reporting biases, the eight odd-numbered items were worded so that agreement with them indicated a pro-ecological view and the seven even-numbered ones so that agreement indicated an anti-ecological worldview.

In this research along with NEP scale a water consumption scale was also used. So the respondents' views on general long-term environmental issues were compared with views on specific and more common day problem of water. However, this paper focuses entirely on general environmental beliefs.

The study is comparative in nature and concentrated in two districts of West Bengal. One of the two, Purulia district, belonging to the arid zone is facing scarcity of water. The other district, North 24 Parganas district, belonging to the alluvial plane and is facing contamination of arsenic in groundwater. The water supply in Purulia is seasonal, based on monsoon rains. During the dry season, existing shallow wells and surface water supplies often dry up. North 24 Parganas district does not have the scarcity of water as such but presents the problem of arsenic contamination that has caused many health issues in the area.

Objectives

The objectives of the present research are three-fold. First, it compares the degree of environmental concern at two different locations: one where people are facing scarcity of water, and another where water is contaminated with arsenic. Second, it examines the reliability of NEP scale used for comparison. Thirdly, it explores the dimensionality of the NEP scale and explores whether the NEP scale is five-dimensional as suggested by Dunlap et al. or in application to rural India it exhibits less or more dimensions.

Hypothesis

This study tests the hypothesis that environmental concerns are determined purely by external socio-economic factors independent of whether risks are visible or not. Thus, the null hypothesis is: visibility of risk (scarcity of water) produces same environmental consciousness as the invisibility of risk (arsenic contamination). Rejection of null hypothesis would lead to thinking regarding the magnitude and direction of relationship between nature of risk and degree of concern about environment.

Method

As said above, the main objective of the present research is to capture the environmental concern of rural people facing the problem of quantity and quality with respect to domestic water consumption. India is a multilingual country and for the field survey knowledge of regional language is necessary. The first author being proficient in Bengali, his mother tongue, selected West Bengal state for fieldwork.

For the selection of sample from the state the first author conducted a couple of meetings with chief engineer and minister-incharge, Public Health Engineering Department (PHED) of West Bengal government.

Along with this, informal meetings were also arranged with environmental science groups of Jadavpur University and Indian Institute of Technology, Kanpur. It may be mentioned here that West Bengal is one of the 29 states of India. It has an area of 89,193 sq km and a population of 80.1 million (Census of India, 2001). Its administrative structure consists of several districts: each district has several development blocks; each block has several *gram panchayats* (GPs), which are basically a cluster of villages. Overall, in the state there are 19 districts, 341 blocks and 37,910 villages.

The groundwater in West Bengal carries various contaminants such as: arsenic, fluoride, iron, copper, calcium, nitrate, sulphate, etc. (National Habitation Survey, 2003). Among all these contaminants, arsenic contamination is posing the greatest threat to health. This deadly inorganic substance is not visible with the naked eye and it takes two to twelve years for the manifestation of symptoms of arsenic poisoning in human body. The arsenic map of West Bengal shows that 3,417 villages in 111 blocks of 12 districts (North 24 Parganas, South 24 Parganas, Kolkata, Hoogly, Howrah, Nadia, Bardhaman, Murshidabad, Malda, Koch Bihar, North Dinajpur, and South Dinajpur) are affected by arsenic pollution in groundwater resources.[2] Among them Murshidabad and North 24 Parganas are most affected districts in which a large number of blocks have this problem. In Murshidabad, 23 blocks are affected and 15 blocks have patients with the symptoms of arsenicosis. In North 24 Parganas district 21 blocks are affected and 16 blocks have arsenic patients. It was decided that North 24 Parganas should be selected as representative of districts facing the invisible risk of arsenic as it has more blocks with arsenic patients in comparison with Murshidabad. Since 1997, over 135 well-head arsenic removal units have been installed in remote villages in several districts bordering Bangladesh. Most of these units are concentrated in North 24 Parganas. Further down, Gaighata block that has the highest number of arsenic affected villages (54 villages) in the district, was selected for the study.[3] The block is located on the Indo-Bangladesh border and has good communication with Bangaon town and Kolkata metropolis. It also has a number of international (Project-well) and national (Arsenic Dushon Protirodh Committee) non-government organisations, working to combat groundwater contamination.

To identify the areas facing scarcity of water hydro-geological map of West Bengal was consulted. Purulia, Bankura and West Medinipur districts are part of arid zone of West Bengal. Among these three districts, Purulia was selected as it has extensive hard rock area with irregular rainfall leading to scarcity of water in most years. In this district, among 14 blocks there are six blocks which fall in hard rock arid zone. They are Jhalda, Bagmundi, Balarampur, Barabazar, Manbazar and Bandwan. Bagmundi block has three different kinds of hydro-geology (upper-tertiary, pre-cambrian, and archaean) and different levels of ground water potential (moderate and limited). This block is practically devoid of ground water for domestic purposes except having a few dug wells (at hilly villages) and a few bore wells.

The final unit of data collection for the present study is 'household'. For the selection of households, household lists collected from local GPs were used. After getting the list, households were selected using computer generated random numbers. If the interviewer failed to get the data from one household for any reason, next randomly selected household was approached. An attempt was made to interview the head of the household. However, in the absence of the head, any adult (male or female) member of the same household was interviewed. During the survey in North 24 Parganas district, many males were absent in the household. In that case female members or younger male members were interviewed. Emphasis was laid on voluntary participation of the respondents. Before the interview, the respondents were informed about the broad objectives of the research. They also ensured that the data would be used for research purpose only. Yet, there were a few people who did not provide consent for the interview.

For the present research, the target sample was fixed at 320 divided equally between the two blocks of the two districts. The survey was first conducted in Gaighata block of North 24 Parganas and then in Bagmundi block of Purulia district. Due to constraints of logistics in the former a total number of 156 people could be interviewed but in the latter district only 127 respondents could be interviewed. In Purulia, the density of the population is low and in the hilly region of Bagmundi block particularly the population is widely scattered. Above all, communication and transportation facilities in the villages are very poor. From Table 1, it is evident that the size of population in Purulia habitations is very low. Here the population is dispersed over a larger area. Further, most of the people in these habitations have been migrants—seasonal and permanent—who have gone to nearby states for employment. For the same reason, in Bagti and Chikan Bagan sampling fraction is rather low and in the other two habitations, Basudi and Nandaramadi, sampling fraction is higher.

Table 1 ***Distribution of Population in Study Area***

District	*Habitation*	*Population*	*No. of Respondents*	*Per cent of Total Sample Size*
North 24 Parganas	Panchpota	1,172	80 (6.8)	28.3
North 24 Parganas	Ghoshpara	645	76 (11.8)	26.9
Purulia	Bagti	598	39 (6.5)	13.6
Purulia	Basudi	181	41 (22.6)	14.3
Purulia	Chikan Bagan	326	12 (3.7)	4.2
Purulia	Nandaramadi	125	35 (28.0)	12.2
Total		3,047	283 (9.3)	100.0

Note: Figures in parentheses represent the sampling fraction in particular habitation.

Results

Socio-economic Profile of the Respondents

Regarding the socio-economic profile of the respondents, it was found that more than half of the respondents are middle-aged, between 30–49 years. It has been noticed that the middle-aged people, particularly men, play a crucial role in decision-making both within and outside family as they are the main bread earners of the family. In North 24 Parganas, water problem came into light during the past two decades only and the middle-aged people have better understanding than the younger members of the family. The age distribution in North 24 Parganas is a little younger than in Purulia. Purulia district has a substantial number of respondents whose age is more than 60 years (17.3%).

Like age, sex too affects opinions and attitudes. As said above, initially, the head of the family was approached for interview. If he was absent then the elder male member was interviewed. When men were away then women were interviewed. There was no separate quota for women. Therefore, in this study 73.1 per cent of the respondents are males but the distribution is not same in the two districts. In North 24 Parganas, 58.3 per cent respondents are males but in Purulia around ninety-two per cent of the respondents are males. Data collection was done in the summer of 2006 when people of Gaighata were busy with cultivation, business, service, etc., whereas in Bagmundi due to lack of regular rain and proper irrigation facility, people involved in cultivation activities used to stay at home or do some part-time work and hence they were available for the interview. Moreover, Gaighata is well-connected with city and people were less apprehensive of participation in survey. Moreover, women respondents in Purulia are less exposed to the outer world. So, it was difficult for the male interviewer to manage the consent of women to participate in the study.

The survey covers both Hindus and Muslims. In North 24 Parganas district 20.5 per cent respondents practice Islam. Here it may be noted that the in-migration rate of North 24 Parganas district, particularly Gaighata block (as it has a long and unsecured border with neighbouring Bangladesh), is quite high. Not only Hindus have migrated from Bangladesh but also poor Muslims have migrated to this region. No Muslim respondent has been has been interviewed in Purulia distinct.

For the present study, caste distribution was made on the basis of four standard categories which are used by the government for official purposes (SC, ST, OBC GEN). No specific question on particular sub-caste was asked. With a rather small sample it is difficult to capture the correlation between environmental concern and sub-caste: there are a large number of sub-castes in any geographical region in India. Overall, around thirty-five per cent respondents belonged to General Castes (GEN) and thirty per cent to Other Backward Castes (OBCs). The rest belonged to Scheduled Castes and Scheduled Tribes (SCs and STs). The proportion of SC and ST respondents is much higher in North 24 Parganas than in Purulia though the proportion of Scheduled Tribe is much higher in Purulia. Representation of Other Backward Castes is 59.1 per cent in Purulia but only 8.1 per cent in North 24 Parganas. Thus, the general caste people are only 6.3 per cent in Purulia whereas in North 24 Parganas they comprise 51.6 per cent of the sample.

In various studies, it has been found that people's attitude and beliefs vary with their occupation because they undergo a process of re-socialisation in their respective occupational environment. People whose daily life is connected with various natural resources or who depend on nature to meet their needs of subsistence are expected to be more concerned about nature. On the other hand, people who earn wages, and those from middle class and upper middle class, are expected to be less concerned about nature. As the number of women is higher in North 24 Parganas, a large proportion of respondents here are housewives (32.1%). Apart from that a few respondents work on others' agricultural land as daily wage labourers. In Purulia, a large percentage of the respondents are cultivators (46.5%). However, if one looks at the amount of agricultural land possessed by the household it can be seen that in Purulia the amount of land is very meagre. People are struggling to survive with this meagre land and lack of water resources for agricultural purposes. Usually, the land is prepared for mono-crop in the rainy season. There are no student respondents in Purulia district. A sizeable number of small businessmen are there in North 24 Parganas (around 14%). It may be noted that overall one-fifth sample of the respondents belongs to semi-skilled and unskilled labour category. They don't have any fixed occupation but they work in different piecemeal jobs in various seasons.

In Purulia, most of the respondents are illiterate. From the earlier studies, it has been pointed out that education is an important impetus behind the beliefs and practices of human behaviour. Purulia not only has scarcity of water but also scarcity of education due to its remoteness and backwardness. However, only 1.6 per cent are having education level of graduate or above. In contrast, in North 24 Parganas an overwhelming majority of respondents are literate and more than 13 per cent have education level of graduate or above.

It is always difficult to find out the real income of people in non-formal rural sector. An attempt was made to ascertain approximate income from all sources to add to monthly income. The table reveals that most of the respondents have monthly income less than Rs 2,000. In Purulia, 90 per cent respondents have household income less than Rs 2,000. That means the general economic condition of this region is poor and most people are living at subsistence level. Although a substantial number of respondents in North 24 Parganas district has income below Rs 2,000, but 23.1 per cent respondents have income between Rs 2,000 and Rs 4,999.

Frequency Distributions and Item-Total Correlations of NEP Scale Items

Table 2 shows the frequency distributions of responses to items of the NEP scale. It helps to examine the variability in the general environmental beliefs in two different regions. Item total correlations are also calculated to examine whether a particular item is significant for the overall scale. Dunlap et al. (2000) were particularly interested in determining if the 15 items can legitimately be treated as measuring a single construct. A high degree of internal consistency is a necessary condition for combining a set of items into a single measure. Hence, this study examines the consistency of responses to the 15 items and for this item-total correlation for each item has been computed. Differences in item-total correlations between the regions show that a particular item may not contribute identically to environmental beliefs in the two regions—arsenic-affected region and scarcity-facing region. However, to have a more generaliseable NEP scale in rural Indian population correlations for the combined sample are also calculated.

Table 2 *Frequency Distributions and Item-Total Correlations of NEP Scale*

	Do You Agree or Disagree That:	*Location*	*SD*	*MD*	*U*	*MA*	*SA*	*ri-t*	*N*
1.	We are approaching the limit of the number of people the earth can support (within limited supply of natural resources such as land, water, air, etc.).	North 24 Parganas	11.5	9.6	14.7	26.3	37.8	.880	156
		Purulia	25.2	11.8	25.2	35.4	2.4	.850	127
		Total	17.7	10.6	19.4	30.4	21.9	.879	283
2.	Humans have the right to modify the natural environment to suit their needs.	North 24 Parganas	3.8	30.8	28.8	16.0	20.5	.753	156
		Purulia	3.9	21.3	41.7	24.4	8.7	.635	127
		Total	3.9	26.5	34.6	19.8	15.2	.674	283
3.	When humans interfere with nature it often leads to disastrous consequences.	North 24 Parganas	12.8	10.3	34.6	32.7	9.6	.793	156
		Purulia	7.1	21.3	40.9	23.6	7.1	.668	127
		Total	10.2	15.2	37.5	28.6	8.5	.732	283
4.	Human ingenuity will insure that we do not make the earth uninhabitables. (They will always be able to make newer discoveries to solve emergent problems of existence.)	North 24 Parganas	7.1	33.3	32.7	12.2	14.7	.781	156
		Purulia	1.6	17.3	37.0	24.4	19.7	.522	127
		Total	4.6	26.1	34.6	17.7	17.0	.701	283
5.	Humans are severely abusing the environment.	North 24 Parganas	4.5	14.7	37.3	28.8	18.6	.734	156
		Purulia	11.8	17.3	32.3	24.4	14.2	.727	127
		Total	7.8	15.9	32.9	26.9	16.6	.724	283
6.	The earth has plenty of natural resources if we just learn how to develop them.	North 24 Parganas	10.3	25.0	28.2	20.5	16.0	.748	156
		Purulia	3.1	13.4	33.9	29.9	19.7	.409	127
		Total	7.1	19.8	30.7	24.7	17.7	.640	283
7.	Plants and animals have as much right as humans to exist.	North 24 Parganas	7.1	13.5	5.8	9.0	64.7	.835	156
		Purulia	7.1	15.7	22.8	18.1	36.2	.677	127
		Total	7.1	14.5	13.4	13.1	51.9	.779	283
8.	Balance of nature is strong enough to cope with the impacts of modern industrial nations (such as UK or US).	North 24 Parganas	12.2	7.7	67.9	8.3	3.8	.558	156
		Purulia	2.4	11.0	70.9	7.9	7.9	.573	127
		Total	7.8	9.2	69.3	8.1	5.7	.575	283

Cont'd...

Cont'd...

9. Despite our special abilities humans are still subject to the laws of nature.	North 24 Parganas	1.9	7.1	32.1	17.9	41.0	.708	156
	Purulia	11.0	11.8	38.6	31.5	7.1	.603	127
	Total	6.0	9.2	35.0	24.0	25.8	.695	283
10. The so-called 'ecological crisis' faced by humankind has been greatly exaggerated.	North 24 Parganas	15.4	12.8	67.3	3.8	0.6	.441	156
	Purulia	1.6	10.2	67.7	13.4	7.1	.445	127
	Total	9.2	11.7	67.5	8.1	3.5	.492	283
11. The earth is a spaceship with very limited rooms and resources (such as water, land and other natural resources).	North 24 Parganas	10.3	9.0	57.1	16.0	7.7	.685	156
	Purulia	8.7	3.9	71.7	9.4	6.3	.644	127
	Total	9.5	6.7	63.6	13.1	7.1	.643	283
12. Humans were meant to rule over the rest of the nature.	North 24 Parganas	13.5	22.4	51.3	12.2	0.6	.529	156
	Purulia	3.1	17.3	29.1	34.6	15.7	.632	127
	Total	8.8	20.1	41.3	22.3	7.4	.609	283
13. The balance of nature is very delicate and easily upset.	North 24 Parganas	11.5	12.2	21.2	41.0	14.1	.792	156
	Purulia	6.3	11.8	63.0	15.0	3.9	.559	127
	Total	9.2	12.0	39.9	29.3	9.5	.725	283
14. Humans will eventually learn enough about how nature works to be able to control it.	North 24 Parganas	10.9	19.9	56.4	9.6	3.2	.568	156
	Purulia	5.5	11.8	31.5	28.3	22.8	.649	127
	Total	8.5	16.3	45.2	18.0	12.0	.631	283
15. If things continue with the present course, we will soon experience a major ecological catastrophe.	North 24 Parganas	12.8	10.3	17.9	34.0	25.0	.765	156
	Purulia	18.9	9.4	33.9	26.8	11.0	.712	127
	Total	15.5	9.9	25.1	30.7	18.7	.751	283

Note:

1. SD = Strongly Disagree, MD = Mildly Disagree, U = Unsure, MA = Mildly Agree, SA = Strongly Agree. All the numbers are in percentage.
2. Wordings in the *parenthesis* are not from original NEP scale. After pilot study these statements are included to clear the meanings of the items. The original scale is developed and tested mostly in developing countries, therefore few concepts are need to be elaborated for the understanding of rural population of India.
3. North 24 Parganas has arsenic affected villages of Gaighata block of North 24 Parganas district and Purulia has water scarce villages of Bagmundi block of Purulia district of West Bengal state of India.
4. Item-total (r_{i-t}) correlations are computed between the total score of NEP (i.e., 15 items) with each item's score.

The above table shows that there are substantial variations in the importance of different NEP items and there are also variations between two different types of villages. As mentioned earlier, the new NEP scale consists of five different dimensions of ecological worldview. They are: limits to growth; anti-anthropocentricism; fragility of nature's balance; rejection of exemptionalism, and possibility of ecocentricism. It is to be noted that eight odd-numbered items are worded so that agreement indicates a pro-ecological view and the seven even-numbered ones so that disagreement indicates a pro-ecological worldview. For the present study, odd number items are recoded so that for all the items a high value (on 1–5 point scale) indicates pro-ecological and a low value indicates anti-ecological beliefs.

Limits to Growth

Items 1, 6 and 11 reveal the 'limits to growth' dimension of the scale. They reflect people's attitudes to the idea of limits. The statement of the first item is "We are approaching the limit of the number of people the earth can support". At the time of pilot study, it was found that respondents are not properly able to understand the inherent meaning of the statement. So, "within limited supply of natural resources such as land, water, air, etc." is added for further clarification. Similarly, in case of item number 11 "such as water, land and other natural resources" is added with the original statement 'The earth is a spaceship with very limited rooms and resources'. Statement of item 6 remains unchanged. It is found that the responses to these statements are different and have regional variations. It may be noted that in Purulia more respondents remained undecided. The number of undecided respondents is highest for item number 11, where more than 71 per cent respondents were undecided in Purulia. In this particular item, respondents are unable to conceptualise the notion of 'spaceship'. In the remote villages of Purulia, people are not aware of the concept of spaceship. That's why they are unable to decide the attitude. For all items, a significant item-total correlation is found which signifies that these items have contributed significantly to the overall scale score. However, in case of item number 6, the correlation in Purulia is only 0.40, much less in comparison with other correlations. Thus, the item "The earth has plenty of natural resources if we just learn how to develop them" contributes less to overall environmental beliefs is an anti-ecological statement and in general people have a general belief that man can overcome the present environmental problem.

Anti-anthropocentricism

Anti-anthropocentric views are depicted in item numbers 2, 7 and 12. In item number 2 it is asked whether humans have the right to modify natural environment. In both the villages more than one-third of people agree with the statement. However, in North 24 Parganas nearly the same proportion of respondents disagree with this proposition. The correlations are significant in each case. Interestingly, in item number 7, human beings' and animals' coexistence are supported overwhelmingly. Ironically, on the one hand people are in favour of animals' right, i.e., giving them equal space to live, on the other they have a strong anthropocentric belief regarding human capabilities. Correlations of them 7 with overall score are significant in the total sample as well as separately for the two types of villages. In case of item number 12 results in the two regions vary. In North 24 Parganas around thirty-six per cent respondents disagree that humans are here to rule over the nature, more than 50 per cent people are undecided, and, therefore, overall agreement percentage is comparatively less than disagreement, On the contrary, in region 2 around 50 per cent people agree with the statement. It revels that arsenic contaminated villagers are facing the disaster and they are more aware than their counterpart in scarcity villages. After revisiting the scarce region, one middle-aged tribal male (a seasonal labourer) made an interesting note in this issue. He said, "human beings are not only meant to rule over the nature but also other human beings. If you are talking about water and scarcity of water you can go to the nearest town. There you cannot find any problem. You do not have to go either that far away, here in our locality you can find people who don't have any problem as such, because they are the leader, powerful people. As our locality does not vote for them they don't give us the proper facility provided by the government. Now you can understand how human beings are ruling over other human beings." This region is a poor and backward region. In general, people living here feel relatively deprived of development and hold traditional views.

Fragility of Nature's Balance

The issue of balance in nature comprises item numbers 3, 8 and 13. People believe that human interference with nature leads to disastrous consequences. In this case both the three items have significant item-total correlation in both types of the villages as well as in the combined sample. However, in majority of the cases percentage of undecided persons is high. In item number 13, Purulia, that is the arsenic-affected area, more villagers agree that the balance of nature is delicate and if human beings interfere much balance may be disrupted. Here an elderly person recalled his younger days and said, "when we were young then we didn't have problems that we are facing today. We never faced the problem of food, water and land although we did not have much prosperity. My days are numbered but my next generations are not properly realising the calamity which is about to come in a few days." Hence, it can be inferred that in arsenic affected villages people are more aware of the fragility of the balance of the nature due to their exposure to media and other urban influences.

Rejection of Exemptionalism

Human exemptionalism is an important issue in new ecological paradigm. According to this premises human beings believe that they are exempt from all the rules of nature. Item numbers 4, 9 and 14 represent this expemptionalist paradigm. The statement in item number 4 is 'human ingenuity will insure that we do not make the earth unlivable'. For further clarification 'they will always be able to make newer discoveries to solve emergent problems of existence' is added with the original statement. In North 24 Parganas, the item-total correlation is higher than in Purulia though both of them are significant. In arsenic-affected villages more than 40 per cent respondents disagree with the statements. They believe that humans cannot solve the problem of present day by means of science and technology. One primary school teacher from Sutia village of North 24 Parganas said, "If humans could solve the problems caused by nature then we would never face problems like cancer, AIDS. If you are talking about environment we can easily see that people are dying due to arsenic contamination in our village. You can find many people to advise, but no one can solve your problem. Government said that they have installed arsenic-free tube well. But after a few days some private organisation tested and found arsenic in the same tube well. Some people say household kit can remove arsenic. Others say that it can not. So how do you decide who is right and who is wrong?" People in both the villages are mostly agreeing with item number 9 that 'despite our special abilities humans are still subject to the laws of nature'. The correlation is also significant in both the cases. On item number 14 while majority of respondents in region 1 were undecided, followed by those who disagreed with the statement, in region 2 majority of people tended to agree. It implies that people affected by scarcity are more optimistic than those affected by arsenic. In arsenic villages solution is not seen to be in the right direction—despite the efforts of government and civil society actors.

The Possibility of an Eco-crisis

The concept of eco-crisis has been newly added in modified NEP scale and items 5, 10 and 15 measure this dimension with three statements. Item number 5 is a pro-ecological statement and if people agree with that they are in favour of ecological beliefs. In none of the villages any person was found who strongly disagreed with this statement. A much higher percentage of the respondents in both locations agreed that people are abusing the environment than disagree with this statement. The item-total correlation is significant in both the regions. Item number 10 states that the so-called "ecological crisis" faced by humankind has been greatly exaggerated. People perceive that this statement is a little bit political and they were hesitant to agree or disagree with the statement. In West Bengal people were a bit hesitant to express political opinions openly. This explains why as large as 67.3 per cent respondents stated that they were undecided about this. This also explains why in this case item-total correlations are low although significant. In the last question on "ecological crisis" around 50 per cent people agreed with the statement 'if things continue with the present course, we will soon experience a major ecological catastrophe' and nearly 25 per cent disagreed with this. The item-total correlation is very high in this case. Overall on eco-crisis issue, in arsenic villages they have a perception that human beings are somehow responsible for the calamity. In water deficit villages, people feel that the earlier generation was more environmental-friendly as they lived a simple life. Contrary to this nowadays people have developed huge aspirations and to fulfil their needs they are heavily abusing the environment.

Figure 1 ***Comparative Analysis of Item-Total Correlation of NEP Scale***

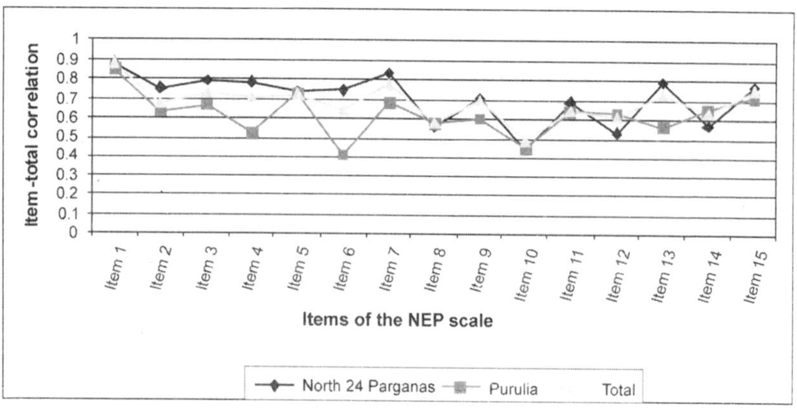

From Figure 1 it can be noticed that except two all the items have correlation with the overall score above 0.5, though it varies from item to item. Even the two items having lower correlation have a value above 0.4 which is statistically significant. Item 1 has the highest correlation with the overall score (0.879). Thus the statement "We are approaching the limit of the number of people the earth can support" is itself a good measure of overall environmental consciousness.

Measures of Reliability

In empirical research involving socio-psychological scales, reliability of the scale is of utmost importance. It is measured through internal consistency. Internal consistency conveys how consistently individuals respond to different items on a scale. Measures of internal consistency are not tests of the unidimensionality of items on a scale. They are measures of "internal consistency reliability" or just "reliability". Also reliability is not the same thing as validity. The latter concept refers to the correlation of an item, scale, or instrument with a hypothetical one which truly measures what it is supposed to measure. To examine internal consistency of NEP, scale Spearman-Brown reliability coefficient (often equated with Cronbach's alpha) has been computed. Spearman-Brown reliability coefficient is the most common form of internal consistency reliability coefficient.

Thus, alpha has been calculated according to the formula:

$$\alpha = (N^* r_{ave})/[1 + (N-1)^* r_{ave})]$$

where,

α = Spearman-Brown reliability coefficient

r_{ave} = The average of inter-item correlations

N = Total number of items

Alpha equals zero when the true score is not measured at all and there is only an error component. Theoretically, alpha varies between –8 and 1. Alpha equals 1.0 when all items measure only the true score and there is no error component. Square of Spearman-Brown reliability coefficient can be interpreted as the per cent of variance, the observed scale would explain in the hypothetical true scale composed of all true items in the universe. Alternatively, it can be interpreted as the correlation of the observed scale with other scales measuring the same thing and using the same number of items. Table 3 represents the alpha of NEP scale as well as five different dimensions of the scale.

Table 3 Reliability of the NEP Scale

	Items	*Arsenic Villages (N=156)*	*Scarcity Villages (N=127)*	*All Villages (N=283)*
1.	***Limits to growth***			
NEP 1	We are approaching the limit of the number of people the earth can support (within limited supply of natural resources such as land, water, air, etc.).	.7942	.5849	.7245
NEP 6	The earth has plenty of natural resources if we just learn how to develop them.			
NEP 11	The earth is a spaceship with very limited rooms and resources (such as water, land and other natural resources).			
2.	***Anti-anthropocentricism***			
NEP 2	Humans have the right to modify the natural environment to suit their needs.	.7258	.6174	.6780
NEP 7	Plants and animals have as much right as humans to exist.			
NEP 12	Humans were meant to rule over the rest of the nature.			
3.	***Fragility of nature's balance***			
NEP 3	When humans interfere with nature it often leads to disastrous consequences.	.7427	.6212	.7092
NEP 8	Balance of nature is strong enough to cope with the impacts of modern industrial nations (such as England or America).			
NEP 13	The balance of nature is very delicate and easily upset.			
4.	***Rejection of exemptionalism***			
NEP 4	Human ingenuity will insure that we do NOT make the earth unliveable (They will always be able to make newer discoveries to solve emergent problems of existence).	.6684	.6104	.6938
NEP 9	Despite our special abilities humans are still subject to the laws of nature.			
NEP 14	Humans will eventually learn enough about how nature works to be able to control it.			

Cont'd...

Cont'd...

5.	***The possibility of an eco-crisis***			
NEP 5	Human are severely abusing the environment.	.5680	.6394	.6259
NEP 10	The so-called 'ecological crisis' faced by humankind has been greatly exaggerated.			
NEP 15	If things continue with the present course, we will soon experience a major ecological catastrophe.			
	Overall NEP scale	.9281	.8865	.9188

The value of Spearman-Brown reliability coefficient for the NEP scale consisting of 15 items is found to be more than 0.9188. This shows a very high reliability of the scale. Spearman-Brown reliability coefficient for the five dimensions varies from 0.6259 to 0.7245. Variations are found between the two regions, i.e., between arsenic villages and scarcity villages. In the case of 'limits to growth' issues (which comprises the items 1, 6, 11) overall alpha score is 0.7245 but in the water-scarce villages this alpha is only 0.5849. This analysis shows that NEP scale is a good measure of environmental beliefs in rural West Bengal in general and arsenic villages in particular.

Comparative Study of Two Regions

Table 4 shows the means and standard deviations (SDs) of items on NEP separately for the two types of villages and for the combined sample. To test for significance of difference in the means of NEP items between the two types of villages t-statistic is used.

Table 4 ***Comparison of General Environmental beliefs in Two Regions***

NEP items	*Arsenic Villages*			*Scarce Villages*			*All Villages*			*t-Value*
	N	*Mean*	*SD*	*N*	*Mean*	*SD*	*N*	*Mean*	*SD*	
1. We are approaching the limit of the number of people the earth can support (within limited supply of natural resources such as land, water, air, etc.).	156	3.69	1.37	127	2.78	1.24	283	3.28	1.39	6.92**

Cont'd...

Cont'd...

2.	Humans have the right to modify the natural environment to suit their needs.	156	2.81	1.19	127	2.87	0.98	283	2.84	1.1	-0.54
3.	When humans interfere with nature it often leads to disastrous consequences.	156	3.16	1.14	127	3.02	1.01	283	3.1	1.09	1.25
4.	Human ingenuity will insure that we do NOT make the earth uninhabitable. (They will always be able to make newer discoveries to solve emergent problems of existence.)	156	3.06	1.15	127	2.57	1.04	283	2.84	1.13	4.41**
5.	Human are severely abusing the environment.	156	3.42	1.09	127	3.12	1.21	283	3.29	1.15	2.70**
6.	The earth has plenty of natural resources if we just learn how to develop them.	156	2.93	1.23	127	2.5	1.05	283	2.74	1.17	3.65**
7.	Plants and animals have as much right as humans to exist.	156	4.11	1.37	127	3.61	1.31	283	3.88	1.36	3.74**
8.	Balance of nature is strong enough to cope with the impacts of modern industrial nations (such as England or America).	156	3.16	0.88	127	2.92	0.77	283	3.05	0.84	2.83**
9.	Despite our special abilities humans are still subject to the laws of nature.	156	3.89	1.09	127	3.12	1.07	283	3.54	1.15	7.16**

Cont'd...

Cont'd...

10. The so-called 'ecological crisis' faced by humankind has been greatly exaggerated.	156	3.38	0.81	127	2.86	0.75	283	3.15	0.83	6.65
11. The earth is a spaceship with very limited rooms and resources (such as water, land and other natural resources.	156	3.02	0.99	127	3.01	0.86	283	3.01	0.93	0.12
12. Humans were meant to rule over the rest of the nature.	156	3.36	0.89	127	2.57	1.05	283	3.01	1.04	8.29**
13. The balance of nature is very delicate and easily upset.	156	3.34	1.2	127	2.98	0.83	283	3.18	1.06	3.28**
14. Humans will eventually learn enough about how nature works to be able to control it.	156	3.26	0.89	127	2.49	1.13	283	2.91	1.08	7.82**
15. If things continue with the present course, we will soon experience a major ecological catastrophe.	156	3.48	1.32	127	3.02	1.25	283	3.27	1.31	3.60**
Average score of General Environmental Beliefs.	156	3.34	0.80	127	2.90	0.65	283	3.14	0.77	5.88**

Note: (**) Significant at 1 per cent level of significance (2 tailed test).

Table 4 shows that for the combined sample mean NEP score is 3.14. Also for most items the value of the mean score for the combined sample is above 3.0. Thus, one can infer that in general people exhibit pro-environmental beliefs. Yet the strength of pro-environmental beliefs is low. This can be explained by the fact that people have started seeing the consequences of unrestrained use of natural resources, but in absence of mobilisation the strength of beliefs is somewhat weak. A high proportion of undecided people for each item is also partly responsible for holding the mean score close to 3. From the table it is evident that arsenic-affected people are environmentally more concerned (mean 3.34) than people facing water scarcity (mean 2.90). The difference is statistically significant.

It is interesting to note that in 14 out of 15 items arsenic villages show greater pro-environmental beliefs than in the water deficit villages. Application of t-test reveals that the respondents from arsenic and water deficit villages differ significantly in environmental beliefs on 12 out of 15 items. For three other items differences are statistically insignificant. Thus, the findings of the study lead to rejection of null hypothesis and lend support to the research hypothesis: arsenic contamination has made people environmentally more conscious than the scarcity. Scarcity of water has long been faced and accepted by people but rise of new risks such as arsenic contamination has made people more concerned about the limits of anthropocentricism.

Factors underlying NEP Scale

Factor analysis is a statistical data reduction technique used to explain variability among observed random variables in terms of a fewer unobserved random variables called factors. The observed variables are modelled as linear combinations of the factors, plus "error" terms. Factor analysis is used for a number of purposes. Two major purposes are: (a) to reduce the number of variables; and (b) to unearth structure of relationships between variables. Factor analysis yields a matrix of factor loadings or regression coefficients on the basis of which variables are classified into a number of groups or factors. Factor analysis also yields communality values which refer to the degree to which all factors

Figure 2 ***Comparison of Mean Value of NEP Scale Items***

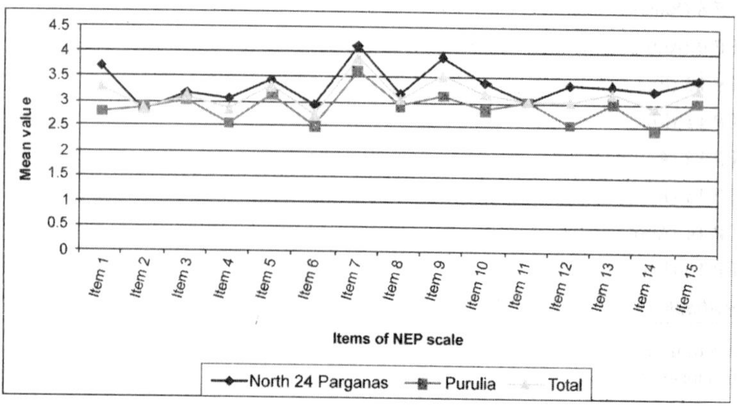

taken together explain the variations in different variables. Variables with high communality values are well-represented in the common factor space, while variables with low values are not well-represented. They are unique.

The first step towards factoring is to go for principal component analysis. It produces the same number of components or factors as the number of variables. Factor analysis, on the other hand, yields a smaller set of factors which may be chosen on the basis of eigenvalue or variance explained. Usually, those factors are retained which have eigenvalue above 1. In this study, varimax rotation method was used to generate orthogonal factors. This helps in maximising the variance of each of the factors, so the total amount of variance accounted for is redistributed over the extracted factors. In arsenic villages, two factors are retained. On the other hand, in water-scarce villages three factors can be retained. For the overall sample only two factors have eigenvalue more than 1. They are retained.

Table 5 ***Factor Loadings of Items—NEP Scale (Arsenic Villages, N=156)***

	Components	
	1	*2*
NEP 1 (Limits)	.769	.428
NEP 2 (Anti-anthrop)	.657	.368
NEP 3 (Balance)	.742	.313
NEP 4 (Anti-exempt)	.769	
NEP 5 (Eco-crisis)	.566	.491
NEP 6 (Limits)	.603	.445
NEP 7 (Anti-anthrop)	.783	.313
NEP 8 (Balance)	.362	.483
NEP 9 (Anti-exempt)	.733	
NEP 10 (Eco-crisis)		.782
NEP 11 (Limits)	.638	
NEP 12 (Anti-anthrop)		.785
NEP 13 (Balance)	.867	
NEP 14 (Anti-exempt)		.652
NEP 15 (Eco-crisis)	.856	
Cronbach's alpha	.9367	.7066

Extraction Method: Principal Component Analysis. Rotation Method: Varimax with Kaiser Normalisation. Rotation converged in 3 iterations.

Table 6 ***Factor Loadings of Items—NEP Scale (Scarce Villages, N=127)***

	Components		
	1	*2*	*3*
NEP 1 (Limits)	.765	.322	
NEP 2 (Anti-anthrop)	.353	.576	
NEP 3 (Balance)	.723		
NEP 4 (Anti-exempt)		.502	.549
NEP 5 (Eco-crisis)	.788		
NEP 6 (Limits)		.790	
NEP 7 (Anti-anthrop)	.720		.313
NEP 8 (Balance)			.678
NEP 9 (Anti-exempt)	.647	.361	
NEP 10 (Eco-crisis)			.724
NEP 11 (Limits)	.538		.382
NEP 12 (Anti-anthrop)	.384	.546	
NEP 13 (Balance)	.657		
NEP 14 (Anti-exempt)	.323	.717	
NEP 15 (Eco-crisis)	.643		.323
Cronbach's alpha	.8765	.7194	.5956

Extraction Method: Principal Component Analysis. Rotation Method: Varimax with Kaiser Normalisation. Rotation converged in 6 iterations.

Table 7 ***Factor Loadings of Items—NEP Scale (All Villages, N=283)***

	Components	
	1	*2*
NEP 1 (Limits)	.730	.493
NEP 2 (Anti-anthrop)	.608	.304
NEP 3 (Balance)	.709	
NEP 4 (Anti-exempt)	.573	.402
NEP 5 (Eco-crisis)	.649	.336
NEP 6 (Limits)	.386	.556
NEP 7 (Anti-anthrop)	.763	
NEP 8 (Balance)	.326	.553
NEP 9 (Anti-exempt)	.661	
NEP 10 (Eco-crisis)		.762

Cont'd...

Cont'd...

NEP 11 (Limits)	.645	
NEP 12 (Anti-anthrop)		.737
NEP 13 (Balance)	.814	
NEP 14 (Anti-exempt)		.697
NEP 15 (Eco-crisis)	.788	
Cronbach's alpha	.9142	.7600

Extraction Method: Principal Component Analysis. Rotation Method: Varimax with Kaiser Normalisation. Rotation converged in 3 iterations.

It is found that ten items load most heavily on the first factor for the overall sample. The second factor loads only five items. In the old NEP scale, there were three broad components—balance of nature, limits to growth and exemptionalism. In the modified scale, there are five dimensions. However, in this study factor analysis identifies only two factors in arsenic villages, three factors in water-scarce villages, and two factors for the overall sample after varimax rotation.

Conclusion

This main conclusion of the study is that the 15-item NEP scale is well-suited to explore environmental consciousness in the rural setting of West Bengal. The reliability scores (i.e., Cronbach's alpha values) of 2nd, 3rd, and 4th dimensions are above 0.6. Only in the case of 5th dimension the score for arsenic villages is less than 0.5680. Hence, it can be said that NEP scale is a good measure of environmental beliefs in rural Indian setting though all factors need not be reliable measures of different dimensions of beliefs. The three factors with eigenvalues greater than one are subjected to a varimax rotation, ten items load most heavily on the first factor for the overall sample. The second factor only loads five items. In the old NEP scale there were three broad components—balance of nature, limits to growth and exemptionalism. In the modified scale, there are five dimensions. However, this study found only two factors in arsenic villages, three factors in water-scarce villages and two factors for overall sample after varimax rotation. For the overall sample, the fist factor has more cognitive component and the second factor has behavioural aspect. So, after the study the factors are renamed as cognitive and behavioural. In the behavioural factors, all the factors have eco-centric items. However, in the cognitive component items are mostly loaded from anthropocentric items, apart from item 2 and 4 where the factor loadings are 0.608 and 0.578 respectively. It is also interesting to note that in these two items the factor loadings in the second component (i.e., behavioural) are 0.304 and 0.402 respectively. It can be inferred that if more studies are to be done in the similar situation with different sample the factors can be divided into two dimensions: anthropocentric and eco-centric. However, it can also be inferred that anthropocentric and eco-centric beliefs are separate aspects of a more comprehensive environmental beliefs construct. The study does not suggest any modification of the NEP scale. For the study scale has not be changed but few words have been added to convey the inner meaning of the items. The study suggests that NEP scale is quite useful in rural West Bengal settings. There is also an evidence to suggest that it is desirable to divide items into forms that express anthropocentric and eco-centric beliefs.

To compare the situation at two different locations, means and standard deviations of scores on items on NEP and water scale are computed. As such the scale contained some positive and some negative statements. They have been scored in such a manner that for each item a higher value of score is indicative of stronger and pro-environmental beliefs and a lower value of anthropocentric beliefs. To compare the means of the two sets of villages t-statistic for difference is calculated. The overall sample mean of NEP scale is 3.14. Also for most items the value of the mean score for the combined sample is above 3.0. Thus, it can be inferred that in general, people are pro-environmental, i.e., they possess ecological beliefs. Yet the degree of pro-environmental beliefs is low. This can be explained by the fact that people have started seeing the consequences of unrestrained use of natural resources but in absence of mobilisation the strength of beliefs is somewhat weaker. From the results it is evident that arsenic-affected people are environmentally more concerned (mean 3.34) about environment than people facing water scarcity (mean 2.90). The difference is statistically significant. In case of general environmental beliefs, the respondents from North 24 Parganas and Purulia districts differ significantly on 12 out of 15 items. Overall, fourteen out of fifteen cases of arsenic villages show greater pro-environmental beliefs than in the water deficit villages.

Notes

1. Dunlap later uses “New Environmental Paradigm” as “New Ecological paradigm”. The present study uses “New Ecological Paradigm” as NEP scale.
2. Data taken from 19 years’ ongoing study of School of Environmental Studies, Jadavpur University. In 1988, when they commenced arsenic survey in West Bengal, there were about 22 affected (As > 50 Fg/L) villages in five

districts. For more information see http://www.soesju.org/arsenic/ wb.htm last visited 1.12.2007

3. http://north24parganas.nic.in/publichealth.html last visited 1.12.2007

References

Adeola, F.O. 1996. Environmental Contamination, Public Hygiene and Human Health Concerns in the Third World: The Case of Nigerian Environmentalism. *Environment and Behaviour* 28(5): 614–46.

Albretch, D., G. Bultena, E. Holberg and P. Nowak. 1982. The New Environmental Paradigm Scale. *Journal of Environmental Education* 13: 39–43.

Axelrod, L.S. and D.R. Lehman. 1993. Responding to Environmental Concerns: What Factors Guide Individual Action? *Journal of Environmental Psychology* 13: 149–59.

Bamberg, S. 2003. How does Environmental Concern Influence Specific Environmentally Related Behaviours? A New Answer to an Old Question. *Journal of Environmental Psychology* 23: 21–32.

Brechin, Steven R., and Willett Kempton. 1994. Global Environmentalism: A Challenge to the Postmaterialism Thesis? *Social Science Quarterly* 75: 245–269.

Buttel, F.H. and D.E. Johnson. 1977. Dimensions of Environmental Concern: Factor Structure, Correlates and Implications for Research. *The Journal of Environmental Education* 9: 49–64.

Buttel, Frederick H. and William L. Flinn. 1978. The Politics of Environmental Concern: The Impact of Party Identification and Political Ideology on Environmental Attitudes. *Environment and Behaviour* 10: 17–36.

Buttel, Frederick H. 1987. New Directions in Environmental Sociology. *Annual Review of Sociology* 13: 465–88.

Catton, William R. Jr. and Riley E. Dunlap. 1978. Environmental Sociology: A New Paradigm. *The American Sociologist* 13(1): 41–9.

——. 1980. A New Ecological Paradigm for Post-exuberant Paradigm. *American Behavioural Scientist* 24(1): 15–47.

Dunlap, Riley E. and Kent D. Van Liere. 1978. The New Environmental Paradigm. *The Journal of Environmental Education* 9: 10–9.

Dunlap, Riley E. and William Jr. Catton. 1979. Environmental Sociology. *Annual Review of Sociology* 5: 243–73.

Dunlap, Riley E., George H. Gallup Jr. and Alec M. Gallup. 1993. Of Global Concern: Results of the Health of the Planet Survey. *Environment* 35: 7–15, 33–9.

Dunlap, Riley E. and Angela G. Mertig. 1995. Global Concern for the Environment: Is Affluence a Prerequisite? *Journal of Social Issues* 51: 121–37.

Dunlap, Riley E., Kent D. Van Liere, Angela G. Mertig and Robert Emmet Jones. 2000. Measuring Endorsement of the New Ecological Paradigm: A Revised NEP Scale. *Journal of Social Issues* 56(3), 425–42.

Dunlap, R.E. and R.E. Jones. 2002. "Environmental Concern: Conceptual and Measurement Issues" in R.E. Dunlap and W. Michelson (eds.), *Handbook of Environmental Sociology*. Westport, CT: Greenwood Press, 482–524.

Fransson, N. and T. Gärling. 1999. Environmental Concern: Conceptual Definitions, Measurement Methods and Research Findings. *Journal of Environmental Psychology* 19: 369–82.

Freudenburg, W.R. 1991. Rural-Urban Differences in Environmental Concern: A Closer Look. *Sociological Inquiry* 61(2): 167–98.

Gagnon-Thompson, S.C. and M.A. Barton. 1994. Ecocentric and Anthropocentric Attitudes toward the Environment. *Journal of Environmental Psychology* 14: 149–57.

Gray, O. 1985. *Ecological Beliefs and Behaviour*. Westport, CT: Greenwood.

Guagnano, Gregory A. and Nancy Markee. 1995. Regional Differences in the Sociodemographic Determinants of Environmental Concern. *Population and Environment* 17: 135–50.

Lewis, T.L. 2003. Environmental Aid: Driven by Recipient Need or Donor Interests? *Social Science Quarterly* 84: 144–61.

Lounsbury, J.W. and L.G. Tournatzky. 1977. A Scale for Assessing Attitudes toward Environmental Quality, *The Journal of Social Psychology* 101: 299–305.

Martinez-Alier, Juan. 1995. Political Ecology, Distributional Conflicts and Economic Incommensurability. *New Left Review* 211: 70–88.

Neiman, Max and Ronald O. Loveridge. 1981. Environmentalism and Local Growth Control: A Probe into the Class Bias. *Environment and Behaviour* 13: 759–72.

Schultz, P.W. 2000. Empathising with Nature: The Effects of Perspective-Taking on Concern for Environmental Issues. *Journal of Social Issues* 56, 391–406.

Schultz, P.W. 2001. The Structure of Environmental Concern: Concern for Self, Other People and the Biosphere. *Journal of Environmental Psychology* 21, 327–39.

Schultz, P.W. and L. Zelezny. 1999. Values as Predictors of Environmental Attitudes: Evidence for Consistency across 14 Countries. *Journal of Environmental Psychology* 19: 255–65.

Schultz, P.W. and L. Zelezny. 2003. Reframing Environmental Messages to be Congruent with American Values. *Human Ecology Review* 10(2): 126–36.

Scott, David and Fern K. Willits. 1994. Environmental Attitudes and Behaviour: A Pennsylvania Survey. *Environment and Behaviour* 26: 239–60.

Seligman, C. 1989. Environmental Ethics. *Journal of Social Issues* 45: 153–68.

Stern, Paul C., Thomas Dietz and Linda Kalof. 1993. Value Orientations, Gender and Environmental Concern. *Environment and Behaviour* 25: 322–48.

Stern, P.C., T. Dietz and G.A. Guagnano. 1995. The New Ecological Paradigm in Social-psychological Context. *Environment and Behaviour* 27: 723–43.

Stokols, D. 1990. Instrumental and Spiritual Views of People-Environment Relations. *American Psychologist* 45: 641–6.

Van Liere, Kent D. and Riley E. Dunlap. 1980. The Social Bases of Environmental Concern: A Review of Hypotheses, Explanations and Empirical Evidence. *Public Opinion Quarterly* 44: 181–99.

——. Environmental Concern: Does It Make a Difference, How It's Measured? *Environment and Behaviour* 13(6), 651–76.

Wall, Glenda. 1995. Barriers to Individual Environmental Action: The Influence of Attitudes and Social Experiences. *Canadian Review of Sociology and Anthropology* 32: 465–89.

Willers, V.A. 1996. Environmental Concern in South Africa. (Unpublished Doctoral Thesis), Department of Psychology, University of South Africa.

10

Projection of Cancer Incident Cases for India till 2016

N.S. Murthy, M. Dhar and K. Chaudhury

Rising longevity, alterations in lifestyle and progressive control of communicable diseases has led to emergence of cancer and other non-communicable diseases as an important heath problem in India and other developing countries. In the country, the life expectancy at birth has steadily risen from 45 years in 1971 to 64 years in 2001, indicating a shift in demographic profile (RGI, 1998). It is estimated that life expectancy of Indian population will increase to 70 years by 2021–25. Due to such changes in age structure, population would face an increase in incidence of cancers and some other non-communicable diseases, which have a higher chance of occurrence among the elderly. At present, for the country as a whole, the magnitude of the cancer incidence cases by site and sex is available till the year 2001 (Murthy et al., 1990). However, no such projections are available for future periods based on data from several Indian registries. A precise knowledge about the magnitude of the cancer problem for the present as well as for the future would help health policy planners to evolve and implement cancer facilities in the country. The present communication presents an estimate of the magnitude of incident cases of cancer at the country as well as at the state levels for quin-quennial years from 2001 to 2016 for "all sites" of cancer as well as for some of the leading cancer sites reported by the population-based cancer registries.

Materials and Methods

The data on the occurrence of cancer in India is available from the population-based cancer registries established in various parts of the country. Although the area and population covered by these registries is small, it gives a fair idea of the extent of the cancer problem in the

Figure 1 ***Location of Cancer Registration Centres in India***

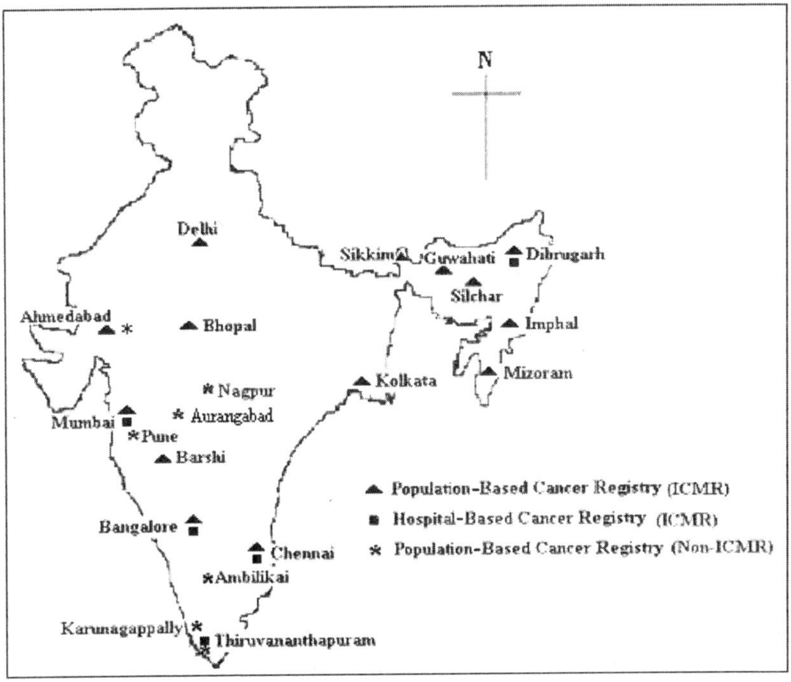

country. A network of 14 population-based cancer registries (including recently established seven registries) is functioning under the National Cancer Registry Programme of the Indian Council of Medical Research (ICMR). They are located at Bangalore, Bhopal, Chennai (earlier known as Madras), Delhi, Mumbai (earlier known as Bombay), Kolkata (earlier known as Calcutta) and a rural registry at Barshi (Maharashtra), six in the north-eastern region, and one in the rural area of Ahmedabad, Gujarat. There are seven population-based cancer registries outside the ICMR network. Those at Pune, Aurangabad and Nagpur operate under the Indian Cancer Society in the state of Maharashtra. The Ahmedabad Urban Cancer Registry is under Gujarat Cancer Research Institute, Ahmedabad, Gujarat. The Karunagappally (rural registry) and the urban registry in the city of Trivandrum are under the Regional Cancer Centre, Trivandrum, Kerala. The Ambillikai population-based registry is under the Cancer Institute, Chennai. The location of various registries is shown in the map. In the near future, all these population-based cancer registries are likely to function under the aegis of National Cancer Registry Programme of Indian Council of Medical Research.

Estimation of Pooled Incidence Rates

The data from various Indian registries are published by the International Agency for Research on Cancer, Lyon, in Cancer Incidence in Five Continents. The volume VIII of cancer incidence in five continents published for the period 1993–1997 contains data for nine Indian population-based registries viz. Ahmedabad (urban), Bangalore (urban), Chennai (urban), Delhi (urban), Mumbai (Bombay) (urban), Nagpur (urban), Karunagapally (rural), Pune (urban) and Thiruvananthapuram (urban) (Parkin et al., 2002). Further, the age and sex wise cancer incidence data by site, for the two-year period, 1997–1998 for Barshi and Bhopal registries and data for the year 1997 for Kolkata registry was also obtained from the published reports (National Cancer Registry Programme, 2002, Chittaranjan National Cancer Institute, 2001). The number of cancer cases by site, sex and five-year age group for each of the registries were obtained by multiplying the age-specific incidence rates with the respective populations. The pooled age, sex and site-wise specific incidence rates of cancer based on 12 registries were calculated.

Population Exposed to Risk

Population of the country as well as for various major states (fifteen) of the country, according to age and sex exposed to the risk at different quin-quennial years from 2001 to 2016 were obtained from the report of population projections carried out for the country for the years 1996 to 2016 by the Registrar General of India (Registrar General of India, 1996).

Estimation of Load of Cancer

The respective age and sex-specific pooled incidence rates by site were multiplied with the corresponding projected age and sex-specific population figures to estimate the predicted number of cases by age, sex and site of cancer at various 5 year periods, viz., 2001, 2006, 2011 and 2016 by site, sex and five year-age groups. The number of new cases of cancer for site "s" (N^s) in a particular year was estimated using the relationship $N = 3_n P_x * {}_n I_x$, where ${}_n P_x$ represents the projected population in the x to x+n age group for a particular year and ${}_{n}I_{x}$ being the pooled incidence rate of cancer by site in the same age group for a particular site. The projections have been carried out for the various selected sites of cancer and tobacco related sites taken together. Estimation of incident cases has been done both at the national level as well as for 15 major states of India which cover 95 per cent of the country's population. Computation of prevalent number of cases is based on the estimate that the average survival of a cancer patient is three years (Dhar et al., 2006).

Assumptions

The projection of number of persons developing cancer has been done with the following assumption (i) rates obtained from these 12 population-based cancer registries represent country's incidence rate as well as for the various states of the country and (ii) age-specific cancer incidence rates available for the latest year will remain unchanged over the next 15 years.

Results

Life Expectancy and Projected Population

The life expectancy at birth of the Indian population has been rising over the last few decades. The life expectancy at birth was 32 years in 1941–51 and increased to 58.7 years during the years 1988–92. Further, it is likely to increase to 68 years during the years 2011–2016. According to the projections based on total fertility rates, the total estimated population of India for the years 2001, 2006, 2011, and 2016 (as of 1st June of the year) would be 1,017, 1,100, 1,184, and 1,270 millions respectively (Table 1). It may be noted that the proportion of Indian population in the age above 40 years, which is more prone to cancer, will increase from 24.1 per cent in 2001 to 29.8 per cent by 2016. In terms of absolute numbers, there will be a massive increase of the population in the age group of 40–59 years from 173 millions to 264 (52.6%) millions from 2001 to 2016. Similarly, the population of elderly (60+ years) will increase from 71 million to 113 million (59.2%) in 2016.

Table 1 ***Projected Population (in 000's) of India for Quin-quennial Years from 2001–2016***

Age (Yrs)	Year							
	2001		2006		2011		2016	
	Male	Female	Male	Female	Male	Female	Male	Female
0–4	55,987	53,060	58,627	55,516	61,706	58,383	63,438	59,994
9–14	59,531	57,206	54,551	51,761	57,235	54,251	60,433	57,232
10–14	63,879	59,653	59,187	56,921	54,219	51,478	56,965	54,031
15–19	57,958	51,661	63,629	59,451	58,928	56,694	54,045	51,334
20–24	47,966	42,714	57,677	51,429	63,294	59,155	58,689	56,485
25–29	41,598	40,289	47,682	42,486	57,315	51,133	62,979	58,896
30–34	37,661	37,894	41,290	40,025	47,320	42,195	56,958	50,860
35–39	33,527	32,215	37,285	37,575	40,877	39,680	46,921	41,896
40–44	29,644	26,792	33,026	31,840	36,740	37,135	40,354	39,286
45–49	24,945	22,047	28,952	26,342	32,278	31,313	35,989	36,591
50–54	20,715	18,384	23,996	21,463	27,890	25,662	31,184	30,580
55–59	16,558	14,729	19,458	17,577	22,590	20,554	26,351	24,655
60–64	12,512	11,671	14,974	13,658	17,655	16,347	20,593	19,203
65–69	9,871	9,567	10,683	10,312	12,848	12,122	15,242	14,598
70–74	6,647	6,473	7,763	7,841	8,461	8,509	10,258	10,087
75–79	4,317	4,035	4,663	4,726	5,497	5,785	6,053	6,352
80+	3,040	2,798	3,958	3,672	4,618	4,526	5,486	5,637
Total	5,26,356	4,91,188	5,67,401	5,32,595	6,09,471	5,74,922	6,51,938	6,17,717

Pooled Age-Specific Incidence Rates

The pooled crude incidence rate (CR), age standardised incidence rate (ASR) and age-specific incidence rate of cancer of all sites for males and females is presented in Table 2. It can be observed that the age-specific rates of cancers increase substantially after the age group of 40 years. The pooled CR and ASR were found to be 66.7 and 76.1 and 100.9 and 108.8 for males and females respectively.

Table 2 Pooled Age-specific Rate, Crude Rate (CR) and Age-Adjusted Rate (ASR) of Cancer Incidence Per 1,00,000 Person Years.

Age Group (Yrs)	*Males*	*Females*
00–04	10.38	7.44
05–09	9.87	5.46
10–14	8.87	6.30
15–19	10.42	8.72
20–24	12.58	12.33
25--29	15.42	21.82
30–34	24.37	41.79
35–39	38.66	80.29
40–44	70.50	145.98
45–49	120.10	214.11
50–54	205.37	289.70
55–59	305.08	326.82
60–64	402.78	397.15
65–69	549.61	462.06
70–74	642.89	476.87
75+	577.45	375.72
CR	66.38	76.06
ASR	100.9	108.8

CR= Crude rate, ASR= Age standardised rate to the world population.

National and State Level Estimates and Projections of Incident Cases (Table 3)

In India, during the year 2001, nearly 0.80 million new cancer cases were estimated. It is estimated that the total number of incident cases of cancer would increase to 1.22 million by 2016 as a result of change in size and composition of population. At any point of time during the year 2001, in the country it was estimated that nearly 2.4 million cancer cases were prevalent and this would increase to 3.7 millions by 2016. The principle factors contributing to this projected increase are the increasing size of the population as well as proportion of the elderly people in the country. Further, state-wise computation of incident cases of cancer during the various years revealed that based on age distribution and size of population the incident number of cases varied amongst the states. States such as Uttar Pradesh, Bihar, Maharashtra and Madhya Pradesh had a large number of incident cases. Kerala had lowest number of cases. There was a 1.5 fold increase in number of incident cases from 2001 to 2016 both at the all Indian level as well as state level.

Table 3 ***Projected Annual Number of New Cases of Cancer During Quin-quennial Years, 2001–2016***

India and States	*Males*				*Females*			
	Year				*Year*			
	2001	*2006*	*2011*	*2016*	*2001*	*2006*	*2011*	*2016*
India	3,91,758	4,47,847	5,12,529	5,87,750	4,05,899	4,71,570	5,46,454	6,31,899
Andhra Pradesh	30,306	34,909	39,999	45,722	33,430	38,783	44,702	51,293
Assam	9,032	10,410	12,104	14,174	8,705	10,432	12,522	15,022
Bihar	37,036	41,580	47,237	54,023	36,865	42,171	48,392	55,626
Gujarat	17,182	19,203	21,844	25,053	19,826	22,927	26,682	31,057
Haryana	7,609	8,363	9,488	11,023	7,361	8,471	9,878	11,614
Karnataka	20,570	23,523	2,6881	30,962	22,149	25,721	29,839	68,978
Kerala	14,229	16,331	18,656	21,336	16,997	19,597	22,477	25,709
Madhya Pradesh	29,492	32,937	37,082	42,041	31,138	35,473	40,632	46,649
Maha-rashtra	35,705	40,109	45,344	51,565	39,499	45,427	52,203	59,928
Orissa	14,180	15,170	17,167	18,999	15,343	16,759	19,460	22,025
Punjab	9,293	10,135	11,077	12,184	9,187	11,006	12,543	14,340
Rajasthan	19,226	22,071	25,411	29,403	19,995	23,101	26,778	31,146
Tamil Nadu	28,246	32,496	37,106	42,190	30,283	35,298	40,737	46,657
Uttar Pradesh	65,672	71,653	79,444	89,173	63,391	72,754	83,874	96,994
West Bengal	30,331	35,712	42,071	49,359	30,822	36,631	43,490	51,229

Patterns of Cancer (Table 4)

The estimated cases were more for females (0.406 millions, 2001) than males (0.392 millions, 2001). Lung, esophagus, stomach, oral and pharyngeal cancers are much higher in men while in women, cancers of cervix and breast are predominant forms followed by oral cancers, stomach and esophagus (Table 4). In the Western world, incidence of colorectal, prostate and lung cancer is higher. In India, in males already lung and colon cancers are increasing, while in women, breast and ovary cancers are showing an upward trend.

Table 4 ***Annual Number (N) of Incident Cases of Cancer by Leading Sites of Cancer During 2001 and 2016, India***

Site	*Male*		*Female*	
	2001 (N)	*2016 (N)*	*2001 (N)*	*2016 (N)*
Oral cavity	42,725	65,205	22,080	35,088
Pharynx	26,555	40,719	6,262	9,783
Oesophagus	24,936	38,536	17,511	28,165
Stomach	20,537	31,538	11,162	17,699
Rectum	8,833	13,444	6,393	10,046
Liver	10,336	15,733	4,539	7,140
Gall bladder	4,435	6,837	10,551	16,913
Larynx	22,776	35,182	2,989	4,767
Lung	39,262	60,730	9,525	15,191
Prostate	17,415	27,215	—	—
Breast	—	—	89,914	1,40,975
Cervix uteri		—	79,827	1,25,821
Urinary bladder	12,707	19,668	3,415	5,454
Others	1,61,241	2,32,943	1,41,731	2,14,857
Total no. of cases	3,91,758	5,87,750	4,05,899	6,31,899

Among males, lung cancer is the leading cancer site in India with the incident cases in 2001 being 42.5 per cent higher than the next leading cancer site (Oesophagus, contributing to 24,936 cases). Lung cancer cases would rise from 0.040 cases to 0.0607 million cases in males. Stomach cancer occupies fourth position with total cases among males increasing from 0.021 million to 0.0315 million (Table 4). It may be seen that all the leading sites shown in Table 4 have revealed an increase of nearly 50 per cent during the fifteen-years time period as a result of change in age structure and size of population. Nearly 40 per cent of cancers seen in Indian females are accounted by cancer of cervix and breast alone. The estimated number of incident cases of breast would increase from 0.090 millions to 0.141 million during the above-mentioned period. Similarly, cancer of cervix cases would rise from 0.0798 million to 0.126 millions.

Table 5 shows the projected number of incident cases of tobacco-related cancers (TRC) in males and females. The sites of cancers included amongst TRCs were lip, tongue, mouth, pharynx, esophagus, larynx, lung and urinary bladder (Table 5). The estimated number of tobacco-related cancer cases in males would rise from 0.171 million to 0.262 million merely as a result of change in size and age structure of the population. Amongst men, tobacco related cancers accounted for nearly 43-45 per cent of all cancers seen amongst men. However, in females, tobacco-related cancers accounted for only 15 per cent of cancers. The incident cases of both sexes combined together would rise from 0.201 million to 0.359 million as a result of change in size and age composition of the population.

Table 5 ***Projected Number of Tobacco Cancers (incident cases) in India During Quin-quennial Years by Site, 2001–2006***

Site	*Year*			
	2001	*2006*	*2011*	*2016*
Males				
Lip	2001	2006	2011	2016
Tongue	1,332	1,535	1,769	2,032
Mouth	19,764	22,775	26,242	30,269
Tonsil	19,645	22,603	26,012	29,962
Oropharynx	5,331	6,139	7,080	8,161
Hypopharynx	3,793	4,377	5,052	5,825
Pharynx unspecified	16,094	18,578	21,478	24,882
Oesophagus	4,451	5,131	5,917	6,839
Larynx	24,936	28,786	33,269	38,536
Lung	22,776	26,252	30,349	35,182
Bladder	39,262	45,292	52,369	60,730
All TRC No.	12,707	14,666	16,941	19,668
All TRC %	1,70,092	1,96,134	2,26,477	2,62,084
All sites	43.4	43.8	44.2	44.6
Females				
Lip	668	779	915	1,071
Tongue	6,337	7,398	8,644	10,103
Mouth	13,764	16,072	18771	21,951
Tonsil	946	1,104	1288	1,510
Oropharynx	618	718	839	987
Hypopharynx	3,914	4,581	5341	6,196
Pharynx unspecified	749	876	1018	1,189
Oesophagus	17,511	20,508	24004	28,165
Larynx	2,989	3,492	4073	4,767
Lung	9,525	11,120	12974	15,191
Bladder	3,415	4,017	4680	5,454
All TRC No.	60,436	70,664	82547	96,584
All TRC %	14.9	15.0	15.1	15.3
All sites	4,05,899	4,71,570	5,46,454	6,31,899

Discussion

It is well known that lifestyles, age composition of the population and total population size are determinants of cancer magnitude. These factors gradually changed in the developed world; as a result, cancer has become one of the greater killer diseases. Several models have been attempted in the developed countries to predict the cancer situation in the years to come by using registry data. The precision of the estimates is made more accurate by taking into account the ecological data.

In the developing countries, the problems are more complex and different from the developed countries. For example, India entered into 'population explosion' era in 1920s and after 1940s mortality rates started falling. In 1980s, a very large cohort born in 1940s has already entered into 'cancer prone' age. The problem is more vexed when society is undergoing a rapid change in lifestyles especially when tobacco consumption is increasing. This is likely to initiate an epidemic of cancers in the midst of already existing heavy load of communicable diseases. In order to plan and develop control measures an accurate estimation of cancer load is essential. Unlike in developed countries we are handicapped because of paucity of essential data to be utilised for making projections with a better degree of precision. Authentic data on cancer incidents for different regions is available only from 1982 when the Indian Council of Medical Research initiated National Cancer Registry Programme (NCRP). In addition to this, a few of the cancer centres started their own population based registries. These registries routinely undertake various exercises to ensure that the data they collect and process is of high quality. A thorough check of data is also done before tabulation. It has been reported that the data collected by the Indian population-based registries are both complete and reliable (NCRP, 2001; Parkin 2002).

Estimation of projection of cancer for the entire country has been done by selecting registries on the basis of availability of published data, stability of registry and location.

The present estimates have been based on the data from average incidence rate of cancer from 12 population-based cancer registries only, although presently there are 21 PBCRs in the country. Detailed published data needed for the present exercise from the two registries Viz: Ambilikai and Aurangabad were not available for the corresponding period. The six registries in the north-east region and the Ahmedabad rural registry were established recently only and are still in the stabilisation stage. Thus, the data of the registries that has accrued over the years is essentially that of selected urban centres and only two are rural registries that cover a part of districts in states of Maharashtra and Kerala. Therefore, the present estimates may not represent a true picture of the estimates of the burden of cancer for the entire country as 70 per cent of the population of India resides in rural areas. Nonetheless, the present exercise provides some idea about the initial number of cases at the national level. The scientists at the ICMR have carried out limited exercises and these figures vary from 700–900 new cancer cases in India every year (Nandakumar and Swaminathan, 2006). Estimation of the population at risk of developing cancer at the country and state level was based on the population estimates provided by the Government of India for the various periods.

The life expectancy at birth for the Indian population crossed 40 years after 1961. Thus, it can be said that cancer started appearing as a health problem in the country after 1961.

In addition to age, there is enough evidence to show that cancer share with major key risk factors such as tobacco use (smoking or chewing), unhealthy dietary habits, physical inactivity, alcohol use, infections and behavioural risk factors (Doll and Peto, 1981). The interactive, additive and synergistic effects of these factors are responsible for a number of cancer cases and untimely death. Tobacco is the single most important risk factor for cancer. The studies carried out by the National Family Health Survey during the year 1998–99 indicates that tobacco use in any form (smoking or chewing) is prevalent in the country to the extent of 46.5 per cent and 13.8 per cent in males and females respectively. In terms of actual numbers, the number of tobacco users in India during the year 1998–99 was estimated to be 149.6 million men and 43.6 million women (IIPS, 2000). There is a strong rise in the incidence of lifestyle-related cancers in India. Of the total cancer cases, nearly 45 per cent and 20 per cent in males and females are due to tobacco use. Tobacco-related cancers account for almost one-third of all cancers in India—predominantly head and neck, lung and esophageal cancers. Spread of tobacco addiction, promoted by commercial interest is responsible for the lung cancer epidemic that is already taking hundreds of thousands of lives annually. Established causes of mouth and pharyngeal cancers are smoking, chewing of tobacco and betel leaf. In addition to above, increasing trends in cancer incidence have also been noted for several other cancers such as colon, rectum, gall bladder, lung, breast, ovary, prostate, brain and leukaemia (Murthy, 2007).

The present projections carried out have not made any adjustments for possible increase in prevalence in the tobacco habit. However, reports are available for increase in tobacco consumption habits. Increasing tobacco smoking instead of tobacco chewing might lead to increase in incidence of lung cancer, which is more difficult to detect and cure. When, suitable adjustments will be made for increasing tobacco habits, the estimates may get further increased. However, the present estimates (without consideration of possible increase in risk factors) do indicate that existing treatment facilities need to be substantially increased to combat this deadly disease.

Accurate information on existing facilities in the country for cancer control is not available. There are 25 regional cancer research and treatment centres and 50 oncology wings in different medical colleges (Gupta et al., 2006; Rao et al., 2002). A total of 345 teletherapy installations existed in 2005 as against a requirement of 1,059 (during the tear 2006) at the rate of one cobalt unit for one million population (Gupta et al., 2006). The availability shown here includes both the private sector and other sources. Most of the populous states in India are without or with very minimum specialised cancer centres. It is really a big question from where and when the resources can be obtained to meet the shortfall of more than these 700 teletherapy machines as of 2006 and would get further increased. Since the governmental funding can support only a fraction of this demand in the immediate future, one has to explore the model of sharing some expensive radiotherapy equipments. The cost of imported equipment of cobalt units and linear accelerators and brachytherapy machines are major problems in making cancer treatment equitable to all. Perhaps, local manufacturing of equipment with cheaper and innovative designs will go a long way in reducing the cost. The current cancer treatment facilities are mostly limited to urban areas of the country with geographical imbalances. Most of the populous states in India are without or with very minimum specialised cancer centres. It may also be mentioned that about 60 to 80 per cent of our cancer patients report at a late stage where radiotherapy is the main mode of treatment often for palliation (NCRP, 2001).

Even, if the age-specific cancer incidence rates remain unchanged, large increase in absolute number of cancer cases in the next one and half decades of the present century is already programmed due to aging of population in the developing countries. With the increasing longevity, the proportion of Indian population in the cancer age will increase substantially. It is envisaged that in years to come cancer morbidity and cancer mortality would rise disproportionately to population increase and therefore strengthening/augmenting the existing diagnostic/management facilities along with primary prevention of tobacco-related cancers should be initiated as early as possible. This approach would help in early detection and linked reduction of mortality. Prevention of cancers through reduction of tobacco use should be an important strategy of National Cancer Control Programme of India. Cancer screening facilities should also be initiated so that leading cancer sites like cervix; breast and oral can be detected at early stages or at pre-cancerous stage. High numbers of cancers of lung, prostate, ovary, oesophagus, stomach, gall bladder (in certain areas) indicate need for augmented research efforts to identify effective screening tools. Incorporating screening activities into peripheral health infrastructure would effectively change the shift of clinical staging to left when less extensive surgical procedures could be attempted. Establishment of adequate treatment guidelines that can effectively be carried out at different levels (district hospitals, teaching hospitals, specialised hospitals, etc.) would also help in reduction of mortality due to cancer.

Increasing trends in cancer incidence have also been noted for several cancers such as colon and rectum, gall bladder, lung, ovary, prostate, brain, leukemia's (Murthy, 2007) etc. However, in the present exercise, no efforts have been made to incorporate the effects of changing trends or dietary practices. The present estimates highlight that existing treatment facilities are woefully inadequate to combat this deadly disease.

References

Chittaranjan National Cancer Institute, Calcutta. 1997. Population Based Cancer Registry, PBCR, Calcutta, Annual Report.

Dhar, M., R. Takiar and N.S. Murthy. 2006. A Comparison of Distribution of Age at Diagnosis with Age at Mortality of Cancer Cases – Does it Help in Estimation of Duration of Disease? *Cancer Registry Abstract*, National Cancer Registry Programme, Indian Council of Medical Research, Vol. XIII, 3–11.

Doll, R. and R. Peto. 1981. The Causes of Cancer: Quantitative Estimates of Avoidable Risks of Cancer in the United States Today. *J Natl Cancer Inst*. 66: 1191–308.

Gupta, S., P.H. Ananthanarayan and R.K. Srivastava. 2006. "National Cancer Control Programmes in South Asia-India, India" in Cancer Awareness, Prevention and Control: Strategies for South Asia. International Union against Cancer, UICC, 171–6.

International Institute of Population Sciences (IIPS) and ORC Macro. 2000. National Family Health Survey (NFHS–2). India 1998–99, Mumbai.

Murthy, N.S., A. Juneja, A. Sehgal and U.K. Luthra. 1990. Cancer Projection by the Turn of Century. *Indian J Cancer*, 27, 74–82.

Murthy, N.S. 2007. Trends and Patterns of Cancer Load in India: An Epidemiological Esιimation and Analysis. (Mimeographed), II Annual Report, Submitted to the Indian Council of Medical Research, New Delhi.

Nandakumar, A. and R. Swaminatha. 2006. "Burden of Cancer" in *Cancer Awareness, Prevention and Control: Strategies for South Asia*. International Union against Cancer, UICC, 17–25.

National Cancer Registry Programme (NCRP). 2001. A Consolidated Study of Population Based Registries Data, Cancer Statistics 1990–96. Indian Council of Medical Research, New Delhi.

——. 2001. A Consolidated Study of Population Based Registries Data, Cancer Statistics 1990–96. Indian Council of Medical Research, New Delhi.

——. 2002. Two-Year Report of the Population Based Registries 1997–1998. Incidence and Distribution of Cancer, Indian Council of Medical Research, New Delhi.

——. 2005. Two-Year Report of the Population Based Registries 1999–2000. Incidence and Distribution of Cancer, Indian Council of Medical Research, New Delhi.

Parkin, D.M., S.L. Whelan and J. Ferlay. 2002. Cancer Incidence in Five Continents. Vol. VIII, International Agency for Research on Cancer, Lyon, France, IARC Scientific Publication, No. 155.

Rao, Y.N., S. Gupta and S.P. Agarwal. 2002. National Cancer Control Programme: Current Status and Strategies. S.P. Agrawal (ed.), Fifty Years of Cancer Control, Director General of Health Services, Govt. of India, pp 41–49.

Registrar General of India. 1996. Population Projections for India and States, 1996–2016. Report of Technical Group on Population Projections Constituted by the Planning Commission, Ministry of Home Affairs, Government of India, New Delhi.

——. 1998. SRS based Abridged Life Tables, 1990–94 and 1991–95. SRS Analytical Report No. 1.

11

Trends in Cancer Incidence in Greater Mumbai

An Epidemiological Assessment

Balkrishna B. Yeole

The information relating to cancer incidence trends forms the scientific basis for the planning and organisation of prevention, diagnosis and treatment of cancer in a community. The trends may also give rise to a hypothesis concerning the etiology and biology of cancer, which can be applicable for testing of various hypotheses made in clinical and experimental oncology. A trend, however, always represents changes that have occurred within different groups of people, living under divergent conditions.

Methods

An attempt has been made to study the trends in age-adjusted incidence rates for the period 1982 to 2001, for prominent sites in Greater Mumbai patients. A model that fits this data is the logarithm $Y=AB^x$ which represents a linear regression model, where Y is the estimated incidence rate per 1,00,000 of the population and X is the calendar year minus the initial year (1982) for the current data. 'A' therefore represents the estimated rate of the initial year and (A–1)*100 gives the average annual percentage change in the incidence rate, during the period. In Table 1, the estimates of average annual percentage change in incidence rates, of various cancers by sex are given for the major sites, during the period 1982 to 2001.

Table 1 ***Estimates of Average Annual Percentage Change in Age-Adjusted Incidence Rate by Site and Sex from Regression Analysis for the 20-year period, 1982 to 2001, Greater Mumbai***

ICD10	*Site*	*Average Annual Percentage Change (apc)*	
		Male	*Female*
C01–C02	Tongue	-2.42***	-0.78ns
C04–C06	Mouth	+0.36ns	-0.02ns
C09–C10	Oropharynx	-2.91***	-1.84ns
C12–C13	Hypopharynx	-3.96***	-3.44**
C15	Oesophagus	-2.83***	-2.67***
C16	Stomach	-2.20***	-2.82***
C18	Colon	+0.86ns	+0.68ns
C19–C21	Rectum	-0.57ns	-0.13ns
C22	Liver	+1.76***	+1.26ns
C23–C24	Gall bladder	+4.22***	+3.89***
C25	Pancreas	+1.01ns	+1.65*
C32	Larynx	-1.11*	-2.78**
C33–C34	Lung	-1.63***	+1.21ns
C50	Breast	—	+1.65***
C53	Cervix	—	-1.04**
C54–55	Uterus	—	+2.65***
C56	Ovary	—	+1.73***
C61	Prostate	+1.27*	—
C62	Testis	-1.33*	—
C60	Penis	-4.69***	—
C66–C68	U bladder	+1.61*	+1.99*
C64–C65	Kidney	+3.40***	+4.02***
C70–C72	Brain	+3.79***	+4.45***
C73	Thyroid	+0.13ns	+0.88ns
C81–C85	Lymphomas	+3.68***	+4.02***
C91–C95	Leukamias	+1.57*	+1.38***
C00–C95	All sites	-0.72ns	0.37ns

ns not significant, * S significant at 0.05 level, ** S significant at 0.01 level,
*** S significant at 0.001 level.

Figure 1 ***Sites Showing Decreasing Trends in Age-Adjusted Cancer Incidence Rates with Corresponding APCs, Greater Mumbai, 1982-2001, Male***

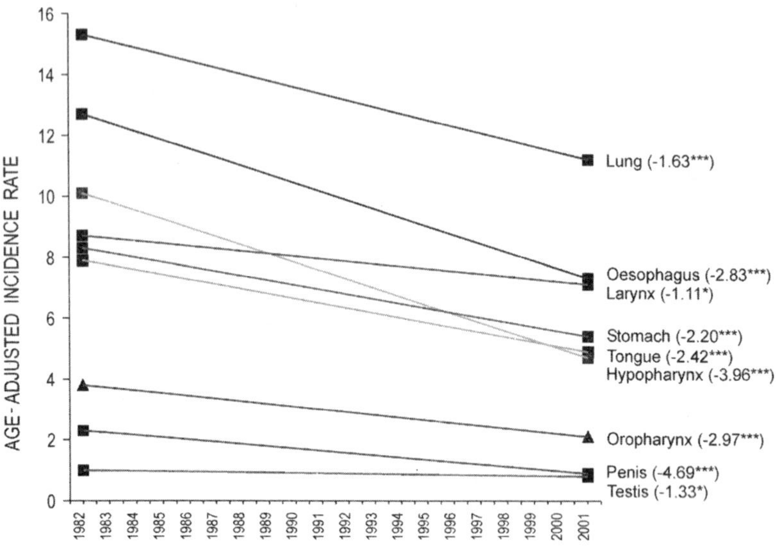

Figure 2 ***Sites Showing Decreasing Trends in Age-Adjusted Cancer Incidence Rates with Corresponding APCs, Greater Mumbai, 1982-2001, Female***

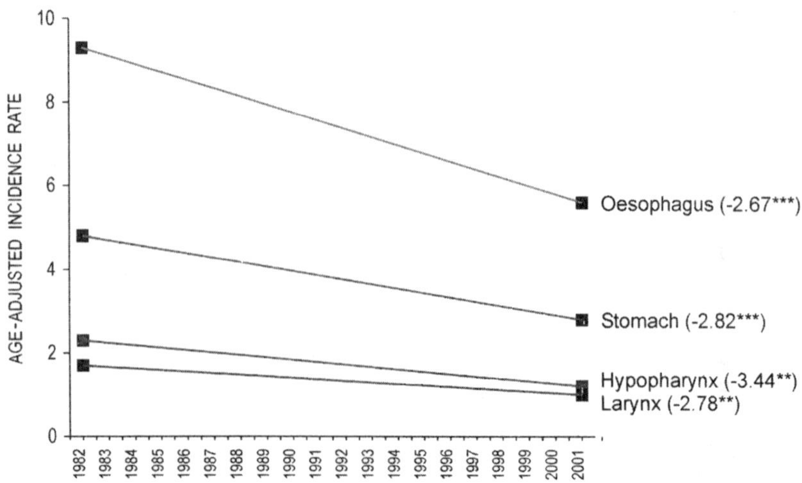

Figure 3 ***Sites Showing Increasing Trends in Age-Adjusted Cancer Incidence Rates with Corresponding APCs, Greater Mumbai, 1982-2001, Male***

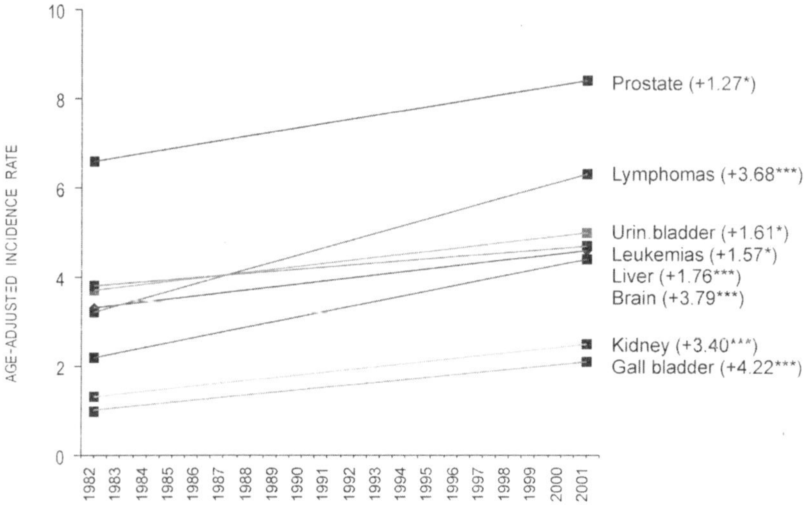

Figure 4 ***Sites Showing Increasing Trends in Age-Adjusted Cancer Incidence Rates with Corresponding APCs, Greater Mumbai, 1982-2001, Female***

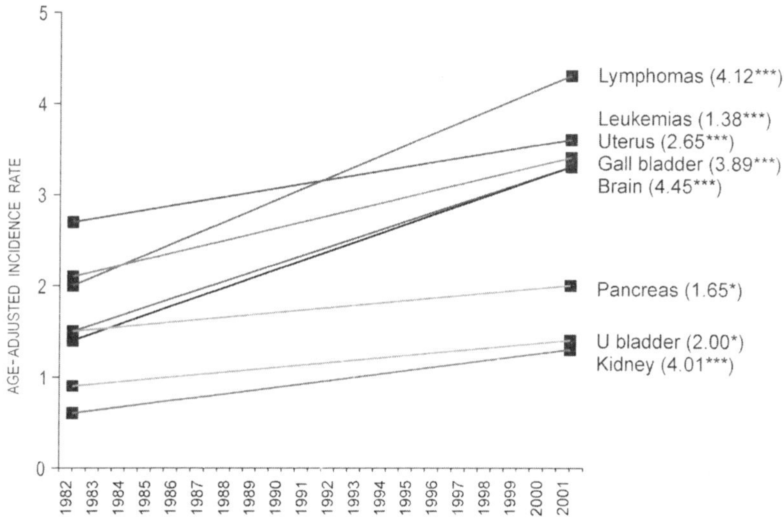

Figure 5 ***Sites Showing No Significant Changes in Trends in Age-Adjusted Cancer Incidence Rates with Corresponding APCs, Greater Mumbai, 1982-2001, Male***

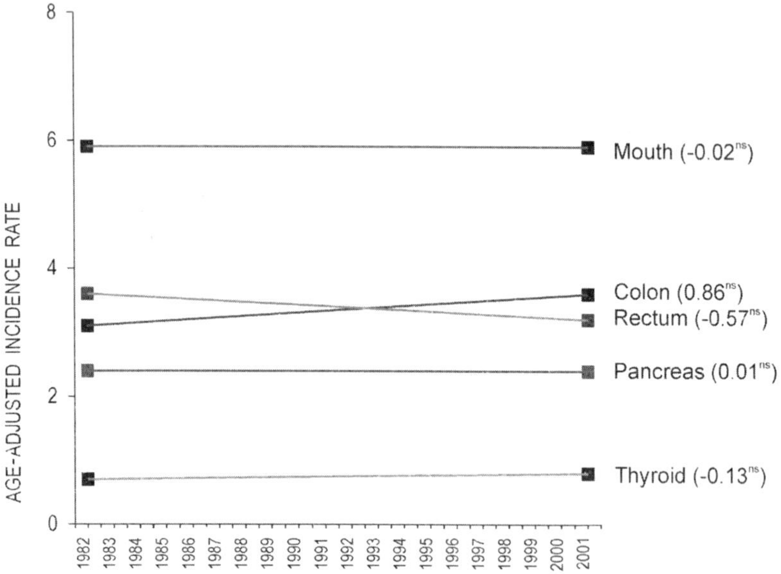

Figure 6 ***Sites Showing No Significant Changes in Trends in Age-Adjusted Cancer Incidence Rates with Corresponding APCs, Greater Mumbai, 1982-2001, Female***

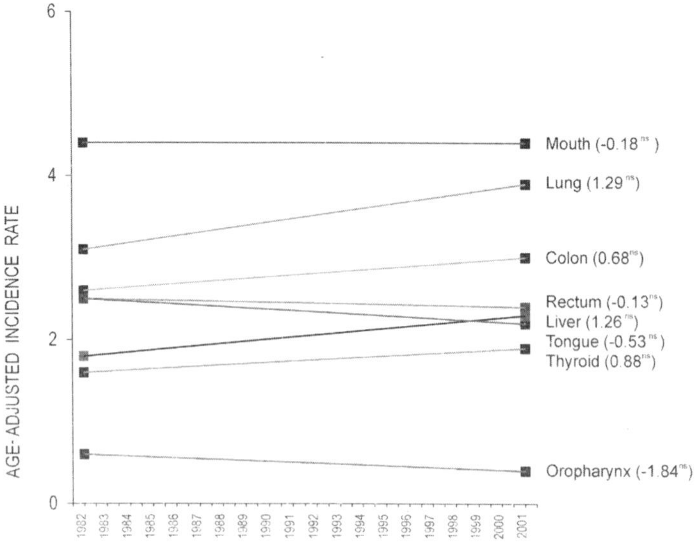

Results

For the period 1982 to 2001, the overall age-adjusted cancer incidence rates are seen to decrease 0.72 per cent per year in males and the increase of 0.37 per cent per year in females (Figure 8). The increase in females is found to be not statistically significant. Increasing trends (statistically significant) in incidence are seen in males for cancers involving the liver, gall bladder, prostate, urinary bladder, kidney, brain, lymphomas and leukemias (Figure 1) and in females for cancers involving the gall bladder, breast, uterus, ovary, urinary bladder, kidney, brain, lymphomas and leukemias (Figure 2). A decreasing trend statistically significant in incidence was found for the oropharynx, hypopharynx, oesophagus, stomach, larynx, lung, testis and penis in males and oropharynx, hypopharynx, oesophagus, stomach and cervix in females (Figure 4).

The incidence was found to be more stable for cancers involving the tongue, mouth, colon, rectum, and thyroid in males (Figure 5) and tongue, mouth, oropharynx, colon, rectum, liver, pancreas, lung and thyroid in females (Figure 6).

For males, the greatest change in incidence over the twenty-year period was for penis, which decreased by 4.69 per cent per year followed by gall bladder (an increase of 4.22% per year) and lymphomas (an increase of 3.68% per year). In females, the greatest change in incidence during the same time period was observed for the brain (an increase of 4.45% per year) followed by gall bladder (an increase of 3.89% per year) followed by lymphomas (an increase of 4.02% per year) (Table 1).

Amongst female, cancer of the breast, cervix, and ovary contribute about 50 per cent of the total incidence. A statistically significant increasing trend was observed for ovarian cancers while decreasing trend was observed for cancer of the cervix.

Discussion

The information behind cancer incidence trends forms the scientific basis for the planning and organisation of the prevention, diagnosis and treatment of cancer in the community. A trend, however, always represents a summary curve of changes that have occurred within different groups of people living under different conditions. A record increase or decrease in incidence, to a large extent, can arise from artifacts such as changes in diagnosis accuracy, changes in coding practice, differences in autopsy rate, and in the percentage of cases examined microscopically.

As a result, there are considerable limitations and errors in the evaluation of trend curves. Interpretation of trends can be effected correctly only by those who are aware of their reliability.

When data is assessed for studying trends from a particular registry, the data should be reliable and complete. From the diagnostic point of view, the cases registered over a period of time should have a high percentage of microscopic confirmation and low percentage of cases diagnosed by death certificate alone. At all times all sources should be tried for collecting the required data.

Strict definition should be adopted for inclusion or exclusion of cancer cases throughout the entire period of study. Much attention should be given to this issue when trends are compared with the trend analysis of other registries.

The difficulty in defining cancer is illustrated by the so-called carcinoma in situ lesions. In some geographical areas, these lesions are registered as malignant tumors. The classification problem of papillomas of the bladder can be used as another example of difficulties in defining cancer. In some registries, sometimes papillomas are included and sometimes they are excluded in the incidence of urinary bladder cancer. Furthermore, in some registries and during the same time periods they are called carcinomas instead of papillomas.

A significant difficulty in the interpretation of cancer trends is created when tumors can be classified on two or more axes. During some time periods, they may be classified topographically and during others, according to morphological or some other criteria. Tumors of lymphatic tissue provide a good example (Barekat et al., 1971; Saxena, 1979). In some series, malignant lymphomas are grouped under tumors of the lymphatic tissue; in other series with reference to the primary site.

Observer variation is another great problem in the histologic classification of tumors and may be of such a magnitude that it seems relevant to raise serious doubts about the validity of many epidemiological studies concerning trends. A considerable level of observer disagreement has been shown in studies dealing with lung cancer (Feinstein, 1970), cervical cancer, malignant lymphomas (Hakama et al., 1973; Symmers, 1968), and thyroid cancer (Saxena et al., 1978).

Mass examinations (screenings) have a definite effect on trend curves and also on the frequency of biologically different tumors included in the trends. The reason for this is simply that slow growing tumors are always more frequently diagnosed through mass examinations than they are under normal conditions.

There should be a practice of census at regular intervals of times for registry areas. Population figures by age and sex should be made available from the census department. Population estimates for required years should be made on scientific way, i.e., taking into consideration the population components such as fertility, mortality and migration.

While interpreting trends, changes in coverage areas under the period of study, problems with the starting registration system and difficulties in the registry conduction should also be taken into consideration.

Several studies in India have shown that chewing and smoking tobacco are the main risk factors for the cancers of the upper areodigestive tract. The changing pattern in these cancers could be viewed in the light of prevalent tobacco habits in the various cohorts and the risk ratios associated with specific tobacco habits. Risk ratios in smokers and chewers for several cancer sites have been estimated in two studies (Jussawalla and Deshpande, 1971; Sanghavi, 1981). It has been shown in the above-mentioned studies that the risk ratios in the *bidi* smokers are higher for cancers of the oropharynx and larynx than in chewers, whereas risk in chewers is higher for cancers of the oral cavity and hypopharynx than in *bidi* smokers. For cancer of the oesophagus, the risk ratio in both smokers and chewers is similar. Those combining the habit of smoking and chewing have a much higher risk—almost multiplicative compared to those indulging in only the single habit. For lung cancer, both *bidi* and cigarette smoking are proven risk factors. (Notani et al., 1977; Jussawalla and Jain, 1979).

Data on tobacco usage in the general population are not available to study the changes, if any, in the habit pattern and their effect on cancer risk in the different cohorts. However, an attempt has been made to explain the observed pattern in the light of prevalent tobacco habits in blue collar workers from a cohort study which was carried out in Bombay between 1971 and 1976 to assess the health consequences of smoking (Jayant et al., 1983). The habit pattern in the various birth cohorts showed that there is a marked decrease in the proportion of both *bidi* smokers (from 21% to 11.8%) and those with dual habit of *bidi* smoking and tobacco chewing (from 9.4% to 4.2%) in the successive younger cohorts, born between 1921 and 1936. Corresponding proportions of cigarette smokers and cigarette smokers plus tobacco chewers show some increase. It has been shown that the trends observed in cancers of the tongue, oropharynx, hypopharynx, oesophagus, larynx and lung in Bombay males are consistent with the observed pattern in the light of prevalent tobacco habits in blue collar workers in Bombay city (Jayant and Yeole, 1987).

Breast cancer is now a leading cancer in women in Mumbai. It has been observed that the incidence has increased over the last two decades. This increase in incidence is significant. Evaluation of breast cancer incidence trends in the light of proven etiological factors suggests that the increase in breast cancer incidence is related to a gradual decrease in the proportion of women having a first child before 20 years of age, and to an increase in the proportion of "never married" women (Yeole et al., 1990).

Cancer of the cervix uteri predominates in India. In Bombay, declining trend in cervical cancer incidence is noted. It was found that this decline could be explained as a cohort effect indicating that it may have been due to an upward shift in age at marriage in the younger cohorts (Yeole et al., 1989).

Bombay data shows decreasing trends in incidence of stomach cancer in both the sexes. The world decline in gastric cancer has been aptly described as an 'unplanned triumph'. This decline was mainly due to a fall in the intestinal type of adenocarcinomas, most closely linked to environmental differences, and that dietary changes were largely responsible. (Hirayama, 1977)

The increasing trend in liver cancer in Bombay data may be attributed to increase in diagnostic facilities and improvement in the coding system. As general increase in pancreatic cancer was observed in European populations, Bombay data also showed increasing trend for this cancer.

The pattern of geographical variation and the main risk factors for endometrial cancer are broadly similar to those for cancers of the breast and ovary. Bombay data shows increasing trends in breast, ovary and endometrial cancers. A marginal increase in incidence for prostate cancer was observed, which may be attributed to improvement in diagnostic practices. The increase in incidence of testis cancer showed a clear increase in the risk in successive birth cohorts. Increase in incidence for bladder cancer may be attributed largely to increased use of tobacco and change in coding practice with respect to incidence of bladder papillomas. Increase in incidence for brain cancer can be due to improvement in diagnostic practice. Increased diagnosis of clinically occult or biologically benign lesions may be the explanation for the increase in incidence of thyroid cancer. No regular trend was observed for lymphomas and Hodgkin's disease. It requires that data should be analysed by histological types separately. The increase in leukemia incidence reported here may reflect improvements in diagnosis.

References

Barekat, A.A., F. Saidi and E. Dutz. 1971. Cancer Survey in South Iran with special reference to Gastrointestinal Neoplasma. *Int. J. Cancer*, 71, 353–63.

Feinstein, A.R., N.A. Gelfman and R. Yesner. 1970. Observer Variability in the Histopathologic Diagnosis of Lung Cancer. *Am., Rev, Resp Dis*, 101–671.

Hakama, M., K. Franssila and E. Saxen. 1973. Reliability of Histopathogenic Diagnosis of Malignant Lymphomas. *Ann. Clin. Res* 5, 104–8.

Hirayama, T. 1977. "Changing Patterns of Cancer in Japan with special reference to the Decrease in Stomach Cancer Mortality" in H.H. Hiatt and J.A. Watson (eds.), *Origins of Human Cancer*. Book A. Incidence of Cancer of Humans, Cold Spring Harbour Laboratory, Cold Spring Harbour, 55–77.

Jayant, K. and B.B. Yeole. 1987. Cancers of the Upper Alimentary and Respiratory Tracts in Bombay, India: A Study of Incidence over Two Decades. *Br. J. Cancer*, 56, 847–52.

Jussawalla, D.J. and V.A. Deshpande. 1970. Evaluation of Cancer Risk in Tobacco Chewers and Smokers: An Epidemiological Assessment. *Cancer*, 24, 11–5.

Jussawalla, D.J. and D.K. Jain. 1979. Lung Cancer in Greater Bombay: Correlation with Religion and Smoking Habits. *Br. J. Cancer*, 40, 437.

Notani, P.N., D. Nagaraj Rao, M.V. Sirsat and L.D. Sanghvi. 1977. A Study of Lung Cancer in Relation to Bidi Smoking in Different Religious Communities in Bombay. *Ind. J. Cancer*, 14, 115.

Sanghavi, L.D. 1981. Cancer Epidemiology: The Indian Scene. J. Cancer Res. *Clin. Oncol.*, 99, 1.

Saxen, E. 1979. Histopathology in Cancer Epidemiology (The Maude Abbott Lecture). Pathol Annu, 14, 203–17.

Saxen, E., K. Franssila, D. Bijarnason, T. Normann and N. Ringertz. 1978. Observer Variation in Histologic Classification of Thyroid Cancer. Acta Pathol Microbiol Scand (A) 86, 483–6.

Symmers, W.S. 1968. Survey of the Eventual Diagnosis in 600 Cases referred for a Second Histological Opinion after an Initial Biopsy Diagnosis of Hodgkin's Disease. J. *Clin Pathol* 21: 650–3.

Yeole, B.B., K. Jayant and D.J. Jussawalla. 1989. Declining Trend in Cervical Cancer Incidence in Bombay, India (1964–1985). *J. Surg. Oncol.*, 42, 267–71.

——. 1990. Trends in Breast Cancer Incidence in Greater Bombay: An Epidemiological Assessment. Bull. World Health Organisation, 68, 245–9.

PART III

Ageing

12

Rapid Fertility Decline and Age-Structural Transition in Iran

Causes and Consequences

Amir H. Mehryar, S. Ahmad-Nia and Shahla Kazemipour

Until recently, the international discourse on population had until recently been dominated by the demographic transition theory and its preoccupation with the consequences of the disturbed balance of births and deaths. The policy and practical objective of this concern was to find out how and how soon developing countries burdened with high rates of population growth could be helped to lower their fertility rates. The impact of the latter, on the age-structure and the composition of the population received little serious attention. The idea of age-structure and its close links with an unavoidable impact on fertility and mortality dynamics had of course been long recognised by demographers like Keyfitz (1985). Such classical writers on population and development as Coale and Hoover (1958) had also offered insightful discussions concerning the impact of changing population age-structure on national savings, investment and economic growth. But little serious note had been taken of problems that the age-structure resulting from lowered fertility and mortality rates would pose for developing countries.

Since the mid-1980s, however, most developing countries have shown promising signs of fertility decline and the potential consequences of the changes in age-structure have received growing recognition by demographers, economists and policy makers. This has led to the emergence of new concepts like age-structural transition, demographic bonus, and the demographic window of opportunity. It has become clear that following fertility decline a period of demographic change will be ushered in during which the number and relative size of the young, working age population will surpass that of children (ages 0–14) and the elderly (ages 65+). This period will present developing countries with a unique opportunity to invest in human capital formation, improve the quality of their labour force and stimulate economic growth.

Iran, like other developing countries, has been deeply concerned with the process of the demographic transition since 1950s. Initial efforts to control fertility and population growth by the establishment of a national family planning programme were interrupted by the eruption of the Islamic revolution in 1979 and the strongly pro-natalist atmosphere created by war at that time postponed Iran's demographic transition for almost ten years. Since 1989, when the government adopted a birth control policy and the family planning programme was revived, however, the situation has changed drastically. The success of Iranian programme, which helped raise contraceptive prevalence to above 60 per cent of eligible married couples in less than five years, has in fact surprised many observers. The equally sharp decline in marital fertility rates to almost replacement level by late 1990s has also taken most observers by surprise. As a result of these developments, the age-structure of Iranian population has begun to change. By 1996, when the last census was held, the share of children aged 0–14 had fallen below 40 per cent of the population while the share of the elderly had risen above 4 per cent. Several large-scale surveys conducted between 1997–2003 strongly suggest that the process of fertility decline is continuing. The demographic window of opportunity thus opened deserves close scrutiny and analysis.

Aim of Study

The primary aim of this paper is to review the process of demographic changes and fertility decline in Iran during the second half of the twentieth century and to forecast their possible course and consequences during the first half of the twenty-first century. Another objective is to review the process of age-structural transition that has resulted from these changes and to discuss their short- and long-term implications for the Iranian society and economy.

Sources of Data

Data used in this analysis consist of two main types: census and survey data for the period 1956–2003 and projections for the period 2000–2050. In addition to decennial censuses conducted between 1956 and 1996 and the combined census survey conducted in 1991 (SCI, 1976–1996), the last decade has witnessed the implementation of several large-scale surveys. Among these, the Population Growth Estimation Survey conducted by the Statistical Centre of Iran (SCI,

1998), in 1997–1998 provides a wealth of data on fertility rates of Iranian couples. The information provided by this survey has been squarely confirmed by the results of the huge, nationwide DHS-type survey conducted jointly by the SCI and Ministry of Health and Medical Education (MoHME) in October 2000 (MoHME, 2001; Mehryar, 2002).

The large-scale Household Survey on Employment and Unemployment (HSCEU) initiated in 1998 and carried out on a quarterly basis since 2000 (SCI, 2004a-b) also provides up-to-date information on such socio-demographic characteristics as education, labour force participation, marital status and age-structure of both urban and rural population. For the period 2000–2050, use will be made of the revised projections of the UN Population Division (2004) published in 2005.

Historical Context

The population of Iran is estimated to have been just under 9 million at the start of the twentieth century (SCI, 2002). By 1956, when the first census was taken it had risen to 18.95 million. Thus, due to the traditional balance between high fertility and mortality rates, Iran's population had taken almost 50 years to double. The age-structure revealed by the 1956 census was indicative of a very young and rapidly growing population.

The second census taken in 1966 revealed a total population of 25.79 million growing at the annual rate of 3.1 per cent. At this rate of growth, Iran's population would double in less than 25 years. Results of the 1966 census also suggested a significant decline in mortality rate accompanied with some rise in birth rate. Partially, in response to the high rate of population growth revealed by the 1966 census, a family planning programme with explicit demographic and health objectives was introduced in 1967. In combination with other development and modernisation processes, the programme was able to bring about some change in the fertility desires and behaviour of married couples, but mostly in urban areas.

These were reflected in the results of the third census taken in 1976 which showed a population size of 34.5 million growing at the average rate of 2.7 per cent per year. The relatively large decline in growth rate (from 3.1 to 2.7%) revealed by the 1976 census was suggestive of the beginning of a new phase of demographic transition in Iran. Comparison of the growth rate indicated by this census with rates demonstrated by the censuses preceding (1966, 3.1%) and following it (1986, 3.9%) has led some demographers to speak of a "stalled transition" in Iran (Aghajanian, 1991).

Shortly after the publication of the results of the 1976 census, Iran went through a period of political protest and rebellion which quickly ended in the establishment of the Islamic Republic of Iran in early 1979. Although some Shiite *ulama* (e.g., Ayatulllah Mahllati of Shirz, 1963) had formally endorsed family planning and contraceptive use even before there was a national family planning programme in Iran and two relatively senior clergy who later emerged as influential leaders of the Islamic revolution in Lebanon and Iran had expressed quite liberal views regarding contraception in general and use of such controversial methods as sterilisation and abortion during the Rabat Conference on Islam and Family Planning in the late 1960s (Bahishti, 1974, Shamsuddin, 1974), the revolutionary atmosphere prevailing in late 1970s was very much against population control and family planning.

The amalgam of religious and secular groups that had joined forces to topple Shah's regime were united in one point. That was a deep mistrust of all modernisation programmes launched by the Shah and or promoted by his Western allies. Family planning programme was one of these which also suffered from having been too closely associated with the Iranian Women's Organisation led by the Shah's unpopular sister, Princess Ashraf. Many groups also believed that given Iran's large area and natural resources the country could accommodate a much larger population. Nevertheless, the liberal-technocratic caretaker government led by the late Mahdi Bazargan which took over the country immediately after the revolution would seem to have been committed to keeping the population control and FP programme alive. To this end, only four months after the triumph of the revolution the minister of health sought an audience with Imam Khomeini, advised him about the need for family planning, and obtained a *fatwa* from him declaring that use of available methods of birth control was not inconsistent with Islamic tenets as long as both husband and wife agreed to their use. Similarly, favourable *fatwas* were obtained from several top ranking Ayaullah and the Ministry of Health sent around a circular announcing that the programme will continue (Ashofteh-Tehrani, 1986; Mehryar, 1999). But the rank and file of the ministry would seem to have disagreed with this decision which seemed to run against the new regime's much publicised preference for early marriage and family formation as basic Islamic values. As a further sign of the Bazargan government's concern with population growth and family planning, it may be of interest to note that the first development plan drafted by the Deputy Prime Minister in charge of revolutionary affairs about a year after the revolution listed high rate of population growth and its control as one of the priority issues to be considered by the revolutionary government.

Despite these efforts, population control soon lost its importance, the family planning programme was merged with the school health programme and its activities were reduced to providing advice and services to couples who sought them. It is however important to note that there was never any formal effort either by the government or the politically powerful *ulama* to officially ban family planning or to limit access to contraceptives through public health facilities and/or the private sector. There were however a variety of efforts to promote early marriage and family formation as major Islamic values and thus to encourage fertility (Mehryar et al., 2001).

With Iraqi aggression and the breakout of the eight-year long war (1981–1988), population size and growth attained new significance. On the one hand, bereft of all sources of international support, the revolutionary government of Iran came to rely on population size as the only measure of comparative advantage in fighting against an enemy politically and financially supported by all Arab states and easily able to buy new armaments from both the Soviet Union and the West. Thus, the creation of a "2,00,00,000 man army" was adopted as one of the rallying slogans of Iranian war-time propaganda. On the other hand, increasing casualties of war persuaded many parents to think of having another child in case their existing ones were lost to war. This fear was quite understandable in view of the average age of the largely volunteer youth that were bearing the brunt of war on the Iranian side. Some families also considered it their religious duty to get their young sons married before sending them to the battle front. This pronatalist environment was provided with tangible economic incentives by the war-time rationing system under which all family members, including new born children, were entitled to an equal share of a variety of rationed goods distributed by the government.

The impact of these forces was clearly reflected in the results of the 1986 census which showed that the population of Iran had risen to 49.4 millions and was growing at the enormous rate of 3.9 per cent per annum (as compared with the figures of 44.9 million and 2.94% projected by the UN in 1975). The heightened rate of growth (from 2.7 to 3.9) was noticeable in both urban (from 4.93 to 5.41%) and rural areas (from 1.11 to 2.39%) of the country.

Publication of the results of the 1986 census coincided with the final years of the eight-year war against Iraq and the depletion of all economic resources. The extremely high rate of growth revealed by the 1986 census was at first hailed as a "god-sent gift" by Iranian authorities. But growing realisation of the social and economic costs and consequences of the high rate of growth for the war-shattered economy of Iran persuaded IRI authorities to adopt an anti-nationalist policy and revive the long-suspended family planning programme in 1989.

Contrary to all expectations, the new policy was enthusiastically received by people in general and the eligible couples in particular. By 1992, that is, in less than three years, the contraceptive prevalence rate (CPR) had risen above 60 per cent of eligible couples and there were clear signs of a precipitous fall in fertility rates. In fact, an analyses of the 1986 census by date of birth suggested that the fertility of Iranian couples had reached its peak between 1984 (in urban areas) and 1985 (in rural areas) (Mehryar and Tabibian, 1997). A twelve-round panel survey on socio-economic characteristics of Iranian households carried out between 1987–1989 indicated some decline in the fertility rates of Iranian couples. A combined census survey conducted in 1991 revealed a population size of 55.8 million growing at the rate of 2.5 per cent per annum. The results were so unexpected that the Plan and Budget Organisation, the parent organisation of the SCI, refused to use them in preparing the Second Five-Year Plan of development then under preparation. (Aghajanian, 1991). (SCI, 2001).

Findings of the 1991 census/survey were strongly supported by the fifth decennial census held in 1996. The latter revealed a total population size of just over 60 million (as compared with the figure of 76 million projected by the UN Population Division in 1996) growing at the modest rate of 1.96 per cent per annum. There were also clear signs of a remarkable drop in both fertility (from a TFR of 6.5 to 2.6) and mortality (from an estimated crude death rate of 12 to 6 per 1,000).

The changing size and growth rates of Iranian population are graphically summarised in Figure 1 which puts together estimates by Iranian demographers, UN experts and census results. As Iran has experienced little international migration during the twentieth century, changes in population size and growth rates presented in Figure 1 are mainly due to variations in fertility and mortality. Estimates of crude birth and death rates are summarised in Figure 2.

Results of the 1996 census which were treated with more than a fair share of caution by both the national and the international demographic

Figure 1 ***Size (in millions) and Annual Growth Rate (%) of Population of Iran between 1901 and 2000 as Estimated (1901-1951 & 2000) and Enumerated (1956-1996)***

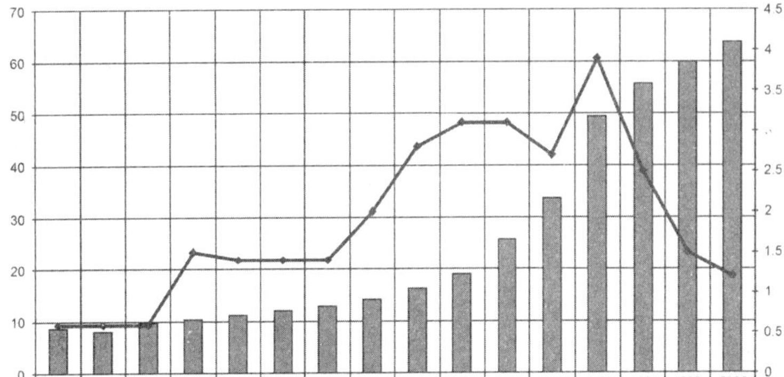

	1901	1911	1921	1926	1931	1936	1941	1946	1951	1956	1966	1976	1986	1991	1996	2000
Population	8.613	8.143	9.707	10.456	11.185	11.964	12.833	14.159	16.237	18.955	25.789	33.709	49.445	55.837	60.005	63.697
Growth Rate	0.6	0.6	0.6	1.5	1.4	1.4	1.4	2	2.8	3.1	3.1	2.7	3.9	2.5	1.5	1.2

Figure 2 ***Estimated Crude Birth and Death Rates of Iranian Population, 1901-2000 (1901-1951, Amani, 1995; 1950-2000, UN, 2005)***

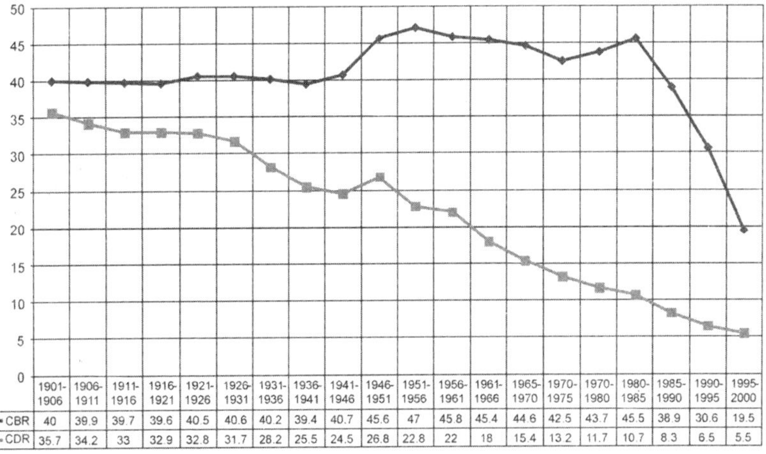

	1901-1906	1906-1911	1911-1916	1916-1921	1921-1926	1926-1931	1931-1936	1936-1941	1941-1946	1946-1951	1951-1956	1956-1961	1961-1966	1965-1970	1970-1975	1970-1980	1980-1985	1985-1990	1990-1995	1995-2000
CBR	40	39.9	39.7	39.6	40.5	40.6	40.2	39.4	40.7	45.6	47	45.8	45.4	44.6	42.5	43.7	45.5	38.9	30.6	19.5
CDR	35.7	34.2	33	32.9	32.8	31.7	28.2	25.5	24.5	26.8	22.8	22	18	15.4	13.2	11.7	10.7	8.3	6.5	5.5

community suggested an almost 40 per cent drop in fertility between 1986–1996. This dramatic drop was, moreover, observable across urban and rural areas of almost all provinces and sub-provinces of the country. A later analysis of the results of the 1986 and 1996 censuses by own-children method indicated that the process of fertility rise had in fact began in mid-1970s, that is, a few years before the revolution and

Figure 3 ***Total Fertility Rates of Iranian Women in Late 2000 by Province and Urban-Rural Residence (DHSI 2000)***

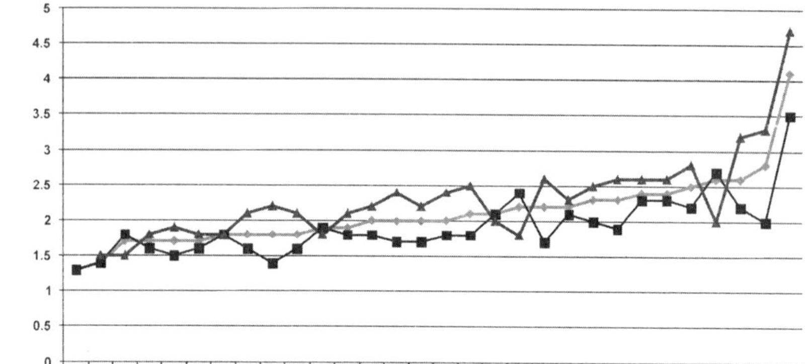

	Tehran MPA	Gilan	Markazi	Mazandaran	Fars	Esfahan	Cazvin	Kermansha	Hamadan	Ilam	Kordestan	Lorestan	Zanjan	Tehran	Ardabil
Total	1.3	1.4	1.7	1.7	1.7	1.7	1.8	1.8	1.8	1.8	1.9	1.9	2	2	2
Urban	1.3	1.4	1.8	1.6	1.5	1.6	1.8	1.6	1.4	1.6	1.9	1.8	1.8	1.7	1.7
Rural		1.5	1.5	1.8	1.9	1.8	1.8	2.1	2.2	2.1	1.8	2.1	2.2	2.4	2.2

	All Country.	Azarbayjan	Semnan	Yazd	Chaharmah	Bushehr	Kohgiluyeh	Golestan	Kerman	Khorasan	Azarbayjan	Qom	Khuzestan	Hormozgan	Sistan &
Total	2	2.1	2.1	2.2	2.2	2.2	2.3	2.3	2.4	2.4	2.5	2.6	2.6	2.8	4.1
Urban	1.8	1.8	2.1	2.4	1.7	2.1	2	1.9	2.3	2.3	2.2	2.7	2.2	2	3.5
Rural	2.4	2.5	2	1.8	2.6	2.3	2.5	2.6	2.6	2.6	2.8	2	3.2	3.3	4.7

had passed its peak point around 1984 (Abbassi-Shavazi, 1999; SCI, 1998).

The results of the 1996 census have been squarely confirmed by two large-scale national surveys specifically designed to assess fertility changes conducted in late 1990s. They are, the population growth estimation survey carried out by the SCI in 1998 and the huge DHS-type survey carried out jointly by the Ministry of Health and the SCI in October 2000. The results of the DHS-type survey are of particular interest because of the wealth of data that it has collected on socio-demographic characteristics and reproductive behaviour of Iranian couples in urban and rural areas of all 28 provinces as well as Tehran municipal area.

These studies not only confirm the results of earlier surveys but they also indicate that the process of fertility decline has continued after 1996. By late 2000, the total fertility rates of Iranian couples had dropped to below replacement level in urban areas of most provinces as well as the rural areas of several provinces (Figure 3). The drop is not surprising in view of the high rates of contraceptive prevalence revealed in almost all provinces (Figure 4).

The most significant achievement of the family planning programme initiated in 1989 is that it has eliminated the traditional gap in CPR of urban and rural couples. The slightly higher CPR of urban couples is mainly due to the fact that a larger proportion of them rely on

Figure 4 ***Proportion of Iranian Couples Using Any Contraceptive Method by Province and***

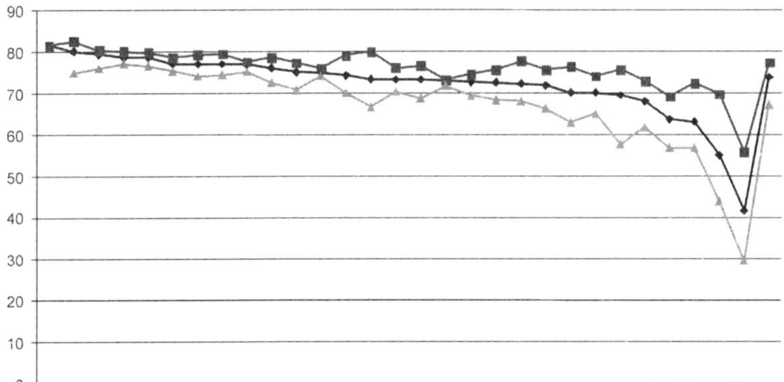

	TE HR AN	SE MN AN	ESF AH AN	MA ZA ND	TE HR AN	KU RDI STA	MA RK AZY	HA MA DA	YAZ D	QA ZVI N	KE RM AN	GIL AN	CH AR MA	ZA NJA N	AR DE BIL
All	81.6	80.2	79.4	78.6	78.6	77.2	77.1	77.1	77	76.1	75.1	75	74.3	73.4	73.3
Urban	81.6	82.6	80.5	80.2	79.9	78.7	79.3	79.5	77.6	78.6	77.4	76	79.2	80	76.1
Rural		74.9	76	77.2	76.6	75.4	74.1	74.5	75.2	72.5	70.8	74.1	70	66.7	70.3

	AZA RB AIJ	QO M	AZA RB AIJ	LO RIS TA	GO LES TA	FA RS	KE RM AN	ILA M	KH UZI STA	KH OR AS	BU SH EH	KO HGI LUY	HO RM OZ	SIS TA N &	TO TAL
All	73.3	73.1	72.7	72.5	72.3	71.9	70.1	70.1	69.5	68.1	63.7	63	55	41.5	73.8
Urban	76.6	73.2	74.6	75.6	77.7	75.6	76.3	74.1	75.6	72.9	69.2	72.4	69.7	55.7	77.4
Rural	68.7	71.7	69.4	68.3	68	66.3	62.9	65.1	57.6	61.8	56.8	56.8	43.8	29.6	67.2

the traditional method of withdrawal not promoted by the national programme. With widespread use of mostly modern methods of contraception by the rural couples, literacy and education have also lost their effect on contraceptive use. If anything, illiterate women are more likely to use modern methods, including female sterilisation, while the better educated women from more developed urban areas tend to rely on the traditional method of withdrawal.

Age-Structural Changes, 1,956–2,000

Changes in Population Pyramids

Changes in fertility and mortality that have taken place since early 1950s are clearly reflected in the age-structure of the population. These age-structural changes have become more noticable since 1976. Age pyramids of different censuses give some indication of these changes (Figure 5). Of the six pyramids shown in Figure 5, those for 1976, 1986 and 1996 are particularly worth the attention. The lowest two ranges of the 1976 pyramid are clearly suggestive of an increase in the number of births and children aged 0–9 years. The five ranges above them (ages 10–34) are also of a broad and regularly declining rectangular shape. In contrast, the age pyramid for 1986 has a broader base and more regularly declining shape until ages 30–34. Although Iran is known to have lost a large number (estimated about 2,50,000) of relatively young

Figure 5 ***Age Pyramids Revealed by Decennial Censuses, 1956–1996 and 2000 DHS***

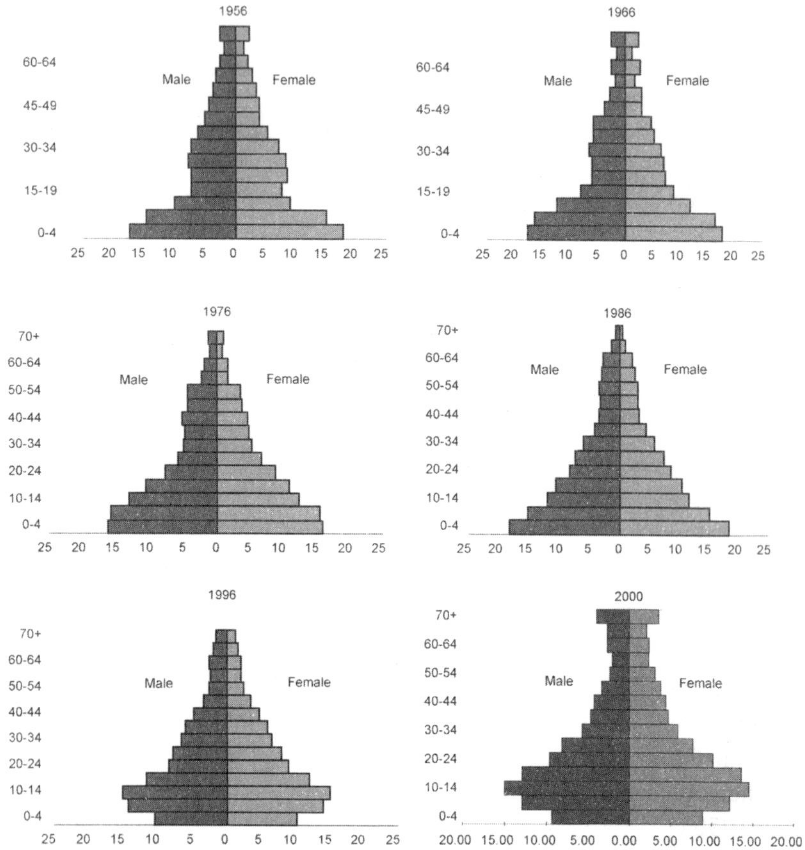

men during the revolution and the eight-year long war (1981–1988), there is little sign of this in the 1986 pyramid. Presumably, the marked decline in general mortality that has taken place since 1980s and the inclusion of a large group of Afghan refugees in the 1986 and 1996 censuses have compensated for the war-related mortality.

The pyramid for 1996 is different from all four previous pyramids in that it reveals a clear fall in the number and relative share of children aged 0–9. The fall is particularly impressive for the age group 0–4 and confirms other evidence regarding the acceleration of fertility decline since 1991. Age pyramids for urban and rural areas in 1996 are very similar and indicate that the huge fertility decline experienced by Iran since late 1980s has not been limited to urban areas only. The age pyramid for the year 2000 is based on a sample survey (DHSI, 2000) of about 5,00,000 individuals and thus is not expected to be as regular as the census-based pyramids. Yet, it strongly confirms the sharp drop of fertility between 1986–1996 and its continuation thereafter.

Judging by the age pyramids for 1956 and 1966, Iran would seem to have experienced a baby boom between 1940–1966. The gradual entry of the large number of children born during this period into reproductive career could have played a role in dampening the impact of the family planning programme between 1967–1979. The large number of women born during the period 1945–1966 was probably also responsible for the sudden rise in fertility after the revolution. The group of 20–40 year old women whose lowered fertility resulted in the surprisingly low growth rate revealed by the 1996 census mostly belong to the cohort born between 1966 and 1976. To what extent the low fertility demonstrated by this birth cohort was influenced by the fact that they were born during a period dominated by an active family planning programme and an anti-nationalist atmosphere remains to be demonstrated.

Changes in the Size and Relative Share of Major Age Groups

As indicated in Figure 7, the number of people falling into each of the three major age groups of 0–14, 15–64 and 65+ years has grown enormously in consecutive censuses taken between 1956–1996. The relative share of these groups of the total population had, however, remained relatively stable until early 1990s (Figure 7). The age-structure of the population enumerated in 1986 differed only slightly from that of the 1956 census. While the proportion of children aged 0–14 had risen (from 42.2 to 45.5) and that of the elderly aged 65+ had dropped noticeably (from 3.9% to 3.1%). The picture changed significantly after 1991. By 2003, the share of children had dropped to 28.4 per cent while that of adults had risen to 66.6 per cent.

These variations are also reflected in the dependency ratios for different years taken from the UN (2004) estimates (Figure 8). Thus, while the total and child dependency ratios of the population had gone up markedly (from 85 and 78 to 99 and 92, respectively) between 1956–1966, the dependency ratio of the elderly had remained constant at 7.

By 1976, the share of children of the total population had dropped slightly (44.5% as compared with 46.1% in 1966) but there was no

Figure 6 *Population Aged 0–14, 15–64 and 65+ Enumerated between 1956–1996*

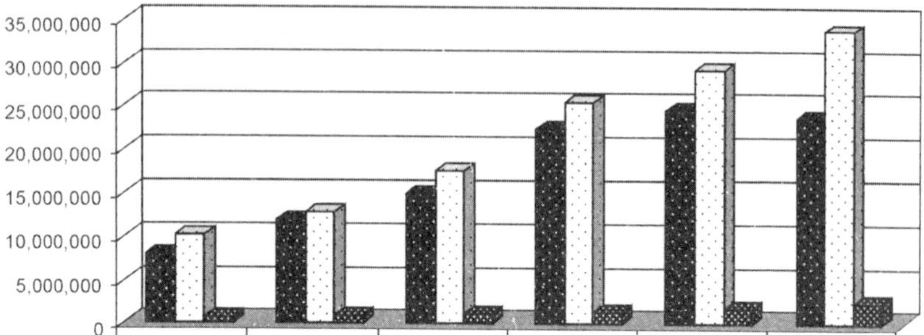

	1956	1966	1976	1986	1991	1996
0-14	7,993,156	11,877,006	15,009,363	22,474,017	24,723,874	23,725,545
15-64	10,202,878	12,908,667	17,512,911	25,445,562	29,164,731	33,702,406
65+	751,597	968,105	1,186,470	1,501,718	1,948,558	2,595,181

Figure 7 *Share (%) of Population of Different Age Groups 0–14, 15–64 and 65+ of the Total Population*

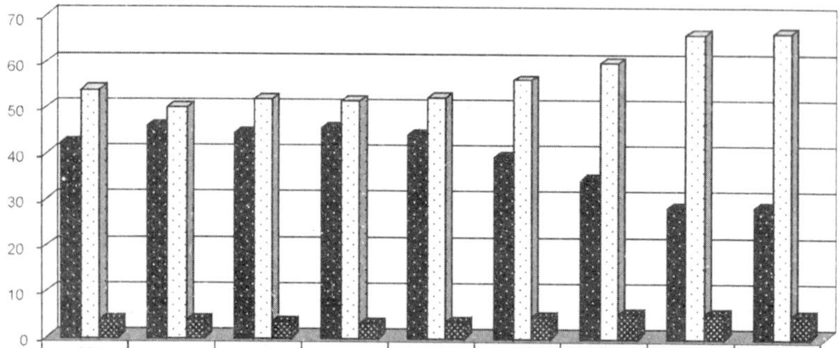

	1956	1966	1976	1986	1991	1996	2000	2002	2003
0-14	42.2	46.1	44.5	45.5	44.3	39.5	34.5	28.5	28.4
15-64	53.9	50.2	52	51.4	52.2	56.1	60.1	66.3	66.6
65+	3.9	3.7	3.5	3.1	3.5	4.4	5.4	5.2	5

commensurate rise in the share of the elderly. If anything, the proportion of population aged 65+ had also declined slightly (from 3.7% to 3.5%). As a result, while the total and child dependency ratios of the population enumerated in 1976 (93 and 86) are lower than those for 1966 (99 and 92), there is virtually no change in the dependency ratios of the elderly (7).

The following decade witnessed a huge increase in the size, fertility, and growth rate of Iranian population. The share of children aged 0–14

Figure 8 ***Child, Elderly and Total Dependency Ratio (%), 1950–2005***

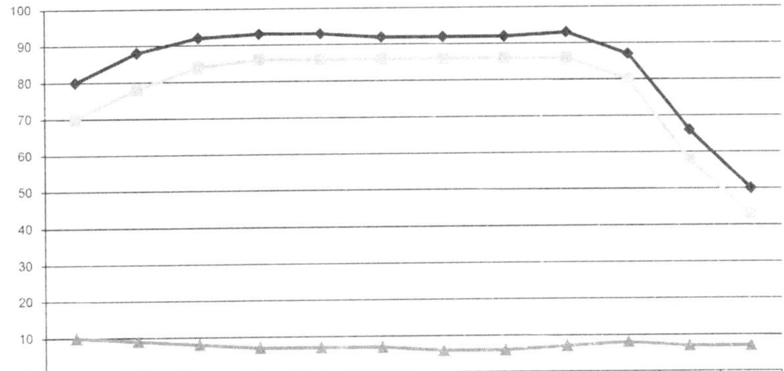

	1950	1955	1960	1965	1970	1975	1980	1985	1990	1995	2000	2005
Total	80	88	92	93	93	92	92	92	93	87	66	50
Child	70	78	84	86	86	86	86	86	86	80	58	43
Old-age	10	9	8	7	7	7	6	6	7	8	7	7

enumerated in 1986 (45.5%) is, however, only slightly higher than that of 1976 (44.5%) but lower than the figure for 1966 (46.1%). At the same time, the proportionate share of the population aged 65+ had fallen to the all time low level of 3.1 per cent.

These ratios may, however, give a misleading impression of the reality. The number of children born during the decade preceding the 1986 census (1,65,70,717) was 1.55 times the figure for 1976 (1,07,06,245). Similarly, the number of the elderly enumerated in 1986 (15,32,795) is almost 30 per cent larger than the number enumerated in 1976 (11,79,806). The total and child dependency ratios for 1986 (94, 88) fall between those for 1966 (99 and 92) and 1976 (93 and 86) while that for the elderly (6) are lower.

The sharp drop in the fertility rate of Iranian population during 1986–1996 is even more clearly reflected in single-year age pyramids for 1976, 1986 and 1996 (Figure 9). From the pyramid for 1976 it would appear that a sharp drop had taken place in the number of children born during the last two years of the decade covered by this census (i.e., 1975 and 1976). A much smaller decline is also detectable in the number of children born during the lat two years of the decade ending in the 1986 census. In the case of 1996 pyramid, not only the total number of children aged 0–9 is smaller than that of 1986 census but also there is clear evidence of a progressive decrease in the number of children born in at least 8 of the 10 years preceding the 1996 census.

The baby boom period following the Islamic revolution thus would seem to have been rather short-lived. In fact, looking at the number of people born between 1976–1986 covered by the 1986 census, it would appear that peak fertility rates were achieved between 1984 (in urban areas) and 1985 (in rural areas). Births registered by the Civil Registration Organisation (CRO) indicate an even earlier date (1981) for the fertility peak. The combined census-survey conducted in 1991 is also clearly indicative of a downward trend in the number of children born after 1987. By this time, the percentage share of children aged 0–4 years of the total population had decreased to 44.3 per cent, while that of the elderly had risen to 3.5 per cent. Nevertheless, the total, child and elderly dependency ratios (92, 85, and 7%) revealed by the 1991 census-survey are hardly different from those of the 1976 census (93, 86, and seven %).

The downward trend in fertility revealed by the 1991 census-survey took a more precipitous form during 1991–1996. This is clearly reflected in the results of the 1996 census which revealed a much smaller population size than generally anticipated. For the first time in the recent history of Iran, the share of children aged 0–14 (39.5%) was less than 40 per cent. Of the latter, only about a quarter (26%) had been born during the preceding five-year period (1991–1996). On the other hand, the 1996 census recorded a small but significant rise in the share of the elderly (4.4% as compared with 3.1% in 1986). Due to these changes, the total and child dependency ratios revealed by the 1996 census (78 and 70) are markedly lower than those derived from earlier censuses while the elderly dependency ratio has risen to 8.

According to the DHS-type survey conducted in October 2000, the share of children in total population had fallen to 34.5 per cent while that of the elderly had risen above 5 per cent. As a result, the total and child dependency ratios had fallen to 66 and 57 (as compared with 78 and 70 in 1996) and the dependency ratio due to the elderly had gone up to nine. The household employment surveys conducted in 2002 and 2003 indicate further declines in the relative share of children (to around 28.5% as compared with the figure of 39.5 in 1996 and 45.5 in 1986) but the relative share of the elderly has remained constant at around 5 per cent. The total and child dependency ratios derived from these surveys (50.5 and 43%) are almost one-half of those obtained by the 1966 census. The dependency ratio of the elderly (7–8%) has, however, remained at almost the same level as in 1956–1976 and 1991.

Figure 9 Comparison of Single-Year Age Pyramids, 1976, 1986 and 1996 Censuses

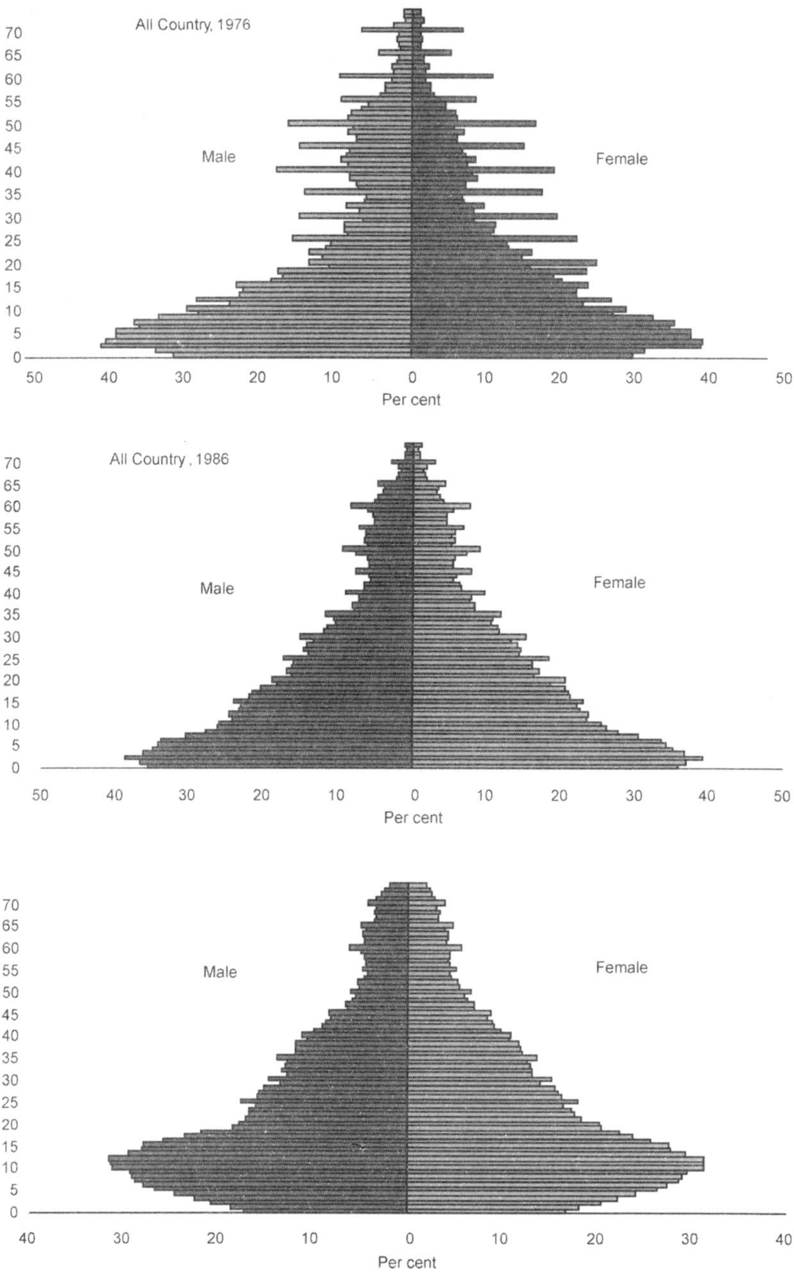

Children Born between 1976–1996 and their Contribution to Age-structural Change

Of the 60 million people enumerated in 1996, 30.84 million (51.0%) had been born during the preceding two decades. Of this group at least 28.5 million had been born since the establishment of the Islamic Republic of Iran, that is, between 1979–1996. This is by far the largest number added to Iran's population within an 18-year period since 1956. By contrast, the number of children aged 0–9 years enumerated in the preceding three censuses (1956–1976), was only 25.6 million. Thus, the cohort born between 1979 and 1996 constitutes a major cohort or *wave* that will strongly affect the future shape of Iranian population during the twenty-first century. In view of the clear evidence of a sharp decline in fertility between 1991–1996, one might even be tempted to exclude children born during the second half of the decade preceding the 1996 census and concentrate on the group of children born between 1977 and 1991 (about 22.2 million in 1996) as the crucial wave to be monitored.

The cohort born between 1976–1996 covers four important sub-groups corresponding to five-year intervals, 1976–1981, 1982–1986, 1987–1991 and 1992–1996. Each of these cohorts is associated with different historical landmarks. The first five-year period (1976–1981) partly overlaps with the final years of the old regime. The third five-year period corresponds to the final years of the war against Iraq and was characterised by devastating signs of war-related damage to the infrastructure, a sharp drop in the national capacity to produce and market oil, a decline in economic growth, and growing doubts regarding the relevance and attainability of the declared objectives of the war.

The fourth and last period (1992–1996) coincides with the development of post-war reconstruction plans calling for economic readjustment, gradual removal of subsidies and government control on prices, privatisation, and the streamlining of state bureaucracy. Continued economic blockade by the United States and mismanagement of resources hampered the achievement of economic growth targets set by the planners, and resulted in higher rates of inflation, unemployment and wide spread economic hardship. These pressures, along with improvements in the levels of education of people, particularly women, media exposure and the modernisation of Iranian society no doubt contributed to the unexpected success of the revived family planning programme and resulted in the tremendous fertility decline that has characterised the last five-year period (1992–1996).

Consequences of Age-Structural Transition

Challenges Posed by Fertility Rise between 1976–1991

As suggested earlier, the trend, size and shape of Iran's population is likely to be strongly determined by the large cohort born between 1976–1996. Obviously, a birth cohort covering two decades will pass through different stages of its life course at different times and its reaction to the particular demands of that stage will be strongly affected by the social, economic and political conditions prevailing at the time. The cohort born between 1976–1981 entered its formal schooling career in 1983 and raised demand for primary education facilities/services considerably. Being constitutionally obliged to provide all children with free education, the government of the IRI responded with increased investment in teacher training, building schools and introducing a two-shift schooling system that allowed use of the same premises by two different groups of children. When this cohort reached age 12 (1987–1989) a similar pressure was experienced by the junior secondary school system. The same happened when the wave reached age 15 and a higher demand for senior secondary school facilities became evident.

Thanks to the experience gained and investments made during this period, the educational system was better prepared for the larger wave coming from the 1982–1986 birth cohort when it reached the age of formal schooling. On the other hand, by the time the much smaller cohort of children born between 1987–1991 reached their school age there were clear signs of excess capacity at the primary school level. This resulted in the closure of a considerable number of primary teacher training centres established during the first decade after the revolution.

Earlier, the sudden increase in the number of young children had presented Iran with the serious problem of feeding them. The problem was partly responsible for the massive and highly successful breast-feeding campaign launched by the Ministry of Health and Medical Education (MoHME). Thanks to the full support of religious leaders and the active participation of grass-roots organisations and public mobilisation systems created during the revolution and war, the campaign proved singularly successful and Iran came to be acknowledged as a regional leader in successfully promoting breast-feeding. Interestingly, the breast-feeding campaign was designed and implemented under the leadership of the same minister of health (a US trained pediatrician) who had played a major role in persuading the government to adopt a birth control policy and revive the family planning programme in 1989.

When the large number of children born between 1976–1986 reached the age of higher education in early 1990s, there was an enormous increase in the number of university applicants. The remarkable expansion of opportunities for higher education through both public and private sector initiatives during the preceding decade was able to absorb the shock, although at the expense of quality. As the process has continued, creation of opportunities for higher education has taken critical dimensions and the problem of finding alternative sources of funding for higher education or further expanding the existing private sector has become a subject of much heated debate. Because of the rising social demand for higher education and the relatively small ratio of secondary school graduates who are currently able to enter universities, the pressure on higher education will most probably continue to rise for decades to come. Currently, the government is seriously studying the ways and means of raising the coverage of higher education to 30 per cent of eligible youth.

The gradual entry of the huge birth cohorts of 1976–1991 into the labour market has also confronted Iran with huge problems of unemployment and job creation in recent years. Again, the problem is unlikely to be solved for decades to come, as is the problem of housing created by the entry of this cohort to family formation and reproductive phases of life.

Signs of the Widening of the Demographic Window of Opportunity

As a result of the sudden decrease in fertility between 1991–1996, the number and relative share of children aged 0–4 dropped significantly. The trend would seem to have continued at least until early 2003 when the last household employment survey was conducted. According to the latter survey only, 7.2 per cent of the population covered was aged 0–4. This is significantly lower than the figures obtained by the 1986 (18.3%) and 1996 (10.3%) censuses. As a result of this change, the total and child dependency ratios have fallen to 50 and 43 as compared with 70 and 78 in 1996. The old-age dependency ratio (7) has, however, remained more or less constant between its 1986 (6) and 1996 levels (8).

Despite its apparent size (3.9% per annum), the growth rate experienced by Iranian population between 1976 and 1988 failed to raise the relative share of children aged 0–14 above its 1966 level. By 1991, it had dropped below its 1976 value (44.3) and by 1996 it was below 40, the conventional cut-off point for considering a population as "young" (Cogwill and Holmes, 1970). The DHS-type survey carried out in late

2000 has given the figure of 34.5 per cent which is very close to that (35.5) used in the 2004 revision of the UN projections. Meanwhile, the share of the elderly (people aged 65+) which had taken a downward trend between 1956–1986 showed an upward rise in 1991 and by 1996 accounted for 4.4 per cent of the total population. Surveys carried out between 2000–2003 indicate that it had continued to grow and had risen above 5 per cent by the end of the century.

On the other hand, the share of the potentially active population aged 15–64 years which had vacillated around 52 per cent between 1956–1986, had risen to 56.1 per cent by 1996 and according to surveys carried out in 2002 and 2003 it now accounts for about two-thirds of the Iranian population. This rise may be taken as a sign that the demographic window of opportunity which began to open in 1996 has grown wider over the past eight years.

As indicated by Figure 6 above, the size of the potentially productive population (ages 15–64) enumerated in 1996 was almost equal to the total population of Iran in 1976. The number of people aged 15–64 exceeded that of those aged 0–14 and 65+ by over seven million which is more than 12 per cent of the enumerated population. This difference may be taken as a sign of the enlarged size of the window of opportunity.

Not all of the people aged 15–64 are in reality economically active and productive. The majority of youngsters aged 15–19 are attending school. In 2003, only about one-third of this age group were considered

Figure 10 ***Relative Share(%) of Five Major Age Groups of Population of Iran, 1956–2003***

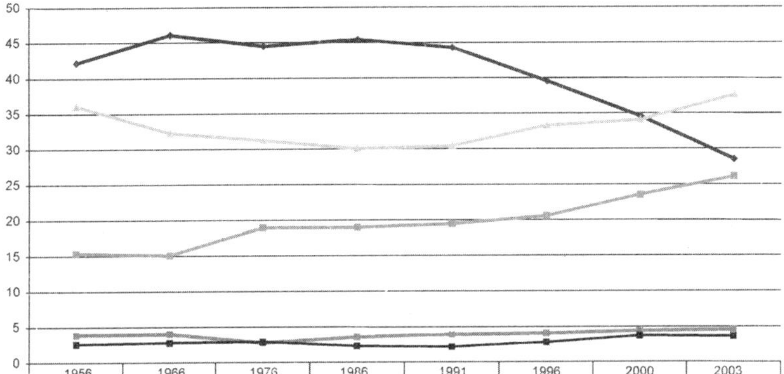

	1956	1966	1976	1986	1991	1996	2000	2003
0-14	42.2	46.1	44.53	45.45	44.28	39.5	34.56	28.51
15-24	15.4	15.1	18.96	18.98	19.44	20.55	23.55	26.11
25-59	36.1	32.3	31.25	30.09	30.45	33.28	34.04	37.58
60-69	3.9	4	2.76	3.56	3.92	4.09	4.41	4.56
70+	2.6	2.8	2.92	2.29	2.15	2.82	3.72	3.61

as economically active, that are employed or looking for employment. A proportion of youth aged 20–24 and 25–29 are also either students or in the process of deciding on a career. Moreover, Iran, like most other countries of Middle East, has a very low rate of female labour force participation which has declined further since the revolution. Labour force participation rate of women which had risen to above 12 per cent in 1976 had dropped to about 8.5 per cent in 1986 and was only 9.4 per cent in 1996. According to the latest survey (2003), it is still below 12 per cent. Assuming that men and women have an equal share of the group aged 25–64 and all of men plus 13 per cent of women participate in the labour force, the ratio of people actually active will be much smaller than the figures given above.

In addition to the three major groups discussed above, one may consider other age groups and explore how their share of the population has changed in the past, and how this will change as the population goes through later stages of transition. In this analysis, the following five age groups will be considered: 0–14, 15–24, 25–59, 60–69 and 70+. These groups in a way represent children (ages 0–14 years) and adolescents and youth (ages 15–24) who need parental care and full-time schooling or part-time vocational training opportunities. The third group covers the young adult population with more or less full-time jobs and contributing to national production of goods and services. In addition to paying for their own expenses and those of the younger members of their family this age group also takes the lion's share in paying taxes, contributing to social security funds and making savings that provide the capital needed for investment in economic growth.

Nevertheless, despite the consistent rise in the share of the elderly (ages 65+ years) of the population since early 1990s, by 2003 only about 8 per cent of the population was aged 60+ years. According to UN (2004), the share of the group aged 65+ of Iranian population in 2005 was only 4.5 per cent which amounted to 3.13 million individuals. Of the latter, only 4,70,000 were age 80+ years.

The fourth group (ages 60–69) covers the relatively younger segment of the aged population. Depending on the local circumstances, a considerable proportion of this group may be economically active and performing all or some of the productive activities carried out by the young adult group. A growing proportion of this group will, however, be retired pensioners whose major demand will be in the areas of health care services and pensions. The fifth sub-group, the "oldest of the elderly", will be predominantly unable to work and will need a good deal of social and health services to continue a relatively autonomous life. Figure 12 gives the share of these five groups of the population enumerated between 1956–2003.

Future Prospects, 2000–2050

In this section, the future course of age-structural transition in Iran will be considered. For this purpose, the medium and low variant projections of the United Nations Population Division (2004 revision) will be used as the basis. It may be of interest to note that, following the unexpectedly huge rise in fertility and population growth rates of 1980s, the United Nations revised its earlier population projections for Iran. The 1996 Revision (published in 1998, that is two years after the completion of the 1996 census) estimated Iran's population in 1995 to be 68.4 millions. Using this estimate as a basis, the population of Iran was projected to rise to 76.2 millions by 2000 and to continue its upward course until 2050. Its final size in 2050 was expected to lie between 143.8 (according to the low variant) and 199.6 millions (according to the high variant), with a medium variant figure of 170.3 million. The constant fertility variant predicted an even higher figure of 414.2 million.

These figures have been drastically scaled down in the 2002 and 2004 revisions of UN projections. Nevertheless, the baseline figure for the year 2000 used by the UN (66.44 million) is somewhat higher than those used by the US Census Bureau (63.5 millions) as well as projections made by the Manpower Bureau of the Management and Plan Organisation of Iran (63.67 million). The UN (2004) estimate for the year 2000 is very close to the medium variant (66.59 million) figure projected by the UN in 1975 while the figure proposed by Iranian authorities is closer to the low variant figure (63.53 million) of the same projections. Judging by recent evidence of continuing fertility decline, the more modest figures obtained by Iranian authorities and the US Census Bureau would seem to be closer to the reality. Our hunch is that the exact size of Iranian population between 2005–2050 will also lie somewhere between the low and medium variants of the UN projections, not too far from the single-variant projection published by the US Census Bureau. UN (2004) projections also differ from those published by the UN in 2002 with respect to both the figures for 2000 (66.365 vs 66.443) and 2005 (69.515 vs 70.675) and projected population for later years. The figures for 2050 are 101.944 vs. 105. 485 and 84.827 vs. 85.052 according to medium and low variant projections, respectively.

Population Size

All variants of the 2004 revision of the UN projections assume a population size of 66.365 million for the end of the twentieth century and a figure of 69.515 for the base year (2005). All of them indicate a relatively sharp rise in population size between 2000–2020. The size attained at this point varies from 80.783 million (low variant) to 89.288 million (high variant). From this point on the medium and low variants indicate a decrease in the tempo of population growth. This is particularly noticeable in the case of the low variant projection which would seem to have reached a plateau by 2025. As a result, there is only a small increase in the projected population size between 2025 (83.114 m) and 2050 (84.827 m). According to the medium variant projection, the population size will continue to rise so that its final value in 2050 (101.944 m) is almost 16 millions higher than the value attained in 2020 (85.036 m) (Figure 13). Even the constant fertility variant predicts a population size of 110.76 million for 2050. This is about one-fourth of the figure obtained by the same variant according to UN projections published in 1998.

Population Growth Rate

The growth rate for the final years of the twentieth century is estimated to be 1.26 which is almost one-third of the growth rate that prevailed

Figure 11 ***Population of Iran (in 1000s) between 2000–2050 according to the Four Variants of UN (2004) Projections.***

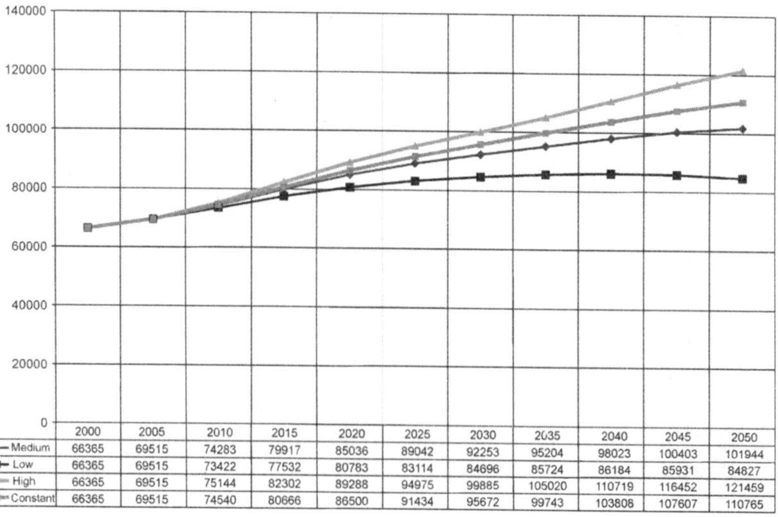

	2000	2005	2010	2015	2020	2025	2030	2035	2040	2045	2050
Medium	66365	69515	74283	79917	85036	89042	92253	95204	98023	100403	101944
Low	66365	69515	73422	77532	80783	83114	84696	85724	86184	85931	84827
High	66365	69515	75144	82302	89288	94975	99885	105020	110719	116452	121459
Constant	66365	69515	74540	80666	86500	91434	95672	99743	103808	107607	110765

between 1980–1990. It is expected to fall to below 1 by 2005 according to both low and medium scenarios. For the next decade, the low variant projection predicts only some slight rise in growth rate (to 1.09) followed by a steady decline terminating at a negative growth rate of –.25 by 2050. The medium variant also predicts some modest rise in the growth rate over the next decade followed by a steady decline leading to a growth rate of 0.31 by 2050.

Components of Growth

The main factors affecting changes in the size of Iranian population during the first half of the twenty-first century are steadily falling birth rates accompanied by slowly rising death rates. The changing balance of mortality and fertility between 1990–2050 is nicely indicated in Figure 12. On the basis of migration trends observed during the last decade, the United Nations (2004) projections also anticipate some out-migration during the twenty-first century which will lead to a loss 276,000 and 120,000 persons per year between 2000–2005 and 2005–2010, and 30,000 per year thereafter.

Changes in Overall Age-Structure

Changes in fertility, mortality and growth rates will result in drastic changes in the age-structure and age pyramids of the population. The low and medium variant age pyramids of the population for the years

Figure 12 ***Crude Birth and Death Rates (per 1000 of Population) according to Medium and Low Scenarios, 1990–2050 (UN, 2004)***

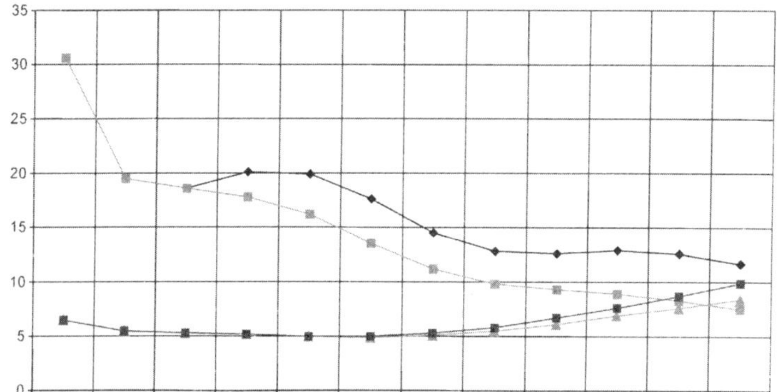

	1990-1995	1995-2000	2000-2005	2005-2010	2010-2015	2015-2020	2020-2025	2025-2030	2030-2035	2035-2040	2040-2045	2045-2050
CBR, Medium	30.6	19.5	18.6	20.1	19.9	17.6	14.5	12.8	12.6	12.9	12.6	11.7
CBR, Low	30.6	19.5	18.6	17.8	16.2	13.5	11.2	9.8	9.3	8.9	8.3	7.5
CDR, Medium	6.5	5.5	5.3	5.2	5	4.9	5.1	5.5	6.1	6.9	7.6	8.4
CDR, Low	6.5	5.5	5.3	5.2	5	5	5.3	5.8	6.7	7.6	8.7	9.9

Figure 13 ***Age Pyramids of the Population of Iran in 2000, 2025 and 2050 (According to United Nations Low and Medium Variant Projections)***

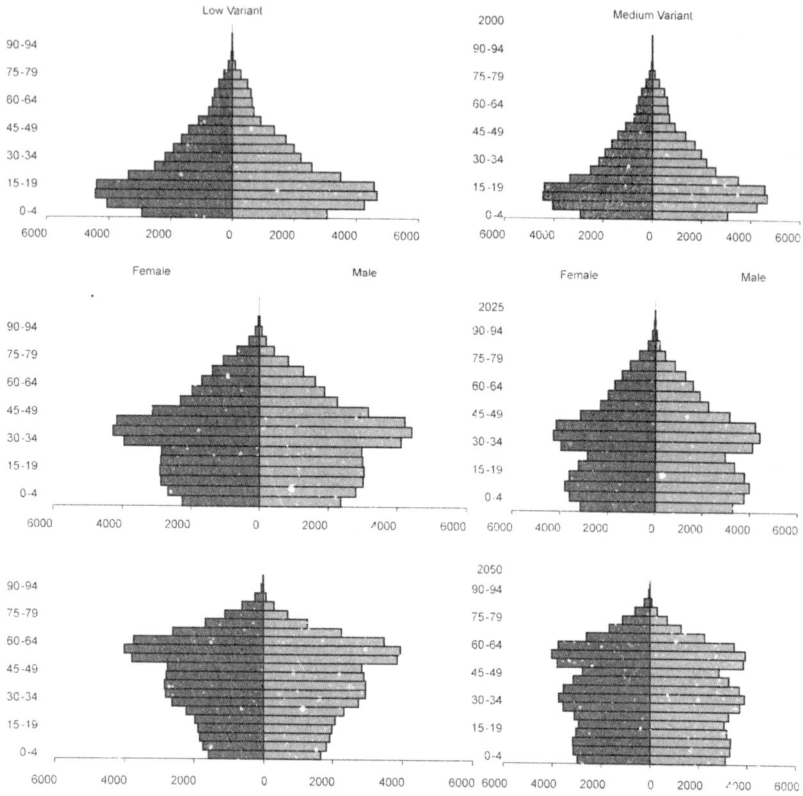

2000, 2025 and 2050 are presented in Figure 13. They clearly show the vast changes that the age-structure of the population of Iran will undergo during its passage from the beginning to the end of the observation period. From the pyramid for 2000 it would appear that the process of fertility decline initiated between 1990–1995 has continued over the next five-year period. The bulges facing age groups 10–14 and 15–19 are reminders of the high rates of fertility experienced during the 1980s.

By the year 2025, the pyramids take quite a different shape. The smaller and more or less equal cohorts born after 2000 have given the bottom of the pyramid a rectangular shape. There are, however, interesting differences between pyramids based on the low- and medium-level projections in this respect. The small bulge between age groups 10–14 to

20–24 in the medium variant pyramid, which is indicative of the momentum effect operating between 2005–2020, is almost entirely absent in the low variant pyramid. This means that sustained low fertility may prevent (or at least overshadow) the momentum effect. The shrunken rectangles representing age groups 0–4 and 5–9 are indicative of the second phase of fertility decline in both variants. From the pyramid for 2050 it is obvious that while the age structure of the population represented by the low variant projection has continued its downward move in a consistent manner, that of the medium level projection has continued to experience changes in relative size of consequent age groups as a result of both primary and secondary momentum effects.

Changes in the Size and Relative Share of the three Main Age Groups

The size of the three main groups aged 0–14, 15–64 and 65+ during the period of observation varies according to the variant considered. All variants, however, indicate a progressive decline in the share of children aged 0–14 years and a consistent increase in the number and ratio of adults aged 15–64 and elderly aged 65+ years. The most important change is the gradual decline in the number of children and a rise in the number and relative share of the potentially active population aged 15–65 years (Figure 13) and the elderly aged 65+ years.

Projected Number of Children Aged 0–14

The projected size of the child population aged 0–14 between 2000–2050 varies according to the scenario used. All four variants

Figure 14 ***Number of Children Aged 0–14 Years according to Medium and Low Scenarios, 2005–2050 (UN, 2004)***

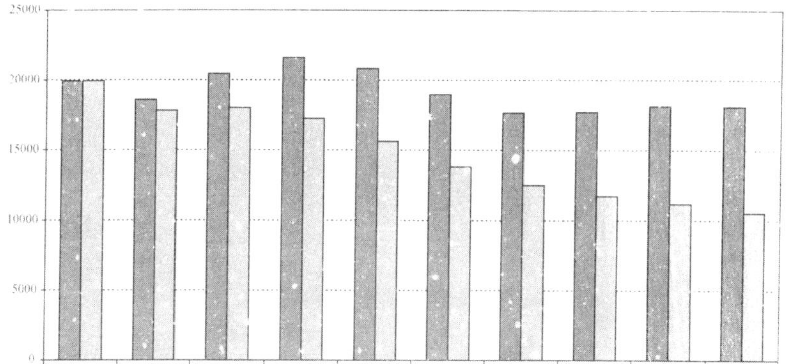

	2005	2010	2015	2020	2025	2030	2035	2040	2045	2050
Medium	19950.805	18645.033	20458.752	21599.144	20835.828	19004.118	17707.944	17742.163	18172.943	18146.632
Low	19950.805	17841.546	18064.956	17287.562	15625.432	13805.448	12515.704	11721.024	11171.03	10518.548

predict a fall in the relative share of this age group of total population between 2000–2010, but the fall is particularly marked and steep in the case of the low variant projection. With regard to the number of children aged 0–14 (Figure 14), the medium variant predicts a slight rise (from 18.645 to 21.599 million) between 2010–2020 which is due to the momentum effect and the entry of large cohorts born between 1980–1990 into their reproductive careers. But the rise is too small to have much impact on the relative share of children of total population. The number is expected to fall back to 20.835 million by 2025 and follow a steady decline until 2035 and remain more or less constant for the rest of the period.

The expected fall in the number of children will have several important consequences. In the first place, it will lead to a decline in the number of children requiring health services, food and pre-school care. Secondly, there will be a sharp drop in the number of consecutive cohorts reaching age of formal schooling and thus a much-reduced pressure on the school system. As these smaller birth cohorts move along time, the reduced pressure will be felt by different levels of the educational system.

Working Age Population (Age 15–64)

According to UN estimates, just over 60 per cent (46.4 million) of Iranian population was aged 15–64 in 2000. The share of this potentially active group of the population will rise to 66.3 per cent by 2005 and will

Figure 15 ***Number of People Aged 15–64 Years according to Medium and Low Scenarios, 2005–2050 (UN, 2004)***

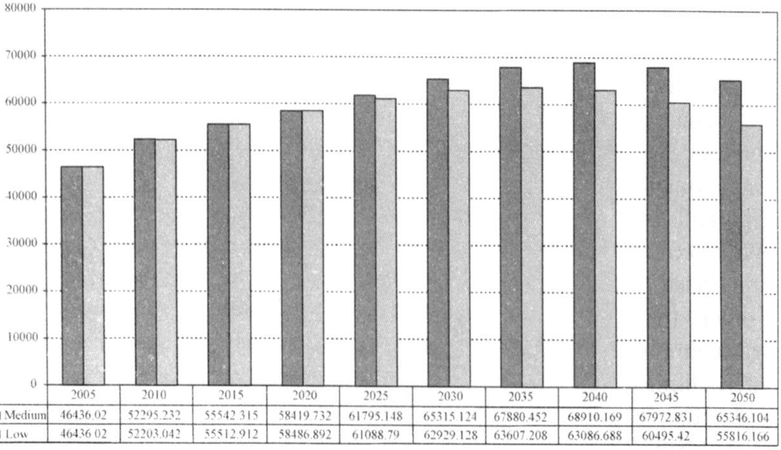

	2005	2010	2015	2020	2025	2030	2035	2040	2045	2050
Medium	46436.02	52295.232	55542.315	58419.732	61795.148	65315.124	67880.452	68910.169	67972.831	65346.104
Low	46436.02	52203.042	55512.912	58486.892	61088.79	62929.128	63607.208	63086.688	60495.42	55816.166

continue to rise over most of the following decades. According to the low scenario, this age group will account for over 74 per cent of the population in 2030 but will gradually decline to account for 65.8 per cent of the population by 2050. The medium level scenario predicts the highest figure (71.3.%) for 2035 followed by a gradual decline that will end in 64.1 per cent in 2050 (Figure 15).

In terms of absolute numbers, according to UN estimates, Iran entered the twenty-first century with a working age population of just over 40 million (60.3% of the population). The number will rise swiftly according to all scenarios. According to the medium scenario, the number of people age 15–64 will exceed 46.4 million by 2005, rise above 52 million by 2010, approach 62 million by 2025, and exceed 69 million by 2040 after which it will decline to 67.97 million by 2045 and lie just above 65.3 million in the middle of the century (2050). If one considers the share of the working age population as the main indicator of a demographic window of opportunity, it may be said that Iran will see this window widen systematically between 2000 and 2040, the widening will be particularly noticeable between 2010 and 2035.

Of the sub-groups making up the working age adult population, youth (ages 15–29) and women of reproductive age (15–49) deserve special attention. The semi-dependent youth aged 20–29 are projected to number 11.9 million at the beginning of the period. This high figure is a reminder of the relatively high fertility rate that prevailed between 1970–1980. As the birth cohorts of the first decade after the revolution reach ages 20–29 the size of this group will go up to 15.4 million and 17.4 million by 2005 and 2010, respectively. It will decline slightly in 2015 (16.9 million) and go down more precipitously over the next decade to reach its lowest level (12.4 million) by 2025. It will go up again to attain a new height (15.1 million) in 2040, remain at the same level for another five years and go back down to its 2005 level by 2025.

The high and fluctuating number of youth aged 20–29 will present services relating to higher education, on-the-job training, and employment creation with enormous challenges. There will also be a high and fluctuating demand for housing by the youth getting married. With a continuing rise in age at first marriage and increasing number of unmarried, mostly well-educated and western oriented urban men and women, the country is likely to face new challenges in the area of living arrangements and sexual relations. A rise in premarital and extramarital interactions, already viewed with increasing concern by Iranian parents and authorities, is likely to lead to social problems such as a rise in illegitimate births, single parent families, abortions, STDS and HIV/AIDS.

The number and relative share of women of reproductive age, one of the major determinants of future fertility trends will go up between 2000–2005 but will decline gradually thereafter so that by 2050 it will be around 42 per cent (Figure 16).

The Elderly (group ages 65 and over)

All variants begin with the same number of elderly (2.962 million) in 2000 which grows at a very low rate to reach four million by 2015. In relative terms, the share of the elderly of the total population will rise from just over 4 per cent in the year 2000 to over 25 per cent by the low variant and about 20 per cent by the medium variant projection by 2050 (Figures 18). As the members of this age group belong to birth cohorts born during the second half of the twentieth century, its size is not much affected by the fertility (and life expectancy) assumptions underlying different scenarios (Figures 17 and 18). As a result, the low and medium variants produce more or less the same numbers. There is a rise in the rate of growth of the elderly after 2015 so that its size doubles between 2015–2030, exceeds 11 million by 2040 and stands at 18.2 million by the end of the period. This means that while the total size of population of Iran will fail to double during the fifty-year period of observation, the number of elderly aged 65 years and over will experience a six-fold increase.

Figure 16 ***Share(%) of Women Aged 15–49 of Projected Population of Iran, 2000–2050 (UN, 2005)***

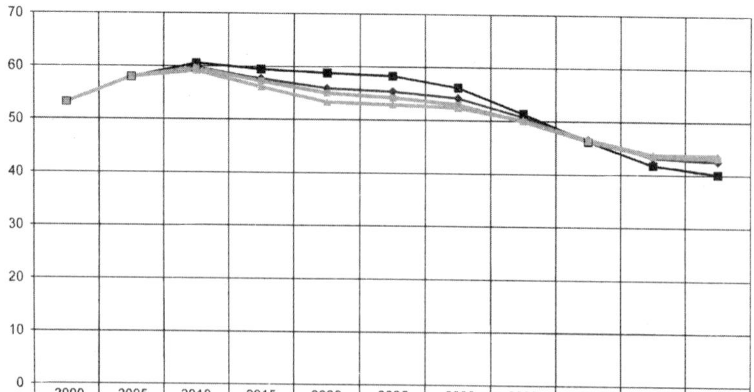

	2000	2005	2010	2015	2020	2025	2030	2035	2040	2045	2050
Low	53.2	58	59.9	57.7	55.9	55.4	54.2	50.8	46.6	43.2	42.5
Medium	53.2	58	60.6	59.5	58.8	58.3	56.2	51	46.2	41.8	40.1
High	53.2	58	59.2	56.1	53.3	52.9	52.4	50.1	46.6	43.8	43.7
Constant	53.2	58	59.7	57.2	55	54.2	53	49.9	46.3	43.5	43.2

Figure 17 ***Percent Aged 65+ of Projected Population of Iran, 2005–2050 (UN, 2004, Different Scenarios)***

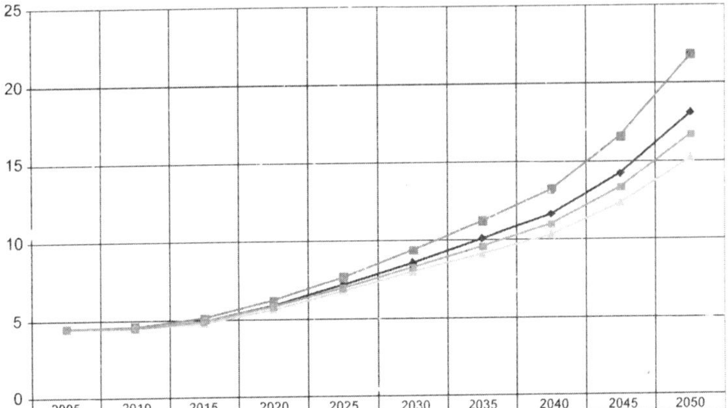

	2005	2010	2015	2020	2025	2030	2035	2040	2045	2050
Medium	4.5	4.5	4.9	5.9	7.2	8.6	10.1	11.6	14.2	18.1
Low	4.5	4.6	5.1	6.2	7.7	9.4	11.2	13.2	16.6	21.8
High	4.5	4.5	4.8	5.6	6.8	8	9.1	10.3	12.3	15.2
Constant	4.5	4.5	4.9	5.8	7	8.3	9.6	11	13.3	16.7

Figure 18 ***Number of People Aged 65+ Years according to Medium and Low Scenarios, 2005–2050 (UN, 2004)***

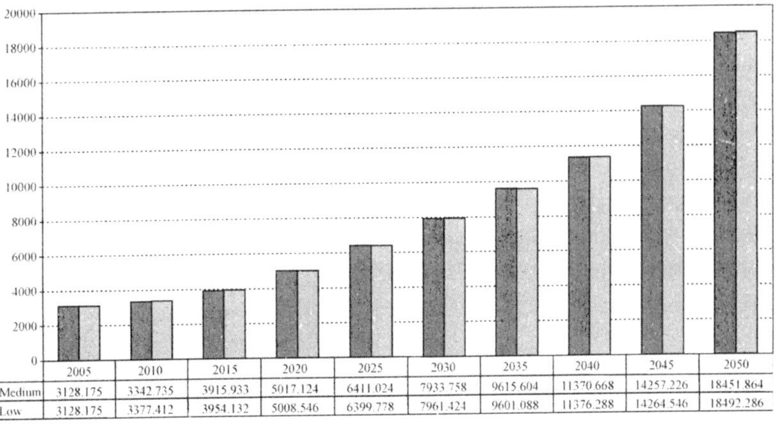

	2005	2010	2015	2020	2025	2030	2035	2040	2045	2050
Medium	3128.175	3342.735	3915.933	5017.124	6411.024	7933.758	9615.604	11370.668	14257.226	18451.864
Low	3128.175	3377.412	3954.132	5008.546	6399.778	7961.424	9601.088	11376.288	14264.546	18492.286

Of the elderly population living in 2050, about one-third (6.1 million) will be aged 75+. Of the latter group 4.8 million will be aged 75–84 and 1.3 million 85+ years. In other words, by 2050, Iran will have to cater for 3.2 million people aged 80+ which is larger than the total number of people aged 65 and over (3.0 million) in the year 2000.

The impact of this huge group of highly vulnerable and dependent elderly on the social security and pension system of Iran deserves careful analysis. As people reaching the age of retirement over the next few decades all will have been born during the last decades of the twentieth century their number is subject to little uncertainty and is unlikely to change significantly. Nor can the enormous problems of coping with an enormous group of aged population, accounting for almost one-fifth of the total population in 2050, be overestimated.

Moreover, due to age differences between husbands and wives and the longer life expectancy of women, the elderly group will include a disproportionately large number of women who are more likely to have been "housewives" without their own income or pension scheme. The "oldest of the old" group is particularly likely to consist of widowed women living on their own. With the gradual disappearance of the traditional family structure and the inability or reluctance of children to look after their parents, this group will need special care in terms of financial support, health services, social relations or some form of homecare. Their increasing number is already being felt by Iran's fledgling social security system whose extension and sustainability have become a matter of national debate and concern.

Changes in Dependency Ratios

Another way of looking at the problem of ageing is to calculate dependency ratios, that is the ratio of people aged 0–14, 65+ and (0–14) + (65+) years to those aged 15–64 years. All four UN projections assume a total dependency ratio of 66 per cent for the year 2000. This is exactly the figure given by the DHS-type survey carried out in October 2000. All four projections also assume a sharp drop in the dependency ratio between 2000–2010 (Figure 19). The drop is sharper for the medium and low variant projections. According to the medium variant projection, the dependency ratio will take a mild upward swing between 2010–2020, but will go down again between 2020–2035 when it attains its lowest projected value of 40. It will rise again between 2035–2050 and stand at 55 by the end of the period of observation. The sharp decline in dependency ratio between 2000–2010 is mainly due to the huge drop in the number of children aged 0–14. According to the medium variant scenario, the child dependency ratio will fall from 58 to 38 between 2000–2010, remain at that level until 2020, fall further (to 26) and rise only slightly to attain its final value of 28 by 2050.

Figure 19 ***Number of People Aged 80+ Yers According to Medium and Low Scenarios, 2005–2050 (UN, 2004)***

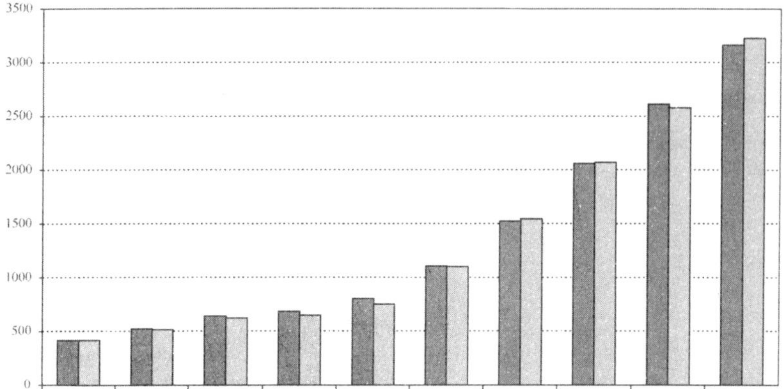

	2005	2010	2015	2020	2025	2030	035	2040	2045	2050
Medium	417.09	519.981	639.336	680.288	801.378	1107.036	1523.264	2058.483	2610.478	3160.264
Low	417.09	513.954	620.256	646.264	748.026	1101.048	1543.032	2068.416	2577.93	3223.426

In contrast, the elderly dependency ratio is expected to rise and constitute a larger share of the total dependency ratio (Figure 20). According to all four variants, the elderly dependency ratio, which is assumed to have been seven in 2000, will remain at the same level until 2015. After this date, all variants predict a relatively sharp upward swing in the elderly dependency ratio. According to the medium variant projection, the elderly dependency ratio will rise steadily between 2015–2035 when its size will be exactly double the figure for the initial year. It will undergo an even sharper upward change in 2040 to reach the figure of 27 per 100 by the end of the period.

If one takes those aged 60+ years as the elderly group, the relative and absolute burden of ageing during the first half of the twenty-first century will acquire even higher dimensions (Figure 22).

Other Measures of Ageing

Using the three new indices of ageing recently proposed by the United Nations (2002) the increasingly heavier burden of ageing on Iranian economy may be better appreciated. These three measures are: the Ageing Index (the number of persons 60 years old or over per one hundred persons under age 15), Potential Support Ratio (the number of persons aged 15 to 64 years per one hundred persons aged 65 years or older), and the Parent Support Ratio (the number of persons 85 years old and over per one hundred persons aged 50–64 years). As indicated in Figure 23, the ageing index of Iran at the end of the twentieth century

Figure 20 ***Dependency Rations (%) of Projected Population, 1995-2050 (UN, 2004, Medium)***

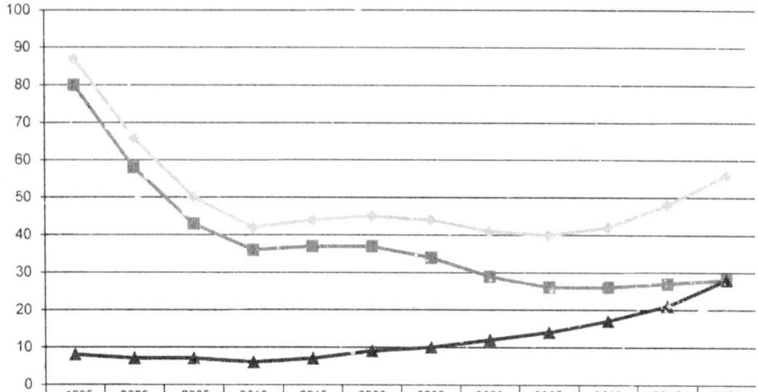

	1995	2000	2005	2010	2015	2020	2025	2030	2035	2040	2045	2050
Total	87	66	50	42	44	45	44	41	40	42	48	56
Child	80	58	43	36	37	37	34	29	26	26	27	28
Old-age	8	7	7	6	7	9	10	12	14	17	21	28

Figure 21 ***Old-Age Dependency Rations according to Different Scenarios, 2000–2050***

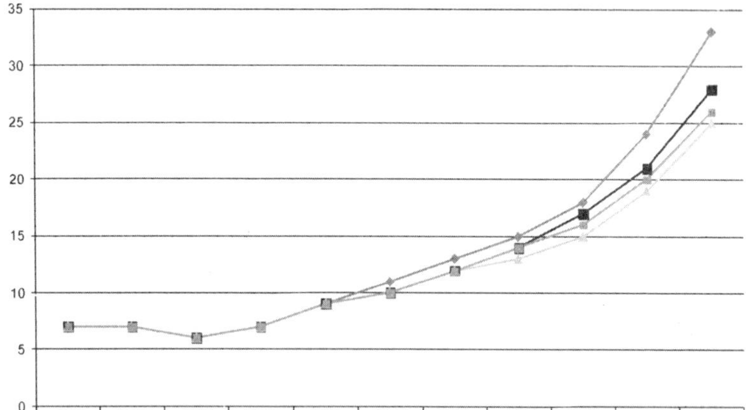

	2000	2005	2010	2015	2020	2025	2030	2035	2040	2045	2050
Low	7	7	6	7	9	11	13	15	18	24	33
Medium	7	7	6	7	9	10	12	14	17	21	28
High	7	7	6	7	9	10	12	13	15	19	25
Constant	7	7	6	7	9	10	12	14	16	20	26

was 18.1, that is, there were 18.1 people aged 60+ years for every 100 child below 15. The index will rise steadily during the first half of the twenty-first century so that by 2050 there will be 145.1 persons aged 60+ for every 100 children under 15 years (Figure 23). During the same period, the old-age dependency ratio (ratio of people aged 65+ to those

Figure 22 ***Number of People Aged 60+ Years According to Medium and Low Scenarios, 2005–2050 (UN, 2004)***

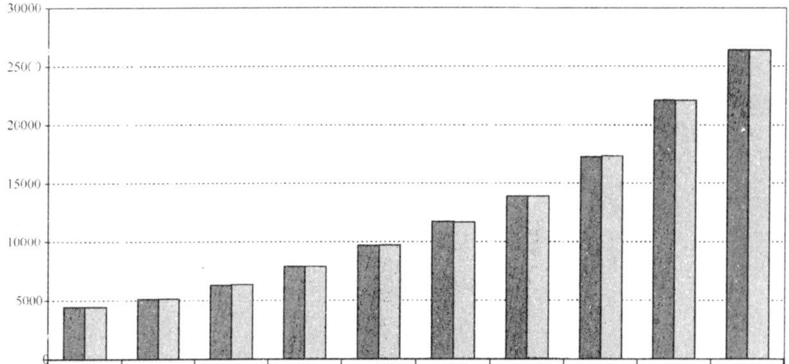

	2005	2010	2015	2020	2025	2030	2035	2040	2045	2050
Medium	4448.96	5125.527	6313.443	7908.348	9705.578	11716.131	13899.784	17252.048	22088.66	26403.496
Low	4448.96	5139.54	6357.624	7916.734	9724.338	11688.048	13887.288	17322.984	22084.267	26381.197

aged 15–64 years) will rise from 7.4 to 28.3, that is an almost four-fold increase.

In contrast, the potential support ratio which was 13.5 in 2000 will decrease steadily over the next fifty years (Figure 24). By 2050, there will be only 3.5 potentially active persons aged 15–64 years for every elderly aged 65+ years. Similarly, the parent support ratio will rise from 1.5 to 6.4. In other words, while at the end of the twentieth century there were 1.5 persons aged 50–64 for every individual aged 85+ years, at the middle of century there will be 6.4 persons aged 50–64 to take care of every person aged 85+ years.

As a result of the changes noted above, the median age of the population will rise steadily from 23.4 years in 2005 to over 35 years by 2030 (Figure 25). By 2050, one half of the population of Iran will be aged above 40.6 years (according to the low scenario) or 47.3 years (according to the medium scenario).

Discussion and Conclusions

The evidence reviewed above leaves no doubt that, following the drastic changes in social values and political orientation ushered in by the Islamic Revolution, Iran experienced a tremendous change in its fertility and population growth rate. The turbulance was however of short duration and by late 1980s there were clear signs of decline in fertility rates, particularly in urban areas. The downward trend was immensely helped by a change in government's population policy and the revival of

Figure 23 ***Ageing Index and Old-Age Dependency Ratios of Iranian Population 1956–2050***

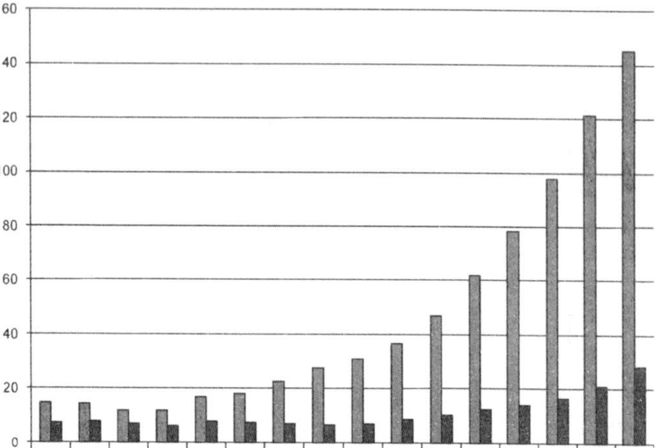

	1956	1966	1976	1986	1996	2000	2005	2010	2015	2020	2025	2030	2035	2040	2045	2050
Ageing Index	14.8	14.2	11.8	11.9	16.8	18.1	22.4	27.4	30.9	36.7	46.9	61.7	78.5	97.7	121.3	145.1
Old-Age Dependency Ratio	7.4	7.7	6.8	5.9	7.7	7.4	6.8	6.4	7.1	8.6	10.4	12.2	14.1	16.5	21	28.3

Figure 24 ***Potential Support Ratios and Parent Support Ratios of Iranian Population, 1956–2050***

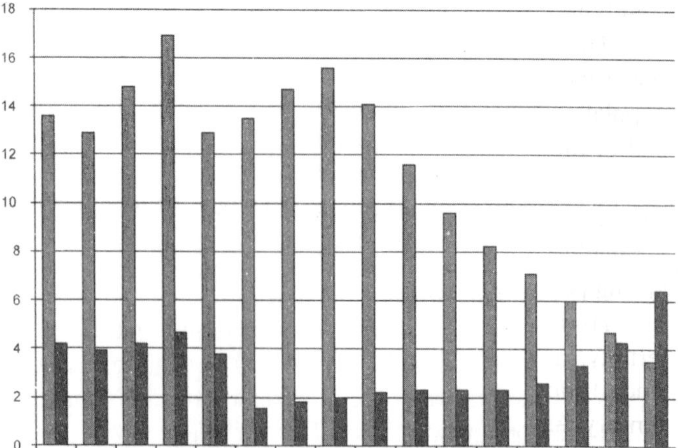

	1956	1966	1976	1986	1996	2000	2005	2010	2015	2020	2025	2030	2035	2040	2045	2050
Potential Support Ratios	13.6	12.9	14.8	16.9	12.9	13.5	14.7	15.6	14.1	11.6	9.6	8.2	7.1	6	4.7	3.5
Parent Support Ratios	4.2	3.91	4.18	4.68	3.77	1.5	1.8	2	2.2	2.3	2.3	2.3	2.6	3.3	4.3	6.4

Figure 25 ***Median Age of Projected Population, 2005–2050, According to Different Scenarios (UN, 2004)***

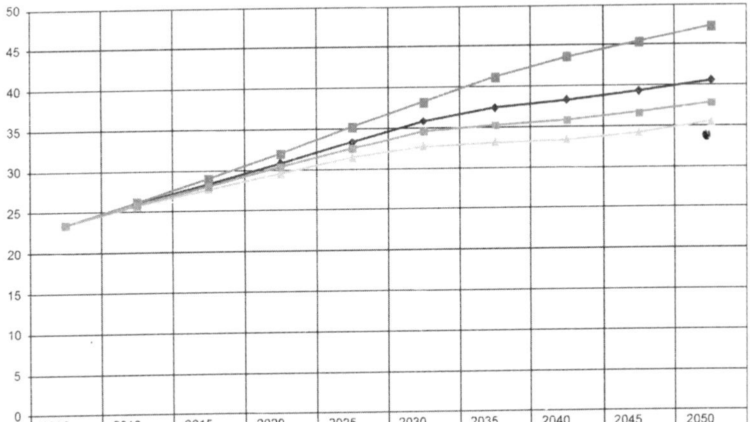

	2005	2010	2015	2020	2025	2030	2035	2040	2045	2050
Medium	23.4	26	28.3	30.8	33.3	35.8	37.4	38.3	39.3	40.6
Low	23.4	26.2	29	32	35.2	38.2	41.2	43.6	45.4	47.3
High	23.4	25.7	27.7	29.5	31.4	32.7	33.1	33.4	34.2	35.5
Constant	23.4	25.9	28.1	30.4	32.6	34.6	35.3	35.8	36.7	37.9

the family planning programme. The national census of population conducted in 1996 provided convincing evidence of a drastic fall in fertility in both urban and rural areas. Large-scale surveys conducted since then leave no doubt that the contraceptive prevalence rate of Iranian couples has risen to surprisingly high levels and fertility rate has continued its sharp downward trend.

Thanks to the drastic fertility decline, the total population will grow very slowly during the first half of the twenty-first century. While the population of Iran experienced a four-fold increase during the second half of the twentieth century, it is unlikely to rise by more than 50 per cent between 2000–2050. The lowered fertility rate in combination with a rise in mortality will result in drastic changes in the age-structure of the population. The population will grow older and the special needs of an ageing population will confront Iran with new problems.

Having successfully managed to control an upward swing in fertility, Iran has entered a definite period of age-structural transition since 1996 which will continue through the first half of the twenty-first century. As a result of this transition, by the end of the twentieth century the ratio of children in total population had dropped significantly while that of the elderly was still under 5 per cent and rising very slowly. The first three decades of the twenty-first century will witness a continuation of this trend and the window of opportunity opened in late 1980s will grow wider. From around 2030, however, a rise in the size and the relative share of the elderly will confront Iran with new challenges. By 2040, the old-age dependency ratio will approach 18 and the ageing index will be just under 100 (as compared with a figure of 18.1 in 2000).

The huge number of children born between 1976–1996 will, however, continue to confront Iran with serious problems during the first decade of the new century. These will be mainly in the areas of training and job creation. As the cohorts of young men and women enter their family building and reproductive careers, the country will be faced with problems of housing and will probably have to handle a new wave of baby boom. The increasing number of people going through their most active and productive period of life (ages 25–59 year) will present a unique opportunity for growth, savings and investment.

If this opportunity is taken seriously and made good use of, Iran will be in a much better position to respond to the looming problem of ageing and the enormous challenges that will be posed by the increasingly large number of elderly that will have to be taken care of in the final decade of the period. In this regard, Iran has to realise that women comprise almost half of the potentially productive age groups and their absence from the labour force can undermine all efforts to speed up and maintain the rate of economic growth needed. The fact that the majority of the elderly demanding care and services in 2040s will also be women making investment in women's labour force participation and coverage by the social insurance system all the more important.

The transition may prove less smooth and more problem-ridden than described above. The gains coming from the demographic bonus during the first quarter of the century (2000–2025) may not suffice to outweigh the effects of turbulence. Certain policies may prove more resistant to change and require a longer period of preparation than others. With the marked reduction in fertility and the number of children, a large number of primary and secondary schools may have to be closed down. But the savings expected may not accrue easily because of the need for keeping teachers employed. The public education system is the largest public employment sector and a large proportion of youth coming out of higher education system depend on this sector for employment. This is particularly true of women who have outnumbered men in university entrance examination since late 1990s. For many of them employment by other agencies, even if available, may not be socially correct and acceptable. This may radically diminish the expected gains from an increase in the proportion of young adults by keeping women's participation in the modern formal sector of the economy at its currently low level.

There is also the possibility that the sharp downward trend of fertility continues and drops below replacement level. This has already been experienced by urban population in a number of better developed provinces. Several large scale surveys conducted between 2000–2004 indicate that the downward trend initiated in mid-1990s is still continuing. According to the latest survey carried out in May 2004 (SCI, 2004b) the share of children aged 0–14 had dropped to 27.1 per cent (as compared with 45.5% in 1986 and 34.5% in 2000). Such a trend is likely to further decrease child dependency ratios and make the window of opportunity wider. But the small number of children reaching age of labour force participation and economic production may prove incapable of raising national productivity and wealth to levels required by the huge increase in old-age dependency after 1935. There are signs that due to forced expansion of social security benefits to a large group of workers who have either paid little contribution or retired at an early age, the social security system is rapidly losing its funds and will have to adopt pay-as-you-go policy in near future. A marked reduction in the number of young workers entering the system is bound to affect the survival of a pay-as-you-go system. Under these circumstances, the younger generation may also feel at a disadvantage in inter-generational struggle for creation and use of resources or their transfer.

References

Abbassi-Shavazi, M.J. 1999. Application of the Own Children Method to Estimate Fertility Rates from Census Data. Tehran: University of Tehran School of Social Sciences (in Persian).

Abbassi-Shavazi, M.J. A. Mehryar, G. Jones and P. McDonald. 2002. Revolution, War and Modernisation: Population Policy and Fertility Change in Iran. *Journal of Population Research 19* (1): 25–46.

Aghajanian, A. 1991. Population Change in Iran, 1966–86: A Stalled Demographic Transition? *Population and Development Review* 17, 703–15.

Aghajanian, A. and A.H. Mehryar. 1999a. Fertility Transition in the Islamic Republic of Iran, 1976–1996. *Asian-Pacific Population Journal* 14: 1, 21–42.

Aghajanian, A. and A.H. Mehryar. 1999b. Fertility, Contraceptive Use and Family Planning Programme Activity in the Islamic Republic of Iran, 1976–1996. International Family Planning Perspectives 25: 2, 98–102.

Ashofteh-Tehrani, J. 1985. Sociology and Future Trends of Iranian Population. Isfahan: University of Isfahan Jahad Daneshgahi Press (in Persian)

Ayatulllah Mahllati of Shirz. 1963. Fatwa on Contraception. (Cited in R. Omran. 1992. *Family Planning in the Legacy of Islam*. New York: Routledge/United Nations Population Fund.)

Bahishti, Shaikh Mohammad Hossein. 1974. "Rules of Sterilisation and Abortion in Islamic Law" in H. Karmi, I. Nazer and M. Zayid (eds.), *Islam and Family Planning:* A Faithful Translation of the Arabic Edition of the Proceedings of the International Conference on Islam and Family Planning, Rabat (Morocco), 1971. Beirut, Lebanon: The International Planned Parenthood Federation, Middle East and North Africa Region, Vol. I, 407–26.

Coale, A. and E. Hoover. 1958. *Population Growth and Economic Development in Low Income Countries.* Princeton, NJ: Princeton University Press.

Cogwill, D.O. and L. Holmes. 1970. "The Demography of Ageing" in A.M. Hoffman (ed.), *The Daily Needs and Interests of Older People.* Springfield, MA: Charles and Thomas.

Keyfitz, N. 1985. *Applied Mathematical Demography*. 2nd edition, New York: Springer Verlag.

Mehryar, A.H. 2002. *Demographic and Health Survey of Iran: A Summary of Main Findings.* Tehran: Population Studies and Research Centre, Working Paper Series in English.

Mehryar, A.H. and S. Ahmad-Nia. 2006. "Age-Structural Transition in Iran: Short and Long-term Consequences of Drastic Fertility Swings during the Final Decades of the Twentieth Century" in I. Pool, L.R. Wong and E. Vilquin (eds.), *Age-Structural Transitions: Challenges for Development.* Paris: Committee for International Cooperation in National Research in Demography, 319–58.

Mehryar, A.H., F. Roudi, A. Aghajanian and F. Tajdini. 2001. Repression and Revival of the Family Planning Programme and its Impact on Fertility Levels in the Islamic Republic of Iran. Cairo, Egypt: Economic Research Forum for the Arab Countries, Iran and Turkey, Working Paper 2022.

Ministry of Health and Medical Education. (MoHE) 2001. Preliminary Report on the Iran DHS Survey, 2000. Tehran: Statistics Unit, Office of the Undersecretary for Public Health, Ministry of Health and Medical Education, (Mimeographed Monograph Persian).

Shamsuddin, Mohammad M. 1974. "Islam and Planned Parenthood" in H. Karmi, I. Nazer and M. Zayid (eds.), *Islam and Family Planning:* A Faithful Translation of the Arabic Edition of the Proceedings of the International Conference on Islam and Family Planning, Rabat (Morocco), *1971*. Beirut, Lebanon: The International Planned Parenthood Federation, Middle East and North Africa Region, Vol. I, 61–88.

Statistical Centre of Iran. 1978. Iran Fertility Survey, 1977. Tehran: Iran Statistical Centre (in Persian).

——. 1978. National Census of Population and Housing of Iran, 1976. Tehran: Iran Statistical Centre (in Persian).

——. 1988. National Census of Population and Housing of Iran, 1986. Tehran: Iran Statistical Centre (in Persian).

——. 1992. Combined Census-Survey of Population of Iran, 1991. Tehran: Iran Statistical Centre (in Persian).

——. 1998. Population Growth Estimation Survey of Iran, 1996–1998. Tehran: Iran Statistical Centre (in Persian).

——. 1998. National Census of Population and Housing of Iran, 1996. Tehran: Iran Statistical Centre (in Persian).

——. 2000. Estimation of Fertility Level and Trends of Iranian Population through the Own Children Method for the Period 1972–1996. Tehran: Iran Statistical Centre (in Persian).

——. 2002. *Statistical Yearbook of Iran, 1381*. Tehran: Statistical Centre of Iran (SCI) Publications.

——. 2004a. Household Employment Survey, 1382. Tehran: Iran Statistical Centre (in Persian).

——. 2004b. Household Employment Survey, 1383. Tehran: Iran Statistical Centre (in Persian).

United Nations Population Division. 1975. Selected World Demographic Indicators by Countries, 1950–2000. New York: Population Division, Department of Economic and Social Affairs of the United Nations Secretariat (ESA/WP. 55).

——. 1998. World Population Prospects: The 1996 Revision. New York: United Nations.

——. 2001. World Population Ageing, 1950–2050. New York: United Nations. Available on line at http:// www.un.org/esa/socdev/ageing.

——. 2002. World Population Prospects: The 2000 Revision. New York: United Nations. Available on line at http://www.un.org/esa/population/publications/wpp2000. pdf

——. 2003a. World Population Prospects: The 2002 Revision. New York: United Nations. Available online at http://www.un.org/esa/population/publications/wpp2002/WPP2002-HIGHLIGHTSrev1.PDF

——. 2003b. World Population Prospects: The 2002 Revision Population Database. Available on-line at http:// esa.un.org/unpp/

——. 2005. World Population Prospects: The 2004 Revision. New York: United Nations. Available online at http://www.un.org/esa/population/publications/wpp2002/WPP2002-HIGHLIGHTSrev1.PDF.

13

Harnessing Human Resource of Older Persons for Promoting Social Interaction and Environment Protection

Ng Sor Tho

With longer life expectancy and low fertility, Malaysian population is growing older. The number of older persons aged 60 and over are expected to increase from 6.6 per cent in 2000 to 13.4 per cent or 4.2 million in the year 2025 (United Nations, 2002). The life expectancy at birth has increased from 67 years for female and 64 years for male in 1975–1980 (United Nations, 2002: 319) to 77 years and 72 years, respectively in 2007 (United Nations, 2007). The life expectancy at age 60 is 19 years and 17 years for female and male, respectively in 2005–2010 (United Nations, 2006). The longer life expectancy implies that there are increasing number of men and women who live longer. The Aging Index (the number of persons 60 years old or over, per hundred persons under age 15) is expected to increase from 19.3 in 2000 to 56.7 in the year 2025 (United Nations, 2002).

With the improvement in educational level, the percentage of older persons aged 60 and over had never attended school declined from 75 per cent in 1970 to 51 per cent in 2000 (Jean, 2005: 18). There is an increasing proportion of the older persons who have completed secondary education and tertiary education. As the educational level of the general population has been increasing over the years, in future older persons will be having higher education and will be better trained. They represent a pool of human resource for the national development.

The mandatory retirement age of 55/56 years in Malaysia greatly affects the work participation of her population aged 55 and above. The greater flexibility of employment in the agricultural sector enables many older persons to continue working after the mandatory age of retirement, especially at family-owned farm (Clark and Anker 1990; 1993). In Malaysia, the 2000 Population Census recorded that older persons aged 55 and above who are still working are mainly engaged in the informal sector, such as agricultural sector, wholesale and retail trade (Department of Statistics, Malaysia, 2003). However, due to the shift in the economic structure from a more agriculture-based economy to non-agriculture based during the 1980s, the proportion of employed persons aged 60 and over declined from 33 per cent in 1980 to 24 per cent in 1991 and 23 per cent in 2000 (Table 1). The percentage of unpaid family workers also has significantly declined from 15 per cent in 1980 to 5.3 per cent in 1991 and 3.2 per cent in 2000 (Jean, 2005). Therefore, higher percentage of older persons are employees, thus more older persons are subject to mandatory retirement and labour force participation rates decline as workers age. Older men tend to be in paid work than older women. The 2000 Population Census shows that the work rate for those aged 50–54 was 84.9 per cent, it fell to 63.2 per cent among those aged 55–59 and further declined to 51.1 per cent among those aged 60–64 (Figure 1).

Table 1 ***Per Cent of Employed Persons Aged 60 and Over by Sex, 1980, 1991 and 2000***

Sex	*1980*	*1991*	*2000*
Male	48.7	39.9	38.1
Female	14.8	9.6	8.8
Total	32.9	23.9	22.8

Source: Jean 2005.

Evidence in Malaysia indicates that the majority of older persons remain fairly well and able, and they can be tapped as potential human resources for the nation instead of being viewed as dependent and requiring assistance (Tan et al., 1999; Ng, et al., 2005; Tan and Tey 2005; 2006). The objective of this paper is to share the experience of Petaling Jaya Community Centre (PJCC) in enlisting older persons to take the lead as coordinators and fully participate in social interaction and environment protection activities.

The next session is a brief description of the National Policy for Older Persons and the existing employment and social security programmes for the older persons. It then follows by the PJCC model of harnessing human resource of older persons for promoting social interaction and environment protection.

Figure 1 ***Work Rate of Male and Female Persons Aged 50–64 by Age and Sex, Malaysia, 2000***

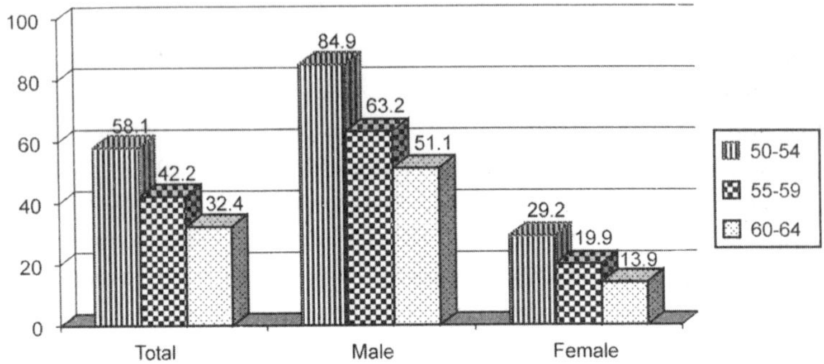

Source: Department of Statistics, Malaysia, 2003.

Policy and Programmes for Older People

National Policy for Older Persons

The National Policy for Older Persons was formulated in 1995 to ensure the social status, dignity and well-being of older persons as members of the family, society and nation by enabling them to optimise their self-potential, have access to all opportunities and have provision for care and protection. The objectives of the policy are:

1. To enhance the respect and dignity of older persons in their family, society and nation;
2. To improve the potential of older persons so that they continue to be active and productive in national development, and to create opportunities to assist them to continue to be self-reliant;
3. To encourage the establishment and availability of specific facilities to ensure the care and protection of older persons towards enhancing their well-being.

The Department of Social Welfare under the Ministry of Women, Family and Community Development has been identified as the agency responsible for coordinating the implementation of the action plans in various areas such as education, employment, participation in the community, recreation, transport, housing, support system for the family, health, social security, media, and research and development.

In conjunction with the International Year of Older Persons in 1999, the Action Plan for the National Policy for Older Persons was implemented during the Seventh Malaysia Plan Period (1996–2000) to ensure the integration and participation of older persons in the society.

Collaborative activities were undertaken by the public and private sectors in health education, training, social and recreational activities (Government of Malaysia, 2001: 516)

In line with the action plan of the National Policy for Older Persons, during the Eighth Plan Period (2001–2005), programmes for the aged shifted from a welfare approach to a developmental approach to ensure active and productive aging. It emphasised on community participation that included promotion of healthy lifestyles, social and recreational activities. These programmes encouraged volunteerism among older person as well as inter-generational activities, life-long learning programmes and learning skills such as ICT to enable their continued contribution to family, society and country (Government of Malaysia, 2006: 311). In the Ninth Malaysia Plan (2006–2010), measures will be undertaken to provide for an environment for the older persons to remain healthy, active and secure while being able to age with dignity and respect as well as leading independent and fulfiling lives as integral members of their families, communities and country. Community level participation will be enhanced through a strong network of community services and the creation of opportunities for their engagement in social and economic activities. The skill, experiences and contributions of senior citizens in national development will be promoted by facilitating partnerships between the government, civil society, NGOs, and the private sector.

Employment and Social Security Programmes

In August 1996, a programme to assist retirees from public sector to work in private sector was implemented under the Service Circulars Year 1996. Retirees from public sector who are interested in getting a job at the private sector are required to register with Department of Manpower under the Ministry of Human Resource. Department of Manpower plays an important role in matching the qualification and experiences of retirees with the job requirement of private sectors. Employment opportunities for older persons were provided by the Ministry of Human Resource whereby employers were allowed to claim 100 per cent tax rebate on retraining costs for older persons taken in as employees (Government of Malaysia, 2006: 311).

The Employees Provident Fund (EPF) scheme provides retirement benefits for members through mandatory savings in the form of monthly contributions from both the employee and the employer. EPF was started in 1952 with the contribution rate of 5 per cent each from employee and employer. The current contribution rate is 11 per cent by the employee and 12 per cent of the monthly wage by the employer. Each member's contributions are separated into three accounts. Account I consists of 60 per cent of contribution, and can only be withdrawn when member reaches age 55, that is mandatory age of retirement. Some 30 per cent of the contributions are deposited into Account II and withdrawals are allowed for the purchase or building a house, or to finance own education or children's education at the institution of higher learning, either locally or abroad. The balance in this account can be withdrawn at age 50. The final 10 per cent is held in Account III and can be withdrawn for medical expenses of critical illnesses, and investment through approved mutual fund (unit trust) institutions.

The government pension scheme is intended to provide financial security for retired government employees. Upon retirement, retirees who opt for the pension scheme will be paid a fixed monthly income of up to a maximum of 50 per cent of the last drawn salary and a service gratuity payment. They also enjoy free medical treatment at government hospitals.

The members of EPF and government pension scheme are mainly from formal sector. Therefore only a small proportion of population enjoys benefits from provident fund and pension. Hence, old-age security would possibly be from pension, provident fund, savings, insurance and other investments as well as from family members particularly children.

With the low coverage and no or very limited protection against inflation or longevity, social security system in Malaysia is quite deficient in providing socially adequate levels of income security in old-age (Asher, 1998). Many older persons are likely to end up in poverty, especially women who live longer and having less access to savings and credit in part due to being out of labour force and/or lower job status and positions. It is therefore community-based programmes that are vehicles for empowerment for older persons to take responsibility for their own welfare. The talents of older persons can then be appropriately tapped in their own interest as well as those of their families and the society at large.

Community Participation

In Malaysia, community development programmes have been implemented to foster harmonious living and nurture the spirit of caring among the various communities as well as to inculcate positive values

(Government of Malaysia, 2006: 312). In the rural area, community development programmes are undertaken by Community Development Department (KEMAS) to provide opportunities for the hardcore poor to improve their socio-economic status. In urban area, the programmes are implemented through the Rukun Tetangga (Neighbourhood Outreach) committee to promote good neighbourliness and national unity. Resident associations as well as social and recreational clubs are also set up to enlist participation from various groups of people for the benefit of all.

A Model Community Centre

The origin of PJCC can be traced to an action-oriented research project on "Evaluating the Needs of Older Persons in Malaysia" undertaken at the University of Malaya. In 1996, the PJCC was set up in Section 17, Petaling Jaya, by a group of researchers headed by the late Prof. Dr Tan Poo Chang from the Faculty of Economics and Administration, University of Malaya, together with the National Unity Department, the Neighbourhood Outreach Committees in Section 17, Petaling Jaya in close cooperation with the local council of Petaling Jaya and other agencies.

Initially, PJCC started with the objective of providing older persons employment opportunities, together with the young, to care for the community. The centre is instrumental in linking the government agencies, non-governmental organisations, the private sector and the communities in implementing various economic, educational, health, social, cultural, information and communication technology (ICT), sports, recreational and environmental activities that involved older people.

The PJCC has the following objectives:

- To promote self-sustaining and ongoing programmes at community level that utilise the expertise and experiences of older persons, with participation from the young;
- To provide an innovative framework to enlist participation and empowerment of older persons in the decision-making process and in providing a support network;
- To operate as a node, and give people a sense of ownership and a feeling of patriotism;
- To act as a coordination and management centre that assists in the identification of vulnerable groups and respond via direct action or referral to other agencies;

- To function as a main resource centre for family members to meet their social, recreational and other needs;
- To enhance good urban governance through smart partnership;
- To improve the quality of life of the people through social and sustainable development; and
- To create a social security alternative for older persons to continue to receive income and maintain independence and live with dignity.

(Tan and Tey, 2005)

The PJCC is managed by a committee together with the Neighbourhood Outreach Committee Members. Monthly meeting is held and account is presented during the meeting. Older persons are given opportunities to take up key positions in decision-making and in running various activities.

Various activities have been carried out to bridge different age groups and enhancing greater social integration and environment protection. Activities are open to all, regardless of age, place of residence or social class. Amongst the activities are:

Social and recreational activities: Most of the social and recreational activities are implemented throughout the year. Social interaction gatherings, such as fellowship nights and line dance sessions are held weekly to further strengthen social cohesiveness among youths, older persons and other family members. From time to time, a community charity party is held to encourage inter-agency and inter-are participation, and cash donations are given out to the needy groups. Older persons share their knowledge and expertise with others through conducting social dancing and line dancing classes. Many have helped in organising tours and visits to places of interest, parties and gatherings, as well as social functions and events.

Physical activity: Physical activity is held to promote regular participation by the young and old in exercise and physical fitness. It includes Tai Chi, Waitankung, yoga, badminton, breakfast run, cleanliness campaign. Older persons are the instructors and coordinators of these activities.

Educational activity: Older persons become the main coordinators to teach the young Mandarin, English, Japanese and art classes. Tuition classes for school children are organised for retired teachers to continue impart their knowledge to the young. On the other hand, the older persons are learning about ICT from younger persons.

Environment activity: PJCC provides employment opportunities to the older persons. The establishment of the Environment Activity Centre in March 1997 with the initial objective of collecting recyclable items such as clothes, papers, glass bottles, aluminium tins, steel tins and plastics, has expended to receive items other than recyclable items when the public began to bring in many useable goods such as books, magazines, toys, decorative items, etc. The Environment Activity Centre is aimed at environment protection and creating awareness on environment issues. It emphasises on waste reduction and the items are first repaired or resorted and only recycled as a last resort (Figure 2). From the items received, older persons sorted out these items in to two categories: useable goods and recyclable items. Usable goods are further sorted out for (a) sales at community shops and sunday flea market; (b) donation to charity homes; and (c) repair if necessary, and sent to community shops and sunday flea market for sale or to charity homes after repairing. Recyclable items are sorted into various categories and grades before selling to recyclers. Recovery of items that have been dumped is a savings of the national resources and a contribution to environmental improvement.

At present, there are six older persons working at the Environment Activity Centre, two older persons are managing the sales centres, eight older persons are working at the weekly flea market with assistance from two university undergraduates, two dance teachers, ten instructors for various exercises, and two language teachers. Funds generated from PJCC activities are being used to pay allowances to older persons (the rate ranges from US$1 to US$5 per hour depending on the type of services provided), to donate to charities and other deserving institutions, and to support community and PJCC activities.

PJCC has facilitated the continued participation of older persons in social and economic activities within the community. Older persons are getting paid for their services in giving tuition and for their work in the Environmental Activities Centre, Neighbourhood Outreach Centre, sales centres and flea market. By involving the senior citizens in the running of the centre, PJCC has reestablished their roles in community development. Older persons are not only the main initiators of these activities, they are the organisers of events, teachers of the dance, instructors of exercises, and also the participants of various activities.

The PJCC model of encouraging and facilitating community participation of older persons has shown great potentials in mobilising the vast human resources of the older persons. The committed older persons have been the key persons in ensuring the continuity of the activities at PJCC. The achievement of PJCC has gained recognition form the

Figure 2 ***The Operation System of PJCC Environment Activity Centre***

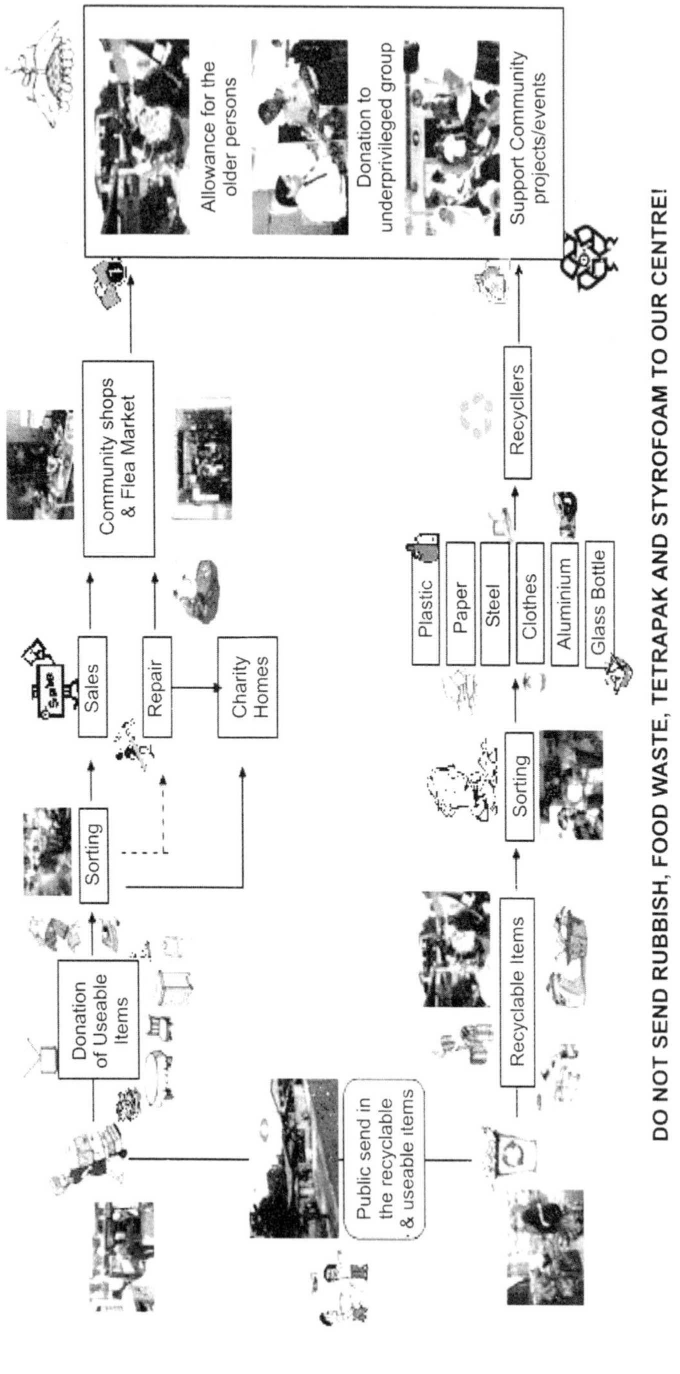

government. PJCC is the only community programme that has been awarded the coveted Public Sector Innovation Award in the year 2000. It was one of the 11 finalists of the 2001–2002 Commonwealth Association for Public Administration and Management (CAPAM) International Innovations Awards. It had been invited to participate at the International Innovation Exhibition, a side event of the sixth Global Forum on Reinventing Government, in Seoul from 24–27 May 2005.

Conclusion

With development and higher education of older persons, the demand will be on maintenance of a high quality of life. It is therefore necessary to ensure that opportunities and choices are provided for all older persons to enjoy independence, participation, care, self-fulfilment and dignity. The PJCC experience on harnessing the human resource of older persons for promoting social interaction and environment protection implies that the expertise and the resource of older persons can be fully tapped and older persons should be integrated in development programmes and as fully participating members of society.

References

Asher, M.G. 1998. The Future of Retirement Protection in Southeast Asia. *International Social Security Review* 51: 3–30.

Clark, R. and R. Anker. 1990. Labour Force Participation Rates of Older Persons: An International Comparison. *International Labour Review* 129(2): 255–71.

Clark, R. and R. Anker. 1993. Cross-national Analysis of Labour Force Participation of Older Men and Women. *Economic Development and Cultural Change* 41(3): 489–572.

Department of Statistics, Malaysia. 2003. *2000* Population Census Report: Economic Characteristics of the Population. Kuala Lumpur.

Government of Malaysia. 2001. Eighth Malaysia Plan, 2001–2005. Kuala Lumpur.

Government of Malaysia. 2006. Ninth Malaysia Plan, 2006–2010. Kuala Lumpur.

Jean, P. 2005. Population Aging Trends in Malaysia. Population Census of Malaysia 2000, Monograph Series No. 1, Department of Statistics, Malaysia.

Ng, S.T., N.P. Tey, Noor Azina Ismail and Others. 2005. *Optimising the Potential of Older Persons As Critical Resources for Development: A Case Study in Urban Malaysia.* Faculty of Economics and Administration, University of Malaya, Kuala Lumpur.

Tan, P.C., S.T. Ng, N.P. Tey and A. Halimah. 1999. Evaluating Programme Needs of Older Persons in Malaysia. Monograph Series No. 1, Faculty of Economics and Administration, University of Malaya, Kuala Lumpur.

Tan, P.C. and N.P. Tey. 2005. PJCC—A Model for Community Participation and Active Ageing in Malaysia. *Journal of Intergenerational Relationships* 3(2): 125–31.

Tan, P.C. and N.P. Tey. 2006. "Empowering Older Adults as Key Resources in Development in Malaysia" in H. Yoon and J. Hendricks (eds.), *Handbook of Asian Aging*. New York: Baywood Publishing Company, 195–210.

United Nations. 2002. World Population Ageing 1950–2050. Population Division, Department of Economic and Social Affairs, United Nations.

United Nations. 2006. Population Ageing 2006. Population Division, Department of Economic and Social Affairs, United Nations.

United Nations. 2007. ESCAP Population Data Sheet. Emerging Social Issues Division, Department of Economic and Social Affairs, United Nations.

14

A Geographical Perspective on the Patterns of Ageing in the Tribal Areas of the North-Eastern Region of India

Debendra Kumar Nayak

The world is in the midst of a major, historically unprecedented demographic transition. This transition is having—and will continue to have—profound effects on the size and age structure of its population. Not only is population growth slowing, but the age-structure of the population is also getting significantly altered. The share of the young is falling and that of the elderly rising. Different countries and regions are at varying stages of this demographic transition. In most advanced countries, the ageing process is already well under way, and a number of developing countries in East and South-East Asia and central and Eastern Europe will also experience significant ageing from about 2020. In other developing countries, however, the demographic transition is less advanced.

World population growth was relatively slow before 1900. The age structure of the population too was broadly constant. Fewer people lived beyond age 65. First half of the twentieth century witnessed dramatic changes in life expectancy and that resulted in unprecedented population growth. Age-structure of the population however did not experience substantive modification at least in the initial period. With fertility rates declining phenomenally in the second half of the twentieth century, population growth slowed down resulting in a decline in the share of the young in the population with a corresponding rise in the share of the elderly.

Thus, the series of unprecedented demographic events overtook the world which is unparalleled in its nature and dimension in human history. The last century has proved to be a watershed in terms of significant demographic transformation of the global population. The most significant of all developments is the phenomenal increment in the total size of the global population accompanied by unprecedented hike in population growth rate. Such an increment is unlikely to be replicated in the coming years. From a meagre 1,650 million people at the turn of the twentieth century, population numbers escalated to over 6,000 millions particularly in the second half of the century. The average annual growth rate of population exceeded 2 per cent for the first time in human history adding over 85 million people annually during 1980s.

The spatial pattern of population growth was however not uniform across the developed and the less developed countries. Most developed countries had by the middle of the twentieth century, witnessed major reduction in both in death rates and then in birth rates leading to not only slower population growth but also a phenomenal decline in child population. Population began to age in such countries. In sharp contrast, the less developed countries continued to experience high fertility rates in spite of large decline in mortality and significant rise in life expectancy particularly in the post-world war years. This contrasting population transitions resulted in significant population redistribution across countries and continents.

By the early twenty-first century, a larger number of countries had joined the ranks of low fertility regime leading to a world-wide fall in growth rates to about 1.2 per cent per annum and is expected to fall further in the years to come as more and more countries shall experience lower fertility. A net outcome of this vital demographic transformation is the slow but a definite change from more youthful societies in many countries to more demographically mature populations—a phenomenon variously described as the process of ageing or greying. In strict demographic terms, the nations witnessing these transitions will be relieved of child dependency to a great extent while they will be faced with a greater burden of old-age dependency. This shift of dependency as reflected in the changing age-structure of such nations may be similar in quantity—decrease in child dependency compensated by increase in old-age dependency—but not in quality. It may be noted that the increase in life expectancy is not only due to greater life expectancy among the younger age group but also rising life expectancy of the older segment.

A significant fact about ageing is that it increases the total number of aged persons compared to other age groups and that the pace of this change is more rapid now in developing rather than the developed countries. Though all countries in the developing world have not equally received the full impact of this rise in the proportion of the aged and a corresponding decline in the young age population, it is expected that nearly all countries will experience, by the beginning of the next century, a gradual demographic shift towards an older segment exceeding the proportion of the young for the first time in history (UNFPA: 1998)—a situation that has already taken roots in more developed countries.

The ageing process in India is no exception but reveals remarkable regional diversity in the manifestation of the process. India presents baffling diversity in its cultural, linguistic, racial and ethnic composition. Modernisation and globalisation have led to a widening of the gap between the rich and the poor and has enhanced the differences in access to social and economic opportunities and resources available to different sections of the society. The resulting intensification of competition among the groups for societal resources has adversely affected older people, especially the poor, who are more vulnerable than others to social and economic hardships. Pervasive poverty and inequalities of income, coupled with a very inadequate safety net, has meant that a majority of older persons become marginalised or even destitute. The poor among elderly people have been losing out even as economic development is taking place in the country as a whole. It is important, therefore, that the ageing process and its impact on society be understood well, so that appropriate measures may be undertaken to minimise the negative effects and to develop appropriate policies and programmes for the welfare of older persons. As the United Nations in its International Plan of Action on Ageing of 1982 states: "Countries should recognise and take into account their demographic trends and changes in the structure of their populations in order to optimise their development" (United Nations, 1999).

The present study aims at assessing the dimension of ageing among the tribal population in the north-east India, a region which experiences a peculiar demographic situation of continuously high fertility rate coupled with an increase in life expectancy resulting in a sizeable number of old people in the total population. However, this trend is not spatially or socially uniform calling for a geographical perspective on the problem. The areas which have experienced a demographic transition are already experiencing a significant alteration in the age-structure that contains a sizeable proportion of aged people and declining proportion of child population. The case of Kerala, Himachal Pradesh and a few states in south India can be cited as examples of this nature of a transition. But this is not true of the North-East India where the fertility rate continues to be high despite a significant decline in mortality. Interestingly, the fertility and mortality indicators illustrate that in some of the states the socio-demographic conditions are at par or close to that of the more developed Indian states such as Kerala. Recent survey data indicate that fertility level has improved in all the states following better health facilities and longer life expectancy. The decline in mortality has been a response to improved medical facility and better spatial coverage in the provision of health care. But the fertility rate has not responded adequately to these improvements and continues to be extremely high in areas that support a sizeable tribal population. As is well known, the north-eastern part of India has very high concentration of scheduled tribes in the hilly areas. The only areas where the tribes are less in number are the plains consisting of the Brahmaputra and Barak valley and the Imphal basin as well as the Tripura plains. The demographic reality coupled with tribal values and social customs create a new situation with these changes in the demographic structure overtaking the tribal areas in recent times. The present study thus aims at assessing the nature of the demographic and social changes in these areas and making an effort to understand the problems of the ever-increasing number of the aged in the context of changing tribal values towards the aged segments of the population.

The Region

The north-east region is taken as the study area. All the seven states included in the region are taken into consideration while assessing the problems of the aged through a spatio-temporal study. The rationale for selecting the region has been the region's peculiarity of demographic reality unfolding in the region in sharp contrast to other regions of the country. The other most important consideration is the fact that the region has a very large concentration of scheduled tribes who have been exposed to urbanisation in recent times only. Topographically, much of the region consists of hills and plateaus although some parts are located in plains notably, the Brahmaputra and Barak plains, the Manipur basin and the Tripura plains. Economically, the region continues to be characterised by subsistence agriculture and the hills have the practice of shifting cultivation. Socially and culturally the region presents extreme diversity characterised by tribal cultures in the hills and peasant culture in much of the plains. The tribal culture extends to the plains too though in many cases the tribal people living in the plains have been assimilated to the peasant cultures in some very important ways.

The region presents the complexities of the sub-Himalayan ranges, the Indo-Burmese hills of Nagaland, Manipur and Mizoram and the eroded surfaces of the Meghalaya plateau, all encircling the Brahmaputra valley. The hills are sharply marked from the plains, physically as well as culturally, though so linked that to some extent they must be treated together (Spate and Learmonth, 1972). The boundaries between the hills and the plains often present themselves as demographic boundaries too. The region presents itself as a replica of the subcontinent, both physically as well as culturally, only on a much smaller scale. The northern mountains are in fact an extension of the Himalayan ranges with modification introduced in the erosional features due to much heavier rainfall. The Indo-Burmese hills are much less imposing as a relief feature. Parts of Tripura and Imphal valley represent area of low relief. The Assam valley is an alluvial expanse laid down by the mighty Brahmaputra and its numerous tributaries. The Meghalaya and Karbi Plateau, a fragment of the peninsular block, is a highly dissected tract.

The overall geographical setting of the region has provided an ideal habitat for a legion of tribal communities. "... the tribes of the north-east India have a world of their own. Having lived in the marchland between India and China and in the triangle where the Indian and the Chinese worlds meet, they have picked up the impression that they belong to none" (Ahmad, 1983). The peculiarity of the geographical and historical conditions of this region has offered relative isolation to the cultural groups who found their way into the region through passes from the north and the east. The northern and eastern mountain ranges and the southern plateau understandably provide more suitable tribal habitats compared to the Brahmaputra valley. However, the valley has not been totally averse to tribal people in providing them with a habitat. They have found suitable sites for settlement in the isolated hill features, forested portions of the valley and in marshy tracts. The northern bank of the river as well as the river islands still retain their predominantly tribal character. The area of the transition between the hills and the plains of Brahmaputra is also largely tribal in its ethnic composition. The plain tribals "generally represent the spill over communities from the hilly regions except for the Bodos who are a big tribal group largely confined to the plains" (Sharma, 1984).

Ageing in India

Incidentally, the growth rate of the elderly population is more rapid in developing countries like India compared to many developed countries. The elderly population in India is the second largest in the world, next only to China and the older population has been steadily increasing in number and proportion. This segment numbered only 12.1 million in the year 1901 and it increased to 24.7 million by the year 1961. The 2001 census recorded 77 million elderly people in India (7.5% of the total population) which is projected to reach around 137 million by the year 2021. In a country where bulk of the population lives in rural areas, 3 out of every 4 elderly persons actually live in rural areas. The fact that the elderly population is growing at a phenomenal rate in India is borne out from their annual growth rate (3%) which far exceeds the growth rate of the total population (1.9%). The proportion of the elderly population is likely to exceed the proportion in the child age group by the year 2050 as projected by the UN. The population of India is ageing in two ways: (i) ageing at the base due to lower fertility and (ii) ageing at the apex due to reduced mortality and dramatic increase in life expectancy. The index of ageing has consequently increased from a mere 14.31 in the year 1901 to 22.7 in the year 2001. The analysis of historical patterns of mortality and fertility decline in India indicate that the process of population ageing intensified only in the 1990s (Bose and Kapoor, 2004).

Looking at regional variations Bose found that three states in India, namely Uttar Pradesh, Maharashtra and Bihar had more than 5 million persons in the 60+ category. It may be noted that in most of the states the population of 60+ males exceeded that of 60+ females, particularly in Bihar, Madhya Pradesh, Rajasthan and Uttar Pradesh. But in Kerala, Maharashtra, Andhra Pradesh, Karnataka and Gujarat, the 60+ female populations exceeded the 60+ male populations. Kerala had the highest proportion of 60+ population followed by Himachal Pradesh, Punjab, Haryana and Tamil Nadu. Among major states, the lowest proportion was in Assam followed by West Bengal, Bihar, Rajasthan, Gujarat, Madhya Pradesh, Andhra Pradesh and Uttar Pradesh.

Ageing in the North-East

The process of population ageing, though less in magnitude than other states, has already begun in the north-eastern region. The population of persons aged 60 or over has almost doubled to 1.7 million persons by the year 1991. In some states like Manipur, Meghalaya and Mizoram, the growth rate of 60+ persons has been faster than that of the overall population. In spite of the fact that the region is characterised by an overwhelming tribal population, majority of the elderly persons in a great number of states are males. In terms of birth rate, total fertility rate (TFR), death rate, infant mortality (IMR) and life expectancy at birth, there have been welcome improvements over the years. It may be thus be interesting to analyse the patterns in the process of ageing in the region with respect to a few important indicators of ageing. The indicators[1] include the proportion of people in the age group of 60 and over, the ageing index, the potential support ratio, old-age dependency rate and the total dependency rate. The patterns have been identified by taking the districts which are dominantly inhabited by the tribal segment of the population. The ethnic divide in population admirably corresponds to a physical division of the region into the hilly and the plain areas, though with a few exceptions. The former category corresponds to the tribal areas while the latter is largely confined to the non-tribal population. A further classification of the districts is made by isolating those districts almost exclusively (over 80%) inhabited by the tribes.

Overall Pattern

Inter-district variation in the process of ageing in the north-east region is analysed below with the help of a series of tables for the region as a whole.

Table 1 ***North-East India: Distribution of Districts according to Proportion of the Aged (60+), 1971–2001***

% Aged	*1971*		*1991*		*2001*	
	Males	*Females*	*Males*	*Females*	*Males*	*Females*
2–2.9	—	—	—	2	1	1
3–3.9	5	15	5	10	4	7
4–4.9	27	19	21	30	15	18
5–5.9	18	25	24	17	31	24
6–6.9	17	13	16	9	17	14
7–7.9	2	—	5	4	4	6
8–8.9	—	—	1	—	—	2
9–9.9	3	—	—	—	—	—
Total	72	72	72	72	72	72

Table 1 reveals the percentage of the aged (60+) for both males and females for the year 1971, 1991 and 2001. It is evident that the proportion of the aged in the population is less than 3 per cent only for females in the year 1991 in two districts whereas in the year 2001, one districts contained a very low proportion of aged population, below three per cent. It is difficult to believe that there is a decline in the absolute old population in these districts over the years. The fall in the proportion of the aged in a few districts is due to excessive increase in child population in these districts characterised by a stable or relatively slow increase in the aged population. It is also evident from the table that in a larger number of districts the aged females constitute a smaller proportion compared to the males. For instance, the aged males constituted less than 5 per cent of the population in 32 of the 72 districts in 1971 compared to 34 such districts in case of the females. The relative position in 1991 changes to 26 districts in case of males as compared to 42 districts in case of females and 20 districts for males in the year 2001 compared to 26 districts in case of females. This shows that the gender gap in ageing was lowered up to 1971, then increased substantially by the year 1991 and shows a decline thereafter. In a large number of districts, the female survival beyond 60 years of age was less compared to that of the males. The aged females constituted a very low proportion (below 8%) in the year 1971. The situation marginally changed in the year 1991 as in some districts the proportion of the aged females increased to 9 per cent. By the year 2001, the aged female component increased in more districts. Another interesting feature that emerges from the table is that there are no districts that fall within 2 per cent in 1971 for both the sexes, but a few in 1991 and 2001. These districts are mostly located in Arunachal Pradesh and Meghalaya. As many as 15 districts in 1971 contained a very low proportion of the aged females (4% or less). The number of such districts however came down to 10 only in 1991 and further reduced to 7 in 2001. These districts are mostly located in Assam, Nagaland, Arunachal Pradesh and Meghalaya. Most of the districts with a greater proportion of the aged are located in parts of Arunachal Pradesh, Mizoram, Nagaland, Assam and Meghalaya. Significant number of districts with a greater proportion of aged females was more in the year 2001 compared to males. For example, there are 8 districts in which the proportion of aged females exceeds 7 per cent. However, in the case of males, the number of such districts is only 4. The extent of inter-district variation in the proportion of the aged population has registered a phenomenal increase over the years and it is much more for the female segment than for the males.

Aged population, particularly of the women is very high, i.e., above 6 per cent in districts of Tripura along with some districts of Manipur, Arunachal Pradesh, Nagaland, Assam and parts of Meghalaya. It is significant that distribution of these districts are highly scattered in the region and hence do not indicate impact of regional factors for such changes in demographic structure.

Table 2 ***North-East: Distribution of Districts in Different Ageing Index Classes, 1971–2001***

Ageing Index (%)	*1971*		*1991*		*2001*	
	Males	*Females*	*Males*	*Females*	*Males*	*Females*
4–7.9	15	13	12	22	2	3
8–11.9	42	48	54	44	16	21
12–15.9	12	11	6	6	26	21
16–19.9	3	—	—	—	20	21
20–23.9	—	—	—	—	7	4
24–27.9	—	—	—	—	1	2
Total	72	72	72	72	72	72

The ageing index is calculated as the number of persons 60 years or over per hundred persons under age 15. The ageing index is a much more sensitive index of ageing as it shows the proportion of the aged relative to the young age population. Table 2 clearly reveals a drastic fall in the number of districts with a lower ageing index over the years. But the fall in the number of such districts in case of males is more uniform, but not so for the females. The number of districts with lower ageing index indeed registered substantial increase by the year 1991 as far as the females are concerned, but fell significantly by the year 2001. Districts characterised by low ageing index (4–7.99%) for both males and females in the year 1971 included nearly whole of Meghalaya; most of Arunachal Pradesh and few districts in Assam. Only a handful of districts in the year 2001 recorded very low ageing index both for males and females. While none of the districts in the year 1971 had an ageing index in excess of 20 per cent, the average in the year 1991 experienced a decline in the index as indicated by the fact that all the districts recorded an index lower than 16 per cent. The situation underwent unprecedented changes in the year 2001 when the ageing index showed substantive improvement with 8 and 6 districts in the region recording an index of over 20 per cent for the males and females respectively.

Table 3 ***North-East India: Distribution of Districts in Different Classes of Dependency Ratio, 1971–2001***

Total Dependency Ratio	*1971*		*1991*		*2001*	
	Males	*Females*	*Males*	*Females*	*Males*	*Females*
50–50.9	3	—	2	1	5	3
60–60.9	5	—	8	4	22	13
70–70.9	13	3	38	19	18	23
80–80.9	8	13	17	33	22	27
90–90.9	27	29	6	10	4	4
100–109.9	12	11	1	5	1	2
110–119.9	4	12	—	—	—	—
120–139.9	—	4	—	—	—	—
Total	72	72	72	72	72	72

The total dependency ratio is the number of persons under the age 15 plus persons aged 60 or older per one hundred persons 15 to 60+. It is the sum of the youth and old-age dependency ratio.

Young age dependency ratio is based on age group of 0–14 years and old-age dependency ratio is based on age group of 60+ years. Hence, if the level of fertility is high, large proportion of population will be in the non-working age group 0–14 years resulting in higher dependency ratios. On the other hand, if the life expectancy improves, a large proportion of the old-age population will increase old-age dependency. Thus, the total dependency ratio generally indicates economic burden on the adult population which has to support these two dependent segments. Table 3 shows a generally declining number of districts over the years with higher dependency ratio. This means that in a large number of districts the overall dependence on the adult population is on the decline.

Table 4 ***North-East India: Distribution of Districts in Different Classes of Old-Age Dependency Ratio, 1971–2001***

Old-Age Dependency Ratio	*1971*		*1991*		*2001*	
	Males	*Females*	*Males*	*Females*	*Males*	*Females*
2–5.9	—	—	—	—	2	3
6–9.9	9	31	5	21	39	41
10–13.9	39	26	32	33	30	26
14–17.9	19	15	22	13	1	2
18--21.9	2	—	10	5	—	—
22–25.9	3	—	2	—	—	—
Total	72	72	72	72	72	72

Old-age dependency ratio is the ratio taken as the number of persons 60/65 years and over per one hundred persons in 15–60 years of age. Table 4 reveals a generally decreasing number of districts with higher old-age dependence. This is indicative of the fact that in many districts the adult population is growing at a much faster rate than the growth taking place in old-age population. In 1971, there were a few districts with higher (over 18 per 100) old-age dependency ratio. However, in 2001 no district shows such a high level of dependence.

Table 5 ***North-East India: Distribution of Districts in Different Classes of Potential Support Ratio, 1971–2001***

Potential Support Ratio	*1971*		*1991*		*2001*	
	Males	*Females*	*Males*	*Females*	*Males*	*Females*
6–8.9	28	16	15	9	16	19
9–11.9	20	39	40	32	40	36
12–14.9	19	17	10	22	12	12
15–17.9	5	—	7	7	3	2
18–20.9	—	—	—	2	—	1
21–23.9	—	—	—	—	1	2
Total	72	72	72	72	72	72

The potential support ratio is the number of persons aged 15–60 per every person aged 60 or older. This is exact opposite of old-age dependency ratio. Table 5 reveals an increasing trend of potential support ratio in most districts for both the sexes from 1971 to 2001.

The Ageing Tribes

Needless to mention the hilly areas in the north-east as also elsewhere in India comprise mostly of the tribal population. Thus, the districts by and large located in the hills contain ethnically differentiated population as compared to the plains which contain a sizeable proportion of the non-tribal segment. There are 38 districts mostly located in the Arunachal, Naga, Mizo and Manipur hills, Meghalaya plateau, parts of Tripura and Assam containing over 50 per cent tribal population in their total.

Table 6 ***North-East India: Ageing in Areas of Tribal Dominance***

	% Aged	*Ageing Index*	*PSR*	*Old-age Dependency*	*Total Dependency*
			1971		
Overall	5.3	9.9	10.5	13.1	86.8
Male	5.5	10	10.7	13.9	86.8
Female	5.2	9.9	10.5	12.2	83
			1991		
Overall	4.8	8.6	12.6	12.6	78.5
Male	5.2	9	13.9	13.9	75.6
Female	4.5	8.2	11.3	11.3	82.1
			2001		
Overall	5	13.3	11.9	8.9	77.6
Male	5.1	13.8	11.8	8.9	76.1
Female	4.9	12.8	12.1	8.8	79.5

Source: Census of India.

As is evident from Table 6, the tribal and hilly areas show the ageing process to be highly muted owing largely to a very high fertility rate experienced in the tribal segment. The proportion of the aged in the year 1971, going by the district average, was 5.3 per cent as against 5.1 per cent in the non-tribal population (see Nayak, 2007) indicating a greater proportion of the aged population among the tribal segment. But the situation changed over the years and the proportion of the aged declined to 4.8 per cent by the year 1991 and marginally increased to 5 per cent of

Figure 1 Changes in the Proportion of the Aged in Tribal Areas of the North-East 1971

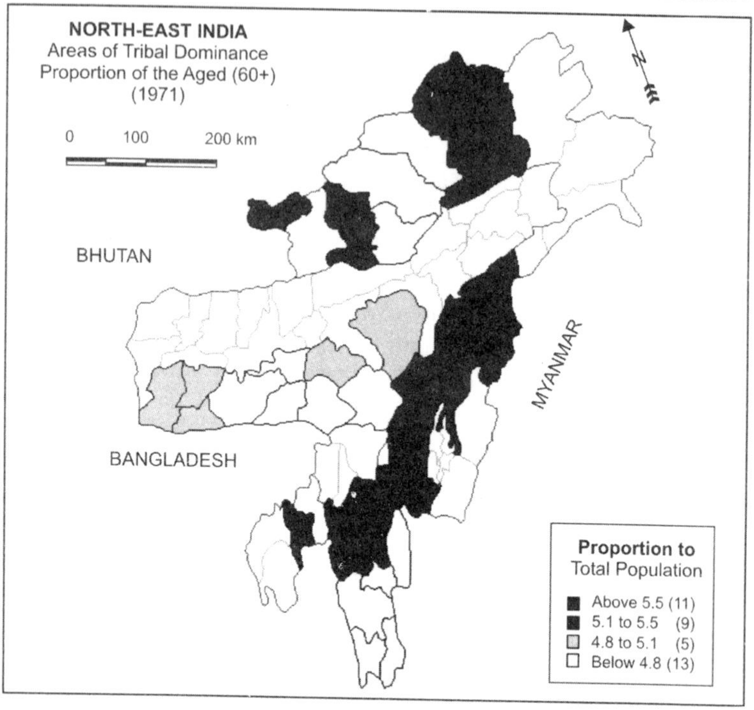

the total population by the turn of the present century. The aged among the males showed a decline over the years in terms of their proportion. So is the case with the females.

This situation is reflected in the ageing index too which experienced a fall during the 1971–1991 period and increased marginally to 13.3 in the year 2001. The ageing index of the females remains lower than that of the males in all the years though follows a similar trend with the population. The overall PSR, a very sensitive index of ageing remained by and large constant over the years, in fact showing an upward trend unlike that for the plain areas. The trend is more or less the same for the two sexes. As regards the old-age and total dependency is concerned, there is a general falling trend comparable with that of areas of non-tribal concentration (Nayak, 2007). The areas of tribal concentration had a greater old-age dependence compared to the non-tribal areas in the year 1971, but the situation reversed by the year 2001 where the old-age dependence was greater in areas of non-tribal dominance (Nayak, 2007). Interestingly, the total dependency ratio was much higher in the

Figure 2 ***Changes in the Proportion of the Aged in Tribal Areas of the North-East, 2001***

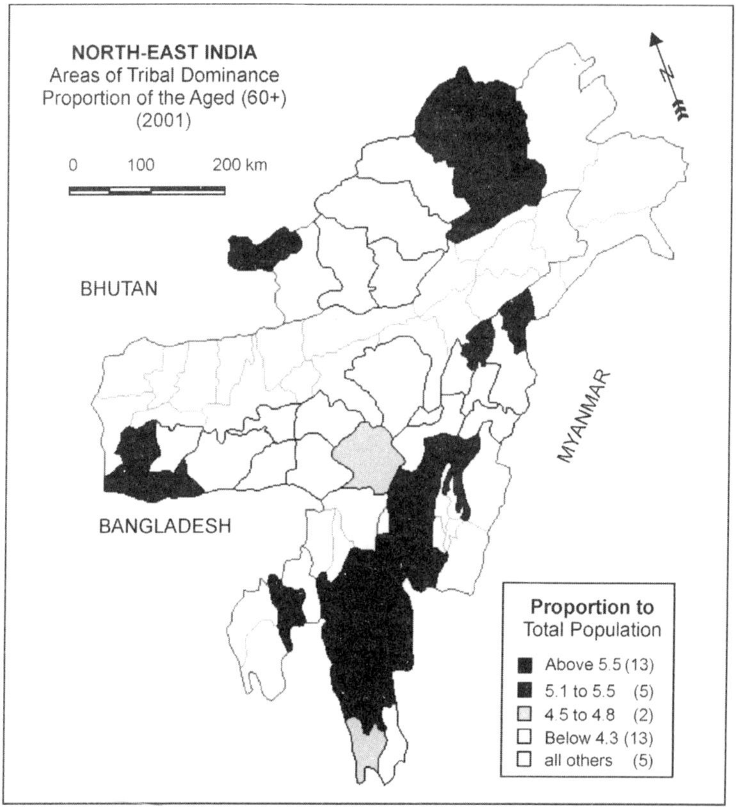

areas of non-tribal dominance in the year 1971 but both the areas exhibited a more or less similar dependency ratio by the year 2001. This reveals a much sharper fall in dependency in the non-tribal areas.

Inter-district variation in the proportion of the aged in the areas of tribal concentration shows a uniform fall in the percentage of the aged during 1971 and 2001. It ranges between 3.8 per cent in Lower Subansiri to a high of 8 per cent in Mon. By the year 2001, it ranged between 3.2 per cent in Dimapur to 7.8 per cent in Upper Siang. This is despite an increase in the number of the aged in all the districts. Such a situation has resulted from an increase in birth rate swelling up the proportion in the young age group. It is significant that the proportion of the aged remained stagnant or declined in a majority of 20 out of 38 districts. In fact the decline took place in over 40 per cent (16) districts.

Figure 3 ***Spatial Patterns in Ageing in the Tribal Areas of the North-East, 1971***

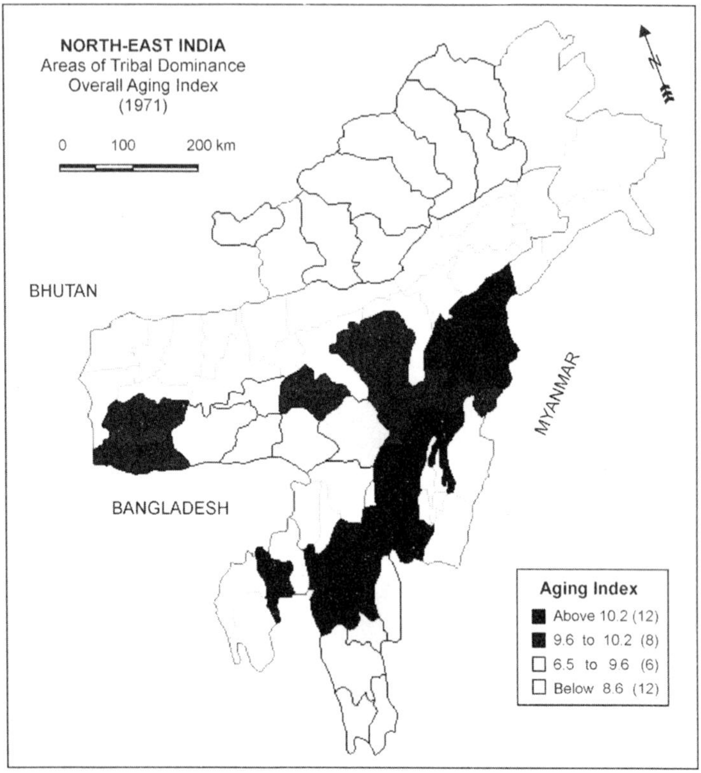

Going by the ageing index, a similar trend and pattern becomes far too evident. The range of variation has indeed widened over the years. The ageing index in 1971 varied between 6.7 in Subansiri, upper Subansiri and Papum Pare to14.6 in Tuensang and Zuneboto. By the year 2001, the index ranged between 5.7 in Papum Pare to a high of 20.4 in Upper Siang. The index registered a decline in 6 districts mostly located in Naga Hills and a few districts of Arunachal Pradesh and Meghalaya. The remaining districts however recorded some increase in the ageing index, the most spectacular increase being noticed in a few districts of Arunachal Pradesh and Mizoram.

In terms of PSR, the 1971 data reveals a range of 6.8 in Mon, Tuensang and Zuneboto to 14.8 in Lower Subansiri. In the year 2001, the PSR shows a general rise with a range of 6.9 in Upper Siang to a high of 25.7 in Papum Pare. Significantly, the PSR index increased in 25 of

Figure 4 ***Changes in Potential Support Ratio in the Tribal Areas of North-East 2001***

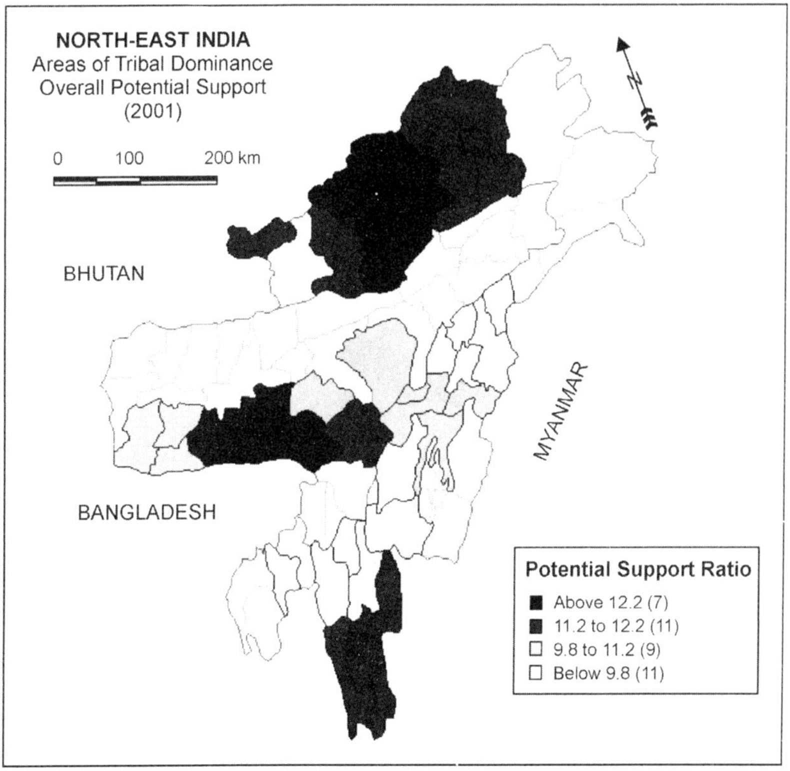

the 38 districts and declined in the remaining 13 districts. Increase in PSR index in such a large number of districts is indicative of substantial rise in the proportion of the population in working age group in relation to the rise in old-age population. The total dependency rate registered a fall in a vast majority of districts numbering 27 whereas nearly all the districts barring three registered an increase in the old-age dependency.

Ageing in Areas of Excessive Tribal Concentration

In this section, the ageing process as is unfolding in the areas of excessive (over 80%) tribal concentration in the North-East is analysed with reference to the indicators mentioned. Needless to mention these areas are exclusively concentrated in the hilly parts in the north-east. There are 27 districts mostly located in the Arunachal, Naga, Mizo and Manipur hills, Meghalaya plateau, parts of Tripura and Assam where the tribes account for more than 80 per cent of the total population.

Figure 5 ***Changes in Potential Support Ratio in Tribal Areas of the North-East, 2001***

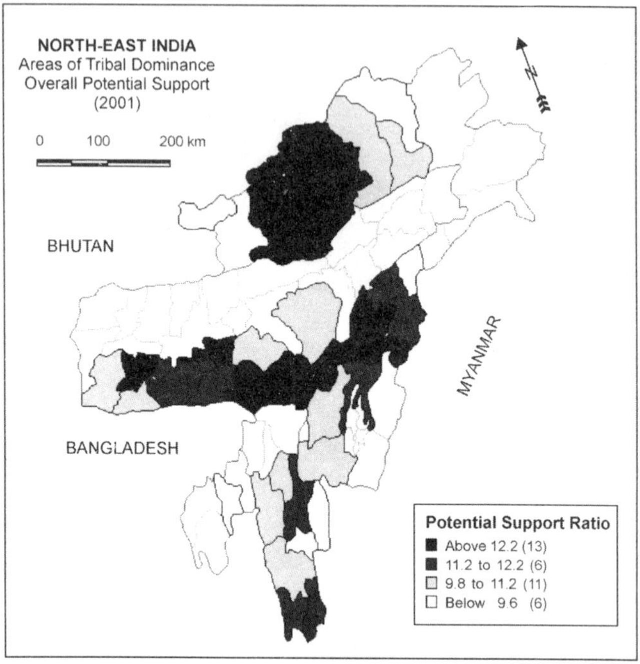

Table 7 ***North-East India: Ageing in Areas of Excessive Tribal Dominance***

	% Aged	*Ageing Index*	*PSR*	*Old-age Dependency*	*Total Dependency*
			1971		
Overall	5.4	10.1	10.3	13.4	87.2
Male	5.6	10.3	10.5	14.2	83.8
Female	5.3	10.1	10.3	12.5	91.6
			1991		
Overall	4.8	8.6	12.0	12.4	79.3
Male	5.1	9.0	11.6	13.6	76.6
Female	4.5	8.2	12.8	11.2	82.5
			2001		
Overall	4.9	13.1	11.7	8.8	78.4
Male	5.0	13.6	11.5	8.9	77.6
Female	4.8	12.6	12	8.6	79.3

Source: Census of India.

Table 7 clearly reveals a trend and a pattern in exclusively tribal areas which is not far too different from the one observed for the tribal districts in general. The only significant feature observed in these districts is that the proportion of the aged has fallen more rapidly in the population residing in these areas than the tribal areas in general. From a district average of 5.4 per cent in 1971 the proportion declined to 4.9 by the year 2001. A similar trend has been observed in the case of ageing index too. It is significant that a great majority (18 of the 27) of districts registered a decline in the proportion of the aged while the remaining districts registered a marginal increase in the proportion.

Discussion and Conclusion

Demographic parametres in the north-eastern region of India have improved remarkably reflecting interesting patterns over space. Population ageing has slowly but surely manifested itself against a background of continued high fertility in the region. However, the patterns are highly varied within different sub-regions and among different ethnic categories making it a highly complex phenomenon not lending itself to an easy explanation.

In terms of the proportion of the elderly population, the entire region lags behind the country average of 7.6 per cent. The areas of tribal concentration show a very low proportion of elderly population in total. The most significant aspect of ageing in the hilly and tribal areas refers to the fact of a declining trend in the proportion of elderly population over the three decades, which is surely linked to continued high fertility among the tribal segment. There is only a marginal increase in the proportion of the tribal elderly population since 1991.

Unlike the all India average, the proportion of the aged among the female segment is lower than that of their male counterparts in the north-east. The elderly among the tribal males constitutes a higher proportion than their female counterparts in all the years. The gap however is reducing over the years.

If one goes by the most sensitive index of ageing, i.e., ageing index, it is significant to note that the ageing process seems to have picked up momentum since the year 1991 in the country as a whole, but is weak in the case of the areas of tribal concentration as evident in such areas of the north-eastern region of the country. There has been indeed a fall in the ageing index till the year 1991.

In terms of PSR, the areas of tribal concentration show a reverse situation of increasing PSR over the years. This is indicative of an increasingly larger proportion of adult population compared to the aged in the areas of tribal concentration. In terms of dependency, there has been a general decline in both the indicators over the years.

Going by international standards and comparing with the developed countries which have a longer history of ageing it is expected that countries/regions beginning to age should experience an increase in the proportion of the aged, in ageing index and in old-age dependency ratio, while there should be a fall in potential support ratio and total dependency ratio. The patterns observed in the north-east do not conform to these parametres with equal vigour. The hilly and tribal areas experience an increase in ageing index only. The proportion of the aged in the total population is showing signs of an increase in recent years only and the PSR too is showing some signs of falling in most recent years. All these indicators only suggest the beginning of the ageing process in hilly and tribal areas. This is supported by a drastic fall in total dependency ratio, but contradicted by equally drastic fall in old-age dependency ratio. These features are perhaps common to a population that has just begun to experience ageing.

Note

1. Elderly Population = 60/64+ years Aging Index (AI):= (Elderly Population/ Youth Population)* 100 Old-Age Dependency Ratio (OADR):= (Elderly Population/Working Population)*100 Potential Support Ratio (PSR):=(Working Population/Elderly Population) Total Dependency Ratio (TDR):= (Young Population+ Elderly Population)/ Working Population * 100.

References

Ahmad, A. 1983. Education of the Scheduled Tribes: Some Aspects of Inequality. Workshop on Indicators of Equity in Education, October 24–28, NIEPA, New Delhi (mimeo).

Bagchi, K. (ed.). 1997. *Elderly Females in India*. New Delhi: Society for Gerontological Research and HelpAge India.

——. 1998. Some Important Areas of Gerontological Research in India. *Research and Development Journal* 4 (2, 3, HelpAge India.

Bali, A. 1997 "Elderly Females: An Ignored Silent Majority" in K. Bagchi (ed.), *Elderly Females in India*. Society for Gerontological Research and Help Age India, New Delhi, Chapter 2.

——. (ed.). 1999*a*. *Understanding Greying People of India*. New Delhi: ICSSR, Inter-India Publications.

——. 1999*b*. "Introduction" in A. Bali (ed.), *Understanding Greying People of India*. New Delhi: ICSSR, Inter-India Publications.

Bhat, Anitha Kumari and Raj Dhruvarajan. 2001. Ageing in India: Drifting Intergenerational Relations, Challenges and Options. *Ageing and Society* 21, 621±640.

Bose, Ashis. 2000. Demographic Transition. Paper presented in Ageing: A Symposium on the Greying of Our Society. Downloaded from website http://www.india-seminar.com/2000/488.htm

Bose, Ashish and Shankardass Mala Kapur. 2002. *Growing Old in India: Voices Reveal, Statistics Speak*. New Delhi: B.R. Publishing Corporation.

International Monetary Fund (IMF). 2004. IMF World Economic Outlook. Downloaded from website www.imf.org/external/pubs/ft/weo/2004/02/

Lee, Ronald. 2007. The Economic Implications of Changing Age-Structure. Downloaded from website www.un.org/esa/population/cpd2007/presentations/lee.hz.shr.ppt

Leete, R. and T. Jacobs. 2002. "The Older Poor and the Excluded in the Developing World" in *Situation and Voice: The Older Poor and Excluded in South Africa and India*. United Nations Population Fund, Population and Development Strategies Series No. 2, New York.

Nayak, D.K. 2007. A Geographical Perspective on the Trends and Patterns in Ageing in India with a special reference to the North-Eastern Region. Research Monograph No. GE/UGC/DKN/7, Department of Geography, North Eastern Hill University, Shillong.

National Institutes of Health, Washington, DC. 2007. Why Population Ageing Matters: A Global Perspective. Downloaded from website http://www.state.gov/g/oes/rls/or/81537.htm#over

Robyn, Stone. 1998. "The Feminisation of Poverty among the Elderly" in *Women The New York Times*, 13 October, A1 and A8. (quoted in U.N. Economic and Social Council. 1999. *Gender and Ageing: Problems, Perceptions and Policies*. Commission on the Status of Women (Report of the Secretary-General). Downloaded from website http://www.un.org/womenwatch/daw/csw/ageing.htm

Sharma, B.D. 1984. *Planning for Tribal Development*. New Delhi: Prachi.

Spate, O.H.K. and A.T.A. Learmonth. 1972. *India and Pakistan*. New Delhi: B.I. Publications.

U.N. Economic and Social Council. 1999. Gender and Ageing: Problems, Perceptions and Policies. Commission on the Status of Women (Report of the Secretary-General). Downloaded from website http://www.un.org/womenwatch/daw/csw/ageing.htm

United Nations. 2001. World Population Prospects: The 2000 Revision. Department of Economic and Social Affairs, Population Division, New York, Population Database. Downloaded from website www.unpopulation.org

UNPFA. 2002. Population Ageing and Development: Operational Challenges in Developing Countries. Population and Development Strategies Series No. 5, New York.

UNFPA. 1998. The State of World Population. New York.

PART IV

Demography of Ethnic Groups

15

Ethnic Differences in Fertility in Uplands of Kanchanaburi, Thailand

Jian Hu

The fertility of human beings is influenced by biological and social factors (Bongaarts and Potter, 1983). Social research on reproductive behaviour of human population focuses on impacts of social norms, socio-economic processes and cultural factors on fertility. Ethnicity refers to a national, racial or tribal group and the sharing of a distinctive cultural tradition (Hornby, 1994). The differences in social class and culture among ethnic groups may result in different fertility patterns. Most social scientists take an assimilationist perspective for research on ethnic fertility (McDaniel, 1996). Bean and Tienda (1987) stated a social characteristics hypothesis and economic hypothesis about fertility differentials between majority and minority populations. The social characteristics hypothesis expects that the fertility of minority groups is closer to that of the majority when structural assimilation of the minority groups into the majority society occurs in terms of socio-economic (education, occupation and income) and residential characteristics. The economic hypothesis states that fertility behaviour is influenced by household decision-making related to cost and value of children, and suggests that when the economic gap between majority and minority narrows, the fertility differences decrease. Minority status explanations suggest that when a minority population has continuing low levels of socio-economic status, they would prefer higher fertility to overcome their numerical smallness and disadvantages in the larger society (McDaniel, 1996).

In Thailand, the total fertility rate (TFR) was as low as 1.8 children per woman in 2002, below 2.1 of the generation replacement level (Institute for Population and Research, 2002). The levels and patterns of fertility differ in the ethnic minorities and in different regions. Ethnic disparities in fertility, socio-economic and culture may exist in the Kanchanaburi province, located in the west of Thailand and sharing a long border with Myanmar.

The TFR was 2.03 in Kanchanaburi in 2002, on average. In the same year, TFR was as low as 1.54 in the mixed economy area and as high as 3.07 in the uplands area in Kanchanaburi, where the greatest proportion of ethnic minorities lived (Thongthai, 2004a). In addition, the fertility pattern in the uplands of Kanchanaburi was quite different from other strata. The age-specific fertility rates were higher at all ages (peak at reproductive age group 20–24), with birth occurrence at age group 45–49 in the uplands (Thongthai, 2004b). Moreover, educational attainment and economic activity of Kanchanaburi were lower in the uplands than in the other strata, such as urban/semi-urban, rice, plantation, and mixed economy. For example, among the female population aged 15 and over in 2002, those not working accounted for about 31 per cent in the uplands and only nearly 22 per cent in the mix economy stratum. The percentage of those with no schooling was just over 41 per cent in the uplands and nearly 18 per cent in the mixed economy stratum among the female population aged 7 and over (Chumpaklai, 2004a). Further, nearly 40 per cent of households in the uplands spoke languages other than Thai in daily life, including 20.2 per cent of Karen/Karang/Pa Ka Yaw; 9.6 per cent of Mon; 5.8 per cent of Burmese, 2.2 per cent of Lao and 1.0 per cent of other ethnic minorities (Chumpaklai, 2004b).

Previous studies show ethnic fertility differentials in Thailand. Religious fertility varies among Thai Buddhists and Muslims (Knodel et al., 1999; Goldstein, 1970; Prasithrathsint, 1985). Fertility differs among the Karen groups (Soottipong, 1995). Also, some researchers reported the factors related to fertility among ethnic minorities, such as female labour force participation and education (Morgan et al., 2002); education and income of population (Kamnuansilpa et al., 1987; Hinton, 1983); son preference, age at marriage, and the role of policy (Soottipong, et al., 1998; Bhruksasri, 1989); and cultural factors (Kunstadter et al., 1987).

However, most previous studies were done in the 1980s and fertility has declined below replacement level in Thailand since then. Therefore, knowledge of fertility differentials among ethnic minorities needs updating. In addition, previous studies on ethnic minorities have mostly been conducted in the north and south Thailand.

The study aims to identify the differences in the number of children ever born (CEB) and related factors such as socio-economic (education, occupation, income) characteristics, the integration of the minority with the Thai in terms of Thai language use, proximate determinants (proportion married, age at the first marriage and contraceptive use), fertility preference, and number of children who had died among married women aged 15–49 from Thai, Karen, Mon, Burmese and other ethnic minorities. This study utilises the data from the uplands of Kanchanaburi Demographic Surveillance System in 2002.

Materials and Methods

Data Source

Individual data set in 2002 in the uplands of round 3 of Demographic Surveillance System (DSS) in Kanchanaburi province, Thailand was utilised in this research. The DSS was conducted by the Institute for Population and Social Research, Mahidol University on 1 July to 18 August 2002, which enumerated 12,680 households with a population of 45,053 (21,673 males and 23,370 females). The DSS study area of 100 villages or census blocks was divided into five strata, such as urban/semi-urban, rice, plantation, uplands and mixed economy, according to the main occupation of the population and land-use patterns.

The uplands stratum included Sai Yoke, Tong Pha Phum and Sangkhla Buri districts, 12,299 population (male 6,182, female 6,117), and 3,399 households in 2002 (Varangrat, 2004a). Of the five strata, the uplands had the highest proportion in the younger age group (35.5%) and the lowest proportion at working age (56.2%) (Varangrat, 2004b). Respondents were 1,581 married women aged 15–49 in the uplands of Kanchanaburi DSS.

Measurement

Mean number of children ever born was a dependent variable, measured as interval scale. Ethnicity was the main independent variable, measured as category scale. Ethnic groups were identified by nationality, which referred to the country or other areas of origin of the ethnic group. The Thai was the majority ethnic group. The Karen, the Mon, the Burmese, and others (Thai Yai, Yao, Khmer, Laotian/Lao Puan, Karang) were ethnic minorities.

Reproductive age, reproductive age square, age at first marriage, number of children who had died and number of additional children women wanted were interval variables. Dummy variables were education (some education as 1, no education as 0), occupation (agriculture sector as 1, non-agriculture sector as 0) and annual income (some income as 1, no income as 0), capability of speaking Thai (yes as 1, no as 0), contraceptive service use (yes as 1, no as 0) and contraceptive method use (use as 1, not use as 0).

Data Analysis

Cross-tabulation for categorical variables and compare means for interval variables were performed to provide comparative descriptions among Thai, Burmese, Mon, Karen and other ethnic minorities.

Multiple regressions with step-wise methods were applied to control the different demographic and socio-economic characteristics of respondents. The age squared term was introduced to control the curvilinear relationship between mean CEB and age of mother. Because CEB was a cumulative measurement relating to some past period, while contraceptive method use and contraceptive service use present current status, they were not included in multiple regression analysis. In addition, cases of the number of additional children women wanted were small, so it could not be covered in multivariate control analysis.

Results and Discussion

Distribution of CEB for Each Ethnic Group

Number of children ever born is a measure of cumulative fertility, measuring fertility accumulated upto the date of the interview. Table 1 shows that in general Burmese, Mon, Karen and other minorities had a higher percentage of four or more live births than Thai. Thai had a higher proportion of two live births than ethnic minorities in the uplands.

In addition, among women aged 30–49, the ethnic minorities accounted for a bigger share than the Thai of three live births and four or more live births, while Thai women had a reproductive peak for two live births in the age group 25–39. In Burmese, Karen and other minorities, about 70 per cent of women aged 40–44 and about 80 per cent aged 45–49 had four or more live births. This suggests that a smaller number of CEB in the Thai than among the ethnic minorities may result from smaller number of live births in high birth order in the Thai than among the ethnic minorities.

Table 1 *Percentage Distribution of CEB by Age Group for Each Ethnic Group (N=1581)*

Age Group	*Number of Children Ever Born*					*Total*	*N*
	Live Births						
	0	*1*	*2*	*3*	*4 or More*		
Thai							
15–19	11.8	88.2	.0	.0	.0	100.0	17
20–24	3.8	67.9	25.6	1.3	1.3	100.0	78
25–29	1.4	35.7	51.0	11.9	.0	100.0	143
30–34	.5	17.6	45.4	27.3	9.3	100.0	205
35–39	.0	7.1	49.5	29.7	13.7	100.0	182
40–44	.0	8.5	31.8	32.3	27.4	100.0	201
45–49	.7	5.6	19.4	28.5	45.8	100.0	144
Total	.9	19.9	37.9	24.1	17.1	100.0	970
Burmese							
15–19	33.3	66.7	.0	.0	.0	100.0	3
20–24	.0	63.6	27.3	9.1	.0	100.0	11
25–29	4.8	28.6	33.3	28.6	4.8	100.0	21
30–34	.0	6.7	20.0	46.7	26.7	100.0	15
35–39	.0	8.3	8.3	16.7	66.7	100.0	24
40–44	.0	5.6	5.6	11.1	77.8	100.0	18
45–49	.0	.0	16.7	8.3	75.0	100.0	12
Total	1.9	18.3	17.3	20.2	42.3	100.0	104
Mon							
15–19	.0	100.0	.0	.0	.0	100.0	1
20–24	15.4	53.8	23.1	7.7	.0	100.0	13
25–29	.0	46.7	30.0	20.0	3.3	100.0	30
30–34	.0	12.2	24.4	36.6	26.8	100.0	41
35–39	.0	4.2	12.5	33.3	50.0	100.0	24
40–44	.0	2.6	13.2	15.8	68.4	100.0	38
45–49	3.6	3.6	10.7	21.4	60.7	100.0	28
Total	1.7	17.1	18.9	24.0	38.3	100.0	175
Karen							
15–19	100.0	.0	.0	.0	.0	100.0	2

Cont'd...

Cont'd...

20–24	14.8	37.0	40.7	3.7	3.7	100.0	27
25–29	.0	12.5	35.4	29.2	22.9	100.0	48
30–34	.0	15.8	33.3	19.3	31.6	100.0	57
35–39	1.8	1.8	27.3	21.8	47.3	100.0	55
40–44	.0	2.6	10.5	18.4	68.4	100.0	38
45–49	.0	2.3	6.8	11.4	79.5	100.0	44
Total	2.6	10.3	25.5	18.5	43.2	100.0	271
Others							
15–19	.0	100.0	.0	.0	.0	100.0	1
20–24	.0	40.0	40.0	20.0	.0	100.0	5
25–29	20.0	30.0	40.0	10.0	.0	100.0	10
30–34	.0	10.0	30.0	40.0	20.0	100.0	10
35–39	.0	.0	25.0	25.0	50.0	100.0	12
40–44	.0	6.3	6.3	12.5	75.0	100.0	16
45–49	.0	.0	.0	14.3	85.7	100.0	7
Total	3.3	13.1	21.3	19.7	42.6	100.0	61

Figure 1 shows higher mean CEB in Burmese, Mon, Karen and others than in Thai in most age groups. In addition, mean CEB had a positive relationship with age. When age increased, mean CEB increased. The positive relationship was not linear. In Burmese and Mon, as a woman's age increased from age group 40–44 to 45–49,

Figure 1 ***Mean CEB by Age Group for Each Ethnic Group***

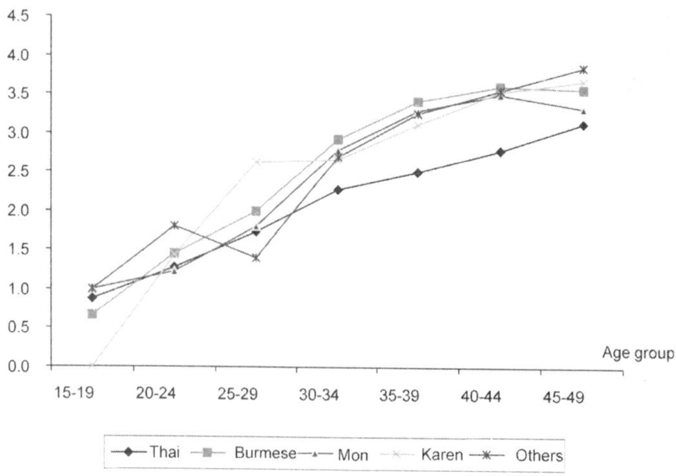

Figure 2 *Marriage Proportion of Respondents by Ethnic Group*

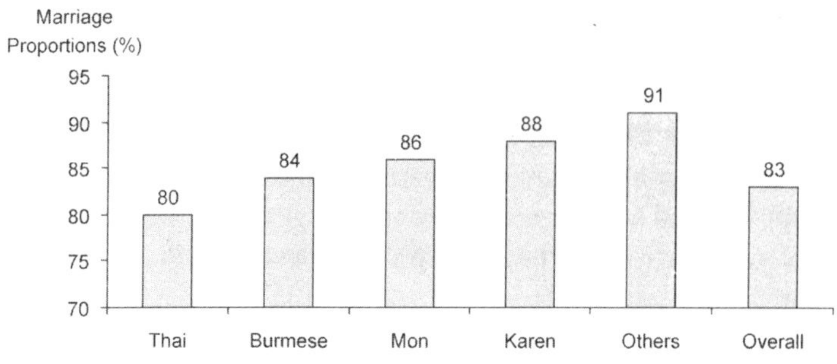

mean CEB decreased. This suggests that mean CEB bears a curvilinear relationship with age, because mean CEB has cumulative effects.

Demographic and Socio-economic Characteristics and CEB

Figure 2 shows the higher proportion of married women in Karen, Mon, Burmese and other ethnic minorities than in Thai.

Table 2 shows the differences in the percentages of education attainment, occupation and annual income among ethnic groups. Thais had a higher percentage of some education, of working in the non-agriculture sector than ethnic minorities. This indicates that Burmese, Mon, Karen and other ethnic minorities have a lower education attainment and economic status than Thai. This may contribute to a higher fertility among ethnic minorities than Thai, since socio-economic characteristics are major factors affecting human fertility behaviour through biological, behavioural and micro-economic decision-making factors.

Table 2 *Percentage Distribution of Education Attainment and Occupation of Respondents by Ethnic Group (N=1581)*

Variable	*Thai*	*Burmese*	*Mon*	*Karen*	*Others*
Education level					
No schooling	12.2	92.3	93.7	67.2	75.4
Some education	87.8	7.7	6.3	32.8	24.6
Total	100.0	100.0	100.0	100.0	100.0
Occupation					
Agriculture	78.8	96.2	94.3	89.3	91.8
Non-agriculture	21.2	3.8	5.7	10.7	8.2
Total	100.0	100.0	100.0	100.0	100.0
N	970	104	175	271	61

Table 3 reveals that Burmese and Karen had a lower mean reproductive age and mean reproductive age square than other ethnic groups. This means that women of Burmese and Karen women may have reproduction at a younger age than other ethnic groups. In addition, Thai had the highest, but Mon had the lowest mean age at the first marriage among ethnic groups. This suggests that ethnic minority, in particular, Mon women tend to marry earlier than Thai women. Moreover, the least number of children who had died were from the Thai, the highest one from the Karen.

Table 3 ***Mean of Explanatory Variables for Mean CEB by Ethnic Groups***

Variables	*Thai*	*Burmese*	*Mon*	*Karen*	*Others*
Reproductive age	35.40	34.04	35.65	34.74	35.25
Reproductive age square	1,314.94	1,221.13	1,333.46	1,271.69	1,303.77
Age at first marriage	19.91	19.58	18.93	19.49	18.93
Number of children who had died	.09	.33	.42	.45	.30
Education	.88	.08	.06	.33	.25
Occupation	.79	.96	.94	.89	.92
N	970	104	175	271	61

Table 4 shows that for each ethnic group the difference in mean CEB was influenced by the differences in the explanatory variables such as reproductive age, reproductive age square, age at the first marriage, number of children who had died, education attainment and occupation. In model 1 to model 5, reproductive age, the number of children who had died and occupation had a positive relationship with mean CEB, which means if these variables increased, mean CEB would increase as well. For example, in model 1, holding other variables constant, Thai married women aged 15–49 had about 0.20 more children when reproductive age increased one year. On the contrary, reproductive age square, age at the first marriage and education had a negative relationship with mean CEB; that is, if they increased, mean CEB would decrease. For example, holding other variables constant, in model 1, Thai married women aged 15–49 had about 0.08 fewer children when age at the first marriage increased one year.

These indicate that lower education level for Burmese, Mon, Karen and other ethnic minorities than for Thai contribute to higher cumulative fertility among them. In addition, a larger number of children had died in the ethnic minorities than in the Thai; this means that infant and child mortality was much higher in Burmese, Mon, Karen and other ethnic minorities than in Thai, which may be attributed to high cumulative fertility among ethnic minorities as well. Richter and Arjun (1989) stated two mechanisms: (1) Biological effect: The death of an infant stops the lactation of the mother and then ovulation could occur as usual. This effect is a main mechanism in the pre-contraception societies. (2) Behaviour effects: Replacement effect: Individual couples whose child has died attempt to replace their dead children. Insurance (hoarding) effect: Individual couples have more children than the number of children they would consider ideal because they want to insure enough surviving children, while there is high infant and child mortality in the community or they have experienced the death of infants and children.

Table 4 ***Multiple Regressions for Mean CEB by Ethnic Groups***

Variables	*Model 1 (Thai)*	*Model 2 (Burmese)*	*Model 3 (Mon)*	*Model 4 (Karen)*	*Model 5 (Others)*
Constant	-0.727	-5.718	-4.441	-2.690	-1.011
Reproductive age	0.203	0.485	0.466	0.333	0.110
Reproductive age square	-0.002	-0.006	-0.005	-0.004	—
Age at first marriage	-0.085	-0.058	-0.122	-0.073	—
Number of children who had died	0.368	0.191	0.193	0.176	—
Education	-0.196	—	—	-0.232	—
Occupation	0.162	—	—	—	—
R	0.67	0.75	0.73	0.68	0.72
R Square	0.45	0.56	0.53	0.46	0.51

Based on the coefficients of the explanatory variable in each model, the predicted mean CEB for each ethnic group was computed when these explanatory variables bore mean values in the Table 3. The predicted mean CEB for each ethnic group was presented as an adjusted mean CEB controlling the demographic and socio-economic characteristics of individuals. Table 5 indicates that the adjusted mean CEB ranked the lowest for Thai and the highest for Mon. This means that

Thais had lower cumulative fertility than ethnic minorities after controlling the above variables.

Table 5 ***Adjusted Mean CEB and Unadjusted Mean CEB by Ethnic Groups***

Variable	*Thai*	*Burmese*	*Mon*	*Karen*	*Others*
Unadjusted mean CEB	2.37	2.82	2.80	2.89	2.85
Adjusted mean CEB	2.13	2.39	3.28	2.37	2.87

Other Factors Related to CEB

Integration of Ethnic Minority with Thai

Patterns of fertility behaviour may vary among ethnic minority groups in various cultural categories. Capability of using Thai as one of the social and cultural factors was examined in the study; this may indicate the assimilation of ethnic minorities into the Thai society. Table 6 shows that most ethnic minority respondents could speak Thai. This may suggest that the integration of the ethnic minorities with the Thai in the uplands was quite good in terms of communication with Thais. Language barriers were not found among respondents of Burmese, Mon, Karen, and other ethnic minorities.

Table 6 ***Percentage of Capability of Speaking Thai by Ethnic Groups***

Speaking Thai	*Thai*	*Burmese*	*Mon*	*Karen*	*Others*	*Overall*
Yes	99.9	98.0	99.2	100.0	98.1	99.7
No	.1	2.0	.8	.0	1.9	.3
%	100.0	100.0	100.0	100.0	100.0	100.0
N	967	51	120	194	52	1,384

Contraceptive Use

Bongaartis (1978) pointed out that a contraceptive use is an important proximate determinant of fertility. Table 3 shows that Thai women had higher contraceptive usage and contraceptive prevalence than Burmese, Mon, Karen and other ethnic minority women. And Thais were more likely to use health centres and government hospitals as sources of contraceptive services than Burmese, Mon and Karen. In addition, of three main contraceptive methods such as female sterilisation, injection and the pill, Thai women were more likely to use the injection method than ethnic minorities. Burmese women were the least likely to use contraceptive pills among the ethnic groups. This suggests that the reasons why they do not use these services should be investigated.

Table 7 ***Percentage of Contraceptive Use by Ethnic Groups***

Characteristics	*Thai*	*Burmese*	*Mon*	*Karen*	*Others*
Contraceptive Service Use					
Use rate	95.9.	74.5	87.5	75.1	87.9
Sources:					
Drug store	9.5	13.8	15.0	11.3	10.3
Health centre	45.3	26.6	36.9	29.2	22.4
Government hospital	36.7	30.9	28.1	25.7	48.3
Private hospital/clinic	2.7	2.1	5.0	4.3	5.2
Others	1.6	1.1	2.5	4.7	1.7
Not use	4.1	25.5	12.5	24.9	12.1
Total	100.0	100.0	100.0	100.0	100.0
N=1516	947	94	160	257	58
Contraceptive Method Use					
Contraceptive prevalence	84.7	58.7	73.1	63.5	77.0
Female sterilisation	28.2	26.9	18.3	14.8	37.7
Norplant	4.1	2.9	5.7	5.2	.0
Injection	21.5	12.5	17.1	18.1	9.8
IUD	2.4	1.0	1.7	1.1	3.3
Pill	26.2	15.4	27.4	22.5	23.0
Others	2.3	.0	2.9	1.8	3.3
Not use	15.3	41.3	26.9	36.5	23.0
Total	100.0	100.0	100.0	100.0	100.0
N=1581	970	104	175	271	61

Fertility Preference

Table 8 shows that there is lowest desire for additional children in Thais and highest desire for additional children in the Karen. This suggests that Karen, Burmese, Mon and other ethnic minorities have a preference for higher fertility than Thai. The reason may be their minority group status. But differences in sex preference of fertility were not found between the Thai and the ethnic minorities, and within the ethnic minorities (Tables not included).

Table 8 ***Desire for Additional Children by Ethnic Group***

Number of Desire for Additional Children	*Thai*	*Burmese*	*Mon*	*Karen*	*Others*
Mean	1.26	1.96	1.61	2.09	2.20
SD	.58	1.24	1.04	2.28	1.55
N=319	170	25	44	70	10

Conclusion

The main findings and recommendations of the study are as follows:

1. There were ethnic differentials in mean CEB in 2002 in the uplands. Mon women had the highest cumulative fertility, whereas Thai women had the lowest one.
2. The Mon, Karen, Burmese and other ethnic minority respondents had lower education attainment and larger number of children who had died than the Thai. These were related to a higher mean CEB in the ethnic minorities than in the Thai. This indicates that human development should be strengthened to reduce infant and child mortality and to improve the education of women among ethnic minorities.
3. The ethnic minority, especially the Mon respondents, had a younger mean age at the first marriage than the Thai; this also affected mean CEB more in the ethnic minorities than in the Thai. Delaying marriage should be encouraged for reduction of fertility.
4. The ethnic minority respondents had lower contraceptive prevalence and usage of contraceptive services than the Thai. This implies that it is necessary to strengthen contraceptive use services for ethnic minorities in the uplands.

Acknowledgements

This study is supported by The Wellcome Trust Foundation of United Kingdom and Institute for Population and Social Research. With the financial support of the conference organiser, the paper was presented in the International Conference of the International Institute for Population Sciences (IIPS) on “Emerging Population Issues in the Asia Pacific Region: Challenges for the Twenty-first Century” in Mumbai, India, under the session of demography of ethnic groups on December 11, 2006. The author thanks Assistant Professor Dr Rossarin Gray and Assistant Professor Dr Pimonpan Isarabhakdi for their valuable comments and suggestions. And the author also appreciates the editorial assistance of Dr Thomas Hoy of the Language Centre, Mahidol University.

References

Bean, F.D. and M. Tienda. 1987. *The Hispanic Population of the United States*. New York.: Russell Sage Foundation.

Bhruksasri, W. 1989. "Government Policy: Highland Ethnic Minorities" in J. Mckinnon and B. Vienne (eds.), *Hill Tribes Today*. Bangkok: White Lotus Co. Ltd.

Bongaarts, J. 1978. A Framework for Analysing the Proximate Determinates of Fertility. *Population and Development Review* 4 (1): 105–32.

Bongaarts, J. and R.G. Potter. 1983. *Fertility, Biology and Behaviour: An Analysis of the Proximate Determinates*. New York: Academic Press.

Chumpaklai, A. 2004a. "Socioeconomic Status" in the Report of Round 3 Census (2002): Kanchanaburi Project. Institute for Population and Social Research, Nakhonpathom, Thailand.

Chumpaklai, A. 2004b. "Socioeconomic Status" in the Report of Round 3 Census (2002): Kanchanaburi Project. Institute for Population and Social Research, Nakhonpathom, Thailand.

Goldstein, S. 1970. Religious Fertility Differentials in Thailand, 1960. *Population Studies* 24(3): 352–37.

Hinton, P. 1983. "Do the Karen Really Exist?" in J. McKinnon and W. Bhruksasri (eds.), *Highlanders of Thailand*. Kuala Lumpur: Oxford University Press.

Hornby, A.S. 1994. *Oxford Advanced Learner's Dictionary of Current English* (4th ed.). London: Oxford University Press.

Institute for Population and Social Research, Mahidol University. 2002. Mahidol Population Gazette 11 (July), IPSR, Nakhonpathom.

Kamnuansilpa, P., P. Kunstadter and N. Auamkul. 1987. Hill Tribe Health and Family Planning: Results of a Survey of Hmong (Meo) and Karen Households in Northern Thailand. Ministry of Public Health, Bangkok.

Knodel, J., R. Soottipong Gray, P. Sriwathcharin and S. Peraccca. 1999. Religion and Reproduction: Muslims in Buddhist Thailand. *Population Studies* 53: 149–64.

Kunstadter, P., C. Kesmanee and P. Pothi-art. 1987. Hmong and Karen Health and Family Planning: Cultural and Other Factors Affecting Using of Modern Health and Family Planning Services by Hill Tribes in Northern Thailand. Ministry of Public Health, Bangkok.

McDaniel, A. 1996. Fertility and Racial Stratification. *Population and Development Review* 22 (suppl.): 134–50.

Morgan, P.S., S. Stash, H.L. Smith and K.O. Mason. 2002. Muslim and Non-Muslim Differences in Female Autonomy and Fertility: Evidence from Four Asian Countries. *Population and Development Review* 28 (3): 515–37.

Richter, K. and A. Arjun. 1989. The Effect of Infant and Child Mortality and Subsequent Fertility. *Journal of Population and Social Studies* 2 (1): 76–89.

Soottipong, R. 1995. Fertility Differentials among the Karen: A Hill Tribe Minority in Northern Thailand. Ph. D. Thesis, The Australian National University, Canberra, ACT, Australia.

Soottipong, R., D. Lucas and A. Gray. 1998. The Role of Policy and Community Organisation in Fertility Reduction of the Karen People in Thailand. Working Papers in Demography, No. 75, The Australian National University, Canberra, ACT, Australia.

Prasithrathsint, S. 1985. Ethnicity and Fertility in Thailand. Research Notes and Discussions Paper, No. 51, Institute of Southeast Asian Studies, Singapore.

Thongthai, V. 2004a. "Fertility and Family Planning' in the Report of Round 3 Census (2002): Kanchanaburi Project. Institute for Population and Social Research, Nakhonpathom.

——. 2004b. "Fertility and Family Planning" in the Report of Round 3 Census (2002): Kanchanaburi Project. Institute for Population and Social Research, Nakhonpathom.

Varangrat, A. 2004a. "General Characteristics of the Population" in the Report of Round 3 Census (2002): Kanchanaburi Project. Institute for Population and Social Research, Nakhonpathom.

——. 2004b. "General Characteristics of the Population" in the Report of Round 3 Census (2002): Kanchanaburi Project. Institute for Population and Social Research, Nakhonpathom.

16

Whom to 'Marry'? Spouse Selection in the Small Tribes of Nilambur Valley, South India

Seetha Kakkoth

Marriage as an institution fulfils a variety of functions in the maintenance and perpetuation of human social life. In almost all societies, spouse selection is restricted by certain rules such as incest taboo, rules of exogamy and endogamy and marriage preferences (Crapo, 1996). Choice of a partner is generally not a personal matter and is influenced by geographic, demographic, social and economic factors. People living in a distinct geographical area at various levels of socio-economic and demographic conditions develop a unique social system and marriage pattern. This article is an attempt to examine the marriage pattern and factors affecting the spouse selection among two numerically small, food gathering and hunting tribes of Nilambur Valley, viz., the Aranadan and the Kattupaniyan of the state of Kerala in South India.

Since the tribes under study are numerically small, a universal coverage is attempted, but in-depth study is limited to a few major settlements. Geographic, demographic and socio-economic factors affecting the marriage pattern were collected through household survey, interview and observation methods. Genealogical and case study methods were used to understand the pattern of spouse selection, family life and marital history. Case studies of intra-tribal, inter-tribal, and tribal-non-tribal marriages were noted. The marital histories of selected men and women were also recorded by case study method. In addition to these, secondary data were also examined.

The paper begins with a brief description of Nilambur Valley and moves on to geo-demographic and socio-economic factors influencing the spouse selection and marital pattern of the Aranadan and the kattupaniyan. A comparative analysis of spouse selection and marital pattern is explained, interpreted and generalised.

Nilambur Valley

Nilambur Valley which lies on the western slope of the Western Ghats, covers an area of 2,72,453.60 acres and has an elevation ranging between 40m and 800m above MSL (Kerala Forests and Forestry Handbook, 1995). The upper reaches of the valley is covered by wet evergreen forests and the lower slopes by semi-deciduous forests, and it is characterised by heavy rainfall, humid climate, moderate temperature and varied flora and fauna. Thus, Nilambur forest having unique geographical features and abundant distribution of natural resources hosts a few, numerically small, food gathering-hunting tribal communities, viz., Aranadan, Kattupaniyan, Pathinaicken and Cholanaicken. It is widely held by anthropologists that the bountiful nature of the Nilambur forests ensures abundant food supply throughout the year to the tribes and thus the tribal communities remain fixated to the food gathering hunting stage (Mathur, 1977). Prior to the commercialisation of forests, these communities occupied distinct geographical areas ranging from upper ghat evergreen forests to lower semi-deciduous forests and their centuries of interaction with the forest ecosystem coupled with relative geographical isolation, small population size, endogamy, etc., resulted in moulding a social system of their own. Thus, the geography of Nilambur forest plays a major role in shaping the life and culture of the forest dwelling tribes, including the Aranadan and the Kattupaniyan.

Aranadan

The Aranadan, one among the 36 Scheduled Tribes of Kerala, inhabit marginal areas of the Nilambur forests, Nilambur taluk, Malappuram district, Kerala state (Figure 1). They are considered to be an autochthonous tribe of Erand taluk (currently Nilambur taluk) and hence also called Ernadan, meaning, people of Ernad (Thurston, 1909; Aiyappan, 1948; Luiz, 1962). The tribes having a population size of 254 are distributed in seventeen locations, interspersed with non-tribes. Most of their settlements are located in the catchment area of the river Karimpuzha, (a major tributary of the river Chaliyar), with a distance of 2–15 km apart from one another. The number of houses in each location varies from 1–12.

Though the Aranadan live in the marginal areas of the forests, they greatly depend on forests and subsist on food gathering, hunting, non-wood forest produces (nwfp) collection, forest labour and wage labour. For food gathering, they roam the lower valley semi-deciduous forests, which are covered by monoculture teak plantation, riverine forest patches, bamboo and reed thickets. The teak plantations and riverine forest patches are rich in edible roots, tubers, medicinal herbs, mushrooms, nwfp, etc. For collection pursuits, husband and wife proceed together to the forests in the morning and return to the settlement in the evening. They also hunt small game, including python.

Figure 1 ***Geographical Location of Study Area (Aranadan)***

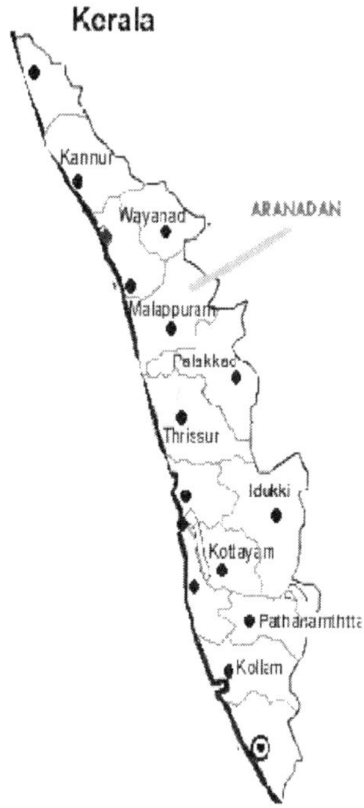

Among the tribes of Nilambur valley, the Aranadan are unique in that they eat the flesh of pythosn. Perhaps, this food habit made the Aranadan a despicable group in the eyes of non-tribes, who had minimum interaction with the Aranadan prior to the commercialisation of forests. At present, python-catching has become rare as their neighbourhood has been converted into agricultural farms and cash crop plantations by non-tribes. Thus, commercialisation coupled with non-tribal influx, deforestation, etc., changed the ecology of the area, thereby changing the food habits, economy, nature of interaction and the social life of the tribe.

Demography

The Aranadan are considered as the smallest scheduled tribe of Nilambur Valley. According to 1971 census their population was only 1. But the 2001 census recorded the population as 153.

An analysis of census records for more than a century, i.e., from 1891 to 2001 (Figure 2) is given above. In the year 1891, the population recorded was 166 constituting 87 males and 79 females. The sex ratio was 908 females per 1,000 males. The census in 1901 recorded only 115 persons, but the sex ratio was 1,053. In 1911 census the population

Figure 2 ***Sex Ratio Population of Aranadan During 1891–2001***

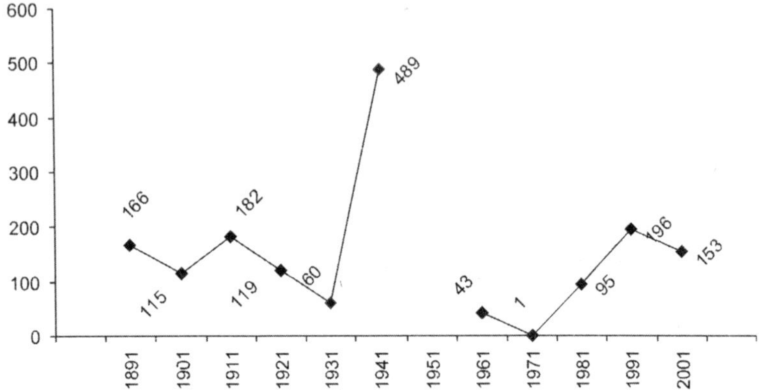

recorded was 182. In 1921, the population of Aranadan declined to 119. In 1931, it further declined to 60. However, the 1941 figure was given as 489, which is 800 per cent more than the 1931 figure. The above census figures are contradictory, but they provide us with a picture of the small size of the community.

A household survey showed the total population of the Aranadan as 254 consisting of 128 males and 126 females (sex ratio: 984 females/1,000 males) with an average family size of 4.03 (Kakkoth 2001). Their literacy rate is 22 per cent. Married people cover 59 per cent of the population and unmarried form 41 per cent (see Figure 3).

Figure 3 ***Marital Status of Population of Aranandan***

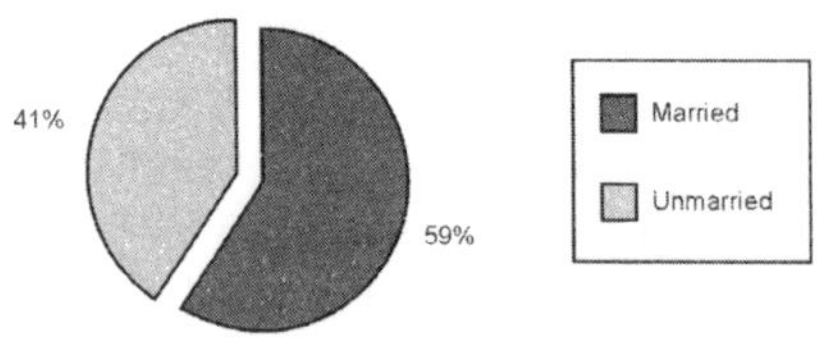

Among the Aranadan, females have relatively low marriage age and are considered eligible for marriage after attaining menarche. In the case of males, the marriage age falls between 20–24 years. There were 62 unmarried males and 42 unmarried females. When we look into the unmarried population above 15 years of age, it is seen that the percentage of unmarried males (68%) is twice than that of females (32%) (Kakkoth, 2001). There are several instances where the female spouse is elder to the male and vice versa. A male marrying a widow or a deserted woman is common.

In this population, the rate of desertions is abnormally high. Among the population of 254 persons, there exist 14 deserted females and 8 deserted males (Figure 4). The deserted female per 1,000 population comes to 55.12. In a study of Paniyan, Kurichiar and Kanikkar the number comes to only 18, 13 and 10 respectively (Viswanathan, 1985). It reveals that the Aranadan marriage unions are very weak and unstable.

Figure 4 ***Marital Desertions Among Population in Aranadan***

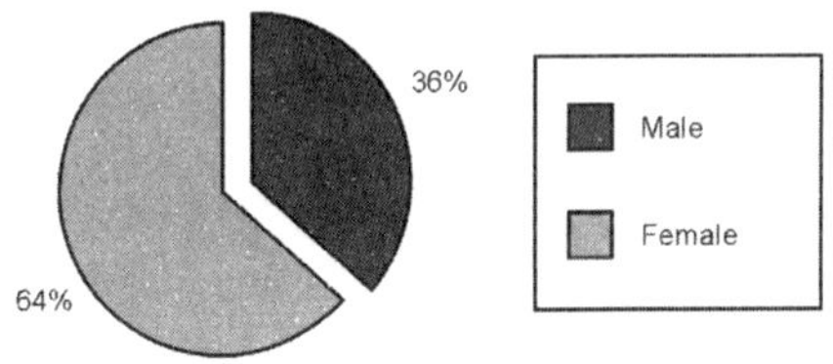

The Aranadan population of 254 people consists of 56 couples and in 16 cases, one of the spouses is a non-Aranadan like Kanakkan, Cheruman, Mannan, Thiyya, Nair, Muslim, Christian, Paniyan, Pathinaicken, Kuruman, etc. Nine males and seven females among the Aranadan have selected spouses from other communities (Kakkoth, 2001). It would appear that the small population size and low female sex ratio results in the non-availability of suitable spouses which lead to alliances with very close relatives and non-tribes as well.

Social Organisation

As mentioned, the Aranadan are distributed in 17 locations, and nuclear family is their basic socio-economic unit. Joint families are rare. The tribe is politically acephalous, though each local group has leaders called *chemmakkaran* (leader of a territorial unit, *chemman*), whose role is determined by age and not by any descent pattern. Search for social institutions like clan divisions is futile. The Aranadan society now-a-days is identified with the colony in which the state government has assigned them land and house. So, the traditional descent pattern based on patrilineal territorial identity no longer exists. Though they worship ancestral spirit, at present they seldom follow common religious observations which give a functional unity to the tribe.

Marriage: Spouse Selection

The Aranadan are monogamous and follow both hamlet exogamy and endogamy. Arranged marriage is the norm and usually a boy's parents find a suitable girl for their son, preferably, a cross-cousin. It is observed that marriage between very close kin often takes place. Marriage by purchase is reported and marriage by exchange was very common earlier. Marriage ties are very weak and often result in desertion, remarriages or alliances (unlike marriage, an alliance is an individual choice made without the consent of society), which finally lead to a kind of

Figure 5 Settlement Patterns in Kottupara, Aranadan

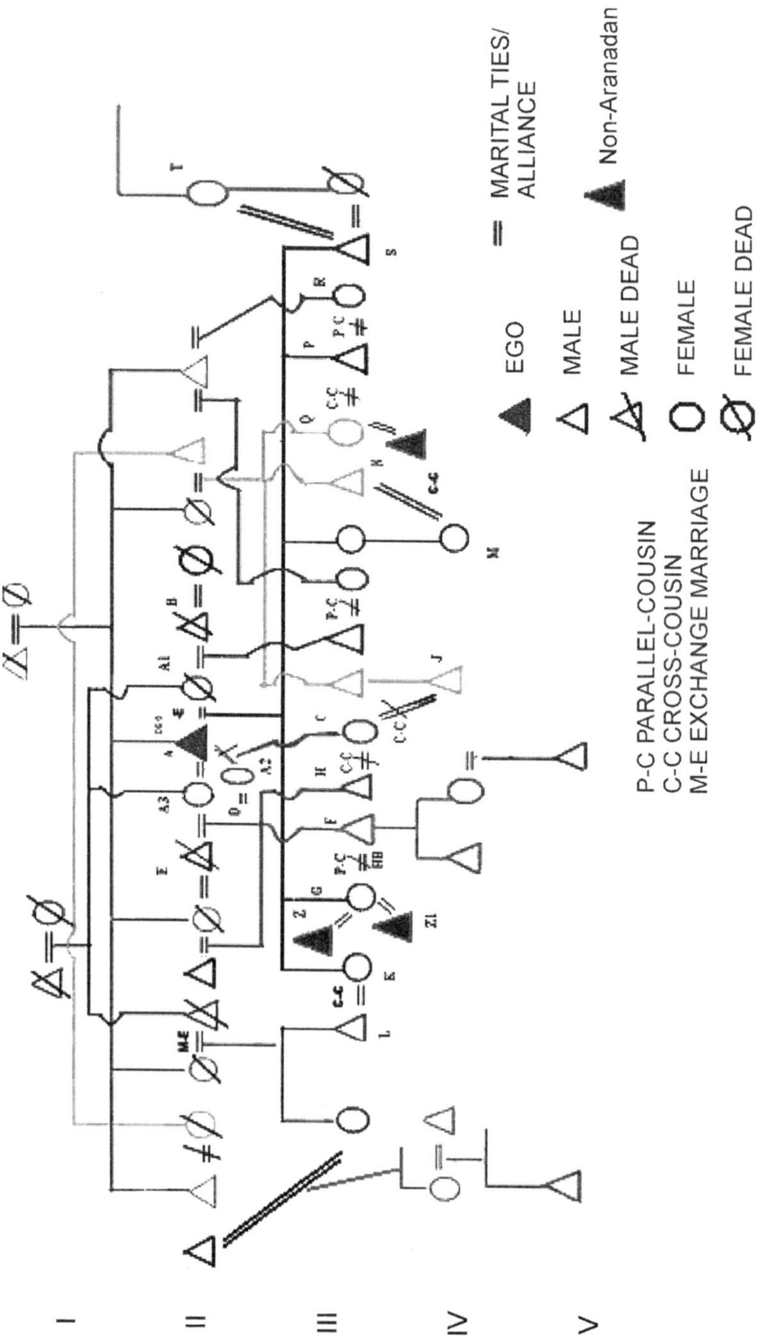

serial monogamy. Though classificatory type of kinship is in vogue, their marriage relationships are neither regulated by any kinship pattern nor restricted with kinship ties of prohibited degree (Thurston, 1909; Luiz, 1962; Stephen Fuchs, 1973). A close examination of the major Aranadan settlements, viz., Kottupara (Figure 5) and Vallikettu (Figure 6) gives a clear picture of the nature of marital ties of the inmates.

Kottupara and Vallikettu Aranadan settlements (rehabilitated) are established at Karulai, Nilambur by the government in 1970s. These two settlements are 2 km apart and situated near Karulai town. The inmates of both colonies are related either consanguineally or affinally.

The Kottupara colony contains 9 families who are patrilineally related. The nature of marital ties of the spouses in this colony is depicted through the genealogical chart of five generations. It is noted that all the spouses are closely related (four cross-cousins, four parallel cousins and one son-in-law–mother-in-law union) and skipping generations for alliances are also noted. It is observed that in the ascending, a kind of serial monogamy is noticed. Marriage by exchange and sororate are also seen. For instance, *A* aged 25 years, married *A1* (marriage by exchange), who was earlier married to *B*. After the birth of two children, *A* made an alliance with *A2* and in that relation, a daughter, C was born. Later *A2* deserted *A* and made an alliance with D. So, *A* returned to his first wife, *A1*. After the death of *A1*, *A* married *A1*'s sister, *A3* (sororate), who already had an alliance with *E* and had a son, *F* in that relationship.

Years later *A*'s daughter *G*, (who was born to his first wife *A1*), married *F* who belonged to the same hamlet and happened to be her half-brother (step mother's son) as well as parallel cousin (mother's sister's son) too. But after a span of three years, she developed relationship with a non-tribe (Muslim) *Z*, who came to her place for construction work and deserted *F*. *Z* stayed with her for almost two years and by that time she gave birth to a daughter. When his work was over, *Z* left the place. A few months later, *G* made alliance with another co-worker, *Z1*, a non-tribe and a son was born in that relationship. Later *Z1* too deserted her. Her two children are living with her.

Another daughter of *A*, *C*, first married her cross cousin, *H* (*A*'s sister's son) and had a son. When *H* deserted her, she made alliance with her another cross-cousin's son, *J* (*A*'s sister's son's son) who is much younger to her and had a son by him. Yet another daughter of *A*, *K*, married her cross cousin, *L* (*A*'s sister's son as well as step-mother's brother's son), a resident of Vallikettu colony. But a couple of years later *L* deserted K, blaming her for barrenness. *K* returned home and now she

Figure 6 Settlement Pattern in Vallikettu, Aranadan

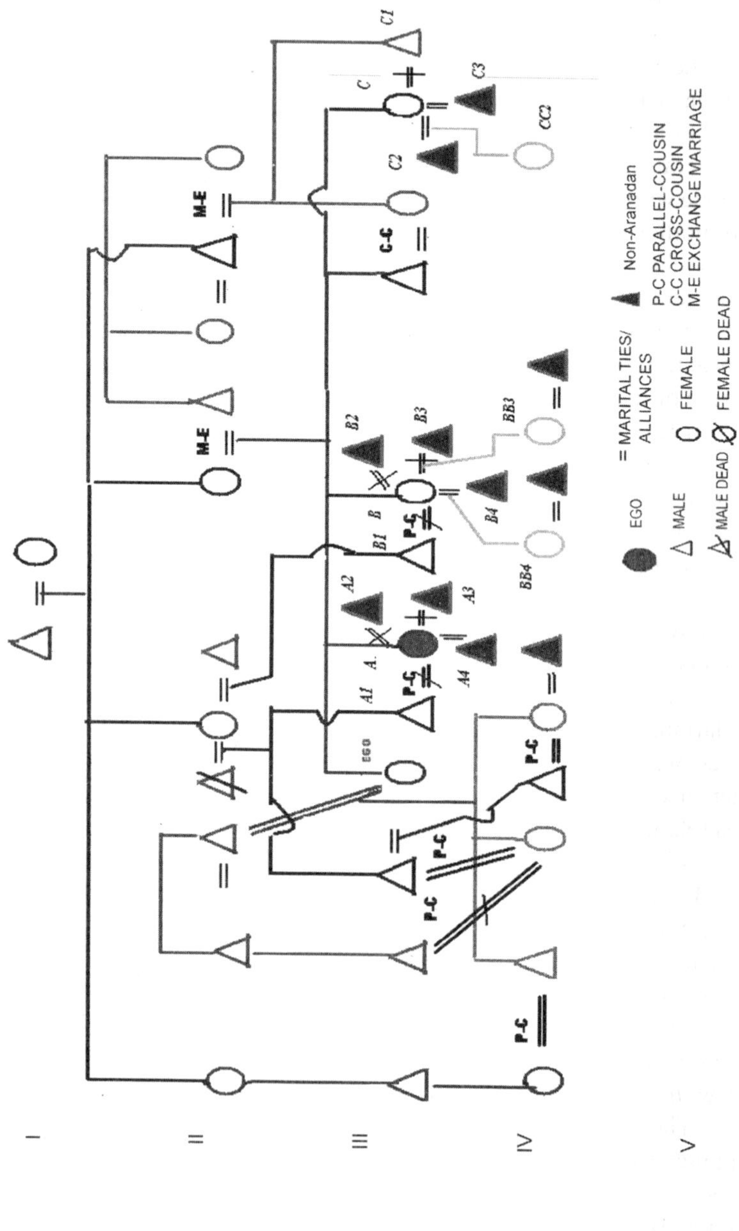

is living with her father. *A*'s daughter's daughter, *M* is given in marriage to *A*'s sister' son, *N*, in the same settlement and it is a kind of cross-cousin marriage by skipping a generation.

A's son *P* married his cross-cousin, *Q*, (Father's sister's daughter) first and when she made alliance with a non-tribe, *P* made an alliance with his parallel cousin, *R* (father's brother's daughter) and started living with her at Chokkad (hamlet exogamy), who was earlier married to her cross-cousin. *S*, another son of *A*, after the death of his wife, made an alliance with his deceased wife's mother, *T* and it is a kind of son-in-law and mother-in-law alliance.

Vallikettu settlement contains six closely related families. As this settlement is situated on the way to Nedumkayam tourist spot, interactions with non-tribes are frequent, which lead to alliances that are transient in nature. The following case studies with genealogy reveal the pattern of spouse selection and the nature of marital life of a few inmates.

A(42) is a resident of Vallikettu colony. Her first marriage took place at the age of 15, with her maternal parallel cousin, *A1*. Her relationship with *A1* did not last for more than a month as she deserted him stating that he was a drunkard. She remained single for almost one year and then struck a relationship with *A2* of Nilambur, who belonged to the Muslim community. They lived together at Vallikettu colony for just a year. *A2* did not have a good relationship with the other male members of the colony and always quarrelled with them. One day after a big quarrel he left the place deserting her. Almost a year later, she formed a relationship with *A3*, belonging to the Cheruman community. *A3* was her co-worker in teak plantations. This relationship ended after a year, when *A* entered into a relationship with *A4* of Kanakkan community. This relationship did not last beyond six months as *A4* consumed poison. Now, *A* is living alone.

A's sister, *B(52)*, was first married at the age of 13, to *B1*, a resident of the Mylampara colony, who happened to be her mother's sister's son (parallel cousin). She remained issueless and her married life ended within a couple of years. She then made alliance with her cross cousin, *B2*, but this relationship lasted only for a fortnight. She says that she did not know the reason behind these two desertions. Her third relationship was with *B3*, who belonged to Thiyya community and was a forest guard then. They remained together for nearly eight years and *B* had a daughter (*BB3*) by him. When their daughter was nearly five years old, *B3* got a transfer elsewhere and he left. After two years, *B* had a registered marriage with *B4*, a medical practitioner in Ayurveda and a native of Ernakulam district. This relationship lasted almost four years and by that time a daughter (*BB4*) was born to them. When *B4* got transferred, he promised to come back but never returned. A couple of years later *B* made relationship with *B5*, belonged to the Kanakkan community who was a labourer engaged by a contractor near the Vallikettu colony. Since then they have been living together. *B*'s daughters, *BB3* and *BB4* are given in marriage to non-tribes.

C(42), another sister of *A*' was first married to her mother's brother's son, *C1*. A few months after their marriage, *C1* deserted her and married another woman. A few months later *C* struck a relationship with her neighbour *C2*, who is a Christian. This relationship lasted till he came to know that *C* had conceived. *C* gave birth to a daughter. After a few years she made an alliance with *C3*, a native of, Palakkad, belonging to the scheduled caste Cheruman community. *C3* came to this place as a forest labourer and was much younger to *C*. Later he too abandoned her. Now *C* is living with her daughter.

The case studies given above demonstrate that among the Aranadan, marriages between very close kin often takes place. It is observed that all the individuals' first marriages were invariably with an Aranadan who happened to be very close relative like mother's sister's son, mother's brother's son, father's brother's son, father's sister's son, step-mother's son, etc. They got married at a very young age, i.e., between 13 and 18. Marriage at a young age and with a close relative much elder to the girl indicates the scarcity of women.

Observations on non-Aranadan men who had married Aranadan women reveal that there is no evidence to show that their ties with Aranadan women are the first of this kind. At the time of marriage these men were living as single away from their natal family. The relationship developed because of constant interaction in a work group or living in neighbourhood. It is widely known that Aranadan women are sexually exploited by non-Aranadan co-workers, in the name of marriage. However, once their work period is over, they leave the place deserting the woman with or without children.

It is observed that both endogamous and exogamous marriages are highly unstable. Spouses have no reluctance in breaking an alliance and forming a new one within a couple of months. Most of the marriage unions are broken within two years. Frequent desertions are noted. Both male and female serial monogamy is the result. A woman with encumbrances is taken as a spouse by a younger man. It is noted that the children born to a woman in her life span can be from more than one marital alliance and the children of such marriages are unaware of their biological father.

Kattupaniyan

The Kattupaniyan too are a numerically small tribe having a population size of 315 (Kakkoth, 2002). They are considered to be an endogamous sub-group of the major tribe, Paniyan. The Kattupaniyan live in four mono-ethnic settlements, viz., Ambumala, Vettilakolli, Chembukadavu and Pathippara.

Figure 7 ***Geographical Location of Kattupaniyan***

Geographically, these settlements are located at the tri-juncture areas of Malappuram, Kozhikode and Wayand districts of the Kerala state (Figure 7). Ambumala and Vettilakolli are situated 8 km apart, at an altitude about 700m above MSL in the upper ghat section, surrounded by virgin forests and are relatively isolated from the mainstream population. The other two settlements, viz., Chembukadavu and Pathippara are situated 4 km apart, at an altitude of 250m above MSL in the marginal forest areas of Kodenchery and Nellipoyil villages respectively, of the Thamarassery range of Kozhikode district.

The Kattupaniyan families living in these settlements opined that they were brought as forest labourers from Ambumala (almost 30km away) to the present sites by the erstwhile owners of these forests. The neighbourhood of Chembukadavu and Pathippara settlements is multi-ethnic and multi-religious. All settlements are located on the banks of the tributaries of the river Chaliyar.

The Kattupaniyan have emerged as a distinct tribe in the forest ecosystem of which they are a part. Their traditional knowledge on forest flora and fauna and adaptation to forests and material culture reveal that this group had centuries of interaction with the forest ecosystem. The devolving of the term 'Kattupaniyan' (*Kadu* in Malayalam means forest) shows that the cultural identity of the tribe took place centuries back. Though there is dialectical variation, the Kattupaniyan and their major tribe Paniyan speak the same language, akin to Kannada and Malayalam. The kinship terms used by them are also similar. They have a pre-agricultural level of technology and subsist on food gathering, hunting, n.w.f.p. collection and wage labour.

Demography

Figure 8 ***Marital Status of Population of Kattupaniyan***

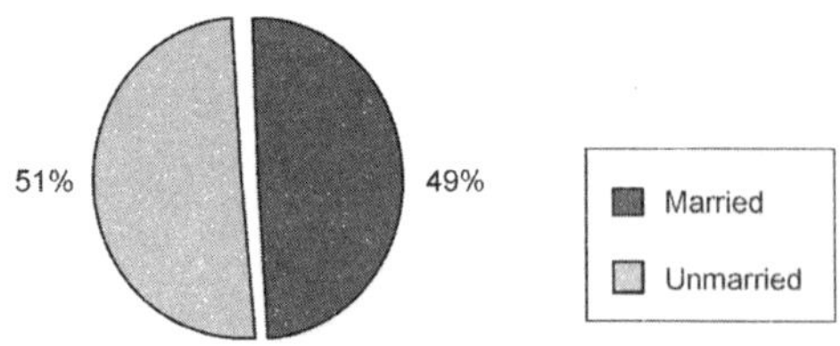

The Kattupaniyan population has not been enumerated separately in the census records. The household survey showed the total population of the Kattupaniyan as 315 consisting of 166 males and 149 females (sex ratio: 897 females/1,000 males) with an average family size of 5.43. Marital status (Figure 8) showed that 49 per cent is married 51 per cent is unmarried (Kakkoth, 2001).

The Kattupaniyan do not conduct marriage before attaining menarche. Females have relatively low marriage age. Within this unmarried population (49%), males form 60 per cent and females form 40 per cent. Again, unmarried female population above 15 years form only 17 per cent, whereas, that of males covers 83 per cent (Kakkoth, 2001). The small population size and low female sex ratio results in the non-availability of suitable spouses, which leads to alliances with very close relatives. More over, older men selecting much younger spouses and vice versa is noticed.

Social Organisation

As mentioned earlier, the Kattupaniyan lead a monoethnic hamlet life and nuclear family forms the basic social and economic unit. The far and wide distribution of the population in four hamlets affects its cohesiveness. The interactions between Chembukadavu and Pathippara sections are more intense than that with Ambumala and Vettilakolli sections and vice versa. The Kattupaniyan of Chembukadavu and Pathippara trace their ancestry from Ambumala hamlet. Like Aranadan, instead of clans, the inmates are identified by their locality and *mooppan* form the headman of a local group. The Kattupaniyan are animist.

Marriage: Spouse Selection

The Kattupaniyan are basically an endogamous society. The families of a hamlet are related to each other in a number of ways as the population is small and due to the practice of hamlet endogamy. The kinship relations at times cut across hamlets. The marital alliances between the Kattupaniyan of Ambumala and Vettilakolli hamlets are common. Likewise, marriage between people of Chembukadavu and Pathippara is more frequent.

Among the Kattupaniyan too arranged marriage is the norm. Out of 66 marriage unions, 63 are endogamous while, for the other three, one of the spouses is a Paniyan. The Kattupaniyan prefer cross cousins as their spouses. But owing to shortage of spouses both cross-cousin and parallel-cousin marriages take place. There are twelve cases of cross-cousin marriages and nine cases of parallel-cousin marriages among these 63 endogamous couples (Kakkoth, 2001).

A genealogical analysis of the five generations in Ambumala settlement (Figure 9) proved that marriage by exchange was prevalent in ascending generations. For instance, there occurred 4 cases of exchange marriages (three cases in the II generation and one case in the ego's generation, i.e., III). Marriages between consanguines are quite common. Here, *A* (Ego) married her mother's brother, *B*. *A*'s brother *C* married his parallel-cousin, *D*, (father's sister's daughter). *A*'s sister *E*, married her paternal cross-cousin's son, *F*, who is much younger to her and it is an example of marriage by skipping generations. Again, *F*'s parents *(G and H)* are parallel-cousins. *J*, a half-brother of *G*, is married to his maternal parallel-cousin (*K*) and another half-brother (*L*) married his maternal cross-cousin (*M*).

It is significant to note that both maternal and paternal cross-cousins and parallel-cousin marriages are taking place within one family itself. Skipping one or two generations for establishing a marital alliance between two members of opposite sex is common. Age difference between spouses is not a deterrent in doing so. Instances of uncle-niece marriage and sororate are noticed. However, when compared to Aranadan, the Kattupaniyan's marital ties (Ambumala) are relatively stable.

Figure 9 Settlement Patterns of Ambumala, Kattupaniyan

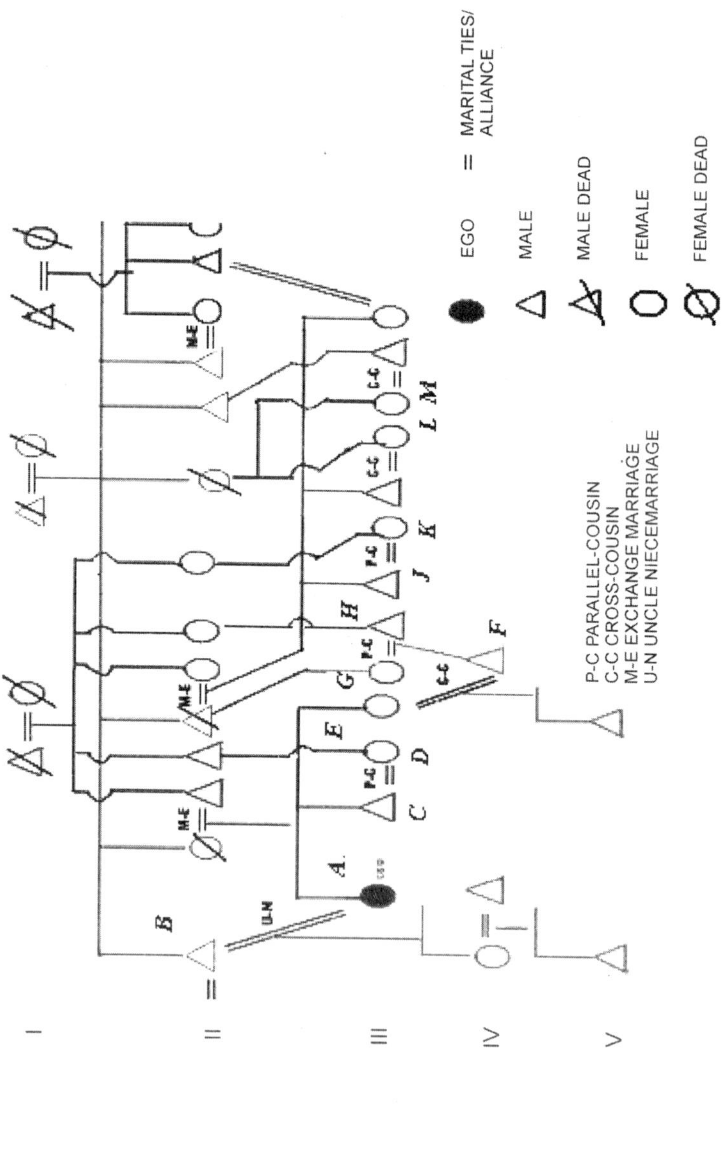

While the Kattupaniyan have been primarily an endogamous community, some changes can be noticed in the past twenty years with the members of the tribe selecting spouses from the Paniyan, their major tribe. Three cases of Kattupaniyan-Paniyan alliances are reported in Chembukadavu colony. It is pertinent to note that only the Kattupaniyan males selected spouses from their major tribe Paniyan and none among the Kattupaniyan females selected Paniyan males. As told earlier, this hamlet is located very close to the mainstream population and the Kattupaniyan work along with other groups. Instances of sexual exploitation of the Kattupaniyan women, which lead to the birth of illegitimate children, are noticed in Pathippara hamlet also.

Analysis and Conclusion

Both the Aranadan and Kattupaniyan of Nilambur Valley live in distinct geographical areas ranging from marginal deciduous to upper ghat evergreen forests and social cohesion of these communities are affected by distant distribution of their colonies. Their way of life revolves round the forest ecosystem and the geography of Nilambur forests plays a significant role in moulding the life and culture of these communities.

Analysis of the demographic aspects of these tribes shows that their smallness in population size limits the scope of mate selection. Both have low sex ratio and unmarried male population is much higher than that of females. This results in the lack of suitable spouses within the marriageable age. The availability of mates with an ideal age difference is limited among these small tribal groups. Younger men are marrying elderly women and elderly men are marrying younger women are not rare. Study on Onge (Coomar and Raha, 1989: 221) is relevant in this situation also. Among the Onge community, a girl may start a marital alliance immediately after puberty with a widower or a divorcee, who may be twice her age. Similarly, a man in his early twenties, after assessing his poor marriage prospects with preferential mates may enter into alliance with a divorcee or a widow, much older than him with encumbrances by her earlier marriages.

These tribes follow both hamlet of exogamy and endogamy. As far as spouse selection is concerned, cross-cousins are considered to be the preferable mates. But due to the lack of cross-cousins within marriageable age, they have no reluctance to marry paternal or maternal parallel cousins, uncles, nieces, deceased wife's sisters, deceased husband's brothers, etc. Skipping generations for an alliance is also observed. When compared to the Kattupaniyan, marital ties of the

Aranadan are found unstable. Frequent desertions and remarriages are common. In the lifetime of an individual, serial monogamous relationship with a number of partners, who are not preferential mates, takes place and such relationships do not give any structure to the society. Moreover, the status and role of the uncle, brother-in-law, sister-in-law, etc., had no relevance in these societies. In other words, there is no effective social control mechanism to regulate these kinds of marital relations.

The ecosystem and economic base of these tribes have been affected by the commercialisation of forest, settler influx and deforestation. Contact with other communities provided an opportunity for developing exogamous alliances. The analysis showed that 90 per cent of such alliances took place with castes/communities with whom the Aranadan and the Kattupaniyan have much commonality. The smallness of the population and the difficulty in finding suitable spouses intensified exogamous unions. Frequencies of such marriages are more among the Aranadan than that of the Kattupaniyan.

The study shows that small endogamous tribal communities have no choice in mate selection within the socially acceptable kin group. As the size of the society becomes larger, the chances of mate selection from preferential kin increase. The society also couldn't impose tribal endogamy and other restrictions usually followed in the selection of spouses. Circumstances make these tribal societies to select their mates even from both patrilateral and matrilateral first cousins.

It is widely held by anthropologists that the population of a society increases when the society practices agriculture and settled life. The clan division and kinship pattern help regulate mate selection in an endogamous society by prohibiting incest and pushing the clan towards exogamy. Thus, inside a given society, certain categories of kin are forbidden to inter-marry (Levi-Strauss, 1949). But as far as these small tribes are concerned they can neither afford endogamy nor restrict their marriage relations within the prescribed categories. Since their marriage pattern does not follow any prescribed rules, these marriages cannot be classified simply by the categories of other societies.

Steward writes:

> ... among the Shoshoni, Bushman, Athapaskans and certain other pre-farming societies, several nuclear families that are consanguineally and affinally related generally comprise the irreducible aggregate, for isolated families would ordinarily not be viable. These basic aggregates

vary with circumstances and may range from ten to fifty persons, but usually average between twenty to thirty persons. Such small groups necessarily intermarry with one another (1968: 322).

Again, it is rightly held by Yengogan in his study on Australian aborigines, that, it is highly improbable for a tribal unit with exceedingly small and fragmented population to maintain stated marriage rules, instead, flexibility in local organisation is a must for their survival (1968: 198). Hence, theoretically, these kinds of alliances without a pattern or structure made for survival can be viewed as *'survival-alliances'*.

To conclude, it is observed that spouse selection of the forest-depended, numerically small tribes is affected by the factors like geography, demography, society and economy. Analysis showed that it is highly improbable for the communities with low population size, low sex ratio, relative isolation, disrupted economic base and weak social control mechanism to follow prescribed marital rules; and, as a survival strategy; they resort to alliance with their consanguine or with the communities with whom they have commonality or frequent interaction.

References

Aiyappan, A. 1948. Report on the Socio-economic Condition of the Aboriginal Tribes of Province of Madras. Government Press, Madras.

Birdsell, J.B. 1968. "Some Predictions for the Pleistocene based on Equilibrium Systems among Recent Hunter-Gatherers" in R.B. Lee and Irven De Vore (eds.), *Man the Hunter*. Chicago: Aldine Publishing Company, 229–40.

Census of India. 1991. Series 12, Kerala, Government of India, New Delhi.

Cohen, Y.A. 1968. *Man in Adaptation: The Cultural Present*. Chicago: Aldine Publishing Company.

Coomar, P.C. and M.K. Raha. 1989. "The Andaman Tribals, Problem of Survival" in M.K. Raha (ed.), *Tribal India: Problem, Development, Prospect*. Vol. 1, New Delhi: Gian Publishing House, 215–26.

Crapo, Richley H. 1996. *Cultural Anthropology*. Boston: McGraw Hill.

Crosby, Alfred W. 1983. *Ecological Imperialism: The Biological Expansion of Europe, 900–1900*. Cambridge: Cambridge University Press.

Fuchs, Stephen. 1973. *The Aboriginal Tribes of India*. New Delhi: Macmillan.

Hiatt, L.R. 1968. "Gidjingali Marriage Arrangements" in R.B. Lee and Irven De Vore (eds.), *Man the Hunter*. Chicago: Aldine Publishing Company, 165–75.

Kakkoth, Seetha. 2002. Three Tribes of Nilambur Valley: A Study in Interrelationship between Habitat, Economy, Society and Culture. Unpublished Ph. D. Dissertation submitted to the University of Calicut, Kerala.

Kerala Forests and Forestry Hand Book. 1995. Kerala Forest Department: Forestry Information Bureau.

Lee, R.B. and Irven De Vore. 1968. *Man the Hunter.* Chicago: Aldine Publishing Company.

Luiz, A.A.D. 1962. *Tribes of Kerala.* Bharatiya Adimjati Sevak Sangh, New Delhi.

Mathur, P.R.G. 1977. *The Tribal Situation in Kerala*. Kerala Historical Society, Trivandrum.

Steward, J.H. 1968. "Casual Factors and Processes in the Evolution of Pre-farming Societies" in R.B. Lee and Irven De Vore (eds.), *Man the Hunter*. Chicago: Aldine Publishing Company, 321–34.

Thurston, Edgar 1909. *Castes and Tribes of Southern India.* Vol. 11, New Delhi: Cosmo Publications.

Viswanathan, Nair N. 1985. Tribal Health and Medicine in Kerala: A Study in Inter-relationship between Habitat, Health, Medicine, Society and Culture. Ph. D. Thesis, Calicut University.

Yengoyan, A.A. 1968. "Demographic and Ecological Influences on Aboriginal Australian Marriage Sections" in R.B. Lee and Irven De Vore (eds.), *Man the Hunter*. Chicago: Aldine Publishing Company, 185–99.
http://en.wikipedia/Alliance_theory

17

Inequality in the Society in terms of Standard of Living Index

R.C. Yadava and Arvind K. Shukla

Development involves mobilisation of natural resources, augmentation of the trained manpower, capital and technical know-how and their utilisation for the attainment of constantly rising national goals, higher living standards and the change over from a traditional to a modern society (Mehmet, 1978).

The economic status of any social group is determined by the amount of wealth and sources of income, social position and the mode of living. This economic measures, to a great extent, determines the standard of living of any group or society. The mode of living in any country depends primarily on the fundamental factors of food, shelter and clothing and an individual's power to get them. But in the different countries the standard of living varies due to the physiography of the various regions, racial characteristics of their people and the differing values of money. Even in the same country the standard of living may vary from region to region and from one group to another due to occupational variation, social stratification and environmental life.

Social inequalities exist in all human societies, but some societies are more unequal than others. The degree of inequality in a society is linked to the stage of social evolution. Original hunter-gatherer societies were typically egalitarian but the later agrarian societies tended to have greater inequality, in particular in the advanced feudal stage (Saderson, 1995). In many countries, there is a strong evidence of disparities in socio-economic status (Rootman, 1988). Drez and Sen (1995) have found the diversities in economic and social development amongst the Indian states which have different capacities of poverty reduction for a variety of reasons. Noorbakhsh (2002, 2003) has analysed regional disparities amongst major states in India to find out if they are on a convergence or a further divergence course. Srinivasan and Mohanty

(2004) have estimated level of deprivation among different caste groups based on possession of some basic social and physical amenities of life at the household level.

Atkinson (1970), Sen (1973) and others have laid the foundations of the modern approach to inequality measurement, the Lorenz curve being widely accepted as the primary measure of relative inequality. Along with associated summary index of inequality, most notably the Gini coefficient, the Lorenz curve has become a staple of applied research. More recently, researchers have measured to capture the contribution to population inequality by sub-groups defined by race, gender or other characteristics (Deutsh and Silber, 1999). Curiously, however, the possibility of decomposing the Lorenz curve itself has been neglected. Butler and McDonald (1987) have proposed ways to compare relative inequality between population sub-groups using inter-distributional Lorenz curves.

The caste especially in rural Hindu society largely determines functions, status, opportunity available for a better life and the handicaps towards greater vertical social mobility, certain caste groups have suffered much since long back and consequently even today they are at the lowest ladder of social hierarchy. A large number of studies have shown greater socio-economic and other development variations according to caste.

The National Family and Health Survey (NFHS) has collected, apart from other information, extensive data at the household level. This information includes items on source of income, housing condition, household facilities, possession of various durable household goods, etc. This information are capable of providing better idea of the socio-economic status of a household. Considering various items, the NFHS has defined a measure called Standard of Living Index (SLI) for a household. Data on certain other basic characteristics of households such as religion and caste, type of residential area, viz., rural/urban have also been obtained. It is a well-known fact that large number of castes exist in India which have their own traditions, values and modes of living. Because of the rigidity in caste system, a person born in a caste normally remains in the same caste till his/her death. Further, these castes occupy normally a rigid position in the social ladder. Consequently, there is a tendency to group various castes into broader caste groups such as Scheduled Castes and Scheduled Tribes (SC/ST), Other Backward Castes (OBC) and remaining castes as 'Other Castes'. The NFHS has also maintained this classification of castes and has tabulated SLI according to caste groups, viz., SC/ST, OBC and Others. The SLI itself has been classified as Low, Medium and High (A description of the computation of SLI is given in the next section).

Broadly, the SLI of a household has been classified by adding scores assigned to various items and the total score representing the SLI of the household. Though the total score of SLI has not been tabulated in NFHS reports but with the help of raw data, the exact score for SLI of a household can be computed.

The Lorenz curve (as a summary graphical representation of the inequality in the population or sub-group of the population) can be obtained if we have the value of SLI for each household of the population (or its subgroups). As discussed above, the raw data of NFHS is capable of providing score of SLI for each household.

The objective of the present paper is to throw some light on relative inequality in terms of SLI for various major states of the country (India), utilising data from NFHS–2. The study is also focused on examining the situation of inequality in different subgroups of the population classified according to caste, religion and type of area, viz., rural and urban. For this purpose Lorenz Curves and their areas have been obtained which provide better idea about the inequalities in various social groups of the present-day Indian society.

A description of the procedure of the computation of the SLI at household level, formation of Lorenz Curve and computation of Gini-coefficient is given in the next section as 'Methodology' while a discussion on the obtained results is presented in the last section as 'Results and Discussion'.

Methodology

The SLI of a household has been computed by giving weights to different items and adding these weights. The weights for different items are as under:

House type:	4 for *pucca*, 2 for semi-*pucca*, 0 for *kachha*;
Toilet facility:	4 for own flush toilet, 2 for public or shared flush toilet or own pit toilet, 1 for shared or public pit toilet, 0 for no facility;
Main fuel for cooking:	2 for electricity, liquid petroleum gas, or biogas, 1 for coal, charcoal or kerosene, 0 for other fuel;
Source of drinking water:	2 for pipe, hand pump or well in residence/yard/plot, 1 for public tap, hand pump or well, 0 for other water source;
Separate room for cooking:	1 for yes, 0 for no;
Ownership of house:	2 for yes, 0 for no;

Cont'd...

Cont'd...

Ownership of agricultural land:	4 for 5 acres or more, 3 for 2.0–4.9 acres, 2 for less than 2 acres or acreage not known, 0 for no agricultural land;
Ownership of irrigated land:	2 if owns at least some irrigated land, 0 for no irrigated land;
Ownership of livestock:	2 if owns livestock, 0 if does not own livestock;
Ownership of durable goods:	4 each for a car or tractor, 3 each for a moped/scooter/motorcycle, telephone, refrigerator or colour television, 2 each for a bicycle, electric fan, radio/transistor, sewing machine, black & white television, water pump, bullock cart, or thresher, 1 each for a mattress, pressure cooker, chair, cot/bed, table, or clock/watch.

The total score ranges from 0 to 67. Accordingly, scores from 0 to 14 have been considered as Low, scores from 15 to 24 have been considered as Medium and scores from 25 to 67 have been considered as High.

Inequalities in terms of standard of living index have been examined with the help of Lorenz curve and Gini-coefficient. In the Lorenz curve technique, usually the households (units) are arranged according to the value of the characteristic (SLI). Then, the values (SLI) of the units (households) and the frequencies are both cumulated and taking the total as 1.0 for both the cases, the values x_i and y_i are computed which are the cumulated proportions of frequencies and SLI up to i^{th} unit (household), (i=1,2,3,...........n), n being the total number of households. These proportions (x_i and y_i) are plotted on a graph paper. If there is proportionately equal distribution of the frequencies over various values of the variate (SLI), the points would lie in a straight line. This line is called the line of 'equal distribution'. If the distribution items are not proportionally equal, it indicates variability, and the curve would be away from the line of equal distribution. The farther the curve is from equal distribution, the greater is the inequality in the series. A higher Lorenz curve implies more social welfare for the same total of SLI. The Gini-coefficient (or the Lorenz ratio as it is frequently called) measures the distance between the line of equal distribution and the Lorenz curve, which is computed as twice the area of the Lorenz curve.

Gini-coefficient is used to attach some absolute measure to the degree of inequality or give some idea whether the inequality is large or small. The Gini-coefficient ranges from 0 to 1, where 0 representing perfect equality and 1 total inequality. It corresponds to twice the area between the Lorenz curve and diagonal. There are different methods to calculate the Gini-coefficient but a simple formula can be as follows.

We know that

$$\text{Gini-Coefficient} = \frac{\text{Area between Lorenz curve and the diagonal}}{\text{Total area under the diagonal}}$$

Obviously, the total area under diagonal is 0.5. Also area under the Lorenz curve can be computed as:

Area of Lorenz curve = 0.5—Area below diagonal excluding area of Lorenz curve

Area below diagonal excluding area of Lorenz curve can be obtained by using suitable quadrature formula because specific form of the curve is not known. For simplicity we may use trapezoidal rule. Under this formula:

$$\text{e}Area = \frac{1}{n}\left[y_1 + y_2 \ldots\ldots \ldots + y_{n-1} + \frac{y_n}{2}\right]$$

$$= \text{A (say)} \qquad \ldots(1)$$

$$\text{Then } G\ (Y) = \frac{0.5 - \frac{1}{n}\left[y_1 + y_2 \ldots\ldots \ldots + y_{n-1} + \frac{y_n}{2}\right]}{0.5}$$

$$= \frac{0.5 - [A]}{0.5} \qquad \ldots(2)$$

Where,

G(Y) = Gini-coefficient; n = Number of units

(y_i) = Proportion of cumulated SLI up to i^{th} unit

This is so because distance between two consecutive points on x-axis is $1/n$.

The area of Lorenz curve can also be obtained as:

$$Area = \frac{1}{n}\sum_{i=1}^{n-1}(x_i - y_i)$$

because at the end point x_i and y_i are equal and then $x_i - y_i = 0$, for $i=n$

where x_i is the cumulated proportion of frequency up to i^{th} unit. (Obviously, $x_i = i/n$ $i=1, 2, 3 \ldots$n)

Results and Discussion

The standard of living index (SLI) can be considered as an overall measure of social and economic development of a household. It is dependent not only on possession of various durable goods but includes some other variables also such as housing condition, drinking water facilities, land holding, etc., and as such is likely to be more influenced by long-term socio-economic development of the household. As mentioned earlier, NFHS has provided weights for various items to compute SLI of a household and the SLI has been computed using these weights for each household selected in the sample.

After computation of total score for each household, the households have been classified in three groups viz. Low, Medium and High with scores 0–14, 15–24 and 25 and above respectively. However, for better presentation of the Lorenz curve, individual SLI score for each household is needed which we have used in drawing the Lorenz curve. For studying the disparity in terms of SLI in Indian society, we have prepared Lorenz curves for major 13 states of the country. Along with the curves, the Gini-coefficients using the formula $G(Y)=2\left[\frac{1}{n}\sum_{i=1}^{n-1}(x_i-y_i)\right]$ have also been obtained. Moreover, for each state, the Gini-coefficient for each sub-population classified according to caste group, religion and type of residential area, viz., rural/urban has also been computed. To have an idea of average development, the average SLI of each state has also been determined.

Table 1 presents the average SLI, two times area of Lorenz curve (Gini-coefficient) and distribution of households in the three categories of SLI for each major state of the country having population more than two crore according to 1991 census. These states are arranged according to their Gini-coefficients in ascending order.

Table 1 ***Disparity in All States (in terms of SLI)***

States	*Gini-Coefficient*	*Average SLI*	*Standard of Living Index (in %)*		
			Low	*Medium*	*High*
Punjab	0.1,876(1)	29.18	6.0	37.9	56.0
Maharashtra	0.2,318(2)	22.24	23.8	47.8	28.5
Kerala	0.2,344(3)	22.80	17.4	53.5	29.1
Rajasthan	0.2,350(4)	20.37	26.8	53.4	19.8
Gujarat	0.2,418(5)	21.95	24.9	46.8	28.3
Uttar Pradesh	0.2,522(6)	18.50	34.4	50.1	15.5
Karnataka	0.2,576(7)	19.13	33.3	46.3	20.3
Madhya Pradesh	0.2,594(8)	18.61	36.8	47.0	16.2
Tamil Nadu	0.2,836(9)	17.72	38.1	45.8	16.1
West Bengal	0.2,840(10)	19.24	35.7	45.7	18.6
Andhra Pradesh	0.2,872	17.67	40.5	44.7	14.8
Bihar	0.2,984	14.68	57.5	34.0	8.50
Orissa	0.3,156	15.50	56.1	32.7	11.2
India	0.2,687	20.25	36.7	44.7	18.6

A critical review of the above table shows that there are wide variations in terms of inequality in SLI among various major states; Punjab shows the minimum while Orissa occupies the status of most unequal state with Gini-coefficients 0.1,876 and 0.3,156 respectively. On the positive side (lesser inequality), Maharashtra gets the second position (Gini-coefficient 0.2,318) while on the negative side (more inequality), Bihar occupies the second position with Gini-coefficient 0.2,984. Uttar Pradesh, Karnataka and Madhya Pradesh occupy almost the middle position ranging their Gini-coefficients from 0.2,522 to 0.2,594.

When we put our eyes on the second column of the table showing average SLI, the situation remains almost similar but in a reverse order. We find that as average development (SLI) increases disparity decreases almost as a rule.

Punjab which shows minimum inequality in terms of SLI occupies the position of maximum development in terms of average SLI. The position for worst condition is interchanged between Bihar and Orissa. Bihar occupies the status of least developed state with average SLI 14.68 while Orissa shows an average SLI of 15.50 representing almost the same level of underdevelopment (we may recall that 15 is the cut-off point between low and medium SLI groups). On the positive side also, Kerala and Maharashtra interchange their positions. Kerala occupies the second position in terms of average SLI (22.80) while Maharashtra gets the third position with average SLI 22.24. As in the previous case, Uttar Pradesh, Madhya Pradesh and Karnataka occupy the middle place with average SLI ranging from 18.50 to 19.13 while West Bengal has a slight edge over these with average SLI of 19.24.

When we observe the distribution of households according to their SLI category (Low, Middle and High) we almost get the similar view. However, the results reveal more striking features. The percentage of households in Low SLI category is only 6.0 for Punjab but this percentage is as high 57.5 and 56.1 for Bihar and Orissa. In reverse order, the percentage of households with High SLI is 56.0 for Punjab while it is only 8.50 and 11.2 for Bihar and Orissa. What a big gap? The other important feature is that Punjab is much ahead of other states. Kerala and Maharashtra which get second and third positions have this percentage as only 29.1 and 28.5; almost half of Punjab. The other feature is that there is almost a continuum for other states except Punjab which is well ahead of other states.

Now we examine the pattern of disparity in various sub-groups of the populations of various states classified according to religion, caste and type of residence, viz., rural and urban. These are examined by computing the value of Gini-coefficients, average SLI and distribution of SLI. The results are presented in Tables 2 to 14.

Table 2 ***Disparity in Punjab (in terms of SLI)***

Characteristics	*No. of Households*	*Gini-Coefficient*	*Average SLI*	*Standard of Living Index (in %)*		
				Low	*Medium*	*High*
Caste Group						
SC/ST	858	0.2,008	21.78	14.2	64.0	21.8
OBC	499	0.1,848	26.32	7.5	50.4	42.1
Others	1,610	0.1,408	34.21	1.3	20.2	78.5
Religion						
Hindu	1,283	0.1,782	27.66	6.5	42.5	51.0
Muslim	68	0.1,528	26.82	5.9	54.4	39.7
Sikh	1,553	0.1,912	30.62	5.5	33.0	61.5
Place of Residence						
Urban	1,066	0.1,162	33.81	0.7	21.8	77.5
Rural	1,901	0.2,124	27.06	9.0	46.9	44.1
Total	2,967	0.1,876	29.18	6.1	37.9	56.0

Table 3 ***Disparity in Maharashtra (in terms of SLI)***

Characteristics	*No. of Households*	*Gini-Coefficients*	*Average SLI*	*Standard of Living Index (in %)*		
				Low	*Medium*	*High*
Caste Group						
SC/ST	1,151	0.2,928	18.06	40.3	44.2	15.5
OBC	1,140	0.2,398	21.09	27.2	51.1	21.7
Others	3,448	0.2,038	24.05	17.0	47.9	35.1
Religion						
Hindu	4,424	0.2,398	21.94	25.9	46.5	27.6
Muslim	759	0.1,842	22.47	14.3	62.0	23.7
Place of Residence						
Urban	3,662	0.1,666	25.90	8.5	51.6	39.9
Rural	2,168	0.2,756	16.06	48.4	41.6	10.0
Total	5,830	0.2,318	22.24	23.8	47.8	28.4

Table 4 *Disparity in Kerala (in terms of SLI)*

Characteristics	*No. of Households*	*Gini-Coefficients*	*Average SLI*	*Standard of Living Index (in %)*		
				Low	*Medium*	*High*
Caste Group						
SC/ST	286	0.2,358	16.15	41.3	52.1	6.6
OBC	1,164	0.2,226	22.58	16.2	56.9	26.9
Others	1384	0.2,258	24.73	12.6	50.4	37.0
Religion						
Hindu	1580	0.2,390	21.87	20.2	54.1	25.7
Muslim	705	0.2,232	22.53	15.9	55.6	28.5
Place of Residence						
Urban	855	0.1,940	25.84	8.1	51.2	40.7
Rural	1,979	0.2,736	21.49	21.5	54.4	24.1
Total	2,834	0.2,344	22.80	17.4	53.5	29.1

Table 5 *Disparity in Rajasthan (in terms of SLI)*

Characteristics	*No. of Households*	*Gini-Coefficients*	*Average SLI*	*Standard of Living Index (in %)*		
				Low	*Medium*	*High*
Caste Group						
SC/ST	2,013	0.2,112	16.25	42.6	51.2	6.2
OBC	1,448	0.2,132	19.77	24.9	59.2	15.9
Others	2,850	0.2,216	23.43	16.5	51.9	31.6
Religion						
Hindu	5,631	0.2,346	20.18	27.1	53.9	19.0
Muslim	542	0.2,254	20.36	27.9	53.1	19.0
Place of Residence						
Urban	1,546	0.1,892	26.92	10.2	44.9	44.9
Rural	4,765	0.2,174	18.17	32.2	56.1	11.7
Total	6,311	0.2,350	20.37	26.8	53.4	19.8

Table 6 *Disparity in Gujarat (in terms of SLI)*

Character-istics	*No. of Households*	*Gini-Coefficients*	*Average SLI*	*Standard of Living Index (in %)*		
				Low	*Medium*	*High*
Caste Group						
SC/ST	1,347	0.2,528	17.71	42.5	48.7	8.8
OBC	929	0.2,310	20.26	27.1	53.0	19.9
Others	1,498	0.1,694	27.64	8.9	39.2	51.9
Religion						
Hindu	3,527	0.2,478	21.60	26.5	45.8	27.7
Muslim	319	0.1,764	23.71	11.7	64.1	24.2
Place of Residence						
Urban	1,709	0.1,802	26.30	10.8	44.8	44.4
Rural	2,223	0.2,580	18.66	35.7	48.3	16.0
Total	3,932	0.2,418	21.95	24.9	46.8	28.3

Table 7 *Disparity in Uttar Pradesh (in terms of SLI)*

Character-istics	*No. of Households*	*Gini-Coefficients*	*Average SLI*	*Standard of Living Index (in %)*		
				Low	*Medium*	*High*
Caste Group						
SC/ST	1,929	0.2,436	17.21	38.5	47.9	13.6
OBC Others	2,160	0.2,322	19.15	32.1	50.9	17.0
	3,702	0.2,356	18.76	32.8	51.1	16.1
Religion						
Hindu	7,282	0.2,524	18.61	34.0	50.3	15.7
Muslim	1,292	0.2,468	17.90	36.3	49.0	14.7
Place of Residence						
Urban Rural	1,835	0.2,170	22.49	9.4	62.2	28.4
	6,847	0.2,310	17.48	40.5	47.2	12.3
Total	8,682	0.2,522	18.50	34.4	50.1	15.5

Table 8 ***Disparity in Karnataka (in terms of SLI)***

Characteristics	*No. of Households*	*Gini-Coefficients*	*Average SLI*	*Standard of Living Index (in %)*		
				Low	*Medium*	*High*
Caste Group						
SC/ST	956	0.2,652	14.49	57.2	36.6	6.2
OBC Others	1,724	0.2,474	19.32	31.0	49.7	19.3
	941	0.2,112	22.99	16.3	49.7	34.0
Religion						
Hindu	3,649	0.2,586	18.98	34.1	46.3	19.6
Muslim	452	0.2,450	17.72	35.3	50.7	14.0
Place of Residence						
Urban Rural	1,552	0.2,068	23.86	14.5	47.0	38.5
	2,721	0.2,516	16.43	44.1	45.9	10.0
Total	4,273	0.2,576	19.13	33.3	46.4	20.3

Table 9 ***Disparity in Madhya Pradesh (in terms of SLI)***

Characteristics	*No. of Households*	*Gini-Coefficients*	*Average SLI*	*Standard of Living Index (in %)*		
				Low	*Medium*	*High*
Caste Group						
SC/ST	5,228	0.2,186	14.99	53.4	42.2	4.4
OBC	2,711	0.2,404	18.88	33.3	52.3	14.4
Others	1,510	0.2,318	25.20	15.1	45.8	39.1
Religion						
Hindu	6,201	0.2,590	18.31	38.1	46.8	15.1
Muslim	401	0.2,278	21.43	24.2	52.4	23.4
Place of Residence						
Urban	1,799	0.2,416	24.22	20.5	42.6	36.9
Rural	4,950	0.2,342	16.69	42.7	48.6	8.7
Total	6,749	0.2,594	18.61	36.8	47.0	16.2

Table 10 ***Disparity in Tamil Nadu (in terms of SLI)***

Characteristics	*No. of Households*	*Gini-Coefficients*	*Average SLI*	*Standard of Living Index (in %)*		
				Low	*Medium*	*High*
Caste Group						
SC/ST	1,265	0.2,886	13.18	59.4	36.6	4.0
OBC	3,828	0.2,682	18.70	32.6	49.4	18.0
Others	171	0.1,584	28.45	5.8	35.7	58.5
Religion						
Hindu	4,664	0.2,868	17.27	40.2	44.7	15.1
Muslim	305	0.2,286	20.95	22.4	56.8	20.8
Place of Residence						
Urban	2,388	0.2,370	21.60	21.8	52.0	26.2
Rural	2,893	0.2,850	14.52	51.5	40.7	7.8
Total	5,281	0.2,836	17.72	38.1	45.8	16.1

Table 11 ***Disparity in West Bengal (in terms of SLI)***

Characteristics	*No. of Households*	*Gini-Coefficients*	*Average SLI*	*Standard of Living Index (in %)*		
				Low	*Medium*	*High*
Caste Group						
SC/ST	1,197	0.2,868	14.09	57.5	37.9	4.6
OBC	202	0.2,280	21.82	24.6	54.8	20.6
Others	2,767	0.2,556	21.81	24.9	49.2	25.9
Religion						
Hindu	3,792	0.2,744	20.20	31.5	47.3	21.2
Muslim	837	0.2,958	15.05	54.2	38.7	7.1
Place of Residence						
Urban	2,335	0.2,134	24.15	14.2	54.6	31.2
Rural	2,390	0.2,874	14.45	56.7	37.0	6.3
Total	4,725	0.2,840	19.24	35.7	45.7	18.6

Table 12 *Disparity in Andhra Pradesh (in terms of SLI)*

Characteristics	*No. of Households*	*Gini-Coefficients*	*Average SLI*	*Standard of Living Index (in %)*		
				Low	*Medium*	*High*
Caste Group						
SC/ST	967	0.2,750	12.79	64.0	33.1	2.9
OBC	1,681	0.2,692	16.93	41.0	48.4	10.6
Others	1,145	0.2,392	22.64	21.0	48.9	30.1
Religion						
Hindu	3,393	0.2,868	17.69	40.4	44.7	14.9
Muslim	244	0.2,426	21.49	25.0	51.2	23.8
Place of Residence						
Urban	1,018	0.2,210	23.46	19.6	48.4	32.0
Rural	2,854	0.2,802	15.60	48.0	43.4	8.6
Total	3,872	0.2,872	17.67	40.6	44.8	14.6

Table 13 *Disparity in Bihar (in terms of SLI)*

Characteristics	*No. of Households*	*Gini-Coefficients*	*Average SLI*	*Standard of Living Index (in %)*		
				Low	*Medium*	*High*
Caste Group						
SC/ST	1,929	0.2,620	11.36	77.7	19.8	2.5
OBC	3,189	0.2,728	14.63	55.2	38.5	6.3
Others	1,227	0.2,888	20.01	31.7	45.0	23.3
Religion						
Hindu	5,277	0.2,980	14.88	56.6	34.4	9.0
Muslim	943	0.2,960	13.42	62.4	32.2	5.4
Place of Residence						
Urban	701	0.2,548	22.95	24.3	43.0	32.7
Rural	5,644	0.2,778	13.65	61.6	32.9	5.5
Total	6,345	0.2,984	14.68	57.5	34.0	8.5

Table 14 Disparity in Orissa (in terms of SLI)

Characteristics	No. of Households	Gini-Coefficients	Average SLI	Standard of Living Index (in %)		
				Low	Medium	High
Caste Group						
SC/ST	1,945	0.2,876	11.22	77.9	20.0	2.1
OBC	1,392	0.2,704	16.39	48.8	41.4	9.8
Others	1,312	0.2,804	20.85	32.0	41.9	26.1
Religion						
Hindu	4,499	0.3,154	15.45	56.3	32.6	11.1
Muslim	92	0.2,888	18.00	40.2	44.6	15.2
Place of Residence						
Urban	932	0.2,992	21.98	29.3	39.9	30.8
Rural	3,757	0.2,910	13.90	62.7	30.9	6.4
Total	4,689	0.3,156	15.50	56.1	32.7	11.2

Table 15 Differences (in upper caste group to lower caste group) of Average SLI of Major States

States	Others-OBC	OBC-SC/ST	Others-SC/ST
Punjab	7.89	4.54	12.43
Maharashtra	2.96	3.03	5.99
Kerala	2.15	6.43	8.58
Rajasthan	3.66	3.52	7.18
Gujarat	7.38	2.55	9.93
Uttar Pradesh	-0.39	1.94	1.55
Karnataka	3.67	4.83	8.5
Madhya Pradesh	6.32	3.89	10.21
Tamil Nadu	9.75	5.52	15.27
West Bengal	-0.01	7.73	7.72
Andhra Pradesh	5.71	4.14	9.85
Bihar	5.38	3.27	8.65
Orissa	4.46	5.17	9.63

Table 16 Differences (in upper caste group to lower caste group) in Percentages in High SLI Group of Major States

States	Others-OBC	OBC-SC/ST	Others-SC/ST
Punjab	36.4	20.3	56.7
Maharashtra	13.4	6.2	19.6
Kerala	10.1	20.3	30.4

Cont'd...

Cont'd...

Rajasthan	15.7	9.7	25.4
Gujarat	32.0	8.8	43.1
Uttar Pradesh	-0.9	3.4	2.5
Karnataka	14.7	13.1	27.8
Madhya Pradesh	24.7	10.0	34.7
Tamil Nadu	40.5	14.0	54.5
West Bengal	5.3	16.0	21.3
Andhra Pradesh	19.4	2.9	27.2
Bihar	17.1	3.8	20.9
Orissa	16.3	7.7	24.0

By and large, when we examine the value of Gini-coefficient we observe more inequality in rural areas than in urban areas though the gap between the two varies from state to state. More developed states like Punjab, Maharashtra and Kerala have larger gaps while less developed states like Bihar and Orissa have smaller gaps though the trend is not that much straight.

When we investigate the values according to religion, we find, as a rule, Hindus have more disparity than Muslims except in case of West Bengal where Hindus show less disparity than Muslims (Gini-coefficients 0.2,744 and 0.2,958 respectively). Here also gaps are not uniform; some where more than the others. For the state of Punjab, we have considered Sikh religion also which shows higher disparity than Hindu and Muslims. As far as the gap is concerned Maharashtra, Gujarat and Tamil Nadu show larger gaps than the others. Kerala, Rajasthan, U.P. and Bihar show very small gaps between disparities in Hindus and Muslims.

As far as castes are concerned, Scheduled Castes and Scheduled Tribes (SC/ST) show more inequality than OBCs and 'Other Castes'. Between OBCs and 'Others', more frequently OBCs show more inequality than 'Others'.

When we examine the values of average SLI, the results are on expected line. 'Other Castes' have highest average while SC/ST have the lowest average in all the states. Averages in urban areas are larger than in rural areas. Results are not that much straight when we examine the figures according to religion. Muslims of eight states viz. Maharashtra, Kerala, Rajasthan, Tamil Nadu, Gujarat, Madhya Pradesh, Andhra Pradesh and Orissa show more development (in terms of average SLI) than Hindus of these states while the reverse is true for the remaining five states. The details are exhibited in the tables.

Thus, after all, we observe striking differentials in inequality as well as development levels among different states as well as within states. This is so even after lapse of more than half a century after independence. Thus, the government has to take steps to form policies aiming reducing inequality in the Indian society for a brighter future of the large country like ours. Then and only then we will have a shining India approaching towards a golden bird of the past.

References

Atkinson, A.B. 1970. On the Measurement of Inequality. *Journal of Economic Theory* 2: 145–200.

Butler, Richard J. and James B. McDonald. 1987. Interdistributional Income Inequality. *Journal of Business and Economic Statistics* 5 (1): 13–8.

Deutsh, J. and J. Silber. 1999. Inequality Decomposition by Population Subgroups and the Analysis of Inter-distributional Inequality. *Handbook of Income Inequality Measurement from Theory to Practice.* New York, USA: Kluwer Academic Publishers.

Deutsh, J. and J. Silber. 1997. Gini Transvariazione and Measurement of Distance between Distributions. *Empirical Economics* 22: 547–54.

Drez, J. and A. Sen. 1995. *India Economic Development and Social Opportunity*. New Delhi: Oxford University Press.

Mehmet, O. 1978. *Economic Planning and Social Justice in Developing Countries.* London: Croom Helm.

National Family Health Survey, 1998–1999. International Institute for Population Sciences, Mumbai.

Noorbakhsh, F. 2002. Human Development and Regional Disparity in Iran: A Policy Model. *Journal of International Development* 14: 927–49.

Noorbakhsh, F. 2003. Human Development, Poverty and Disparity in the States of India. Paper presented at the United Nations University/WIDER conference on Inequality, Poverty and Human Well-being, 30–31 May, Helsinki, Finland.

Rootman, I. 1988. Inequality in Health: Source and Solution, Health Promotion. *Health and Welfare, Canada* 26(3): 2–8.

Sandarson, S.K. (ed.). 1995. *Civilisation and World System, Studying World Historical Change.* Walnut Creek, CA: Altamira Press.

Sen, A. 1973. On the Economic Inequality: Income after Tax Distribution by Size in Canada. Statistics Canada, Oxford UK: Clarendon Press.

Srinivasan, K. and S.K. Mohanty. 2004. Deprivation of Basic Amenities by Caste and Region, Empirical Study using NFHS Data. *Economic and Political Weekly* 39 (7).

PART V

Population Policies and Programmes

18

Reproductive Health Services Remain Missing at the Grassroots Level

Evidence From a Time-Use Study of Service Providers in Rural Gujarat

N.P. Das and Urvi Shah

Background

The National Family Welfare Programme and the Child Survival and Safe Motherhood Programme have been combined and formulated as the Reproductive and Child Health (RCH) Programme, which is being implemented in the country since 1997. In addition, the RCH programme also envisages identifying and managing infections of the reproductive tract and sexually transmitted infections. It also lays emphasis on quality of services and ensuring satisfaction of service users. The RCH programme has also made a strategic shift from being a provider-driven centralised programme to a decentralised, target-free and client-centred programme. To this end, various management strategies namely bottom-up planning, improved management, information and evaluation system (which monitors programme performance beyond contraceptive targets to include the complete range of RCH indicators), enhancing the role of IEC campaigns, ensuring community participation and establishment of a workable GO-NGO partnership have been articulated and translated into programmatic action.

It, therefore, becomes important to understand how effectively the various aspects of the RCH programme have been integrated in actual service provision within the existing health delivery system and to identify the weak components, which need to be redressed under the programme. Several evaluations of the functioning of the RCH programme have already been undertaken (RCH household surveys, facility surveys, sub-project evaluations) which provide data on district level parametres of fertility, mortality, maternal and child health, contraceptive use and reproductive health and status of service delivery outlets. However, there is not enough information to understand the extent to which medical and health care providers are successful in translating the RCH philosophy in their day-to-day interactions with the clients visiting service delivery points. There is also not enough known regarding the time spent by health workers on purely family planning, maternal health and immunisation services vis-à-vis other services which fall under reproductive health. For example,

- How much time, on an average, is spent by the medical officers, health supervisors and health workers of PHCs on various activities related to day-to-day service provision?
- Are service providers including "non-contraceptive" and "non-maternal" groups in their service provision (e.g., young, unmarried, adolescent boys and girls, menopausal women or women with RTIs)?
- Are service providers talking to both men and women about varied reproductive health needs?
- Do they include identification and management of RTIs/STIs or anemia prophylaxis for adolescent girls?

Answers to these queries would therefore help to establish how successful the programme has been in addressing the varied health needs of both men and women across the life cycle, as envisaged under the RCH programme.

Objectives

The present study was therefore undertaken with the main objective of understanding how effectively the RCH philosophy has been integrated in service provision within the health delivery system, particularly at the primary health centres, in the state of Gujarat, through utilising a time-use analysis approach.

The specific objectives of the study were:

1. To obtain the daily work pattern of the various health and medical staff of primary health centres for a period one week prior to the interview.
2. To analyse the work pattern to understand the proportion of time spent by the different cadre of the staff on various components of the RCH programme particularly adolescent health (including anaemia control among girls), promoting male involvement in family planning, reproductive health issues (including identifying

and managing RTIs/STIs, infertility), safe motherhood, child care, infant and child immunisation, family planning and management of diseases.

3. To study the work pattern of the selected PHCs in order to ascertain institutional functioning with regard to service provision under a target-free and community needs assessment approach.

Study Design

This study was carried out in the rural areas of the state of Gujarat. The state can be broadly divided in the following five regions based on the natural geographical position of the districts.

1. Saurashtra, including the desert area of Kachchh (Rajkot, Bhavnagar, Amreli, Surendranagar, Junagadh, Jamnagar, Porbander and Kachchh).
2. North Gujarat (Banaskantha, Sabarkantha, Mehsana and Patan).
3. Central Gujarat (Ahmedabad, Gandhinagar, Nadiad, Anand).
4. East Gujarat (Dahod, Panchmahals).
5. South Gujarat (Vadodara, Bharuch, Narmada, Surat, Navsari, Valsad, Dangs).

A total of 24 Primary Health Centres (PHCs) covering these 5 regions were selected such that proportionately more number of PHCs was selected from those regions which have a greater number of PHCs. The required numbers of PHCs were selected from the respective region by covering at least one district from each region, as depicted below:

Region	*No. of Districts in the Region*	*No. of PHCs in the Region*	*No. of PHCs Selected*
Saurashtra	8	280	6
North Gujarat	4	204	4
Central Gujarat	4	166	4
East Gujarat	2	125	3
South Gujarat	7	295	7
Total	25	1,070	24

The selection of PHCs was done by the method of systematic sampling from the selected district in the region. The six districts selected for the study were Bhavnagar, Mehasana, Nadiad, Panchmahals, Vadodara and Bharuch.

Data were collected from all the staff of the selected PHCs (MOs, LHVs, MPHS, ANMs/FHWs and MPWs). They were interviewed to obtain their individual time-use work pattern using the appropriate tools. A description of the tool as well as a brief overview of time use technique is given in the following section.

Time Studies

Time studies, also known as time budgets and task allocation studies are one of the most frequently used methodologies in social science research to understand the work pattern of households, individuals, communities and institutions. It has also been successfully used with rural communities to understand the agricultural production cycle. The advantage of time-use studies is that data can be obtained from populations who have a clear concept of time as a measurable, finite resource with a linear flow from the past to the future as well as those population groups who are not dependent upon the 'clock' for a sense of time, but who have their own 'time scale' in terms of seasonality or the rising and setting of the sun. Time-use data can be obtained from both literate as well as non-literate groups.

Time-use data provide an understanding of the proportional allocation of time spent on various activities and for a given reference period. When used with programme managers, it makes it possible for them to see time allocated to various activities, whether such allocations are giving necessary programme benefits, where time is not productively utilised so that remedial action can be taken.

In the health care set-up, time use method has been utilised to understand the pattern of time spent on various activities with the aim to improve quality of services and increase the productivity of service providers. Studies have also compared results obtained from different approaches of measuring time-use. (West et al., 2001; Janovitz et al., 2001 and Janovitz, 2006). However, there appears to be little evidence of the application of this technique in the Indian health delivery system.

The various techniques of obtaining time-use data include:

1. One-day recall method
2. Time diaries/records of the respondents
3. Non-participant observation
4. Participant observation, wherein the observer actually participates in the activities of the household over a period of time to obtain the necessary data.

The one-day recall and time diaries are two methods, which are able to yield the required data fairly quickly at a reasonable cost, and are therefore preferred over the two types of observation methods, particularly for survey research. The respondents or the interviewers or both can complete either the recall method or time diaries.

The present study therefore utilised the recall method through interviews for obtaining the necessary time-use data from the various cadres of staff of the selected PHCs in Gujarat. The main focus of the interview was to obtain the work pattern of the medical and para-medical staff during a typical week. They were also asked to recall the various activities they had carried out during each day of the week in reference and the time they spent in doing the same. It was ensured that the time spent in travelling to their work area is also accounted for while obtaining details of their daily work. A period of one week prior to the interview date was the reference to minimise errors in recall. Data were also obtained to ascertain knowledge of the PHC staff on the various components of the RCH programme, the new initiatives under the same, the difficulties they faced in carrying out various activities and comments and suggestions about the RCH programme.

Results and Discussion

Sample Implementation

As per the study design, 24 PHCs were visited across the state, covering six districts. A total of 174 medical and para-medical staff of these 24 PHCs, who were in position and available on the date of visit, were interviewed to obtain the required data. Out of 174, 109 (62.6%) were female staff while the remaining 65 (37.4) were males (Table not given). Table 1 provides the distribution of staff by their designation and sex which shows that all except one medical officer of the selected PHCs could be interviewed. Out of 23 MOs, the majority (19) are males while the remaining 4 are females. However, not all the LHVs/FHSs and MPHSs (24 each) could be interviewed primarily due to vacancy of this post.

As expected, majority of the health workers interviewed were ANMs/FHWs (91) followed by 23 multi-purpose workers (MPWs). Other staff interviewed included sanitary inspector (5), leprosy/TB worker (1) and 8 other health staff, particularly vaccinators (Table 1).

Experience and Training

The results on the experience and training of the PHC staff, presented in Table 2 indicates that a little over three-fourths of the staff interviewed had been in service for 10 or more years. A careful examination of this data further reveals that the LHVs/FHSs, MPHSs, FHWs and SIs, can be considered to be 'more experienced' as more than 86 per cent of this category of staff reported that they had been in service for 10 or more years, as against only 26 per cent of medical officers. Regarding the training(s) received by the staff under the RCH programme, it is satisfying to note that 81 per cent had received training under the RCH programme (Table 2). However, majority of the sanitary inspectors, multi-purpose health supervisors, vaccinators, leprosy/TB workers and malaria surveillance workers had not received any training which indicates that they are least involved in RCH programme activities.

The staff who had received some training was asked about the duration and adequacy of the trainings. As can be noted from Table 2, majority of the MOs (83%), LHVs (85%) and 90 per cent of ANMs had received at least one week of training under the RCH programme. Similarly, 83 to 100 per cent of the staff also found the training to be adequate.

Knowledge of Components of RCH Programme

All the PHC staff was next asked to state the various components of the RCH programme, irrespective of whether they had undergone any training under the programme. Their responses, presented in Table 3, reveal that the majority of the staff interviewed (80 to 98%) could recall the important aspects of women's health such as early registration of pregnancy, antenatal, natal and post-natal care, anaemia control among adolescent girls/women, prevention and treatment of RTI/STI and HIV/AIDS. Similarly, majority of the staff also reported about important components under child health such as newborn care, timely immunisation and management of diarrhoea and ARI. A similar level of knowledge can also be seen with regard to family planning/contraception and men's reproductive health (Table 3).

In view of the greater involvement of female staff under the RCH programme, it is not surprising to note that this cadre of staff is found to have an edge regarding knowledge about the components of the RCH programme compared to their male counterparts.

Table 1 ***Per Cent Distribution of PHC Staff Interviewed by Sex according to Designation, Gujarat, 2001***

Designation	*Sex*		
	Male	*Female*	*Total*
Medical Officer	82.6(19)	3.7(4)	100.0(.23)
LHV/FHS	—	100.0(15)	100.0(15)
MPHS	100.0(8)	—	100.0(8)
ANM/FHW	—	100.0(92)	100.0(92)
MPW	95.7(22)	—	100.0(22)
SI	100.0(5)	—	100.0(5)
Leprosy/TB worker	100.0(1)	—	100.0(1)
Other health staff+	87.5(7)	12.5(1)	100.0(8)
Total	37.4 (65)	62.6 (109)	100.0(174)

* LHV—Lady Health Visitor; FHS—Female Health Supervisor
MPHS—Multi-Purpose Health Supervisor; ANM—Auxiliary Nurse Midwife
MPW—Multi-Purpose Worker (male); SI—Sanitary Inspector

\+ Includes vaccinator, malaria surveillance worker and staff nurse under RCH

Table 2 ***Percentage Distribution of PHC Staff by their Years of Service, RCH Training Received and its Adequacy, according to Designation, Gujarat, 2006***

Designation	*Per cent of PHC staff*				
	Working for more than 10 Years	*Received RCH Training*	*Received at least One Week of RCH Training**	*Found the RCH Training to be Adequate**	*Total*
Medical Officer	25.7	78.3	83.3	94.4	100.0 (23)
LHV/FHS	100.0	86.7	84.6	84.6	100.0 (15)
MPHS	87.5	37.5	33.3	100.0	100.0 (8)
ANM/FHW	85.7	96.7	89.9	83.0	100.0 (91)
MPW	60.8	65.2	20.0	66.7	100.0 (23)
SI	100.0	20.0	0.0	100.0	100.0 (5)
Leprosy/TB worker	0.0	0.0	—	—	100.0 (1)
Other health staff	87.5	37.5	33.3	100.0	100.0 (8)
Total	75.9	81.0	78.0	83.7	100.0 (174)

\+ Out of those who received any training under the RCH programme, 46 per cent of LHV/FHS, 31 per cent of ANMs/FHWs and overall 26 per cent of PHC staff had attended 2 or more RCH trainings.

* Out of those who received any training under the RCH programme.

Table 3 ***Knowledge of Various Components of RCH Programme among PHC Staff, Gujarat, 2006***

Components of RCH Programme	*Per Cent of Respondents Reporting at least Some Knowledge*		
	Male	*Female*	*Total*
Women's Health			
Antenatal care	95.4	100.0	98.3
Intra-natal care	78.5	89.0	85.1
Post-natal care	80.0	92.7	87.9
Provision of emergency obstetric care	69.2	79.8	75.9
Provision of safe abortion service	61.5	81.7	74.1
Prevention and treatment of RTIs/STIs	67.7	89.0	81.0
Provision of adolescent sexual and reproductive health services/information	67.7	83.5	77.6
Early registration of pregnant women	76.9	99.1	90.8
Anaemia control among adolescent girls/women	81.5	95.4	90.2
Nutrition and health education for women and children	84.6	95.4	91.4
Identify and refer women with high risk pregnancies	76.9	87.2	83.3
HIV/AIDS	78.5	90.8	86.2
Promote condom use	67.7	89.0	81.0
Child Health			
Management of newborn and neo-natal care	75.4	92.7	86.2
Ensure timely immunisation	98.5	98.2	98.3
Management of sickness among children	75.4	82.6	79.9
Management of diarrhoea	83.1	92.7	89.1
Management of ARI	81.5	92.7	88.5
Promote nutritional supplementation	75.4	82.6	79.9
Family planning/contraception			
Promote small family	87.7	98.2	94.3
Promote a range of contraceptive choices and services	87.7	98.2	94.3
Promote NSV	80.0	84.4	82.8
Men's reproductive health			
STI	72.3	71.6	71.8
HIV/AIDS	83.1	93.6	89.7

Routine Weekly Work Schedule

Having established the knowledge and experience of the PHC staff under the RCH programme, it was thought necessary to understand their weekly work pattern. They were therefore first asked the number of days they spent at the clinic and in the field.

Their responses are presented by the designation of the staff in Table 4. The overall time-use data reveal that the staff works for 5 ½ days (8 hours per day) on an average, in service provision (Saturday was reported to be a half working day), out of which they are spending 4 days' worth of time in a week at the field while the remaining days (i.e., 1.5 days' worth of time) are spent at the clinic (Table 4). The data on this aspect further shows that all the PHC staff is spending some time at the clinic and some time in the field every day. However, the time spent by the staff in the field and at the clinic obviously varies by designation of staff. For example, the medical officers devote more time at the clinic, i.e., on an average 3.4 days' worth of time per week while they spend the remaining days (i.e., 2.1 days' worth of time) in the field. As expected the LHVs/FHSs as well as ANMs/FHWs are also spending some time at the clinic (less than 2 days' worth of time per week) although more of their weekly time is spent in the field (4 days' worth of time on an average). The other health staff, i.e., male health supervisors, workers and sanitary inspectors are spending most of their time in the field (4.6 days).

In order to understand the type of activities the staff is carrying out both at the clinic as well as at the field, the respondents were further asked to state the number of hours they spent in a typical week on each activity both at the clinic and field level. The analysis of these data is based on the assumption that an officer/worker spends, on an average, 44 hours in a week, carrying out various activities in service provision (Saturday was reported to be a half working day by the staff).

These responses of the PHC staff by their designation are summarised in Table 5. It is evident from Table 5 that the PHC staff spends almost 50 per cent of the time in a week on service provision for routine MCH and FP activities like immunisation, family planning, ANC and child care (also see Figure 1) apart from OPD activity (almost 10%). Another significant proportion of their time (10%) is spent on maintaining records or other administrative work. As Table 5 and Figure 1 further show a very small proportion of time is spent on reproductive health for adolescents, women and men (about 6% of the time in a

Figure 1 ***Average Number of Hours Spent by PHC Staff in a Typical Week on Various Activities Under the RCH Programme***

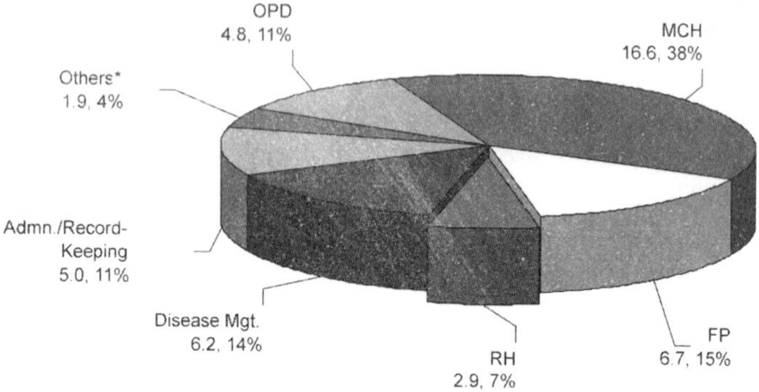

week). It is however important to note that the time spent on various activities in a week varies by the designation of the staff. For example, the medical officers spend more time on OPD, supervision and administrative activities in a week (Table 5). The male health supervisors (MPHS) are spending more time in identification and management of diseases (like leprosy, TB, malaria and other chronic diseases) and record-keeping work followed by their role in supervising MCH care activities particularly immunisation. On the other hand, the LHVs/FHSs as well as ANMs/FHWs spend a major part of their time in MCH care and family planning activities, indicating once again the low priority given to reproductive health activities for various community groups.

Table 4 ***Average Number of Days Spent by the PHC Staff at the Clinic and the Field to Carry Out Various Activities Under the RCH Programme in a Typical Week, Gujarat, 2006***

Staff Structure	*Average Number of Days Per week**		
	Clinic	*Field*	*No. of Respondents*
Medical Officer	3.4	2.1	23
LHV/FHS	1.5	4.0	15
MPHS	0.8	4.7	8
ANM/FHW	1.4	4.1	91
Other Health Staff	0.9	4.6	37
Total	1.5	4.0	174

* The working days of the PHC staff were found to be 5½ days per week, as the staff reported Saturday to be a half working-day.

Table 5 ***Time Spent in a Typical Week on the Various Activities that the PHC Staff Carry Out at the Clinic and in the Field Under RCH Programme, Gujarat, 2006***

Activity	*Average Number of Hours Spent Per Week on Each Activity**						
	MO	*LHV/ FHS*	*MPHS*	*ANM / FHW*	*Other*	*Total*	*Per cent of Time Devoted by PHC Staff in a Typical Week on Each of the Activities Under RCH Programme*
OPD	24.9	3.1	0.0	1.5	2.1	4.8	9.9
Immunisation	1.6	8.2	8.2	8.3	7.7	7.2	15.1
ANC	1.3	7.3	2.6	7.3	3.1	5.4	11.3
Child care	0.9	4.2	4.1	5.2	3.0	4.0	8.4
Family planning	2.0	8.6	4.2	8.2	5.8	6.7	13.9
Reproductive health for:							
Adolescents	0.3	1.4	0.3	1.4	0.8	1.1	2.3
Women	0.3	1.7	0.3	1.9	0.5	1.3	2.7
Men	0.3	0.3	1.2	0.1	1.3	0.5	0.9
Identification and management of leprosy, TB, malaria and chronic diseases	0.8	2.0	10.1	2.2	7.1	3.4	7.1
Treatment of minor ailments and collection of blood slides	0.4	1.4	4.0	2.3	5.6	2.8	5.7
Record-keeping/Adminis trative work	4.1	5.0	7.7	4.8	5.2	5.0	10.4
Other (such as supervision of all activities at the field, village sanitation, IEC and epidemic management)	7.1	0.8	1.4	0.8	1.8	1.9	4.0
Total	44.0 (23)	44.0 (15)	44.0 (8)	44.0 (91)	44.0 (37)	44.0 (174)+	100.0 (44)*

+ Figure within parentheses indicates number of respondents

* Based on 44 hours of work in a week assuming 8 hours of work per day, on an average, on a full working day (i.e., Monday to Friday and half that time on Saturday)

Pattern of Time-Use During the Reference Week

An important objective of the present time-use study was to understand the timing of various activities carried out by the PHC staff during each day of the reference week and to assess the amount of time spent on different activities of service provision. The study had therefore obtained detailed data on time diary of activities, individually carried out by the PHC staff, during the one week prior to the interview. This time recall diary obtained data on the activities carried out by the staff with regard to the initiation and completion time of each activity for every day of the week in reference. It may be noted that the timing of an activity sometimes varied across the selected PHCs as well as across the different categories of the staff within a PHC. However, to understand the overall picture of time utilisation for various activities for each day of the week, the timing of an activity was decided on the basis of responses of a majority or a significant group, of the staff.

The results of this daily time-use diary indicate that OPD, antenatal clinic and outreach sessions are essentially conducted during the morning hours for almost all days of the week (Table 6). The respondents appear to be silent on the conduct of afternoon OPD at the PHC. On probing, some respondents, particularly the MOs, defended this lapse by stating that after morning OPD, they leave for field supervision and are unable to return on time to conduct afternoon OPD, due to remoteness of the villages. Moreover, they also stated that attendance at afternoon OPD generally used to be thin due to poor public transport facilities to reach the PHC village. These ground realities appear to be in the knowledge of the district health authorities, as reported by the PHC staff. Home visits are conducted both in the morning as well as in the afternoon depending on the other work carried out by the staff during that day, while major community level activities like village sanitation, chlorination of wells, attending Gram Sabha meeting and contact with the Anganwadi worker for growth monitoring of children and coordinating immunisation sessions are usually carried out during the afternoon. Supervision of these village level activities (by MOs, LHVs and MPHS) therefore also takes place during the afternoon of all the six working days as does administrative work including maintenance of service records.

It may also be noted from Table 6 that antenatal clinic and outreach sessions are reported to be held on Wednesday as a full day activity, as per the "fixed day, fixed time" immunisation strategy and therefore this activity is supervised by the supervisory staff in addition to the medical officer during the whole day on Wednesday. Family planning activity has been reported to be a full-day activity which had been carried out on

Table 6 ***A Consolidated Time Schedule of Various Activities Carried Out by the PHC Staff Based on Time Recall Diary of All Staff for the One Week Prior to the Interview, Gujarat, 2006.***

Activity	*Timing of Activity on a Particular Day+*					
	Mon.	*Tue.*	*Wed.*	*Thu.*	*Fri.*	*Sat.*
OPD	a.m.	a.m.	a.m.	a.m.	a.m.	a.m.
ANC (ANC, immunisation, child care, FP, RH, etc.)	a.m.	a.m.	f.d.	a.m.	a.m.	a.m.
FP camp	—	f.d.	—	—	f.d.	-
Outreach session (ANC, immunisation child care, FP, RH, etc.)	a.m.	a.m.	f.d.	a.m.	a.m./p .m.*	-
Home visits (household survey/blood slide collection/minor ailments/chronic diseases, etc.)	a.m./ p.m.*	a.m./ p.m. *	p.m.	a.m./ p.m. *	a.m./ p.m. *	a.m.
Other village level activities (like sanitation, IEC, epidemic management, Gram Sabha, block level meeting, contact with AWW, other meetings at the community level)	p.m.	p.m.	p.m.	—	a.m./ p.m. *	p.m.
Supervision of various activities and organising meetings by supervision staff including MO.	p.m.	p.m.	f.d.	p.m.	p.m.	a.m.
Administrative work/maintenance of records/record-keeping	p.m.	p.m.	p.m.	p.m.	p.m.	a.m.
Special activity/programme (such as leprosy camp, Vit. A meeting and training of staff)	f.d.	f.d.	—	f.d.	—	—

a.m. – Morning activity, p.m. – Afternoon activity, f.d. – Full day activity

\+ Time of activity for a day is approximately derived based on actual time of initiation and completion of a particular activity from the time recall diary of all staff for the one week prior to the interview (reference period). It is important to note that timing of an activity may vary from PHC to PHC as well as across the health staff even within a PHC. Therefore, it is likely that a particular activity may have been carried out by some staff in the morning (a.m.), while others might have carried out the same activity in the afternoon (p.m.), or during the day (f.d.). Nevertheless, timing of an activity is decided on the time schedule reported by the majority of the staff or by a significant group.

* Some of the PHC staff reported this as a morning activity, while another group reported to have carried out the same activity in the afternoon.

Tuesday and Thursday, by all the respondents due to their involvement in the ongoing sterilisation camps. Certain special programmes or activities such as vitamin A training/meeting and reconstructive surgery camp, which had been organised during the study period, were also reported to be full-day activities on Monday, Tuesday and Thursday, indicating that a substantial portion of the working week of majority of the staff is devoted to these activities. Saturday stands out as all the activities are carried out during the morning hours, as Saturday was reported to be a half working day.

The time recall diary has also enabled the assessment of average time spent on various activities by all the staff for each day of the week under reference, as well as the time spent on such activities by different cadre of staff. As can be noted from Table 6, all the respondents together spend a total of about 15 hours (less than two days) per week on clinic-based activities and almost twice this time (a little over 28 hours or about 3½ days) on outreach or community level activities, which means that they are spending a little over 43 hours (that is almost 5½ days) per week in service provision.

Further examination of Table 7 also shows that for each day of the week, the time spent on clinic activities is about 2–3 hours as against 5–5½ hours for field-based activities indicating that a lot of outreach/community level activities, as expected, are carried out by the PHC staff. The total average time spent on Saturday is less than other days, as this was reported to be a half day by the female staff. Another reason for the drop in average time was that the male staff reported that they had a holiday on every second and fourth Saturday. So, if the time recall week for the male staff included such a non-working Saturday the overall hours showed a decline. From Table 7, it may be noted that Thursday also shows a drop in average working hours, i.e., about 5 hours of time, which is less than other days. This is attributed to the fact that a particular Thursday (in some of the PHCs), in the time recall diary, happened to be 26 January which is a national holiday.

An examination of the total average weekly time devoted to various activities reveals that about four hours were spent by the staff in service provision at OPD (which includes major time of the medical officers and other staff on duty to assist him in service provision like the LHVs, ANMs/FHWs (and sometimes the male health workers), antenatal care services (2 hours 13 minutes), immunisation (4 hours), and about 1 ½ hours each for management and treatment of chronic diseases such as TB, leprosy, malaria and treatment of minor ailments and collection of blood slides (Table 7). It is not surprising to note that family planning activities, especially sterilisation camp duty continues to dominate service provision as 9 hours of the week were reported to be spent by the PHC staff on this activity. An equal proportion of the time (9 hours) was spent in conducting school health programme (which was ongoing during the study period), attendance at Gram Sabha meetings, and liaisoning with Anganwadi workers. In one of the PHCs, an outbreak of gastroenteritis had been reported during the reference period, whereas in another PHC, a suspected case of measles had been reported. In these two PHCs, therefore a majority of the health workers under the medical officers' direction was deployed in the management of these diseases.

An important finding from the time recall diary is the fact that reproductive health related service provision, whether at the clinic or at the field level is extremely poor as the total time spent on this activity by the PHC staff during the whole week is only 29 minutes (day-wise range, on an average, is about 1–8 minutes). Educational activities also are low priority activities as only 16 ½ minutes are reported to be spent on IEC activities at the village level (Table 7).

An assessment of time spent by the different categories of staff on the various activities indicates that medical officers had spent 45 ½ hours per week in carrying out their various duties in the field and at the clinic (Table 8). A major part of the time of the medical officers (21 hours) had been spent in conducting the OPD clinic, followed by carrying out the school health programme (11 hours). Family planning work (especially duty at sterilisation camps) took up 3 hours of the weekly working time while record-keeping and administrative work took up two hours (Table 8). With regard to time spent on various activities by the male and female health workers and their supervisors, it is noted that the supervisory staff had devoted about 40–43 hours weekly in carrying out their responsibilities while the health workers had spent about 41 to almost 43 hours in service provision (Table 8). However, it is important to note that the supervisors, particularly the male supervisors, claim to have spent a major part of their working week in administrative work/record-keeping, school health programme, attending meetings, etc. The male and female health workers, on the other hand, claimed to have spent a large part of their time in FP activities, immunisation work and antenatal care services.

Thus, the one-week time recall diary matches well with the data on time-use for a typical week (see Tables 4, 5, 7 and 8), indicating that MOs are spending a major part of their time in OPD activity, followed by administrative and record-keeping work while the other staff of the PHC are largely engaged in family planning work, immunisation, antenatal care services, followed by other service provisions like school health programme, epidemic management, attendance at Gram Sabha meeting, etc., and record-keeping. More importantly, the envisaged focus on service provision for meeting reproductive health needs of men, women and adolescents has been ignored by the PHC staff not only during the family planning campaign months but also throughout the year, as noted in the typical week of activities.

Table 7 ***Time Spent on Various Activities by PHC Staff During the One Week Preceding the Interview at the Clinic and in the Field Under the RCH Programme, Gujarat, 2006.***

Activity	*Average Number of Hours Spent on Each Activity+*						
	Monday	*Tuesday*	*Wednesday*	*Thursday**	*Friday*	*Saturday***	*Total*
		Clinic					
OPD	0:54:12	0:47:18	0:39:06	0:37:48	0:34:18	0:35:00	4:07:42
ANC	0:14:54	0:05:36	0:08:18	0:05:24	0:06:48	0:03:30	0:44:30
Immunisation	0:14:06	0:04:12	0:51:48	0:00:30	0:01:24	0:00:12	1:12:12
FP	0:03:36	0:08:30	0:05:12	0:14:48	0:10:36	0:03:48	0:46:30
Child care	0:02:06	0:00:18	0:01:24	0:00:12	0:00:36	0:00:18	0:04:54
RH	0:00:30	0:00:00	0:00:42	0:01:00	0:00:00	0:00:30	0:02:42
Management and treatment of leprosy, TB, malaria and chronic diseases	0:04:00	0:00:36	0:01:30	0:04:12	0:00:18	0:03:00	0:13:36
Record-keeping/Administrative work	0:30:36	0:08:48	0:13:06	0:17:54	0:20:12	0:54:12	2:24:48
Other clinic activity (leprosy camp, vitamin A meeting/training of staff, etc.)	1:42:54	1:37:36	0:07:24	0:28:24	1:06:24	0:08:18	5:11:00
Total	3:46:54	2:52:54	2:08:30	1:50:12	2:20:36	1:48:48	14:47:54
		Outreach/Community level					
ANC	0:16:18	0:11:18	0:19:00	0:14:54	0:19:30	0:12:48	1:33:48
Immunisation	0:20:06	0:12:36	2:14:06	0:07:18	0:03:42	0:05:06	3:02:54
FP	0:43:36	2:19:18	0:40:18	1:30:12	2:19:30	0:56:42	8:29:36
Child care	0:08:12	0:05:54	0:10:36	0:04:48	0:07:24	0:10:48	0:47:42

Cont'd...

Cont'd...

RH	0:02:30	0:01:18	0:07:42	0:06:54	0:03:42	0:04:36	0:26:42
Management and treatment of leprosy, TB, malaria and chronic diseases	0:13:24	0:16:00	0:10:24	0:12:48	0:16:18	0:15:48	1:24:42
Treatment of minor ailments/blood slide collection	0:16:24	0:22:30	0:13:30	0:07:48	0:17:24	0:16:48	1:34:24
Village sanitation/Chlorination of wells/DDT spraying	0:04:54	0:07:36	0:06:48	0:00:54	0:03:18	0:05:12	0:28:42
IEC activities	0:02:00	0:03:18	0:03:30	0:02:06	0:04:24	0:01:18	0:16:36
Record-keeping/Administrative work	0:08:30	0:03:36	0:10:06	0:04:30	0:03:48	0:16:48	0:47:18
Other activities (school health/*gram sabha*/survey/home visits/epidemic management/*anganwadi* workers' meeting, other meetings, etc.)	3:14:42	2:00:18	1:10:06	0:53:24	1:16:36	0:49:18	9:24:24
Total	5:30:36	5:43:42	5:26:06	3:25:36	4:55:36	3:15:12	28:16:48
	Total						
OPD	0:54:12	0:47:18	0:39:06	0:37:48	0:34:18	0:35:00	4:07:42
ANC	0:31:12	0:16:54	0:27:18	0:20:18	0:26:18	0:16:18	2:18:18
IMM	0:34:12	0:16:48	3:05:54	0:07:48	0:05:06	0:05:18	4:15:06
FP	0:47:12	2:27:48	0:45:30	1:45:00	2:30:06	1:00:30	9:16:06
Child care	0:10:18	0:06:12	0:12:00	0:05:00	0:08:00	0:11:06	0:52:36
RH	0:03:00	0:01:18	0:08:24	0:07:54	0:03:42	0:05:06	0:29:24
Other clinic activity (leprosy camp, vitamin A meeting/training of staff, etc.)	1:42:54	1:37:36	0:07:24	0:28:24	1:06:24	0:08:18	5:11:00
Management and treatment of leprosy, TB, malaria and chronic diseases	0:17:24	0:16:36	0:11:54	0:17:00	0:16:36	0:18:48	1:38:18

Cont'd...

Cont'd...

Treatment of minor ailments/blood slide collection	0:16:24	0:22:30	0:13:30	0:07:48	0:17:24	0:16:48	1:34:24
Village sanitation/Chlorination of wells/DDT spraying	0:04:54	0:07:36	0:06:48	0:00:54	0:03:18	0:05:12	0:28:42
IEC activities	0:02:00	0:03:18	0:03:30	0:02:06	0:04:24	0:01:18	0:16:36
Record-keeping/Administrative work	0:39:06	0:12:24	0:23:12	0:22:24	0:24:00	1:11:00	3:12:06
Other activities (school health/*gram sabha*/survey/home visits, epidemic management/*anganwadi* workers' meeting, other Meetings, etc.)	3:14:42	2:00:18	1:10:06	0:53:24	1:16:36	0:49:18	9:24:24
Total	9:17:30	8:36:36	7:34:36	5:15:48	7:16:12	5:04:00	43:04:42

\+ Average time spent is completed in terms of hours, minutes and records

* The average hours spent by the staff is relatively low on Thursday because this day happened to be a public holiday for some PHCs (26 January).

** Saturday was reported to be a half working day by female staff, while male workers reported to have holiday on second and fourth Saturday.

In other words, family planning work, especially attendance at sterilisation camp continues to dominate in-service provision of the health staff (22% of their time in a week). Another activity, which was found to take up more than one-fifth of their weekly time, i.e., again 22 per cent, was in conducting the school health check-up, (which was ongoing during the study period) and attendance at Gram Sabha meetings (Table 8). Other components which have taken up a significant proportion of time are immunisation (10%), antenatal care (5), treatment of minor ailments and management of chronic diseases (4% each), apart from the time devoted to administrative work and record-keeping (7%). The one-week time recall diary has also attested to the low priority given to reproductive needs assessment (such as identifying and managing or treating reproductive infections) at the community level especially among men and unmarried, adolescent girls as only 1 per cent of the weekly time was noted to be spent on this activity. A comparison of time spent on various activities in a typical week vis-à-vis the spent during one week prior to the interview (Tables 5 and 8 respectively) clearly reveals that almost all the activities during the reference week are affected as a result of intensive family planning campaign period as well as the special school health programme, during this period. Nevertheless, the data clearly reveals that the RCH programme still continues to function as the earlier family welfare programme with regard to service provision. A new focus which is more visible is that of identification and management of diseases like TB, leprosy and malaria.

Adequacy of Time Spent on Various RCH Activities

In response to a query on adequacy of time spent on various RCH activities, it is noted that more than half (55%), of the respondents were not satisfied with the amount of time they could devote to various activities under the RCH programme while the remaining 45 per cent expressed satisfaction with the time they spent on RCH activities (Table 9). Those who expressed that they could not give enough time were further asked to state the activities which demanded more time for effective service provision. In response to this, almost 39 per cent felt that all the activities are affected under the RCH programme due to shortage of time. Additionally, another 39 per cent felt that record-keeping, followed by immunisation (33%) and family planning (18%) require more time than they are able to devote at present (Table 10). These responses thus reveal that none of the staff could specifically perceive that they are spending very little time to meet reproductive health needs of men, women and adolescents, and that this important component (RH activity) demands more time than they are able to devote at present.

Table 8 ***Time Spent on Various Activities by Each Cadre of PHC Staff During the One Week Preceding the Interview at the Clinic and in the Field Under the RCH Programme, Gujarat, 2006.***

Activity	*Average Number of Hours Spent on Each Activity*						*Per cent of Time Devoted by PHC Staff in a Week on Each of the Activities Under RCH Programme*
	MO	*LHV/ FHS*	*MPHS*	*ANM/ FHW*	*MPW*	*Total*	
		Clinic					
OPD	21:05:24	2:27:18	—	1:23:12	1:55:24	4:07:48	27.9
ANC	0:34:36	1:50:18	—	0:54:42	0:07:48	0:44:36	5.0
Immunisation	0:16:30	4:26:00	0:52:30	1:08:12	0:41:24	1:12:06	8.1
Family planning	0:16:06	2:25:42	1:44:24	0:42:00	0:23:12	0:46:30	5.2
Child care	0:04:36	0:16:18	—	0:05:30	—	0:04:54	0.6
RH	0:04:36	0:02:18	0:15:00	0:02:18	—	0:02:42	0.3
Chronic diseases	0:09:06	0:17:42	2:33:48	0:05:48	0:03:06	0:13:30	1.5
Administrative work/Record-keeping	1:46:30	2:12:00	7:00:00	2:17:48	2:11:42	2:24:54	16.3
Other	2:19:36	8:48:00	6:22:30	5:53:48	3:24:36	5:10:54	35.0
Total	26:37:00	22:45:36	18:48:12	12:33:18	8:47:12	14:47:54	100.0 (14:47:54)

Cont'd…

Cont'd...

Outreach/Community Level							
ANC	0:24:18	0:59:18	0:13:48	2:29:42	0:27:06	1:33:42	5.5
Immunisation	1:57:24	1:58:42	1:54:24	3:34:18	3:06:24	3:02:54	10.8
Family planning	3:05:12	5:15:00	5:59:24	10:11:00	9:32:12	8:29:36	30.0
Child care	0:16:30	0:09:42	0:35:36	1:01:06	0:51:54	0:47:42	2.8
RH	0:39:06	0:31:00	0:31:54	0:31:12	0:04:54	0:26:48	1.6
Chronic diseases	0:24:36	0:27:18	1:53:06	1:07:54	3:04:18	1:24:48	5.0
Treatment of minor ailments/blood slide collection	0:19:48	0:25:18	0:40:36	1:12:54	3:57:24	1:34:24	5.6
Sanitation	—	—	3:28:48	0:04:42	1:20:18	0:28:42	1.7
IEC	—	0:02:42	0:15:00	0:19:54	0:25:18	0:16:42	1.0
Administrative work/Record-keeping	0:12:48	1:09:00	2:26:18	0:49:24	0:32:30	0:47:12	2.8
School health/*Gram Sabha*/survey/home visits/ other meetings	11:28:54	6:26:00	9:15:00	8:26:30	11:49:18	9:24:24	33.3
Total	18:48:36	17:24:00	27:13:54	29:48:36	35:11:36	28:16:54	100.0 (28:16:54)

Cont'd...

Cont'd…

			Total				
OPD	21:05:24	2:27:18	—	1:23:12	1:55:24	4:07:48	9.6
ANC	0:58:54	2:49:36	1:08:30	2:37:30	1:11:42	2:18:18	5.4
Immunisation	2:13:54	6:24:42	2:46:54	4:42:30	3:47:48	4:15:00	9.9
Family planning	3:21:18	7:40:42	7:43:48	10:53:00	9:55:24	9:16:06	21.5
Child care	0:21:06	0:26:00	0:35:36	1:06:36	0:51:54	0:52:36	2.0
RH	0:43:42	0:33:18	0:46:54	0:33:30	0:04:54	0:29:24	1.1
Chronic diseases	0:33:42	0:45:00	4:26:54	1:13:42	3:07:24	1:38:18	3.8
Treatment of minor ailments/blood slide collection	0:19:48	0:25:18	0:40:36	1:12:54	3:57:24	1:34:24	3.7
Sanitation	0:04:54	0:07:36	0:06:48	0:00:54	0:03:18	0:28:42	1.1
IEC	0:02:00	0:03:18	0:03:30	0:02:06	0:04:24	0:16:42	0.6
Administrative work/Record-keeping	1:59:18	3:21:00	9:26:18	3:07:12	2:44:12	3:12:06	7.4
School health/*Gram Sabha*/survey/home visits/ other meetings	11:28:54	6:26:00	9:15:00	8:26:30	11:49:18	9:24:24	21.8
Other clinic level activities: leprosy camp/vitamin A meeting/training	2:19:36	8:48:00	6:22:30	5:53:48	3:24:36	5:10:54	12.0
Total	45:32:30	40:17:48	43:23:18	41:13:24	42:57:42	43:04:42	100.0 (43:04:42)

Among the reasons cited by them for reporting inadequate time to carry out various activities are, staff vacancies which increase the workload on existing staff, inadequate involvement of male health workers including vaccinators and sanitary inspectors in RCH activities (which puts greater stress on female staff), lack of vehicle for supervision in the field and poor sub-centre facilities including accommodation for the ANM/FHW and for service provision (Table not shown).

Table 9 ***Opinion of PHC Staff Regarding Adequacy of Time Spent on Various RCH Activities, Gujarat, 2006***

Designation	*Whether Time Spent on Various Activities was Adequate*		
	Yes	*No*	*Total*
Medical officer	60.9(14)	39.1(9)	100.0(.23)
LHV/FHS	33.3(5)	66.7(10)	100.0(15)
MPHS	50.0(4)	50.0(4)	100.0(8)
ANM/FHW	37.4(34)	62.6(57)	100.0(91)
Other health staff	56.8(21)	43.2(16)	100.0(37)
Total	44.8(78)	55.2(96)	100.0(174)

Table 10 ***Opinion of PHC Staff Regarding Various Programme Activities which they Feel Require More Time than Spent on them for Effective Service Provision, Gujarat, 2006***

Activity(s) which Require More Time	*Per cent Distribution+*		
	Male	*Female*	*Total*
Record-keeping	25.0 (7)	44.1 (30)	38.5 (37)
Family planning	17.9 (5)	17.6 (12)	17.7(17)
Immunisation	28.6 (8)	35.3 (24)	33.3(32)
Supervision work	21.2 (6)	4.4 (3)	9.4(9)
Home visits	7.1 (2)	4.4 (3)	5.2(5)
IEC activities (including health education)	7.1 (2)	7.4 (5)	7.3(7)
TB/DOTS programme	21.4 (6)	10.3 (7)	13.5(13)
Natal and post-natal care service provision	—	13.2 (9)	9.4(9)
All activities are affected	32.1 (9)	41.2 (28)	38.5(37)
Total	100.0 (28)	100.0 (68)	100.0*(96)

\+ Based on number of respondents who reported that time spent on various RCH activities was not adequate (refer Table 15), while the remaining respondents were excluded from the analysis in this table.

Percentages may add to more than 100 due to multiple responses.

Perceptions and Opinions about the RCH Programme

To ascertain the perception of the health staff regarding the nature of RCH programme activities that they carry out, they were asked to state whether they had carried out these same activities before the introduction of the RCH programme. In response to this query, it is satisfying to note that more than 70 per cent of the respondents see a definite change in the nature of activities carried out by them as a result of a shift in programme focus, while the remaining 30 per cent did not perceive any change in the nature of activities carried out by them prior to and after the introduction of the RCH programme (Table 11). This clearly indicates the need to provide some refresher training to enable this group to appreciate and understand the new approach of the RCH programme so that the same gets reflected in the execution of their role responsibilities.

Table 11 ***Perception of RCH Programme Among PHC Staff, Gujarat, 2006***

Designation	*Whether Carried out Same Activities before the Introducing RCH Programme*		
	Yes	*No*	*Total*
Medical officer	52.2(12)	47.8(11)	100.0(.23)
LHV/FHS	13.3(2)	86.7(13)	100.0(15)
MPHS	37.5(3)	62.5(5)	100.0(8)
ANM/FHW	14.3(13)	85.7(78)	100.0(91)
Other health staff	56.8(21)	43.2(16)	100.0(37)
Total	29.3(51)	70.7(123)	100.0(174)

Those who felt that there has been a change in the nature of activities after the introduction of the RCH programme, justified their responses by stating that new activities or initiatives such as adolescent health (41%), newborn care/identification and referral of high risk infants (39), early registration of pregnancy/ensure safe delivery, RTI/STI detection and promotion of condom use for protection against HIV/AIDS (20% each) were carried out by them (Table 12). The staff also perceived that ensuring "quality of services not merely quantity", (21%), surveillance and control of other diseases such as malaria, TB and leprosy (20%) and stress on IEC activities to create awareness and demand at the community level (11%) to be the other new initiatives under the RCH programme. As expected, the change in programme activities is better reflected in the responses of the female staff than the male staff (Table 12).

Table 12 *Perception of RCH Programme Activities Among PHC Staff, Gujarat, 2006*

New Activities/Initiatives Undertaken After the Introduction of RCH Programme	*Per cent Distribution+*		
	Male	*Female*	*Total*
Adolescent health	37.5 (12)	41.8 (38)	40.7(50)
Early registration of pregnancy	12.5 (4)	36.3 (33)	30.1(37)
Newborn care/neo-natal care/identification of high risk infants and referral	34.4 (11)	40.7 (37)	39.0(48)
Ensure safe delivery/five 'cleans' technique/safe delivery kit to be used	21.9 (7)	33.0 (30)	20.3(37)
RTI/STI detection among men and women	15.6 (5)	22.0 (20)	20.3(25)
Promote condom use for protection against HIV/AIDS/educate about HIV/AIDS	12.5 (4)	23.1 (21)	20.3(25)
Surveillance of other diseases and control of diseases like TB, leprosy	15.6 (5)	20.9 (19)	19.5(24)
Provide all services/ensure quality of services, not merely quantity	9.4 (3)	25.3 (23)	21.1(26)
Vitamin A programme	9.4 (3)	2.2 (2)	4.1(5)
Stress on IEC to create/awareness and demand at community level	21.9 (7)	6.6 (6)	10.6(13)
Infertility and its management	3.1 (1)	11.0 (10)	8.9(11)
School health programme	3.1 (1)	4.4 (4)	4.1(5)
Malnutrition among children/women	3.1 (1)	2.2 (2)	2.4(3)
Promote NSV	—	1.1 (1)	0.8(1)
Others	6.3 (2)	9.9 (9)	8.9(11)
Total	100.0*(32)	100.0*(91)	100.0*(123)

+ Based on those respondents who felt that RCH programme has certain additional or new activities/initiatives (refer Table 17).

* Percentages may add to more than 100 due to multiple responses.

Finally, the PHC staff was asked for their comments and suggestions regarding the RCH programme and its activities. Their responses, which are summarised in Table 13, reveal that quite a few respondents consider the RCH programme to be good because it is more organised and systematic/more effective for the reduction of IMR and MMR (14%), programme emphasises all aspects of maternal and child health (6%) and stress is on reproductive health (5%). On the other hand, some respondents felt that the programme is good but MCH activities are affected because of multiple workload (6%), female health workers have more workload than male health workers (6%) and PHC staff need refresher training under RCH (5%). However, a large proportion of respondents (32%) felt that while the programme is good, there is a need for improvement in logistics, supply and equipment. It is also disheartening to note that a little over one-third of the respondents did not express any opinion about the RCH programme, which is indicative of their apathy to the programme and which is likely to affect their work performance. This warrants the need to periodically include short refresher training programmes for the PHC staff.

Table 13 *Overall Comments/Suggestions of the PHC Staff Regarding RCH Programme, Gujarat, 2006*

Comments on RCH Programme and Its Activities	*Per Cent Distribution of the Respondents#*		
	Male	*Female*	*Total*
Programme is good...			
More organised and systematic/more effective for reduction of IMR and MMR	13.8 (9)	14.7 (16)	14.4 (25)
Stress on adolescent health	—	1.8 (2)	1.1 (2)
Stress on reproductive health	3.1 (2)	6.4 (7)	5.2 (9)
Emphasis on all aspects of maternal and child health	7.7 (5)	4.6 (5)	5.7 (10)
New components like leprosy/TB are good for health maintenance	1.5 (1)	—	0.6 (1)
Stress on management of ARI and other childhood diseases is a good feature	3.1 (2)	0.9 (1)	1.7 (3)
Programme is good but...			
MCH activities are affected because of multiple workload	4.6 (3)	6.4 (7)	5.7 (10)
PHC staff need refresh training for RCH.	1.5 (1)	6.4 (7)	4.6 (8)
Female health workers have more workload than male health workers	1.5 (1)	8.3 (9)	5.7 (10)
Government should improve residential facilities so that ANM can stay at sub-centre for effective service provision.	—	6.4 (7)	4.0 (7)
There is need for further improvement in logistics, supply, equipment, vehicle provision, staff availability and payment of incentives to grassroots workers on time.	24.6 (16)	35.8 (39)	31.6 (55)
There is not much change in programme activities.	6.2 (4)	0.9 (1)	2.9 (5)
No comments/cannot say	40.0 (26)	31.2 (34)	34.5 (60)
Total	100.0 (65)	100.0 (109)	100.0 (174)

Percentages may add to more than 100 due to multiple responses.

Summary and Policy Implications

The strategic shift in the implementation of the national family welfare programme and the inclusion of addressing reproductive health needs of men, women and adolescents under the RCH programme warrants the need to understand whether reproductive health components have been assimilated by the medical and health staff and how effectively these have been translated in service delivery. The present study was therefore undertaken with the main objective of understanding how effectively the RCH philosophy has been integrated in service provision within the health delivery system at the PHC level and to identify the weak components, which need to be addressed under the programme. A study of the time-use pattern of the PHC staff involved in service provision was considered appropriate to meet the primary research objective.

This time-use study was carried out in the rural areas of the state of Gujarat and covered 24 PHCs from the five natural geographical regions of the state, viz., Saurashtra, North Gujarat, Central Gujarat, East Gujarat and South Gujarat. The 24 PHCs were selected such that proportionately more number of PHCs was selected from those regions which have a greater number of PHCs. Data on time-use and other aspects of RCH programme were obtained by individual interviews with all the staff of the selected PHCs (MOs, LHVs, MPHSs, ANMs/FHWs, MPWs and vaccinators). A total of 174 medical and health staff, who were in position and available on the date of visit, could be interviewed to obtain the required data.

Knowledge of and Training Under RCH

The salient findings of the study in the first place reveal that the PHC staff had adequate knowledge about the various components of the RCH programme, which have to do with maternal and newborn health, anaemia control among women and adolescent girls, prevention and treatment of RTI/STI and HIV/AIDS, in addition to aspects related to infant and child care (such as timely immunisation, diarrhoea and ARI management), contraception and addressing men's reproductive health.

The results also bring to light certain important gaps with regard to training and service delivery, under the RCH programme. For example, majority of the male health supervisors and workers had not received any training under the RCH programme, probably indicating their lack of involvement in the new programme or if they are engaged in certain RCH activities, they are probably not carrying out service delivery as envisaged under the programme. The female health supervisors and workers appear to be better trained with regard to number of trainings and duration of training. Majority of the PHC staff, who had received some training found it to be adequate and four-fifths or more of them could rightly recall some of the important components of the RCH programme (covered in their training) such as early registration of pregnancy, identification and referral of high risk pregnant women and newborns, adolescent health, RTI/STI and nutrition. Less proportion of workers could recall aspects regarding gender and male involvement, interpersonal communication, IEC activities and behaviour change communication strategies.

Pattern of Time-Use

The analysis of time-use pattern at the PHC level, in a typical week, has revealed that the staff works for 5½ days in a week, on an average, (Saturday was reported to be a half working day) in service provision, with major part of time (about four days' worth of time) in outreach/community level service delivery, and about 1½ days in clinic (OPD/antenatal clinic). This time obviously varies by designation of the staff since the medical officers devoted more time (3–4 days) at the clinic against about two days in field level supervision. The female health staff is also spending some time at the clinic in conducting/supervising antenatal and immunisation services while more of their time (4 days) was spent in outreach activities. On the other hand, the male health supervisors and workers spend almost all their time in community/outreach activities. With regard to the type of activities carried out at the clinic and field level, in a typical week, the results highlight the fact that a major part of the time of the health workers in a week is spent on service provision for routine MCH and family planning activities (such as immunisation, family planning, ANC and child care) while that of the MOs is spent in conducting OPD. Another significant proportion of the time of the PHC staff was found to be spent on administrative work and maintaining records. The male staff was essentially spending time in the identification and management of diseases such as malaria, TB and leprosy. Very little time was reported to be spent by the male and female staff in reproductive health activities for adolescents, men and women.

An important objective of the present time-use study was to understand the timing of various activities carried out by the PHC staff during each day of the reference week and to assess the amount of time spent on different activities of service provision. The study had therefore obtained detailed data on time diary of activities, individually carried out by the PHC staff, during the one week prior to the interview. This time recall diary obtained data on the activities carried out by the staff with regard to the initiation and completion time of each activity for every day of the week in reference.

A similar pattern of activities observed in a typical week, has also emerged from the analysis of their time recall diaries of one week prior to the date of interview. The staff were found to spend 15 hours (less than two days of work) per week on clinic based activities and almost twice that time (a little over 28 hours or 3½ days) on field/outreach activities, which means that they are spending a little over 43 hours (that is almost 5½ days) per week in service provision. For each day of the week, the time spent on clinic activities is about 2–3 hours as against 5–5½ hours for field-based activities indicating that a lot of outreach/community level activities, as expected, are carried out by the PHC staff. An important finding from the time recall diary is the fact that reproductive health-related service provision, whether at the clinic or at the field level, is extremely poor as the total time spent on this activity by the PHC staff during the whole week is only 29 minutes (daywise range, on an average, is about 1–8 minutes). Educational activities also are low priority activities as only 16 ½ minutes are reported to be spent on IEC activities during the whole week at the village level.

An assessment of time spent by the different categories of staff on the various activities indicates that the medical officers had spent 45 ½ hours per week in carrying out their various duties in the field and at the clinic. A major part (21 hours) of the time of the medical officers had been spent in conducting the OPD clinic, followed by carrying out the school health programme (11 hours). Family planning work (especially duty at sterilisation camp) took up 3 hours of the weekly working time while record-keeping and administrative work took up two hours.

With regard to time spent on various activities by the male and female health workers and their supervisors, it is noted that the supervisory staff had devoted about 40–43 hours weekly in carrying out their responsibilities while the health workers had spent about 41 to almost 43 hours in service provision. However, it is important to note that the supervisors, particularly the male supervisors, claim to have spent a major part of their working week in administrative work/record-keeping, school health programme, attending meetings, etc. The male and female health workers on the other hand, claimed to have spent a large part of their time in family planning activities, immunisation work and antenatal care services.

Thus, the one-week time recall diary clearly reveals that medical officers are spending a major part of their time in OPD and other clinic level activity, followed by school health programme, *gram sabha* and other meetings, FP camps and administrative and record-keeping work, while the other staff of the PHC are largely engaged in family planning work, immunisation, antenatal care services, followed by other service provisions like school health programme, epidemic management, attendance at Gram Sabha meeting, etc., and record-keeping. More importantly, the focus envisaged in service provision for meeting reproductive health needs of men, women and adolescents has been ignored by the PHC staff not only during the family planning campaign months but also throughout the year, as noted in the typical week of activities.

In other words, family planning work, especially attendance at sterilisation camp continues to dominate in service provision of the health staff (22% of their time in a week). Another activity, which was found to take up more than one-fifth of their weekly time, i.e., again 22 per cent, was in conducting the school health check-up, (which was on-going during the study period) and attendance at Gram Sabha meetings. Other components which have taken up a significant proportion of time are immunisation (10%), antenatal care (5), treatment of minor ailments and management of chronic diseases (4% each), apart from time devoted to administrative work and record-keeping (7%). The one-week time recall diary has also attested to the low priority given to reproductive needs assessment (such as identifying and managing or treating reproductive infections) at the community level especially among men and unmarried adolescent girls as only 1 per cent of the weekly time was noted to be spent on this activity. A comparison of time spent on various activities during the one week prior to the interview vis-à-vis that spent in a typical week, clearly reveals that almost all the activities during the reference week are affected as a result of intensive family planning campaign period as well as the special school health programme, during this period. Nevertheless, the data clearly reveal that the RCH programme continues to function as the earlier family welfare programme with regard to service provision. A new focus which is more visible is that of identification and management of diseases like TB, leprosy and malaria.

Adequacy of Time Spent on Various RCH Activities

In response to a query on adequacy of time spent on various RCH activities, it is noted that more than half (55%), of the respondents were not satisfied with amount of time they could devote to various activities under the RCH programme while the remaining 45 per cent expressed satisfaction with the time they spent on RCH activities. Those who expressed that they could not give enough time were further asked to state the activities which demanded more time for effective service provision. In response to this, almost 39 per cent felt that all the activities are affected under the RCH programme due to shortage of time. Additionally, another 39 per cent felt that record-keeping, followed by immunisation (33%) and family planning (18%) require more time than they are able to devote at present. It is important to note from their responses that none could specifically perceive that they are spending very little time to meet reproductive health needs of men, women and adolescents, and that this important component (RH activity) demands more time than they are able to devote at present.

Perceptions and Opinions about the RCH Programme

To ascertain the perception of various cadres of health staff regarding RCH programme activities that they carry out, they were asked to state whether they had carried out these same activities before the introduction of the RCH programme. In response to this query, it is satisfying to note that more than 70 per cent of the respondents see a definite change in the nature of activities carried out by them as a result of a shift in programme focus, while the remaining 30 per cent did not perceive any change in the nature of activities carried out by them prior to and after the introduction of the RCH programme. This clearly indicates the need to provide some refresher training to enable this group to appreciate and understand the new approach of the RCH programme so that the same gets reflected in the execution of their role responsibilities.

Those who felt that there has been a change in the nature of activities after the introduction of the RCH programme, justified their responses by stating that new activities or initiatives such as adolescent health (41%), newborn care/identification and referral of high risk infants (39), early registration of pregnancy/ensure safe delivery, RTI/STI detection and promotion of condom use for protection against HIV/AIDS (20% each) were carried out by them. The staff also perceived that ensuring "quality of services not merely quantity", (21%), surveillance and control of other diseases such as malaria, TB and leprosy (20%) and stress on IEC activities to create awareness and demand at the community level (11%) to be the other new initiatives under the RCH programme. As expected, the change in programme activities is better reflected in the responses of the female staff than the male staff.

Finally, based on the opinions of the PHC staff about RCH programme, it is satisfying to note that they feel that the programme is good because it addresses new activities/initiatives like adolescent health, reproductive health, early and timely antenatal services and focusses on provision of high risk newborn care. Some have also reported that service delivery is more organised and systematic and that the focus is on ensuring quality of services rather than merely quantity. However, they have also expressed their views on the lack of time available to carry out various activities due to staff vacancies as well as poor involvement of male health staff under the RCH programme, which has increased the workload, particularly on existing female staff. They have also expressed the view that they need refresher training in RCH programme to carry out these activities effectively. A large proportion of the staff also felt that the RCH programme is good, but suffers due to inadequacies in logistics, supplies and inadequate sub-centre facilities.

Policy Implications

The results of the present study have clearly indicated that a change in nomenclature of a programme does not necessarily result in a change in the nature of service provision. The primary health centre staff is spending a major part of their time on family planning (especially sterilisation camp), immunisation, antenatal care services and OPD and clinic-related activities. The desired focus on reproductive health of women, men and adolescents is glaringly absent in day-to-day service provision. There is also a need to organise training under the RCHs programme to highlight the important aspects of the same in service provision. Needless to say, the programme cannot function effectively if the existing lapses in infrastructural facilities, logistics, supplies and equipments, as well as the critical human resources, (particularly staff vacancies and poor involvement of male health workers), remain unaddressed.

References

Caroline, W. et al., 2001. Measuring Staff Time Use in Public Sector Family Planning Clinics in Kingston Jamaica: A Comparison of Four Methods. Family Health International Final Report, Research Triangle Park, NC: Family Health International.

Janowitz, Barbara et al., 2001. How do Providers Spend their Time: Implications for the Costs and Quality of Reproductive Health Services. Paper presented at the 2001 Annual Meeting of the Population Association of America.

Janowitz, Barbara. 2006. Making Better Use of Provider Time in Reproductive Health Clinics. FRONTIERS Programme Brief No. 7, Washington D.C.: Population Council.

19

Health Modernity and Utilisation of Health Services

A Pilot Study in Madhya Pradesh

A.S. Dey and A. Shrivastava

Health status in India is distressingly low and is reflected in several health, fertility and mortality related indicators. The latest RCH round 2, 2002–04 (India, 2006) data available show that in 31 districts of India more than 60 per cent of girls are marrying below the legal minimum age of marriage. Of all births third and higher order births constitute more than 60 per cent. Full antenatal check-up is limited to a mere 16 per cent women. Similarly, only less than half (48%) of children are getting all vaccinations, about three-fifths (59%) of deliveries are being conducted at home, and in case of 57 per cent of newborn children mothers squeeze out milk from their breasts. The reported prevalence rate of tuberculosis, malaria, and complete blindness is 326, 556, and 337 per 1,00,000 population respectively.

The low health status has been identified as one of the important obstacles to human resource development and it is also a well-known fact that improvement of health status of population is an essential requirement for reduction of fertility and stabilisation of population. If proper knowledge about different services is poor then demand for services will also be very limited.

According to philosopher Kant, knowledge is based on the perception of external world. He further says that mind is active and forms into a system of knowledge all the materials brought in by the senses. There exists a difference between common sense knowledge and scientific knowledge. The common sense knowledge is viewed by 'man in the street', whereas the scientific knowledge is based on systematic knowledge. Conan (1951) defines scientific knowledge as an interconnected series of concepts and conceptual schemes that have developed as a result of experimentation and observation and are fruitful of further experimentation and observation. Reddy (1988) opined that common sense knowledge as acquired by direct sense perception and experience need not be wrong, but its limitation is that it will not be able to explain the inter-relatedness of a given phenomenon in a scientific manner.

It seems there exists a difference between cultural perception of knowledge and scientific perception of knowledge. Rappaport (1971) observed that one should prepare two models of the subject matter. One is cognised model and another operational model. The cognised model may be considered as part of a population's distinctive means of maintaining itself in its environment. The 'cognised model' includes components, such as supernaturals, where existence cannot be demonstrated by empirical procedures, but whose putative existence moves the actors to behave in particular ways. On the other hand, the 'operational model' is description of the same ecological system in accordance with the assumptions and methods of the science of ecology. Rappaport elucidates further by saying that this does not mean however a less accurate or more ignorant view of the world than is represented by an operational model.

Reddy (1988) gives example of tribe who tries to stop a typhoid epidemic by organising large scale witch-hunts operates logically in terms of the culturally established fact that witches are responsible for diseases. When people try to achieve the same end by inoculation and boiling drinking water, they also are acting logically on the basis of our culturally-established knowledge that disease is caused by bacteria. Most members of society have never seen a germ. By performing magician-religious ceremonies the tribals get the mental satisfaction that they've done everything in their power to cure a sickman or for a good harvest. A large part of the knowledge of social organisation, religion and rituals, etc., is transmitted orally from generation to generation.

Population Education Resource Centre (PERC) at Ranchi conducted an ICMR-sponsored Development of Modernity Scale Project (DMSP) and a Health Modernity Education Project (HMEP) covering four ethnic/religious groups in South Bihar (presently Jharkhand state). The study demonstrated that there exists widespread ignorance and misconceptions about family planning, child care, breast-feeding in different communities. It is suggested that low health status can be improved by scientific health education intervention in the community. Health modernity has been defined (Singh et al., 1987) as scientifically correct information, attitudes and behaviours in relation to physical health, mental health, family planning, and child care, personal hygiene and environmental sanitation and such other issues which are essential prerequisites for healthy living, and therefore, for human and social development. In this context, an emphasis on health modernity is much relevant. In this paper, an attempt has been made to administer a Health Modernity Scale, in the form of a interview-schedule in a pilot survey in Madhya Pradesh.

Objectives of the Study

- To assess health modernity attitudinal and behavioural scale.
- To study different components of health modernity.
- To observe factors influencing poor quality of health modernity.
- To study relationship between level of health modernisation and utilisation of health services.
- To identify area of ignorance and misconceptions in the community.

Location of the Study

The present study was done in the Sagar district of Madhya Pradesh state in India. Madhya Pradesh which was the largest state of India area-wise, is presently the second largest state after creation of Chhattisgarh as a separate state in 2000. The state is divided into 9 revenue divisions, which are further divided into 48 districts, 259 tehsils, 313 community blocks, 55, 393 villages and 394 towns. The entire state is divided into six geographical regions, namely Malwa Plateau, Northern, Central, South Central, South Western and Vindhya region. Madhya Pradesh is physically characterised by scattered settlements, sparsely populated, and difficult and inaccessible terrain and has the largest forest cover.

Sagar District

The district has 1.4 million population staying in 17 towns and about 2,000 villages in 10 thousand sq km area. The age at cohabitation is very low. Less than half of women use a family planning method. Only 28 per cent of births are attended by a skilled person. Full immunisation is limited to 32 per cent women. Half of the births are of third or above order. In short, Sagar district is characterised by low utilisation of health services.

Relevant information regarding attitudinal and behavioural aspect were collected from 500 eligible women in the age group 15–44 yrs from Sagar district of Madhya Pradesh covering equally from rural and urban area. Table 1 shows the background characteristics of women. About three-fourths of women belonged to households having joint family set-up. About half of women belonged to households having poor standard of living or poor economic group. A little less than one-third (30%) of women are illiterate. About one-fifth of women have no exposure to any mass media (newspaper/radio/TV).

Table 1 ***Characteristics of Women by Place of Residence***

Characteristics		*Rural*	*Urban*	*All*
Caste	SC/ST/OBC	76.8	71.2	74.0
	Higher caste	23.2	20.8	22.0
	Other	0.0	8.0	4.0
Type of family	Nuclear	14.8	66.0	40.4
	Joint	85.2	34.0	59.6
HH amenity	Poor	35.2	39.2	37.2
	Moderate	53.2	40.8	47.0
	Good	11.6	20.0	15.8
Per person income (Rs)	350 or less	47.2	45.6	46.4
	351–1,500	49.6	45.6	47.6
	1,501+	3.2	8.8	6.0
Standard of living	Poor	58.4	36.0	47.2
	Moderate	34.4	31.6	33.0
	Good	7.2	32.4	19.8
Age	15–24	18.8	24.0	21.4
	25–34	40.4	41.6	41.0
	35+	40.8	34.4	37.6
Education	Illiterate	35.2	24.8	30.0
	Primary/Middle	56.8	44.4	50.6
	High school	8.0	30.8	19.4
Engaged in any economic activity	Yes	34.0	33.2	33.6
	No	66.0	66.8	66.4
Exposure to mass media	Yes	77.2	81.2	79.2
	No	22.8	18.8	20.8
		100.0	100.0	100.0
N		250	250	500

Methodology

In this study an attempt has been made to administer a health modernity scale in the form of an interview schedule in a pilot survey in the Sagar district of Madhya Pradesh. Health Modernity Scale has two components, health modernity attitudinal scale and health modernity behavioural scale. The basic framework of the scale is done in an ICMR-sponsored study The first component has eight dimensions, physical health, mental health, diet and nutrition, obstetric care, immunisation, child care and growth of child, breast-feeding, and family planning. The second component is related to health habits and has two dimensions, personal hygiene and food habit. The themes included in physical and mental health are scientific understanding of the etiology, treatment and prevention, ignorance, and misconception. The diet and nutrition dimension deals with scientific understanding about nutritional values of food, cleanliness, etc. The family planning dimension deals with scientific understanding of child birth, son preference, birth control, etc. The obstetric care deals with correct knowledge about ANC/NC/PNC care. The child care dimension deals with knowledge about signs of dehydration, ORT, and milestones of development of children. The breast-feeding dimension deals with misconceptions about breast-feeding, advantages of breast-feeding, etc. There are ten items in each of the dimension scale and each of the items is measured on a five-point scale. A mixture of Likert and non-Likert type questions were considered. A maximum score of 50 in each of the dimension is allotted. The extent of health modernity has been reported in relation to percentages of the 'modern' scores. A 'modern' response is a scientifically correct answer representing information, attitudes and behaviours. Each of the eight dimensions of health modernity attitudinal scale, physical health, mental health, diet and nutrition, obstetric care, immunisation, family planning, and child care, and growth of child one who obtains a score of 40 or more is considered as 'modern' score. Similar scores are provided for each of the two dimensions of health modernity behavioural scale, personal hygiene and food habit.

Results and Discussions

Health Modernity

As mentioned earlier health modernity has two components, health modernity attitudinal scale and health modernity behavioural scale. The first component has eight dimensions, physical health, mental health, diet and nutrition, obstetric care, immunisation, child care and growth of child, breast-feeding, and family planning. The second component is related to health habits and has two dimensions, personal hygiene and food habits. The study shows that 40 per cent of women have 'very poor' health modernity having modernity scores less than 25 per cent of total score. Only 7 per cent of women have 'good score' having 75 per cent or more of the total score as can be seen from Table 2. Among the eight dimensions of health modernity attitudinal scale, immunisation modernity is found 'very low'. As high as more than four-fifths (82%) of the women have 'very low' level. Hardly 2 per cent of women have 'good' immunisation modernity. Further, it is seen 40–42 per cent of women have 'very low' child care modernity, obstetric care modernity, and diet and nutrition modernity. About 29–39 per cent of women have 'very low' breast-feeding modernity, mental health physical health, and physical health modernity. Very low level of family planning modernity is limited to 18 per cent of women. In health modernity behavioural scale, more than half (54%) of the women have 'very poor' level of personal hygiene modernity and also food habit modernity. Personal hygiene modernity is seen good by only 2 per cent of the women. A graphical presentation can be seen from Figure 1.

Figure 1 ***Level of Different Dimensions of Health Modernity***

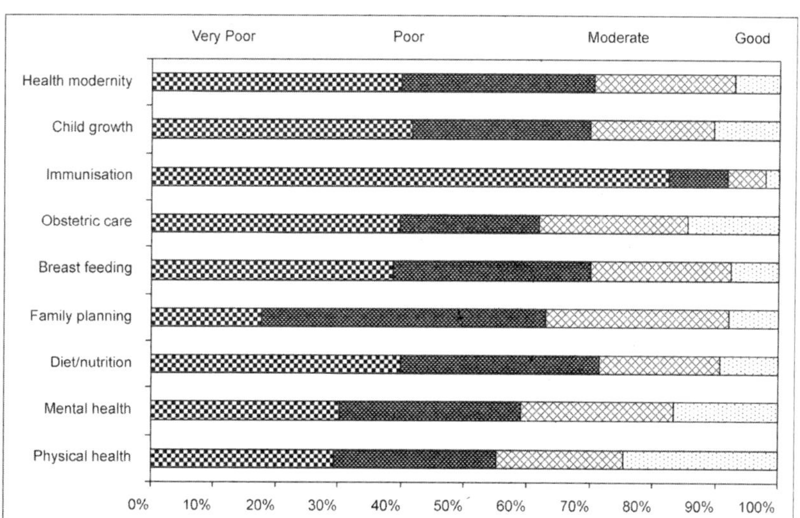

Table 2 Percentage Distribution of Women by Level of Modernity in the Different Dimensions of Health Modernity Attitudinal Scale and Behavioural Scale

Dimension of Modernity	*Proportion of Women Having Health Modernity*				*Total*	*N*
	Very Low	*Low*	*Moderate*	*Good*		
Health Modernity Attitudinal Scale						
Physical health	29.4	25.8	20.0	24.8	100.0	500
Mental health	30.4	28.6	24.4	16.6	100.0	500
Diet/nutrition	39.8	31.6	19.2	9.4	100.0	500
Family planning	17.6	45.2	29.2	8.0	100.0	500
Breast-feeding	38.6	31.4	22.4	7.6	100.0	500
Obstetric care	39.6	22.2	23.8	14.4	100.0	500
Immunisation	82.4	9.4	6.0	2.2	100.0	500
Child growth	41.6	28.2	19.8	10.4	100.0	500
Health modernity	39.8	30.6	22.4	7.2	100.0	500
Health Modernity Behavioural Scale						
Personal hygiene	53.8	34.2	10.0	2.0	100.0	500
Food habit	54.2	22.2	0.6	23.6	100.0	500

Health Modernity Differentials

Table 3 presents distribution of women in the three categories, 'low', 'moderate', and 'good' in the different dimensions of health modernity by their background characteristics. It is seen Illiteracy and poverty (which is reflected in poor level household income, standard of living index (SLI), and household amenity) are the main reasons of 'low' level health modernity. About three-fifths (72%) of illiterate women have 'low' health modernity. Nearly 70 per cent of women who are not exposed to any mass media are also seen to have low health modernity. More than half (58–63%) of women belonging to poor economic group have low modernity. Also, about half (48–49%) of women in rural area or women belonging to SC/ST/OBC community have low health modernity. In urban area, low health modernity is limited to 31 per cent of women. Health modernity is found 'good' among women having high school level education (34%), higher household income group (30%). However, immunisation modernity is found 'low' even among 44 per cent of high school level educated women. Table 3 also presents personal hygiene modernity and food habit modernity among different categories of women. It is seen about three-fifths (74%) of women belonging to poor health modernity have poor personal hygiene and food habits.

Table 3 ***Percentage Distribution of Women by Different Dimensions of Health Modernity Attitudinal Scale and Behavioural Scale by Background Characteristics of Women***

Characteristics		*Health Modernity Attitudinal Scale*								
		Physical Health			*Mental Health*			*Diet and Nutrition*		
		Low	*Moderate*	*Good*	*Low*	*Moderate*	*Good*	*Low*	*Moderate*	*Good*
Place of residence	Rural	33.6	49.6	16.8	30.4	58.0	11.6	54.0	44.8	1.2
	Urban	25.2	42.0	32.8	30.4	48.0	21.6	25.6	56.8	17.6
Caste	SC/ST/OBC	35.1	45.9	18.9	36.8	53.5	9.7	45.9	47.3	6.8
	Higher caste	9.1	44.5	46.4	8.2	51.8	40.0	21.8	60.9	17.3
	Other	35.0	50.0	15.0	35.0	50.0	15.0	25.0	60.0	15.0
Type of family	Nuclear	21.3	44.6	34.2	26.7	49.5	23.8	24.8	62.4	12.9
	Joint	34.9	46.6	18.5	32.9	55.4	11.7	50.0	43.0	7.0
HH amenity	Poor	45.2	45.2	9.7	46.2	48.4	5.4	52.2	42.5	5.4
	Moderate	23.8	48.9	27.2	24.3	60.0	15.7	37.0	55.3	7.7
	Good	8.9	38.0	53.2	11.4	43.0	45.6	19.0	57.0	24.1
Per person income (Rs)	350 or less	47.0	42.2	10.8	44.0	49.6	6.5	55.2	40.9	3.9
	351–1,500	16.0	51.3	32.8	20.2	59.7	20.2	29.0	58.4	12.6
	1,501+		30.0	70.0	6.7	26.7	66.7	6.7	66.7	26.7

Cont'd...

Cont'd...

		1.0	2.0	3.0						
Standard of living	Poor	43.6	46.2	10.2	42.4	51.3	6.4	55.1	41.9	3.0
	Moderate	23.6	49.7	26.7	26.1	57.0	17.0	34.5	55.8	9.7
	Good	5.1	38.4	56.6	9.1	50.5	40.4	12.1	63.6	24.2
Age	15–24	23.4	46.7	29.9	34.6	50.5	15.0	29.9	58.9	11.2
	25–34	24.4	48.8	26.8	25.4	54.1	20.5	38.5	50.7	10.7
	35+	38.3	42.0	19.7	33.5	53.2	13.3	46.8	46.3	6.9
Education	Illiterate	64.0	33.3	2.7	50.0	47.3	2.7	68.0	31.3	0.7
	Prim/Middle	20.2	60.1	19.8	28.9	58.9	12.3	35.2	59.7	5.1
	High school		27.8	72.2	4.1	46.4	49.5	8.2	57.7	34.0
Engaged in any economic activity	Yes	41.7	41.7	16.7	38.7	50.6	10.7	45.8	45.8	8.3
	No	23.2	47.9	28.9	26.2	54.2	19.6	36.7	53.3	9.9
Exposure to mass media	Yes	24.5	46.2	29.3	25.8	54.5	19.7	33.3	55.3	11.4
	No	48.1	44.2	7.7	48.1	47.1	4.8	64.4	33.7	1.9
All		**29.4**	**45.8**	**24.8**	**30.4**	**53.0**	**16.6**	**39.8**	**50.8**	**9.4**

Cont'd...

Cont'd...

Characteristics		*Health Modernity Attitudinal Scale*								
		Family Planning			*Breast-feeding*			*Obstetric Care*		
		Low	*Moderate*	*Good*	*Low*	*Moderate*	*Good*	*Low*	*Moderate*	*Good*
Place of residence	Rural	17.6	78.4	4.0	35.2	61.6	3.2	51.2	39.2	9.6
	Urban	17.6	70.4	12.0	42.0	46.0	12.0	28.0	52.8	19.2
Caste	SC/ST/OBC	21.1	71.6	7.3	43.8	52.2	4.1	44.6	45.7	9.7
	Higher caste	4.5	84.5	10.9	16.4	64.5	19.1	20.9	47.3	31.8
	Other	25.0	70.0	5.0	65.0	25.0	10.0	50.0	45.0	5.0
Type of family	Nuclear	16.3	73.3	10.4	35.6	53.5	10.9	26.7	52.5	20.8
	Joint	18.5	75.2	6.4	40.6	54.0	5.4	48.3	41.6	10.1
HH amenity	Poor	31.2	63.4	5.4	57.0	39.8	3.2	52.2	42.5	5.4
	Moderate	9.8	82.6	7.7	31.9	62.1	6.0	37.0	49.8	13.2
	Good	8.9	75.9	15.2	15.2	62.0	22.8	17.7	43.0	39.2
Per person income (Rs)	350 or less	26.3	70.7	3.0	54.7	42.7	2.6	56.0	40.1	3.9
	351–1,500	9.7	77.7	12.6	26.9	62.6	10.5	25.6	53.4	21.0
	1,501+	13.3	76.7	10.0	6.7	70.0	23.3	23.3	33.3	43.3

Cont'd...

Cont'd…

Standard of living	Poor	25.4	71.2	3.4	53.0	43.2	3.8	54.2	40.3	5.5
	Moderate	13.3	77.6	9.1	32.1	60.6	7.3	35.2	52.1	12.7
	Good	6.1	76.8	17.2	15.2	67.7	17.2	12.1	49.5	38.4
Age	15–24	21.5	71.0	7.5	43.0	52.3	4.7	35.5	57.9	6.5
	25–34	15.6	75.1	9.3	32.2	60.0	7.8	34.6	42.9	22.4
	35+	17.6	75.5	6.9	43.1	47.9	9.0	47.3	42.6	10.1
Education	Illiterate	31.3	68.0	0.7	64.0	35.3	0.7	66.0	34.0	
	Prim/Middle	15.0	79.8	5.1	36.8	59.3	4.0	36.8	52.6	10.7
	High school	3.1	70.1	26.8	4.1	68.0	27.8	6.2	47.4	46.4
Engaged in any economic activity	Yes	25.0	67.9	7.1	47.6	44.0	8.3	50.0	39.3	10.7
	No	13.9	77.7	8.4	34.0	58.7	7.2	34.3	49.4	16.3
Exposure to mass media	Yes	14.4	75.5	10.1	32.8	58.1	9.1	34.3	48.2	17.4
	No	29.8	70.2	0.0	60.6	37.5	1.9	59.6	37.5	2.9
All		**17.6**	**74.4**	**8.0**	**38.6**	**53.8**	**7.6**	**39.6**	**46.0**	**14.4**

Cont'd…

Cont'd...

Characteristics		*Health Modernity Attitudinal Scale*								
		Immunisation			*Child Growth*			*Health Modernity*		
		Low	*Moderate*	*Good*	*Low*	*Moderate*	*Good*	*Low*	*Moderate*	*Good*
Place of residence	Rural	94.4	4.8	0.8	47.6	47.6	4.8	48.8	49.2	2.0
	Urban	70.4	26.0	3.6	35.6	48.4	16.0	30.8	56.8	12.4
Caste	SC/ST/OBC	86.8	12.4	0.8	47.0	45.9	7.0	47.6	48.9	3.5
	Higher caste	69.1	24.5	6.4	20.9	57.3	21.8	11.8	69.1	19.1
	Other	75.0	20.0	5.0	55.0	35.0	10.0	50.0	40.0	10.0
Type of family	Nuclear	70.8	26.2	3.0	37.1	47.5	15.3	28.7	59.4	11.9
	Joint	90.3	8.1	1.7	44.6	48.3	7.0	47.3	48.7	4.0
HH amenity	Poor	91.4	8.6	0.0	56.5	39.2	4.3	63.4	35.5	1.1
	Moderate	83.0	15.7	1.3	35.3	56.2	8.5	29.4	65.1	5.5
	Good	59.5	30.4	10.1	25.3	44.3	30.4	15.2	58.2	26.6
Per person income (Rs)	350 or less	93.1	6.9	0.0	52.2	43.1	4.7	59.1	40.1	0.9
	351–1,500	75.6	20.6	3.8	32.4	54.2	13.4	24.8	64.7	10.5
	1,501+	53.3	40.0	6.7	33.3	36.7	30.0	10.0	60.0	30.0

Cont'd...

Cont'd...

Standard of living	Poor	93.2	6.8	0.0	53.8	42.8	3.4	58.5	39.8	1.7
	Moderate	83.6	14.5	1.8	37.6	50.9	11.5	33.3	60.6	6.1
	Good	54.5	37.4	8.1	19.2	55.6	25.3	6.1	71.7	22.2
Age	15–24	88.8	11.2	0.0	57.0	39.3	3.7	41.1	57.9	0.9
	25–34	75.6	22.0	2.4	33.2	54.1	12.7	33.7	56.6	9.8
	35+	86.2	10.6	3.2	42.0	46.3	11.7	45.7	46.3	8.0
Education	Illiterate	98.0	2.0	0.0	62.0	36.0	2.0	72.0	28.0	0.0
	Prim/Middle	87.7	11.1	1.2	40.3	56.1	3.6	35.6	63.2	1.2
	High school	44.3	47.4	8.2	13.4	45.4	41.2	1.0	64.9	34.0
Engaged in any economic activity	Yes	85.1	11.9	3.0	49.4	42.3	8.3	53.0	39.9	7.1
	No	81.0	17.2	1.8	37.7	50.9	11.4	33.1	59.6	7.2
Exposure to mass media	Yes	78.8	18.4	2.8	34.1	53.3	12.6	31.8	59.1	9.1
	No	96.2	3.8	0.0	70.2	27.9	1.9	70.2	29.8	0.0
All		**82.4**	**15.4**	**2.2**	**41.6**	**48.0**	**10.4**	**39.8**	**53.0**	**7.2**

Cont'd...

Cont'd...

Characteristics		*Health Modernity Behavioural Scale*					
		Personal Hygiene			*Food Habit*		
		Low	*Moderate*	*Good*	*Low*	*Moderate*	*Good*
Place of residence	Rural	68.4	30.8	0.8	36.4	63.6	0.0
	Urban	39.2	57.6	3.2	20.4	78.4	1.2
Caste	SC/ST/OBC	57.8	40.5	1.6	34.6	65.1	0.3
	Higher caste	36.4	60.0	3.6	10.0	88.2	1.8
	Other	75.0	25.0	0.0	15.0	85.0	0.0
Type of family	Nuclear	43.1	55.4	1.5	26.7	72.8	0.5
	Joint	61.1	36.6	2.3	29.5	69.8	0.7
HH amenity	Poor	58.6	39.8	1.6	47.8	51.6	0.5
	Moderate	57.4	40.9	1.7	18.3	81.3	0.4
	Good	31.6	64.6	3.8	12.7	86.1	1.3
Per person income (Rs)	350 or less	63.4	34.9	1.7	42.2	57.3	0.4
	351–1,500	48.7	49.2	2.1	16.8	82.4	0.8
	1,501+	20.0	76.7	3.3	13.3	86.7	0.0

Cont'd...

Cont'd...

Standard of living	Poor	66.9	31.8	1.3	41.9	58.1	0.0
	Moderate	50.9	47.9	1.2	22.4	76.4	1.2
	Good	27.3	67.7	5.1	6.1	92.9	1.0
Age	15–24	54.2	43.9	1.9	25.2	73.8	0.9
	25–34	51.7	46.3	2.0	28.3	70.7	1.0
	35+	55.9	42.0	2.1	30.3	69.7	0.0
Education	Illiterate	72.0	27.3	0.7	48.7	51.3	
	Prim/Middle	55.3	44.3	0.4	25.3	74.3	0.4
	High school	21.6	70.1	8.2	5.2	92.8	2.1
Engaged in any economic activity	Yes	62.5	35.1	2.4	36.3	63.7	0.0
	No	49.4	48.8	1.8	24.4	74.7	0.9
Exposure to mass media	Yes	47.0	50.5	2.5	23.2	76.0	0.8
	No	79.8	20.2	0.0	48.1	51.9	0.0
Health modernity	Poor	74.4	24.6	1.0	54.3	45.7	0.0
	Moderate	44.9	54.0	1.1	12.5	86.4	1.1
	Good	5.6	80.6	13.9	2.8	97.2	0.0
All		**53.8**	**44.2**	**2.0**	**28.4**	**71.0**	**0.6**

Ignorance and Misconceptions

Table 4 presents different types of ignorance and misconceptions in different types of health modernity. It is seen women believe in certain myths or misconceptions and are ignorant. In physical health modernity, the misconceptions are seen as: during an illness a patient should fast because he does not have the power to digest, HIV/AIDS is a curable disease, leprosy disease is due to curse of God. In diet and nutrition modernity, the misconceptions included: vegetables should be diced into small pieces so that they can be boiled/cooked properly, refined rice or *atta* is good for health than coarse one. In family planning modernity, the ignorance or misconception is seen about: any method of family planning should not be used before getting the first child, a son is necessary for the continuation of the lineage. In breast-feeding modernity, the myths are: HIV/AIDS women can't breast-feed the child, A mother should not breast feed her child during her illness as this may cause harm to the child. In obstetric care modernity, the ignorance is found in pregnancy is God's gift and its growth within womb is His wish, there is no need of any check during pregnancy by anybody and another as, delivery should be done by traditional experienced *dai* even if she is not trained for that. For immunisation modernity it is seen majority of women have very poor knowledge about different aspects of vaccination like number of doses to be given, interval between the doses, when to be given, etc. About personal hygiene modernity, a very little proportion of women did: brushing teeth in the night before sleep, washing mouth before sleep, washing hand with soap after toilet. In food habit modernity, less consumption of meat/fish/egg, milk, fruit, salad, etc., is seen (Table 5).

Table 4 ***Proportion of Women Having Very Low Score in Health Modernity Attitudinal Scale About Different Myths***

S. No.	*Item*	*Proportion*
I	*Physical Health Modernity*	
1.	During an illness, a patient should fast because he does not have the power to digest.	37.2
2.	HIV/AIDS is a curable disease.	33.0
3.	Unless there is some emergency or helplessness, one should try to keep away from a hospital.	29.2
4.	Leprosy disease is due to curse of God.	26.8

Cont'd...

Cont'd...

II	*Mental Health Modernity*	
1.	Persons who have been once insane should never be can entrusted with a responsible job.	43.8
2.	Pilgrimage can cure mental illness.	42.4
3.	One becomes a criminal due to insanity.	39.6
4.	Insanity is caused by evil spirits.	25.8
III	*Diet Nutrition Modernity*	
1.	Vegetables should be diced into small pieces so that they can be boiled/cooked properly.	84.6
2.	Drinking liquor in public does not look nice but if someone wants to, he can drink at home.	50.0
3.	Refined rice or *atta* is good for health than coarse one.	25.4
IV	*Family Planning Modernity*	
1.	Any method of family planning should not be used before getting the first child.	52.0
2.	A son is necessary for the continuation of the lineage, therefore even after the birth of several daughters until a son is born the birth of children should not be checked.	42.2
3.	Oral pill does not contaminate breast milk.	40.2
V	*Breast-Feeding Modernity*	
1.	HIV/AIDS women can breast-feed the child	51.2
2.	A mother should not breast-feed her child during her illness as this may cause harm to the child.	43.6
3.	Whether a child is breast-fed or bottle-fed it has a sense of oneness with its mother because a mother looks after the child.	27.6
4.	Even if a child is only breast-fed upto the age of one or one and a half years he can remain healthy.	27.2
VI	*Obstetric (ANC/NC/PNC) Modernity*	
1.	Pregnancy is God's gift and its growth within womb is His wish, there is no need of any check during pregnancy by anybody.	79.6
2.	Other health care (regular weight/blood pressure/green vegetables, milk, etc.) should be taken during pregnancy	44.0
3.	Delivery should be done by traditional experienced *dai* even if she is not trained for that.	37.6
4.	Proper knowledge of TT injection.	31.8
VII	*Immunisation Modernity*	
1.	Proper knowledge about IFA tablets	99.0
2.	Proper knowledge about DT/TT booster doses	98.2

Cont'd...

Cont'd...

3.	Proper knowledge about Vitamin A drops	95.0
4.	Proper knowledge about DPT booster dose	87.0
5.	Proper knowledge about Measles	62.0
6.	Proper knowledge about Polio	58.2
7.	Proper knowledge about DPT	56.4
8.	Proper knowledge about BCG	50.8
VIII	*Child Care Modernity*	
1.	What should be given to a child during diarrhoea.	64.0
2.	Signs of diarrhoea.	47.6
3.	Awareness about age at which solid food should be introduced to a child.	39.6
4.	Average weight of a healthy child.	30.2
5.	First milk of mother to a newborn child should be given.	27.6
6.	Age at walking by himself/teething of child speaking words	27.2

Table 5 ***Item-Specific Proportion of Women having Very Low Score in Health Modernity Behavioural Scale***

S. No.	*Item*	*Proportion*
I	*Personal Hygiene Modernity*	
1.	Brushing teeth at the night before sleep	90.4
2.	Using oil before bath	90.2
3.	Washing mouth before sleep	84.8
4.	Washing hand with soap after toilet	34.0
II	*Food Habits Modernity*	
1.	Meat/fish/egg	89.4
2.	Milk	84.0
3.	Fruit	61.0
4.	Salad	33.4

Health Modernity and Utilisation of Services

Table 6 shows level of health modernity and utilisation of different health services. Here, among the couples who had given birth during last their years, there level of health modernity and utilisation of different health services is seen. The table shows that among couples who have low level of obstetric modernity also utilised obstetric services in a limited way. Couples who had low score, only 46 per cent did 3 or more ANC check-ups, 49 per cent did first check-up during first-trimester. The corresponding figures for 'good' modernity score women are 87 and 88 per cent respectively. About three-fourths (73%) of low-scored women had not taken IFA tablets as compared to 22 per cent among relatively high scoring women. A little above one-fourth (26–27%) of low scoring women suffered any health problem during pregnancy or during the post-delivery period as compared to 13–17 per cent of better scoring women.

Table 6 ***Level of Different Health Modernity and Utilisation of Services***

Obstetric Care (ANC/NC/PNC) Modernity			
*Services**	*Low (N=74)*	*Good (N=54)*	*All (N=128)*
Three or more ANC check-ups done	46.0	87.0	63.3
First check-up done during first trimester	48.6	77.8	60.9
IFA tablets not taken	73.0	22.2	51.5
TT not taken	13.5	5.6	10.2
Delivery is done in a health institution	44.6	70.4	55.5
Suffered any health problem during pregnancy	27.0	13.0	21.1
Suffered any health problem during post-delivery period	25.7	16.7	21.9
Breast-feeding Modernity			
*Services**	*Low (N=96)*	*Good (N=32)*	*All (N=128)*
Breast-feeding by squeezing	30.3	10.3	24.2
Breast-feeding same day	69.7	87.2	75.0
Immunisation Modernity			
*Services**	*Low (N=101)*	*Good (N=32)*	*All (N=133)*
BCG not given	12.9	0.0	9.8
Any DPT dose not given	17.3	6.2	14.6
Any polio dose not given	14.3	6.2	12.3
Measles vaccination not given	37.8	37.5	37.7
Family Planning Modernity			
Services	*Low (N=314)*	*Good (N=186)*	*All (N=500)*
Current users of any family planning method	47.1	57.5	51.0

* Among women who have given a birth during last three years.

Among women who have 'low' breast-feeding modernity, 30 per cent breast-fed the child after squeezing as compared to 10 per cent women having 'good' breast-feeding modernity. About 70 per cent of women belonging to the first category of women breast-fed the same day as compared to 87 per cent from the second group. About immunisation modernity, a lesser difference among the two groups of women is noticed. In about 13 to 17 per cent of women belonging to 'low' immunisation modernity group any dose of BCG, DPT, or Polio was not taken, whereas, in the second group 6 per cent or less did not receive any service. Further, among women who had 'low' score in family planning modernity, 47 per cent are current users of any family planning method as compared to 57 per cent couples having better family planning modernity.

Risk Factors

Due to inter-relationship among many of the influencing factors, the health modernity differentials so far discussed among different sub-groups could provide only crude differentials. Many studies have used logistic regression analysis as a best-fitting and most parsimonious model that describes the relation between the dependent variable and a set of predictor variables. Three logistic analyses are carried out with the dependent variables as 'poor' health modernity, 'poor' personal hygiene modernity, and 'poor' food habit modernity. Women having score less than 50 per cent of the total score in the modernity scale were considered as 'poor'. The list of independent variables included place of residence, caste, type of family, standard of living, per person household income, household amenities, age, education, engaged in any economic activity, and exposure to mass media. For the second and third analysis, level of health modernity is also included in the list of independent variables.

Poor Health Modernity

Among the 10 variables considered here two variables, place of residence and education are the factors seen to negatively influence health modernity and are statistically significant at 1 per cent level. It is seen that the urban women have 62 per cent less chance of poor health modernity as compared to rural women. Also, women having primary/middle level education have 88 per cent less chance of poor health modernity, high school level educated women have 99 per cent less chance of poor health modernity as compared to illiterate women. Women who are exposed to mass media have 51 per cent less chance of poor health modernity as compared to those women who are not exposed to any mass media, although statistically insignificant. Similarly, it is seen women having poor economic condition (which is reflected in SLI, household income, household amenity) have less chance of poor health modernity as can be seen from Table 7.

Table 7 ***Estimated Logit Coefficients and Odds Ratio for Poor Health Modernity***

Characteristics		*Coefficients*	*Odd Ratio*
Place of residence	Rural	—	—
	Urban	-0.971	0.379**
Caste	SC/ST/OBC	—	—
	Higher caste	-0.278	0.757
	Other	1.830	6.235*
Type of family	Nuclear	—	—
	Joint	0.071	1.074
Standard of living	Poor	—	—
	Moderate	-0.532	0.588
	Good	-0.326	0.722
Per person income (Rs)	350 or less	—	—
	351–1,500	-0.649	0.523
	1,501+	-0.806	0.447
HH amenity	Poor	—	—
	Moderate	-0.187	0.829
	Good	-0.479	0.619
Age	15–24	—	—
	25–34	-0.539	0.583
	35+	-0.277	0.758
Education	Illiterate	—	—
	Prim/Middle	-2.156	0.116**
	High school	-4.381	0.013**
Engaged in any economic activity	No	—	—
	Yes	0.102	1.107
Exposure to mass media	No	—	—
	Yes	-0.718	0.488

* Significant at 5 per cent level ** Significant at 1 per cent level.

Poor Personal Hygiene

The logistic regression analysis with 'poor' personal hygiene modernity as dependent variable shows four variables, level of health modernity, education, SLI, and household level amenities are statistically significant in influencing personal hygiene. It can be seen from Table 8 that women belonging to 'good' health modernity group have 66 per cent less chance of 'poor' personal hygiene as compared to women belonging to 'low' health modern group. Women belonging to high school level education have 89 per cent less chance of 'poor' personal hygiene modernity as compared to illiterate women. Both the variables are seen statistically significant at 1 per cent level. Urban women have 23 per cent less chance of 'poor' personal hygiene as compared to rural women, although statistically insignificant. Women having better household income have 29 per cent less chance although statistically insignificant.

Table 8 ***Estimated Logit Coefficients and Odd Ratio for Poor Personal Hygiene and Food Habits***

Characteristics		*Personal Hygiene*		*Food Habits*	
		Coefficients	*Odd Ratio*	*Coefficient*	*Odd Ratio*
Place of residence	Rural	—	—	—	—
	Urban	-0.259	0.772	0.579	1.784
Caste	SC/ST/OBC	—	—	—	—
	Higher caste	0.076	1.079	0.461	1.585
	Other	1.170	3.221	0.681	1.976
Type of family	Nuclear	—	—	—	—
	Joint	-0.163	0.849	-0.063	0.939
Standard of living	Poor	—	—	—	—
	Moderate	1.005	2.731*	0.557	1.746
	Good	1.188	3.279*	0.948	2.579
Per person income (Rs)	350 or less	—	—	—	—
	351–1,500	0.083	1.086	-0.422	0.656
	1,501+	-0.217	0.805	-0.172	0.842
HH amenity	Poor	—	—	—	—
	Moderate	-1.059	0.347*	0.009	1.009
	Good	-1.130	0.323	0.435	1.546
Age	15–24	—	—	—	—
	25–34	0.368	1.444	-0.952	0.386**
	35+	0.173	1.189	-1.546	0.213**

Cont'd...

Cont'd...

Education	Illiterate	—	—	—	—
	Prim/Middle	-0.790	0.454	0.120	1.128
	High school	-2.166	0.115**	0.446	1.562
Engaged in any economic activity	No	—	—	—	—
	Yes	-0.626	0.535	-0.480	0.619*
Exposure to mass media	No	—	—	—	—
	Yes	-0.631	0.532	-0.734	0.480*
Health modernity	Low	—	—		
	Good	-1.090	0.336**	0.388	1.475

* Significant at 5 per cent level ** Significant at 1 per cent level.

Poor Food Habit

Here, three variables, age, engaged in any economic activity, and exposure to mass media are found to significantly influence food habit modernity. Women belonging to middle-age group (25–34) is found to have 61 per cent less chance of 'poor' food habit modernity, women belonging to relatively older age group (35–44) have 79 per cent less chance of 'poor' food habit modernity as compared to younger women (15–24). Women engaged in any economic activity are found to have38 per cent less chance of 'poor' food habit modernity as compared to women who are not engaged in any economic activity. Women who are exposed to any mass media have 52 per cent less chance of 'poor' food habit modernity. Strangely, it is noticed that variables like health modernity, education, SLI did not have a clear-cut relationship with food habit modernity.

Summary and Conclusion

In this paper an attempt has been made to administer a health modernity scale, in the form of a interview-schedule in a pilot survey in Madhya Pradesh. The objectives of the study are to assess health modernity attitudinal and health modernity behavioural scale. Eight dimensions of health modernity attitudinal scale, physical health, mental health, diet and nutrition, obstetric care, immunisation, child care and growth of child, breast-feeding, and family planning; and two dimensions of health modernity behavioural scale, personal hygiene and food habits are studied. Also, relationship between level of health modernisation and utilisation of different health services is seen. Various myths, ignorance and misconceptions prevailing in the community are observed.

The study shows that 40 per cent of women have 'very poor' health modernity having modernity score less than 25 per cent of total score. Only 7 per cent of women have 'good' score having 75 per cent or more of the total score. Among the eight dimensions of health modernity attitudinal scale, immunisation modernity is found 'very low'. As high as more than four-fifths of the women have 'very low' level. Further, it is seen 40–42 per cent of women have 'very low' child care modernity, obstetric care modernity, and diet and nutrition modernity. More than half (54%) of the women have 'very poor' level of personal hygiene modernity and also food habit modernity.

About factors influencing health modernity it is seen illiteracy and poverty (which is reflected in poor level household income, standard of living index (SLI), and household amenities) are the main reasons of 'low' level health modernity. About three-fifths of illiterate women have 'low' health modernity. 70 per cent of women who are not exposed to any mass media are also seen to have low health modernity. It is further seen about three-fifths of women belonging to poor health modernity have poor personal hygiene and food habit.

It is seen women believe certain myths or misconceptions and ignorance. In physical health modernity, the misconceptions are seen as 'during an illness a patient should fast because he does not have the power to digest', 'leprosy disease is due to curse of God', etc. In diet and nutrition, the misconceptions included 'vegetables should be diced into small pieces so that they can be boiled/cooked properly', 'refined rice or *atta* is good for health than coarse one'. In family planning, the ignorance is seen as 'any method of family planning should not be used before getting the first child'.

A linkage between health modernity and utilisation of different health services is seen. It is seen that among couples who have low level of obstetric modernity also utilised obstetric services in a limited way. Couples who have low score, only 46 per cent did 3 or more ANC check-ups, 49 per cent did first check-up during first trimester. About three-fourths of low scoring women had not taken IFA tablets as compared to 22 per cent among relatively high scoring women. Further, among women who have 'low' score in family planning modernity, 47 per cent are current user of any family planning method. The logistic regression analysis shows that place of residence (rural/urban) and education negatively influence health modernity and are statistically significant. Also, in personal hygiene, four variables, level of health modernity, education, SLI, and household level amenities are statistically significant in influencing personal hygiene.

The study suggests that there is a need to educate people to impart scientifical values about different myths, misconceptions, ignorance, etc., which are prevailing in the community. Perceived benefits about different aspects of obstetric care, immunisation, family planning, etc., need to be imparted to the community through entertainment education or self-help groups (SHGs).

References

Conan, James Bryant. 1951. *Science and Common Sense*. New Haven: Yale University Press.

India Summary Report. 2006. International Institute for Population Sciences, Mumbai and Ministry of Health and Family Welfare, Government of India, New Delhi.

Pappaport, Roy A. 1971. "Nature, Culture and Ecological Anthropology" in Harry Shapiro (ed.), *Man, Culture and Society*. Galaxy Book, New York: Oxford University Press.

Reddy, G.P. 1988. Socialisation for Modernisation in the Tribals. *Social Change,* Vol. 18, No. 1.

Singh, Amar Kumar, Meera Jayaswal and Azariah Hens. 1991. Understanding the Health of the Tribals. *Social Change*, Vol. 21, No. 1.

20

The Road Map to Hospitalisation

Tackling Health Problem in Rural Meghalaya

Sandip Mitra, Chaiti S. Biswas, Dilip C. Nath, Manoranjan Pal and Biswanath Bhattacharya

A study by National Council for Applied Economic Research (NCAER, 2002) has indicated that majority of the people in the N.E. depend heavily on public hospitals for treatment of major morbidity cases unlike most of the states in India. It further reasserts that poor patients depend heavily on public health services because the cost of treatment of illness is higher in private health facilities. This is rather a gross statement about the actual situation prevailing in this region. This may possibly be true for the critical conditions of morbidity cases when poor people have no other option but to go to the public hospitals, because they cannot afford to spend so much money to avail the facilities of private health institutions. But for other cases this may not be the actual practice. Do the common people in this locality avail the public facilities as frequently as they should? In order to answer this question one has to understand the problem in a more comprehensive manner. A deeper probing of the issue of dependence is required. A study on the health issues of the villagers in Meghalaya was conducted in 2004–05 to answer such questions. Though the detailed study was done on the households having had at least one member being hospitalised during last one year prior to the survey, the information collected from those households and from other sources shows the precarious condition of the people of villages in Meghalaya.

Before we go into the details of village conditions regarding the health facilities through the windows of the hospitalised cases, it is better to see the position of Meghalaya in a broader perspective. Economic condition of Meghalaya has deteriorated in the recent past and there are enough signals that the situation is worsening day-by-day (see Table 1).

Table 1 *Percentage of People Below Poverty Line in Different States in India*

State	*1987–88*	*1993–94*	*1999–2000*	*2006–07 (Projection)*
Andhra Pradesh	25.9	22.2	15.8	08.5
Bihar	52.1	55.0	42.6	43.2
Gujarat	31.5	24.2	14.1	02.0
Haryana	16.6	25.1	08.7	02.0
Himachal Pradesh	15.4	28.4	07.6	02.0
Karnataka	37.5	33.2	20.0	07.9
Kerala	31.8	25.4	12.7	03.6
Madhya Pradesh	43.1	42.5	37.4	29.5
Maharashtra	40.4	36.9	25.0	16.2
Orissa	55.6	48.6	47.2	41.0
Punjab	13.2	11.8	06.2	02.0
Rajasthan	35.2	27.4	15.3	12.1
Tamil Nadu	43.4	35.0	21.1	06.6
Uttar Pradesh	41.5	40.9	31.2	24.7
West Bengal	44.7	35.7	27.0	18.3
Manipur	31.4	33.8	28.5	30.5
Meghalaya	33.9	37.9	33.9	31.1
Mizoram	27.5	25.7	19.5	20.8
Nagaland	34.4	37.9	32.7	31.9
Sikkim	36.1	41.4	36.6	33.8
Tripura	35.2	39.0	34.4	31.9
Arunachal Pradesh	36.2	39.4	33.5	29.3
Assam	36.2	40.9	36.1	33.3
All India	38.9	36.0	26.1	19.3

Source: Tenth Five-Year Plan 2002–2007, Planning Commission, Government of India.

Percentage of poor in Meghalaya was less than that of all India average till 1987–88. After 1987–88, the situation has deteriorated. In 1999–2000, the percentage of poor persons was 33.9. The all India percentage was then only 26.10. The difference is more than 7 per cent. The projected figure in 2006–07 is much worse than this when compared to all India figures. The percentage of poor people in Meghalaya has been projected as 31.1 and the corresponding all India percentage is only 19.3. The difference has increased to 11.8 per cent. Meghalaya could not cope up with the other states in India. The condition is similar for other north-eastern states in India. This may be a reflection of the sustained neglect of the north-east zone.

Public health facilities per individual show a better picture for the north-east region in India when compared with the other states (Table 2). The average rural populations covered by one sub-centre, PHC and CHC were respectively approximately 4,500, 21,800 and 1,43,000 whereas the corresponding all India figures are approximately 5,400, 32,500 and 2,44,000 (Table 2). Again, this gives a wrong message to the general public. The states in the north-east region in India are on the eastern side of the Himalayan range. The people do not have easy access to many places of day-to-day necessity like schools, post offices, dispensaries, hospitals, etc. The population density in these places is also very low compared to other states in India. Thus the number of these establishments per unit area is also less. People have considerable difficulty to access the available public health system. This situation especially affects adversely the poor people in the society. (see Table 2)

Table 2 ***Government Health Facility for Rural Population***

State/union Territory	*Health Facility (number)*			*Average Rural Population (2001) Covered by One*		
	Sub-Centre	*PHC*	*CHC*	*Sub Centre*	*PHC*	*CHC (Lakh)*
Andhra Pradesh	10,568	1,386	219	5,226	39,844	2.52
Bihar	10,337	1,648	101	7,178	45,024	7.35
Gujarat	7,274	1,001	242	4,358	31,666	1.31
Haryana	2,299	401	64	6,511	37,329	2.34
Himachal Pradesh	2,069	302	65	2,650	18,154	0.84
Karnataka	8,143	1,676	249	4,275	20,772	1.40
Kerala	5,094	944	105	4,627	24,970	2.24
Madhya Pradesh	8,129	1,178	228	5,447	37,591	1.94
Maharashtra	9,725	1,768	351	5,731	31,523	1.59
Orissa	5,927	1,352	157	5,226	23,085	1.99
Punjab	9,926	484	105	5,625	33,148	1.53
Rajasthan	2,852	1,674	263	4,359	25,847	1.65
Tamil Nadu	8,682	1,436	72	4,016	24,282	4.84
Uttar Pradesh	18,629	3,551	287	7,061	37,043	4.58
West Bengal	8,126	1,262	99	7,105	45,749	5.83
Manipur	420	69	16	4,329	26,351	1.14
Meghalaya	413	85	13	4,488	21,805	1.43

Cont'd...

Cont'd...

Mizoram	346	58	9	1,301	7,759	0.50
Nagaland	302	46	9	5,417	35,561	1.82
Sikkim	147	24	2	3,269	20,020	2.40
Tripura	539	58	11	4,913	45,656	2.41
Arunachal Pradesh	273	65	20	3,181	13,360	0.43
Assam	5,109	610	100	4,551	38,113	2.32
All India	1,37,311	22,842	3,043	5,401	32,469	2.44

Source: Tenth Five-Year Plan 2002–2007, Planning Commission, Government of India.

Poor people have hardly any access to the costlier private health care system generally available in the towns.

In the current literature on development economics, health parametres are not treated in isolation with other development parametres. In this connection, literacy rate, gender issues may be mentioned along with the health parametres. Literacy is one of the most important development indicators. The literacy profile of Meghalaya is not better when compared with all India and other north-eastern states. Literacy rate of Meghalaya has been less than the all India rate throughout the period. On the contrary, other states in the north-east (NE) region are in a better position than Meghalaya and the percentage of literate people in most of these states is higher than the all India percentage (Table 3). Fortunately the gender gap in the education is much less in Meghalaya (5.7%) than the all India level (21.7%) as in 2001.

Table 3 ***Literacy Rate, FMR and IMR: Meghalaya vs All India, 2001***

Devt. Indicators	*Literacy Rates (%)*						*FMR*		*IMR*	
	1981			*2001*			*1981*	*2001*	*1981*	*2001*
	M	*F*	*All*	*M*	*F*	*All*				
Meghalaya	37.9	30.1	34.1	66.1	60.4	63.3	0.954	0.975	80	52
India	56.4	29.8	43.6	75.9	54.2	65.4	0.934	0.933	77	71

Source: Census of India, 2001.

The improved situation of gender bias is also reflected by female-male ratio (FMR) defined as the ratio of female population to male population. According to the 2001 census, the FMR in Meghalaya was been found to be 0.975 as against 0.933 in all India. Here it should be pointed out that Meghalaya is a matriarchal society. The female population gets equal if not more opportunities and freedom of movement. It is thus reflected through the indices of gender bias. Infant mortality rate (IMR) also shows considerable improvement from 80 in 1981 to 52 in 2001, whereas the all India figures for the same years are 77 and 71 respectively (Table 3).

The study was conducted in a small area of Meghalaya. Survey was conducted on the households that have had at least one case of hospitalisation in the year 2003–2004. Self-Reported Health Status (SRHS) data which records people's own perception of their health status have been collected. Studies with such SRHS data have been done by many Demographers like Allison (2004) for different kinds of research. After deep probing, it was observed that majority of these cases did depend on private facilities at the community level before hospitalisation. Over and above, the period of such dependence was quite significant compared to the period of hospitalisation. Thus a study on hospitalised cases reveal that the patients depend on private facilities at various stages before actual hospitalisation. This clearly explains how the management of diseases takes place due to poor accessibility to public health facilities of Northeast states.

This short study was undertaken in "West Khasi Hills", the largest district in Meghalaya. In addition, this district has the highest number of villages (914) in Meghalaya. Since we are more interested in understanding the rural health scenario, the selection of West Khasi Hills was perhaps appropriate. West Khasi Hills have a total geographical area of 5,247 square kilometres, which is found to be the largest among all other districts of Meghalaya. According to the 2001 census report, the population of West Khasi Hills was 2,94,115, with density as low as 56 people per square kilometre, the lowest among all the blocks in Meghalaya.

It was generally observed that most of the primary health centres in the West Khasi Hills were non-functional. We did concentrate on four community health centres at Nongflow, Nongstong, Moirang and Mokrah. The indoor registers of the concerned hospitals were consulted to find out the hospitalisation cases for the said reference period. Another independent study was undertaken at the household level around Moirang and Nongflow community health centres. The villages covered under the study were Nonkrem, Mawkarah, Sdodduki, Nongpriang Uming, Nonglang and Jakhong.

When investigating only the hospitalisation cases, one should try to address the problem by examining both pre-hospitalisation and post hospitalisation treatments simultaneously without concentrating on post hospitalisation treatments only. More specifically, one has to clearly understand the road map to hospitalisation in order to understand the aspect of dependence. In fact, we have observed in this paper that, the dependency of the people on private facilities is quite significant in the pre-hospitalisation period. Besides, we have also tried to understand the profile of the families with at least an incidence of hospitalisation. In this context, our interest centred on the patterns of diseases, the types treatments undergone and the extent of economic burden faced by the associated families. Some indices have been constructed to understand the hygiene conditions and standard of living of the people. The study has thus tried to examine broadly the technological view of health in some sense. Green (1997), Obrein (1995) have thrown some light on these aspects in a different context.

To summarise, the objectives of this study were to see:

1. the socio-demographic profile including standard of living and the hygiene profile.
2. the pre-hospitalisation efforts made for the treatment of the disease and the expenditures incurred thereof, and
3. the inter-relations between these variables of the affected households.

Collection and Compilation of Data

Our study was based on household surveys in the villages around four CHCs in the West Khasi Hills district. In all these villages, we had undertaken total enumeration exercise in order to find all the cases of hospitalisation from the village during the last one year, i.e., during 2002–2003. Only the households with at least a single case of hospitalisation in the preceding one year were considered for the study.

If we want to identify the people from the hospital records who visited the four CHCs from the six villages, it would be a gross under-enumeration because people from the six villages also have the possibility of visiting other hospitals. The household study is expected to depict a more clear picture. The aim of the survey is not only to find out the number of hospital cases by total enumeration, but also to find the inter-relations between variables using correlation and regression analysis. Since the villages were not selected by a proper sampling procedure, we refrain ourselves from drawing generalised conclusions. This study tries to open up the difficulties and problems faced by the patients and their family members at different stages of hospitalisation.

By complete enumeration of six villages, we could identify only 135 cases of hospitalisation admitted during one year preceding the date of survey. Schedules were canvassed among 135 households in order to get an idea about the health-related issues affecting these families. Our interest was to explain the road map, which was followed by the affected persons (target person) families prior to and during hospitalisation.

Economic condition is possibly the most important factor towards taking decision on the treatment of diseases. Since income data are not reliable enough, monthly per capita expenditures (MPCEs) of the households have been taken as proxy to the income. Type of dwelling unit, possession of durable items, land holding, etc., also reflect economic standard. In order to assess the standard of living, we had enquired whether the households were in possession of assets like chair, table, watch, radio, television, mattress, pressure cooker, etc., in addition to taking data on MPCE. Agricultural land was also considered an important factor in order to judge SLI of the households. Possession of livestocks was also taken into account, since many of the households had cattle, pigs, or chicken though not commercially bred. Possession of land, livestock and durable assets of the households has been combined giving appropriate weights to these items to get an overall index known as Standard of Living Index (SLI). The weights to these items reflect the importance of these items in the day-to-day life of the households and have been arrived at after consultation with the local people.

It is rather difficult to get a clear idea of the household assets of these families. We had to rely on the response of these households in order to get some idea about the level of living. Poor households dominated the village selected under the study. The concerned villages had very limited infrastructural facilities and scope of employment. Availability of agricultural land, livestock and some other household articles along with mattress, pressure cooker, chair, cot/bed, table, clock/watch, electric fan, bicycle, radio/transistor, television, bullock cart, hand cart, taxi/three or four-wheelers and many others were considered to get an idea about the standard of living of the concerned households.

It is expected that with the process of development people become more and more conscious, people are expected to adopt better health and hygiene habits. The habits of individuals play an important role in the decision-making process relating to health of an individual. Washing hands before meals, consumption of uncooked eatables, consumption of alcohol, use of mosquito net and footwear, brushing teeth and taking bath daily are some of the important habits in this respect. A Hygiene Habit Index (HHI) has been constructed taking into account different behavioural patterns which have direct bearing on the hygienic aspect of any individual. Appropriate weights have been considered in consultation with local authorities. Besides hygiene habit there are other aspects of hygiene, e.g., whether there is enough ventilation in the rooms, whether drinking water available is upto the mark, etc. Thus, we have constructed another index known as Hygiene Index (HI) reflecting all these factors.

Our main focus was on the profile of the target person and his health-related decision-making process. In absence of the target person (in case he is not alive) responsible member of the family was requested to respond. Since, this survey is not related to the clinical diagnosis of the disease we wanted to know the symptoms of the disease for which the patient needed hospitalisation. We were interested in knowing the history of illness of the target person and steps taken by the family to manage the crisis. We were keen to understand whether there was any gender bias in health-related decision-making of the family or not.

In addition to this, we are interested in knowing about his level of education and occupation in order to get a fair idea about the awareness level of target person.

In order to capture the series of activities by the family of the target person right from the start of the illness, data were collected about the time of illness and questions were asked regarding pre-hospitalisation activities in details. The practitioners/institution consulted at every stage was noted. The time, period of visit, diagnosis and total expenses incurred were recorded. In general, allopaths, homeopaths, ayurveds, pharmacy and quacks were the practitioners consulted besides the government hospitals. The government hospitals included PHCs, CHCs and district hospitals. In addition to this the expenses incurred for each visit were expected to play an important role in choosing the consultant visited. The sources of funds of the family were also recorded to examine if the illness has caused deterioration in the economic condition of the family. It was rather interesting to see if the target person or his family has changed the course of treatment quite often before hospitalisation. We also wanted to know whether hospitalisation was resorted to at an advanced stage of illness or not.

Focus was then shifted to post-hospitalisation episodes. The primary diagnosis (as known to the patient family) was recorded, the duration of stay and expenditures on hospitalisation were also recorded.

Expenditures on hospitalisation were collected under two broad headings—medical and non-medical. Admissions, bed charges, cost of medicines, cost of pathological test, surgery, blood, etc., were included under medical expenses. On the other hand, non-medical expenditure included lodging charges of patient families and other related expenses. We were eager to know about the outcome of this hospitalisation. It was enquired if the person got cured or not after his release from the hospital. The extent of indebtedness (if any) of these diseased families was also under examination. At last, we wanted to know if the target person was benefited in any way by the government or from his place of work.

Results and Findings

Profile of the Villages

The distribution of 135 cases across the villages is shown below along with the some features of the concerned villages. It is observed that Jakhong had the largest number of hospitalisation cases (Table 4).

Table 4 ***Summary Profile of the Six Villages***

Villages Investigated	*No. of Households*	*No. of Cases Found*	*Percentage*
Nonkrem	95	22	23.16
Mawkarah	385	35	9.09
Sdodduki	34	13	38.24
Nongpriang Uming	35	11	31.43
Nonglang	43	12	27.91
Jakhong	89	42	47.19
Total	681	135	19.82

Profile of the Affected Households

The study tries to capture in brief the characteristics of the households in which there were hospitalisation cases. The profile is neither an attempt to generalise the cause nor indicate the effects of the disease for which the individual was hospitalised. It only tries to highlight the demographic, socio-cultural and economic characteristics of the affected households.

Age and sex composition of the affected households have been described in the following table (Table 5). Out of 918 persons, there were 470 males and 448 females. As expected, most of the members of these households represented the 15 to 69 age group.

Table 5 ***Age and Sex Composition of the Members of the Affected Households***

Age	*Number of Males*	*Number of Females*	*Total Number of Patients Hospitalised*
<5	104	114	218
5–14	147	126	273
15–59	205	193	398
60+	14	15	29
Total	470	448	918

It may be noted that all the households under study belonged to Khasi community. However, it was observed that the decision makers in most of the households were males. Out of 135 households, only 30 households (22.2%) were headed by female members.

In order to find the level of education of the households, highest education in each of the households was recorded. The number of households against the level of education is presented in Table 6. Most of the households were illiterate.

Table 6 ***Level of Education of the Members of Households***

Level of Education	*Sex*		
	Male	*Female*	*Total*
Illiterate	56	12	68
1–4	19	10	29
5 or more	30	08	38
Total	105	30	135

Most of the households had more than one source of income. The main source of income was found to be agriculture. As many as 118 households earned their livelihoods from agriculture. The next important source was the daily wage labourer. Livestock also generated income significantly for many of the households. There was a clear seasonal pattern of monthly per capita consumption expenditure (MPCE). During winter, the maximum number of households had MPCE in the interval (Rs 2,200–3,000) and during winter it came down to about half of the summer expenditure. Almost 92.6 per cent of the households reported to have agricultural land. But, majority of land owners were small and marginal possessing land area of less than 0.5 acres only (96%).

About 51 per cent out of 135 households had semi-*pucca* houses. 43 per cent houses were *pucca*. Majority of the houses were two-room houses. There were three, four or more rooms also in some houses. The highest number of rooms found in a house was 15. But the housing conditions, so far as health is concerned, were not so good for the target households. There were some rooms without any ventilation. Nearly 44.4 per cent houses had at least one room with no ventilation at all. About 20.7 per cent houses did not have separate rooms for kitchen. Majority of the households (57%) did not have proper toilet facility. Only 5.2 per cent households had flush toilet. The rest 37.8 per cent either had the low-cost latrine facility or had the pit toilet facility. Our data also reveal that many of the households (35.6%) consumed rain water preserved in ponds. An equal number of households consumed water after precipitation. Only 3 per cent consumed water strained by cloth. No indigenous filter was used to purify water.

The source of lighting for a majority of the households was kerosene. Only 35.6 per cent of the households were fortunate to have electricity. Fuel wood was the only source of fuel for cooking. The cooking oil consumed was mainly mustard oil. Almost all the sampled households used mustard oil for cooking.

In order to understand awareness about hygiene among the people in the villages we-collected information on certain health habits. This is summarised in the Table 7.

Table 7 ***Health Habits of the Households in the Six Villages of Meghalaya***

Type of Health Habits	*Per cent of Households*
Did not wash hands before meal	11.1
Consumed uncooked food	10.4
Did not use mosquito net	38.5
Did not use footwear	2.2
Did not brush teeth daily	75.6
Did not take bath daily	3.0

Consumption of alcohol is usually very much frequent in hilly areas. Meghalaya is also not an exception. However, it was found that only 26.7 per cent consumed foreign liquor. And 71.9 per cent consumed country liquor. There were some households who possibly could not afford to consume even country liquor. They satisfied themselves with low grade of liquor of local make.

The villagers mainly depended on local/private allopathic doctors (45.9%) or visited the local CHC and PHC (44.4%), especially for their children. Poor households consulted local health workers or the chemists in the medicine shops.

Profile of the Target Persons

One of the objectives of the study was to know about the history of the illness of the target persons and the steps adopted by their families in the process of providing treatment to the affected person. We were also concerned about the basic demographic data.

Out of 135 persons, who were hospitalised during the year prior to the interview, there were 54.1 per cent males and 45.9 per cent females. There were 116 cases, who survived during the time of interview. So the survival rate was hopefully more than 85.9 per cent. More than half of these persons were married. More than 57 per cent of the target persons were illiterate.

According to the records of illness found to be diagnosed four distinct groups were identified after proper clubbing which was done based on the symptoms and in consultation with the doctors.

1. Cold, cough and asthma.
2. Cholera, gastric, dysentery and jaundice.
3. Diphtheria, malaria, fever and tuberculosis.
4. Others.

The places that were visited before hospitalisation were Community Health Centres (CHC), Primary Health Centres (PHC), and Health Workers (HW), Chemists (CH), Midwifes (MW), Mystics, etc. It was found that the target persons had gone through three stages of treatments on an average before being hospitalised. Most of them went to chemists as the first visit (59.2%). These chemists not only kept allopathic medicines but also kept homeopathy and tribal medicines. Along with maintaining the shops, these chemists also practice treatments of diseases. A portion of the patients was forced to visit CHC or hospitals on their second visit. In the third visit, there were more cases of hospitalisation or visit to CHC. Attempts were made to see if level of education has any relation with the pattern of visits. However, no clear pattern emerged.

It was assumed that the standard of living of the affected families would play a considerable role in the decision-making at various stages. It was found that people with high SLI depended more on CHCs compared to people with low CHCs at least for the first visit (Table 8). But there was no such relation with the HI (Table 9).

Table 8 ***Visits to Health Clinics vs SLI of the Households in the Six Villages of Meghalaya (First Visit)***

Type of Health Clinic	*Institution Visit*	
	Low SLI	*High SLI*
CHC and Hosp.	8	21
Chemist	53	27
Others	14	12

Table 9 ***Visits to Health Clinics vs HI of the Households in the Six Villages of Meghalaya (First Visit)***

Type of Health Clinic	*Institution Visit*		
	Low HI	*High HI*	*Total*
CHC and Hosp.	15	14	29
Chemist	35	45	80
Others	12	14	26
Total	62	73	135

It was also noticed that the medical expenditures increased with the stages of visits. Also the pattern of visits at different stages depended heavily on the monthly per capita expenditures (MPCEs) of the families (Table 10).

Table 10 ***MPCE vs Type of Visit to Health Clinics***

Stage of Visit	*Type of Health Clinic*	*MPCE*	
		Less than Rs 350	*More than Rs 350*
Ist Visit	CHC	21	5
	Hosp.	2	1
	Others	60	46
	Total	83	52
2nd Visit	CHC	53	40
	Hosp.	10	4
	Others	9	7
	Total	72	51

The study was conducted in an area where most of the people are below poverty line. We tried to understand how they managed their funds for medical treatment. Nearly 54 households out of 135 households managed the expenditures of their own, i.e., without taking any loan from others. Families of the majority of the patients (79), however, had to depend on the friends and relatives for funds. There was no significant involvement of money lenders. It shows how strong the inter-personal bondage is among the people in the tribal community.

In our study on the Khasi community, the female members were found to go to CHC more frequently than the male members, especially as the first visit. The amount spent for female patients was also more than that of males. This might be due to the specific kinds of diseases that usually need more expenses for the females.

Inter-relations among these variables can be best judged by correlation and regression analysis. For this, we selected a few of the variables collected from the villages, which are thought to be important for the purpose. The variables taken were as follows:

1. *Hhsize:* Household size.
2. *TotExHH:* Total monthly expenditure of the household.
3. *PcExHH:* Per capita monthly expenditure of the household.
4. *MedExp:* Medical expenditure of the target person due to the disease for which hospitalisation was necessary.
5. *NonMdExp:* Non-medical expenditure of the family of the target person due to the disease for which hospitalisation was necessary.
6. *TotExHos:* Sum of MedExp and NonMdExp.
7. *SexHoH:* Sex of head of household.
8. *AgeHoH:* Age of head of household.
9. *EduHoH:* Education of head of household.
10. *EduMo:* Education level of mother of the target person.
11. *EduFa:* Education level of father of the target person.
12. *Inc1:* Primary monthly income of the household.
13. *Inc2:* Secondary monthly income of the household.
14. *Land:* Total land possessed by the household.
15. *SLI:* Standard of living index of the household.
16. *HI:* Hygiene index of the household.
17. *HHI:* Hygiene habit index of the target person.
18. *Survival:* Survival status of the target person.

These variables can be put in some groups. Different expenditures of the household and the target person can be put in one group (S. Nos. 2–6). Sex, age and education of the head of household and education of mother and father of the target person can be put in a group (S. Nos. 7–11). Primary and secondary incomes of the household constitute another group (S. Nos. 12 and 13). The three indices signifying standard of the family form another group (S. Nos. 15–17). Besides, we had household size (S. No. 1), total land possessed by the household (S. No. 14) and the survival status of the target person (S. No. 18).

The product moment correlations between pairs of variables for different pairs have been computed and are shown in Table 11. Some variables like sex of head of household (SexHoH) and survival status of the target person (Survival), are binary and the product moment correlations using these variables, strictly speaking, are not valid for testing significance with usual test statistic. We have thus restrained ourselves from making any significance tests of the correlation coefficients. It should also be noted that apart from binary variables there are also some variables which are discrete in nature (e.g., level of education of head of household and the parents of the target person—EduHoH, EduMo, EduFa). But these variables do not pose much problem since these variables take a wide range of discrete values. Again income from primary source (Inc1) and income from secondary source (Inc2) are not continuous in our case. Instead of actual values we have taken codes for income intervals. However, in all these cases the values of the correlation coefficients give us an idea of associations and the degree of such associations. This helps us in selecting appropriate variables in regression analysis especially when there is a restriction in increasing the number of regressors beyond a certain point because of multicollinearity problem related with his/her age. Older members had less income than the younger members who were heads of households. Age of head of household was also negatively correlated with income but positively correlated with land possessed. Younger heads of households did not depend much on land. Elder members of the families are prone to earn their livelihood through traditional means, i.e., through agricultural lands. Surprisingly, the standard of living and hygiene level were more for households with older heads. As expected, level of education has positive correlations with standard of living of the household (SLI) and hygiene habit index (HHI).

There was another interesting finding. Medical expenses for the surviving patients were less compared to the medical expenses for the patients who did not survive. This was because the medical expenditures were usually high for critical conditions.

Some striking features came out from the correlation analysis. First, though the usual test of significance for the product moment correlation is not valid for binary variables, SexHoH was not found to have high values of correlations with any of the other variables. Was it because there was less gender disparity in this region? Since SexHoH is a binary variable, interpretations should be made accordingly. The binary variable assumed the value '1' for male and '2' for female. Thus, a positive correlation implies the value to be more for female than for male.

Household size had high positive correlation with total monthly expenditure of the household (HH) but negative correlation with per capita monthly expenditure of the HH. It means that increase of income could not match increase of the family size. It was positively correlated with the age of head of the household which is quite expected. Household size was also found to be positively correlated with land possessed. As HHSize was also positively correlated with the age of head of the household it explained why HHSize was also positively correlated with land possessed. Elder members were more likely to be more dependent on land whereas newly married couples with small HHSize earned their livelihood through some other non-traditional means. The value of the correlation coefficient between age of head of household and land possessed was significantly positive. Two other significant correlations found with HHSize were survival status of the target person and hygiene habit index both being negative. The explanation for these can be sought in some other common variable(s) acting simultaneously on these variables.

Primary income has been found to be directly related with the level of education of the head of the family. But it is negatively related with land possessed. Is it because income from land goes to secondary income? Observe that primary and secondary incomes are strongly negatively correlated. Primary income is also negatively related with the three indices SLI, HI and HHI whereas secondary income is positively related with SLI, HI and HHI, which calls for further investigation. The three indices SLI, HI and HHI are correlated to each other and are related with many other variables. These are mostly positively correlated with other variables except survival status and primary income. Also HHI has been found to be negatively correlated with HH Size.

Besides correlations, we have carried out some regression analysis to see the dependency of a variable on a set of other variables. To start with we have taken the three indices SLI, HI and HHI. To see the variables which have influence on SLI, HI and HHI we have regressed each of these three variables on a set of other variables. Since we have initially taken a large number of regressors test for multicollinearity was necessary for each regression. This was done through the condition index. Depending on the value of the condition index we have removed some variables one by one until we got satisfactory level of condition index. For this we had to remove that variable which has most

Table 11 ***Product Moment Correlations Between Different Pairs of Variables***

	HH Size	*ToTE xHH*	*PcEx HH*	*Med Exp*	*NonMd Exp*	*Tot ExHos*	*Sex HoH*	*Age HoH*	*Edu HoH*	*EduMo*	*EduFa*	*Inc1*	*Inc2*	*Land*	*SLI*	*HI*	*HHI*	*Survival*
HHSize	1.00	0.62	-0.59	0.06	0.03	0.05	-0.12	0.40	-0.14	-0.09	-0.11	-0.21	0.09	0.28	0.04	0.13	-0.19	-0.17
TotExHH	0.62	1.00	0.14	-0.09	-0.12	-0.10	-0.15	0.46	-0.14	-0.21	-0.12	-0.06	0.06	0.23	0.02	0.28	-0.01	-0.02
PcExHH	-0.59	0.14	1.00	-0.16	-0.16	-0.16	-0.02	-0.02	0.08	-0.15	-0.03	0.22	-0.04	-0.15	-0.03	0.08	0.26	0.19
MedExp	0.06	-0.09	-0.16	1.00	0.93	1.00	-0.03	0.03	-0.02	-0.08	-0.06	-0.01	-0.03	0.05	0.07	0.07	-0.00	-0.32
NonMdEp	0.03	-0.12	-0.16	0.93	1.00	0.96	-0.00	0.02	-0.08	-0.11	-0.11	-0.05	0.01	0.04	0.08	0.09	0.05	-0.33
TotExHs	0.05	-0.10	-0.16	1.00	0.96	1.00	-0.03	0.02	-0.03	-0.09	-0.07	-0.02	-0.02	0.05	0.07	0.08	0.01	-0.33
SexHoH	-0.12	-0.15	-0.02	-0.03	-0.00	-0.03	1.00	0.05	-0.03	0.09	-0.12	-0.04	0.03	0.09	0.09	0.05	0.10	-0.04
AgeHoH	0.40	0.46	-0.02	0.03	0.02	0.02	0.05	1.00	-0.28	-0.17	-0.22	-0.24	-0.01	0.27	0.21	0.35	0.07	-0.03
EduHoH	-0.14	-0.14	0.08	-0.02	-0.08	-0.03	-0.03	-0.28	1.00	0.29	0.59	0.25	-0.11	-0.19	0.22	0.17	0.23	0.11
EduMo	-0.09	-0.21	-0.15	-0.08	-0.11	-0.09	0.09	-0.17	0.29	1.00	0.41	0.05	-0.07	0.05	0.30	0.06	0.11	0.12
EduFa	-0.11	-0.12	-0.03	-0.06	-0.11	-0.07	-0.12	-0.22	0.59	0.41	1.00	0.16	-0.20	-0.03	0.23	0.01	0.08	0.05
Inc1	-0.21	-0.06	0.22	-0.01	-0.05	-0.02	-0.04	-0.25	0.25	0.05	0.16	1.00	-0.64	-0.25	-0.35	-0.29	-0.17	0.05
Inc2	0.09	0.06	-0.04	-0.03	0.01	-0.02	0.03	-0.01	-0.11	-0.07	-0.20	-0.64	1.00	-0.01	0.24	0.18	0.15	-0.08
Land	0.28	0.23	-0.15	0.05	0.04	0.05	0.09	0.27	-0.19	0.05	-0.03	-0.25	-0.01	1.00	0.16	0.18	-0.18	0.02
SLI	0.04	0.02	-0.03	0.07	0.08	0.07	0.09	0.21	0.22	0.30	0.23	-0.35	0.24	0.16	1.00	0.58	0.49	-0.13
HI	0.13	0.28	0.08	0.07	0.09	0.08	0.05	0.35	0.17	0.06	0.01	-0.29	0.18	0.18	0.58	1.00	0.43	-0.11
HHI	-0.19	-0.01	0.26	-0.00	0.05	0.01	0.10	0.07	0.23	0.11	0.08	-0.17	0.15	-0.18	0.49	0.43	1.00	-0.02
Survival	-0.17	-0.02	0.19	-0.32	-0.33	-0.33	-0.04	-0.03	0.11	0.12	0.05	0.05	-0.08	0.02	-0.13	-0.11	-0.02	1.00

non-significant coefficient or high variance inflation factor. Ultimately, the following regression equations were arrived:

$$\text{SLI} = \underset{(.353)}{2.081} + \underset{(.001)}{0.099}\,(\text{AgeHoH}) + \underset{(.458)}{0.536}\,(\text{SexHoH}) + \underset{(.000)}{0.307}\,(\text{EduHoH}) - \underset{(.342)}{0.145}\,(\text{HHSize}) - \underset{(.303)}{0.00398}\,(\text{PcExpHH}) \quad \ldots (1.1)$$

(R square = 0.139, p-value = 0.002)

$$\text{HI} = \underset{(.030)}{1.140} + \underset{(.000)}{0.0383}\,(\text{AgeHoH}) + \underset{(.449)}{0.181}\,(\text{SexHoH}) + \underset{(.000)}{0.103}\,(\text{EduHoH}) - \underset{(.246)}{0.0521}\,(\text{HHSize}) + \underset{(.026)}{0.000414}\,(\text{TotExpHH}) \quad \ldots (1.2)$$

(R square = 0.230, p-value = 0.000)

$$\text{HHI} = \underset{(.000)}{2.507} + \underset{(.067)}{0.0161}\,(\text{AgeHoH}) + \underset{(.285)}{0.235}\,(\text{SexHoH}) + \underset{(.004)}{0.078}\,(\text{EduHoH}) + \underset{(.002)}{0.00287}\,(\text{PcExpHH}) - \underset{(.447)}{0.000112}\,(\text{TotExpHH}) \quad \ldots (1.3)$$

(R square = 0.148, p-value = 0.001)

Observe that age, sex and education level of head of household have positive influence on these indices. Though there is a positive marginal influence of head of 'family being female compared to head of family being male' (SexHoH =1 for male and SexHoH=2 for female) on these indices, the effect is not pronounced. Because the coefficients of SexHoH are not significant for any of the regression equations, we can only say that there is a slight positive marginal influence of the gender of head of family in favour of female on these indices. HHSize has negative influence on these indices. But none of the coefficients are significant. Total expenditure of the household has positive influence on HI. In the other cases, it is not significant. Per capita expenditure also has positive influence whenever significant. Thus, older generation and educated families are more prone to observe hygiene conditions and habit and raise the standard of living of the families.

We were also interested in looking at the variables which influences the expenditure on hospitalisation. The most important variable is the type of illness. There is no way to incorporate this variable into the regression analysis. This is because the sample size is too small to analyse for so many diseases. We have performed the regression of the hospital expenditure on many other variables like SLI, HHI, PcExpHH, TotExpHH, etc. But in none of the cases we got significant coefficients.

Another interesting case is the HHSize. To see the variables which may influence HHSize of the household we have regressed HHSize on different variables. The ultimate result after eliminating the highly non-significant variables is as follows:

$$\begin{aligned} \text{HHSize} = {} & \underset{(.000)}{9.703} + \underset{(.000)}{0.0876}\,(\text{AgeHoH}) - \underset{(.264)}{0.0699}\,(\text{SLI}) \\ & + \underset{(.093)}{0.298}\,(\text{HI}) - \underset{(.450)}{0.143}\,(\text{HHI}) + \underset{(.323)}{0.0000286}\,(\text{TotExHos}) \\ & - \underset{(.000)}{0.00169}\,(\text{PcExpHH}) - \underset{(.013)}{1.016}\,(\text{SexHoH}) \qquad \ldots (1.4) \\ & (R\ \text{square} = 0.521,\ p\text{-value} = 0.000) \end{aligned}$$

None of the SLI, HI or HHI has significant effect on HHSize. Standard of living as expected has a negative influence. Most significant influences were due to age of head of household and per capita expenditure of the household. Per capita expenditure is a proxy variable to income of the household. Household size is known to be negatively related with the income. The positive effect of age of household head is plainly due to its direct relation with the duration of married life. We have not found sex of head of household significantly correlated with any other variables. Interestingly enough, the partial effect of this variable on household size has been found to be significant at 5 per cent level. If we fix the standard of living, hygiene level, age of head of household, etc., to be constant then the household size in female-headed households is less than the household size in male-headed households. This may be because the female heads in most cases took charge of the families after the death of their male counterparts.

The most interesting part of regression analysis in this case is to see the effect of relevant variables on the survival status. Again, here we could not take type of illness due to small sample size. Since survival status is a binary variable the usual regression analysis is not advisable. We have performed the logistic regression. The final result of the logistic regression is as follows:

$$\begin{aligned} P\,(\text{Survival}) = {} & \underset{(.791)}{0.295} - \underset{(.030)}{0.163}\,(\text{SLI}) + \underset{(.014)}{0.008}\,(\text{PcExpHH}) + \underset{(.813)}{0.0001}\,(\text{TotExHos}) \\ & + \underset{(.058)}{0.384}\,(\text{EduMo}) + \underset{(.746)}{0.037}\,(\text{EduFa}) \ldots (1.5) \end{aligned}$$

(-2 Log likelihood value = 96.064, and Cox and Snell R square = 0.096).

The regression gives expected results. The coefficients have right signs except for standard of living index. Standard of living index reduces probability of survival of a person whereas all other variables namely per capita expenditure of household, total expenditure at hospital and education of mother and father raise the probability of survival. Per capita expenditure of household and total expenditure at hospital has pronounced effect on survival probability. The effect of other two variables is not so pronounced. We may however replace education levels of the parents by education level of mother only with no significant changes in the result. But the coefficient of level of education of mother of the family becomes marginally significant at 5 per cent level. This is because the education level of father does not have much effect on the survival status as is seen by the significance level. The logistic regression is then

$$\begin{aligned} P\,(\text{Survival}) = {} & \underset{(.767)}{0.327} - \underset{(.033)}{0.155}\,(\text{SLI}) + \underset{(.014)}{0.008}\,(\text{PcExpHH}) + \underset{(.757)}{0.0001}\,(\text{TotExHos}) \\ & + \underset{(.044)}{0.399}\,(\text{EduMo}) \ldots \quad (1.7) \end{aligned}$$

(-2 Log likelihood value = 96.172, and Cox and Snell R square = 0.095 and Nagel kerke R square = .171)

Conclusion

The study has attempted to show the various stages of treatments of diseased persons followed in the villages of Meghalaya. It has been found that a large unorganised private sector is active in the north-east.

There are some interesting findings which resulted from correlation analysis. Total monthly expenditure (TotExHH) and per capita monthly expenditure (PcExHH) did not go together because of the intervening HHSize. AgeHoH was very much positively related with TotExHH but showed almost no relation with PcExHH. On the other hand, primary income was positive with PcExHH and had no relation with TotExHH. The same comments hold for HI, HHI and survival status. Medical and non-medical expenditures were not much related with other variables except on themselves. However, they have been found to be negatively related with survival status. Those who succumbed to death did actually cost a lot to the family.

From regression analysis, it has been seen that older generation and educated families are more prone to observing hygiene conditions and habit and raise the standard of living of the families. Most significant and well-known influences on the household size were due to age of head of household with a positive effect and per capita expenditure of the household having a negative effect. Standard of living index reduces probability of survival of a person whereas all other variables namely per capita expenditure of household, total expenditure at hospital and education of mother and father, raise the probability of survival.

Due to lack of accessibility, public medical facilities people increasingly depend on the private sector. The socio-economic profile of the diseased families is illustrated without any real motive of generalisation. A more comprehensive study is essential to understand the health profile of individuals. Hospitalisation cases may not reflect the exact scenario unless dealt together with all the facilities available in the area. Proper understanding of the culture and tradition becomes essential to implement any policy. To assess the possible impact of such a policy is left to future researchers of health economics.

It is well known that in an underdeveloped area a vast unorganised sector coexists with the organised sector. Under a process of development the organised sector is expected to grow at a faster pace. However, in areas, which are too backward, the process of transformation is rather slow. The role of NGOs is felt at this crucial juncture. It is felt that the so called 'barefooted doctors' may influence the health scenario significantly. In the NE states it may be more relevant as the area is dominated by tribal communities.

References

Central Bureau of Health Intelligence, Ministry of Health and Family Welfare. 2002. Health Information of India (2002).

Manpower Profile India Year Book. 2004. Institute of Applied Manpower Research, New Delhi.

Selvaraju, V. 2003. Health Care Expenditure in Rural India. National Council of Applied Economic Research, New Delhi.

Stevens, A. 2000. *Advance Handbook of Methods in Evidence Based Healthcare.* New Delhi: Sage Publications.

Wilson, R.A. and J.F. Foster. 2003. Measuring Health Inequality. *Journal of Health Economics.*

Contributors

Abbi, Rita, Head, Department of Statistics, City and Industrial Development Corporation (CIDCO), Navi Mumbai.
E-mail:abbirita@gmail.com

Ahmad-Nia, Shirin, Assistant Professor of Sociology, Allameh Tabatabaee University, Tehran, Iran.
E-mail: shirin.ahmadnia@gmail.com

Begum, Semim Wara, Research Scholar, Department of Geography, Guwahati University, Guwahati, Assam.
E-mail: semim24@yahoo.co.in

Bhattacharya, Biswanath, Honorary Visiting Professor, Indian Statistical Institute, Kolkata, West Bengal.

Biswas, Chaiti Sharma, Researcher, Economic Research Unit, Indian Statistical Institute, Kolkata, West Bengal.
E-mail: chaitisb@hotmail.com

Chaudhury, K., Scientist-F, Division of Non-Communicable Diseases, Indian Council of Medical Research, New Delhi.

Das, K.C., Associate Professor, Department of Migration and Urban Studies, International Institute for Population Sciences, Deonar, Mumbai.
E-mail: kcdas@iips.net

Das, N.P., Director, Population Research Centre, Faculty of Science, The Maharaja Sayajirao University, Vadodara, Gujarat.
E-mail: prcbaroda@yahoo.com

Dey, A.S., Deputy Director, Population Research Centre, Dr. H.S. Gour University, Sagar, Madhya Pradesh. E-mail: asdeyprc@yahoo.co.in

Dhar, M., Assistant Professor, Department of Community Medicine, J.S.S. Medical College, Mysore.

Hu, Jian, Associate Professor, School of Public Administration, Guizhou University of Finance and Economics, Yun Yan District, Guiyang City, Guizhou Province, People Republic of China.
E-mail: jianhu61@yahoo.com

Kakkoth, Seetha, Field Assistant, Department of Anthropology, Kannur University, Thalassery Campus Palayad, Kannur, Kerala.

Kapoor, Deepak, IAS, Joint Managing Director, City and Industrial Development Corporation(CIDCO), Navi Mumbai.

Kar, Bimal K., Reader in Geography, Guwahati University, Guwahati, Assam.
E-mail: bimalkar@yahoo.com

Kazemipour, Shahla, Deputy Director (Research), Regional Center for Population Studies and Research in Asia and the Pacific, Ministry of Science, Research and Technology, Tehran, Iran.
E-mail: shkazemi@ut.ac.in

Lahiri, S., Professor and Head, Department of Public Health and Mortality Studies, International Institute for Population Sciences, Deonar, Mumbai.
E-mail:slahiri@iips.net

Lakshmana, C.M., Associate Professor, Population Research Centre, Institute for Social and Economic Change (ISEC), Bangalore.
E-mail: lakshmana@isec.ac.in

Lam, Nguyen Tran, National Programme Officer, UNESCO, Hanoi, Vietnam.
E-mail: lamnt63@yahoo.com.

Mathews, Elizabeth, Head, Department of Commerce, C.K. Thakur A.C.S. College, New Panvel, Navi Mumbai.
E-mail: emathew@vsnl.net

Mehryar, A.H., Emeritus Professor, Institute of Research on Management and Development Planning, Former Director, Asia and Pacific Population Studies Centre, Ministry of Science and Technology, Tehran, Iran.
E-mail: ahmehryar@gmail.com

Mitra, Sandip, Associate Scientist, Indian Statistical Institute, Kolkata, West Bengal.
E-mail: sandip@isical.ac.in

Mukherji, Dipti, Reader, Department of Geography, University of Mumbai, Mumbai.
E-mail: diptimukherji@yahoo.com

Murthy, N.S., Professor and Research Coordinator, Department of Community Medicine, M.S. Ramaih Medical College, Bangalore.
E-mail: nsmurthy44@yahoo.com

Nayak, Debendra Kumar, Professor of Geography, North-Eastern Hill University, Shillong. Meghalaya.
E-mail: dknak@rediffmail.com

Nath, Dilip C., Professor, Department of Statistics, Guwahati University, Guwahati, Assam.

Pal, Manoranjan, Professor, Indian Statistical Institute, Kolkata, West Bengal.

Paswan, Balram, Professor, Department of Population Policies and Programmes, International Institute for Population Sciences, Deonar, Mumbai.
E-mail: brpaswan@iips.net

Pelletier, Adeline, Economist, Institute of Political Sciences (Sciences – Po Paris), France.
E-mail: adeline.pelletier@sciences.po.org

Phadke, V.S., Research Guidance, Department of Geography, University of Mumbai, Mumbai.

Shah, Urvi, Research Investigator, Population Research Centre, Faculty of Science, The Maharaja Sayajirao University, Vadodara, Gujarat.

Shanthi, K., Professor, Department of Econometrics, University of Madras, Chennai.
E-mail:santi49@yahoo.com

Sharma, Arun K., Professor, Department of Humanities and Social Sciences, Indian Institute of Technology, Kanpur.

Shrivastava, Akshay, Research Fellow, Population Research Centre, Dr. H.S. Gour University, Sagar, Madhya Pradesh.

Shukla, Arvind K., Director, Shree Satya Institute of Management, Moradabad, Uttar Pradesh.

Swarnakar, Pradip, Assistant Professor of Sociology, ABV Indian Institute of Information Technology and Management, Gwalior, Madhya Pradesh.
E-mail: swarnakar@gmail.com

Tho, Ng Sor, Senior Lecturer, Department of Applied Statistics, Faculty of Economics and Administration, University of Malaya, Kuala Lumpur, Malaysia.
E-mail: ngst@um.edu.my

Viswanathan, Brinda, Associate Professor, Madras School of Economics, Chennai.
E-mail: brinda@mse.ac.in

Yadava, R.C., Professor, Department of Statistics, Banaras Hindu University, Varanasi, Uttar Pradesh.
E-mail: rcyadava@banaras.ernet.in

Yeole, Balkrishna B., Deputy Director, Bombay Cancer Registry, Indian Cancer Society, Mumbai.
E-mail: bcrics@vsnl.com